MARKETING COMMUNICATIONS

AN IRISH PERSPECTIVE

LECTURERS!
SUPPORT MATERIAL

For your support material check our website at www.gillmacmillan.ie

Support material is available to lecturers only within a secure area of this website. Support material for this book consists of teaching slides and case study notes.
To access support material for *Marketing Communications*:

1. Go to www.gillmacmillan.ie
2. Click on the 'logon' button and enter your username and password.
   (If you do not already have a username and password you must register. To do this click the 'register' button and complete the online registration form. Your username and password will then be sent to you by email.)
3. Click on the link 'Support Material'.
4. Select the title *Marketing Communications*.

MARKETING COMMUNICATIONS

An Irish Perspective

Patricia Medcalf

Gill & Macmillan

This book is dedicated to Dave Nelson, Des Medcalf and Aileen Medcalf.

Gill & Macmillan
Hume Avenue
Park West
Dublin 12
with associated companies throughout the world
www.gillmacmillan.ie

07171 3575 6

Design and print origination in Ireland by O'K Graphic Design, Dublin

The paper used in this book is made from the wood pulp of managed forests. For every tree felled, at least one is planted, thereby renewing natural resources.

A catalogue record is available for this book from the British Library.

Extract from *Channel4/Sunday Times 100 Greatest TV Ads* reprinted by permission of HarperCollins Publishers Ltd. © Mark Robinson 2000.

Extract pages 370–2 reprinted with permission from the 3 January 2003 issue of *Advertising Age*. © Crain Communications Inc. 2003.

For permission to reproduce cover photographs grateful acknowledgment is made to the following: Concern Ireland, Renault Ireland, the Department of the Environment and Local Government.

For permission to reproduce interior photographs grateful acknowledgment is made to the following: the Department of the Environment and Local Government, the Department of Education and Science, AXA Insurance, Response Productions, Tesco Ireland, Guinness, The Advertising Archive, Vodafone, MS Ireland, Eircom, GAA, Irish Distillers, William Grant and Sons Ltd, Renault Ireland, Concern Ireland, Ballygowan, D.I.D Electrical, Bank of Scotland (Ireland), Irish Cancer Society, GOAL, Specsavers Optical Group, An Post, CIE, Irish Ferries, Unicef, Allianz, the Department of the Marine and Natural Resources, Superquinn, Lyons, The Animal Foundation.

CONTENTS

ACKNOWLEDGMENTS

This book was written with the assistance and support of many of my colleagues, family members and friends.

I would like to thank many of my colleagues at the Institute of Technology Tallaght – Bláth McGeough, Ethna O'Connor, Hilda Burton and Joyce Byrne Walsh for reviewing various chapters and providing valuable feedback. I am particularly indebted to Joe MacDonagh who rigorously edited some of my work as it neared completion. My thanks also to Adrian Payne for his incisive input into the chapter on personal selling. I would like to thank Donal Rogan for contributing his award-winning Jameson case study and Garrett Murray for allowing me to use key excerpts of his case study on the 2003 Special Olympics World Summer Games.

My friends, Julie Fossitt and Martin Fahy, did not escape the chores of editing and provided an invaluable outsider's perspective.

Some experts in the marketing communications industry were very generous with their time and provided valuable insights into their specialist fields – Nula Bermingham on the advertising industry, Douglas Nicol on the direct marketing sector and Tracey Stafford on the public relations industry. My thanks also to Ernie Parker of the IDMA for furnishing me with very up-to-date information on data protection, to Mark Cassin of DMA for his expert view on direct marketing in Ireland, and to Pat Costello of the National Safety Council for providing the 'Shame' case study and for taking an interest in the entire book.

My thanks to three past students of the Institute of Technology Tallaght – Ian Lamon and Amanda Finnegan, who contributed their case studies on Multiple Sclerosis Ireland and Carrolls Tobacco Company respectively; and Fiona Heffernan, who worked tirelessly sourcing images of Vodafone's advertising.

My thanks to the team at Gill & Macmillan, particularly Ailbhe O'Reilly for persuading me to write this book and to my editor Hubert Mahony for all his help.

Finally, special thanks to my husband, David Nelson, for all his support, encouragement and understanding. Without him, I may never have completed this book.

FOREWORD

Marketing communications is perhaps the most pervasive element of the marketing mix. None of us are ever too far away from its messages as they infiltrate all parts of our lives. As markets become more competitive, marketing communications offers firms the opportunity of being noticed, and more and more firms are availing of this opportunity.

Marketing Communications: An Irish Perspective takes the reader through the key aspects of marketing communications with, as its title suggests, particular emphasis on applications in an Irish context. Each chapter starts with a number of key aims and objectives which serve as an important contextual setting for the student. Key terms are explained and highlighted in the margins. Throughout the book, checklists are provided to reinforce key aspects. Review questions test the reader's understanding, while practical exercises are included at the end of each chapter. These can be completed individually or in groups. Most importantly, they require the participant(s) to go out and investigate the marketing communications industry.

When work on this book started, the Internet was still being singled out as a revolutionary innovation in marketing and the marketing communications industry. Since then, the hype has calmed down and the importance attached to the Internet is more measured. Undeniably, it has the potential to transform the marketing communications industry. Consequently, technological and Internet references are made throughout the book and Chapter 14 is dedicated to online marketing communications.

While marketing communications is largely associated with commercial endeavours, it is now increasingly used by not-for-profit organisations. This is illustrated in Chapter 15 by concentrating on the charity sector.

1

MARKETING COMMUNICATIONS – AN INTRODUCTION

The aims and objectives of this chapter are to provide greater understanding of:

- the meaning of marketing communications and how it relates to the other elements in the marketing mix
- the objectives that can be achieved using marketing communications
- the marketing communications tools available to the practitioner (these will be explored in greater detail in later chapters)
- the factors that influence the composition of an organisation's marketing communications mix
- the concept of integrated marketing communications (IMC) and the reasons behind the growing interest in it
- the benefits that IMC brings to an organisation
- the barriers to implementing integrated marketing communications and practical ways of challenging them.

Introduction

Marketing communications enjoys the highest profile of all the elements in the marketing mix. To some, it is better known as the 'promotion' element of the four 'P's (product, price, promotion, place). Many marketing students are attracted to the discipline because of their early exposure to marketing communications tools such as advertising and sponsorship. When members of the general public are asked to explain the term 'marketing', they often use words like advertising, selling, publicity and PR. This is hardly surprising because the general public and aspiring marketers are merely reinforcing the fact that the promotion element of the marketing mix is the one to which they are most obviously exposed. Practitioners estimate that people are exposed to anything between 500 and 3,000 messages every day. This figure is, if anything, on the increase. Most individuals only notice a very small proportion of these messages. This illustrates the immensity of the challenge facing organisations with regard to marketing communications. How can they grab the attention of their target audience, and once they have done that, how can they keep it?

Defining marketing communications

Many definitions of marketing communications have been proposed. According to Pickton and Broderick (2001), marketing communications comprises 'all the promotional elements of the marketing mix which involve the communications between an organisation and its target audiences on all matters that affect marketing performance'.

According to de Pelsmacker *et al.* (2001), 'marketing communications try to influence or persuade the potential consumer by conveying a message.'

Fill's (2002) definition recognises marketing communications' importance as 'a management process through which an organisation enters into a dialogue with its various audiences. To accomplish this, the organisation develops, presents, and evaluates a series of messages to identified stakeholder groups. The objective of the process is to influence the perception, understanding and actions the target audience has towards the organisation and/or its products and services.'

Fill's definition is the most comprehensive but the key points to emerge from a combination of all three definitions are as follows:

- Marketing communications is an activity that occurs between an organisation and its various target audiences.
- It is a management process that involves the development and presentation of various messages, followed up with the evaluation of their success.
- It sets out to influence the perceptions, understanding and actions of an organisation's target audiences.

Marketing communications messages are delivered directly to individuals by individuals or through various media such as television, radio and newspapers.

Marketing communications and the marketing mix

One of the best known sets of tactical tools available to marketers is the marketing mix, more commonly referred to as the four 'P's. It comprises product, price, promotion and place and enables the marketer to execute the marketing plan. The marketing mix has evolved and expanded over time in response to changing consumer demands, the dramatic growth in the service industry since the 1980s, and the emergence of a much greater service element within physical product sectors. Many commentators now incorporate physical evidence, people and process into a revised version of the marketing mix, popularly referred to as the seven 'P's.

Unlike external forces, such as economic, political, legal and environmental forces, all of the tools within the marketing mix can and should be controlled by the organisation. Those who fail to manage the marketing mix miss out on significant opportunities to position their business in a way that they prefer.

Promotion, also known as marketing communications, has a significant role to play as part of the marketing mix. It enables companies to communicate with its key stakeholders in a planned and strategic way. Consequently, most organisations set out to assist target audiences to form expectations about their products or services. They portray a favorable image of the staff who deliver the products or services and the environments where they are delivered. They communicate key points about their customer service ethos, and thus help shape the target audience's expectations regarding the way in which their queries or complaints are likely to be handled. Organisations use marketing communications to inform audiences about price levels and special offers. If these promises are not met, it usually means that some or all of the elements in the marketing mix are contradicting each other. Take, for example, Ryanair's marketing communications programmes. They are in harmony with the other elements of its marketing mix. Customers are attracted by low prices and are not led to expect the extras that some other airlines promise. This is because Ryanair does not make such promises. What you see in the advertisements and sponsorship messages is what you get.

The role of marketing communications

Marketing communications has many functions (see Table 1.1).

Table 1.1 The role of marketing communications

- Inform
- Persuade
- Remind
- Reassure
- Differentiate

Inform

Commercial and not-for-profit organisations use marketing communications to inform target audiences.

In February 2003, the Department of Education and Science used advertising to inform second-level teachers about a series of information meetings to deal with the proposed supervision and substitution scheme. Venues and dates were included in the advertisement.

Exhibit 1.1

INVITATION TO AN INFORMATION MEETING FOR SECOND LEVEL TEACHERS ON THE SUPERVISION AND SUBSTITUTION SCHEME

I would like to invite second level teachers who may shortly be voting on the above scheme to one of a series of meetings which I will attend and where information will be provided to teachers on the scheme.

I hope that these meetings will be of assistance to teachers in reaching decisions on their participation in the scheme.

Dates	**Time**	**Venue**	
Tuesday	February 18	7.30 pm	Spa Hotel, Lucan, Co.Dublin
Wednesday	February 19	7.30 pm	Ardboyne Hotel, Navan, Co.Meath
Thursday	February 20	7.30 pm	Corrib Great Southern Hotel, Galway
Friday	February 21	7.30 pm	Tower Hotel, Sligo
Monday	February 24	7.30 pm	South Court Hotel, Limerick
Tuesday	February 25	7.30 pm	Rochestown Park Hotel, Cork
Wednesday	February 26	7.30 pm	Shamrock Lodge Hotel, Athlone
Thursday	February 27	7.30 pm	River Court Hotel, Kilkenny

For those who may not be in a position to attend any one of the meetings, I am organising for the distribution of information to teachers through schools and through the Department's website.

Noel Dempsey T.D.,
Minister for Education & Science

AN RIONN OIDEACHAIS AGUS EOLAÍOCHTA | DEPARTMENT OF EDUCATION AND SCIENCE

Persuade

While target audiences may be informed of a company's offering, they may not be committed to purchasing it. Sales promotions are often used in conjunction with advertising in such situations. For example, in an attempt to persuade Eircom's domestic customers to switch telephone companies, Esat offered 1,000 Tesco clubcard points to those who changed. They also committed to giving customers one point for every euro's worth of calls made each month.

Exhibit 1.2 illustrates how Marks & Spencer use marketing communications as a way of persuading target audiences to take action.

Exhibit 1.2

Remind

Some organisations, who are market leaders in Ireland, are also the biggest spenders when it comes to marketing communications. This resembles a virtuous cycle in that they remain successful because they continue to invest heavily in reminding their customers that they are still there. They argue that, unless they actively promote their products and services, competitors will take their place. Examples of such companies include Kellogg's, Coca-Cola, Guinness and Nestlé. Government bodies also use marketing communications to remind the general public of important information.

When the Department of the Environment and Local Government introduced a 15-cent levy on plastic shopping bags, most consumers were aware of it. The levy meant that they had to change their habits and initially they needed reminding to bring their own shopping bags when they went shopping.

Exhibit 1.3

Reassure

It is not unusual for purchasers to experience stress and discomfort (post-purchase dissonance) after purchasing a product or service. This is particularly true for high-involvement, expensive products. Companies selling these products often engage in direct marketing programmes in order to maintain contact with their customers and to allay any post-purchase worries.

Car companies such as Opel, Ford and BMW regularly contact customers directly to reassure them that they have made the right decision.

Differentiate

Competition in many industries is intense and the differences between rival products and services are difficult for consumers to appreciate. Marketing communications is utilised by many organisations in order to build brands and create points of difference. This is very evident in the fast-moving consumer goods (FMCG) sector.

It is not unusual for the public to enthusiastically anticipate the advertising campaigns of certain companies. This in itself creates difference, and more importantly, competitive advantage. For example, Heineken's and Kitkat's advertisements are usually very entertaining. More importantly, core brand values are highlighted and conveyed to their audiences, thus differentiating them from their competitors.

Consumers often find it difficult to differentiate between the offerings of service providers in the insurance and financial sectors. Firms in these sectors often use advertising to highlight key differences. In Exhibit 1.4, AXA Insurance even use the word 'unique' to convey their difference.

Exhibit 1.4

The marketing communications mix

Promotions mix
Umbrella term to describe the tools available to organisations communicating with their target audiences.

The marketing communications mix (illustrated in Figure 1.1), otherwise known as the **promotions mix**, is an umbrella term for the tools that are available to organisations wishing to communicate with their target audiences. It is usual for organisations to use a combination of some or all of the tools in the mix to achieve specific communications objectives.

Figure 1.1 The marketing communications mix

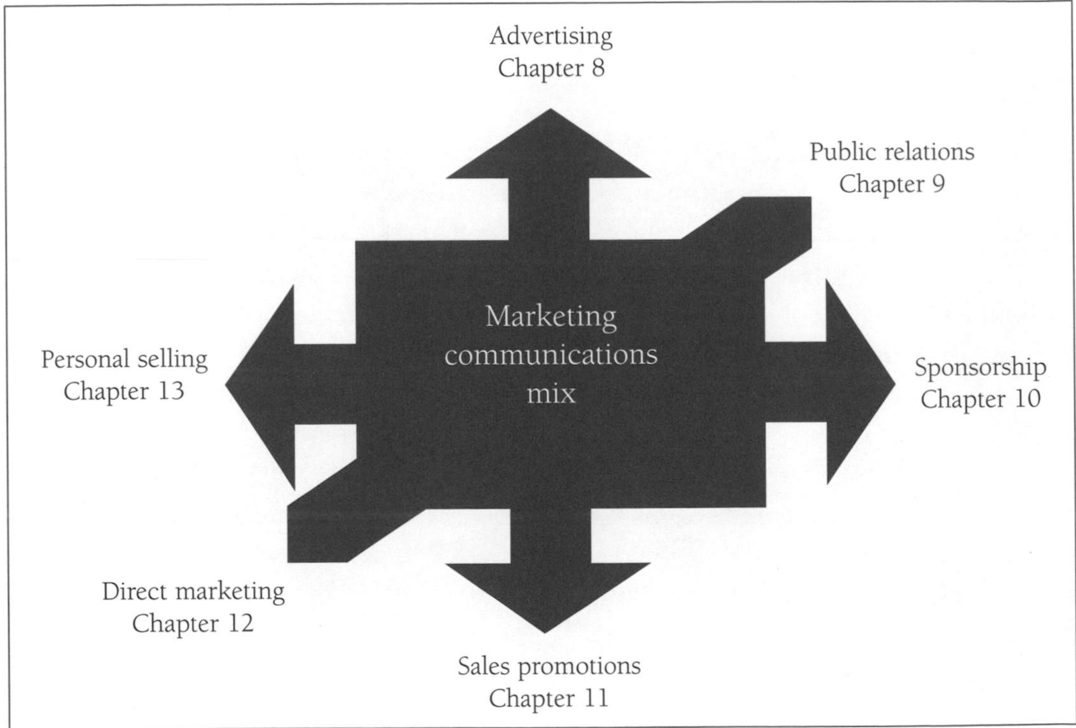

Advertising
Non-personal form of mass communication transmitted through various media.

Advertising

Advertising is a non-personal form of mass communication that transmits its messages through various media. Common forms of mass media include television, radio, newspapers, magazines, outdoor and cinema. In addition to these high-profile media, many advertisers place their messages in catalogues and directories, and on packaging.

From the advertiser's point of view, advertising affords control over the message in terms of content, timing and place. On the downside, some forms of advertising, in particular, television, are expensive to produce. Also the cost of placing an advertisement can be very expensive, for example, daily national newspapers might charge anywhere between €7,500 and €22,500 for a full-page advertisement. Media options are explored in detail in Chapter 6.

Sometimes advertising lacks credibility with target audiences because the source of the message does not necessarily offer a completely objective viewpoint.

Another area of concern for advertisers is the fact that the effectiveness or success of advertising can be difficult to measure. Environmental factors or other aspects of the marketing mix influence sales levels. For example, good weather may coincide with an advertising campaign for ice cream, thus causing sales levels to soar. Therefore, unless there is some form of feedback mechanism built into advertising (for example, a free phone number), the true measure of its effectiveness may be over- or understated. These issues are dealt with in detail in Chapter 8.

Public relations

Public relations *A variety of programmes used to generate goodwill among an organisation's various audiences, known as 'publics'.*

Public relations (PR) is the collective term for a variety of programmes used to generate goodwill among an organisation's various audiences, known as 'publics'. PR has at its disposal a range of tools including press releases, site visits, speeches, in-house advisory services, lobbying and publicity. Publicity involves 'drawing attention to something by highlighting the issue, event or occasion in the media' (Gunning, 2003).

Like advertising, PR is impersonal in that it is not addressed directly at any one individual. Consequently, it is difficult to directly measure its effectiveness because it does not usually involve two-way communication.

PR messages are often delivered as news items. This lends them credibility and objectivity in the eyes of the target audience. However, in these circumstances, journalists and editors usually govern timing and content. This means that the organisation often lacks control over the message.

PR is considered relatively inexpensive but there are many hidden costs associated with it. For example, it requires a high level of staff input to make it happen and in some organisations the cost of this input is not taken into account. PR is dealt with in detail in Chapter 9.

Sponsorship

Sponsorship *A mutually beneficial exchange of cash, time and/or products or services for the right to exploit a particular activity, person or place.*

Sponsorship is a mutually beneficial exchange between two parties. The sponsor contributes cash, time and/or products or services to an activity, person or place in exchange for the right to exploit that activity, person or place. Nowadays, an increasing number of activities are sponsored, but sport, popular music and the arts are particularly popular areas for sponsorship.

Ireland's Celtic Tiger economy in the 1990s created a positive environment for sponsorship because consumer spending on leisure activities increased. While advertising is facing up to the challenge of being able to attract the attention of its intended target audiences, sponsorship offers the advantage of delivering a captive audience to the sponsor. Part of the terms of many sponsorship agreements might be that no two competing organisations can sponsor the same activity.

One of the criticisms frequently made about advertising is the level of wastage it incurs due to targeting constraints. In contrast, sponsorship enables organisations to reach very specific target audiences.

In general, sponsorship tends to be a one-way communication making its effectiveness difficult to measure. While it is relatively straightforward to measure the amount of press coverage enjoyed by a sponsored event, it is not so easy to measure the level of sales directly attributable to the activity. Some organisations utilise sales promotions techniques at sponsored events in order to motivate audiences to buy products at a later date and to gather names and contact details of attendees. Sponsorship is dealt with in Chapter 10.

Sales promotions

Sales promotions *The use of incentives to encourage potential and existing customers to try and ultimately to purchase a product or service.*

Sales promotions involve the use of incentives to encourage potential and existing customers to try and ultimately to purchase a product or service. Common techniques used are free gifts, money-off coupons, discounts, free samples, competitions, support with advertising. Exhibit 1.5 shows a 2003 sales promotion used by Tesco Ireland.

Exhibit 1.5

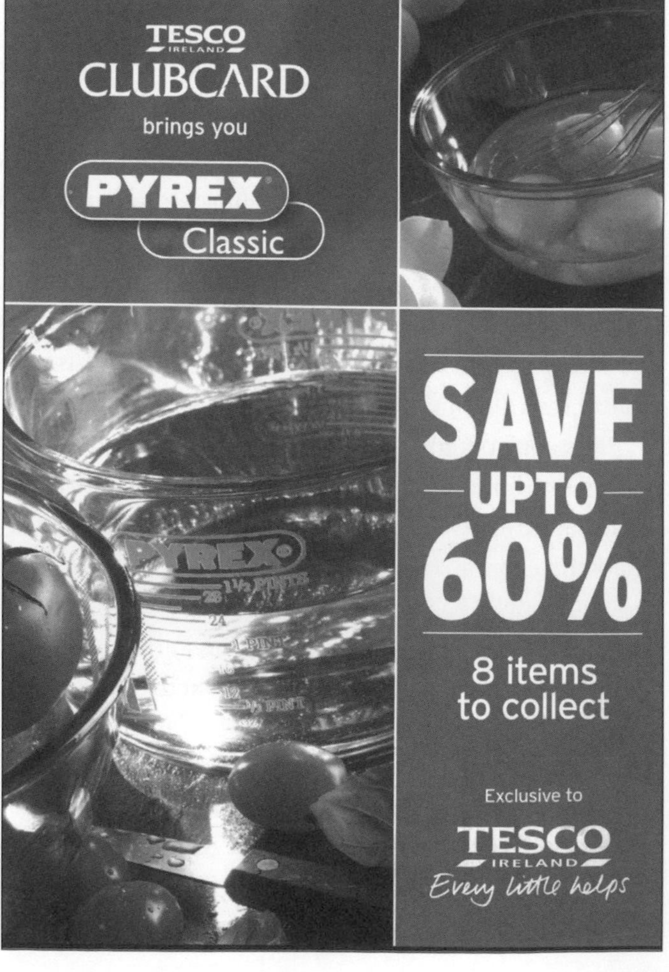

Sales promotions are often used as a short-term, tactical tool but, with the widespread exploitation of customer databases, they are also used in conjunction with direct marketing techniques (see below), thus giving it a role in relationship marketing. Sales promotions are aimed at the end consumer or at staff and distributors whose involvement is vital for the sale of products to the end consumer.

Some sales promotions can be implemented quickly, thus making them well suited to dealing with unexpected competitive and economic forces. For example, in the aftermath of the 11 September 2001 attacks in the United States, the Irish hotel sector put together a number of very attractive offers in order to fill their rooms with Irish holidaymakers and to counter the lack of overseas tourists.

Organisations like sales promotions because uptake is easily measured. For example, the number of redeemed coupons or the number of competition entries can be counted. However, it is not so easy to measure how many repeat sales occur after a particular sales promotion.

Sales promotions can damage a brand if they are used too frequently. Where price discounts have been used on an ongoing basis, consumers might subsequently be reluctant to pay the full price for the product or service. Another downside of prolonged sales promotions activity is that consumers might think there is something wrong with the product. Sales promotions are examined in Chapter 11.

Direct marketing

Direct marketing involves two-way communication and uses one or more media to elicit a measurable response from the target audience. It uses personal media such as mail, telephone and the Internet, and non-personal media such as television, radio and press, to communicate with existing and prospective customers. The main objective of direct marketing activity is to elicit a response from the target audience and to use these responses to form long-lasting, mutually beneficial relationships with the respondents. Database management is a key success factor in direct marketing and this is examined in Chapter 12.

***Direct marketing** uses various personal and non-personal media to communicate with existing and prospective customers in order to elicit a response.*

When an organisation communicates through personal media, it may be possible to tailor the messages to suit each individual. Not everyone needs or wants the same thing and the information on databases often allows organisations to take this into account when communicating with known individuals. Also, if the name of the target is known, the communication can be personalised, for example, 'Dear Mrs Smith ...'.

Direct marketing is one of the most accountable elements of the marketing communications mix. Response rates are easily calculated and subsequent behaviour and purchase patterns of respondents can be tracked with the aid of a database.

On the downside, there is much debate about the ethical aspects of direct marketing. Due to the unscrupulous behaviour of a small number of organisations, some consumers have suffered what they consider an invasion of privacy and are worried as to how these organisations might have gained access to their personal information. Chapter 12 deals with the many aspects of direct marketing.

Personal selling *Face-to-face interaction with one or more prospective customers for the purpose of making a sale and building long-term mutually beneficial relationships.*

Personal selling

According to Kotler (1994) **personal selling** involves 'face-to-face interaction with one or more prospective purchasers for the purpose of making sales'. While this definition is still correct, the role of the sales representative has developed in recognition of the fact that sales should no longer be transaction-based (i.e. a one-off sale) but relationship-oriented. Armstrong and Kotler (2003) have since identified a number of tasks over and above pure selling that are carried out by sales representatives. These tasks include:

- searching for prospective customers
- communicating information about the company's products and services
- providing additional services to customers such as consulting, technical support and advice on finance
- gathering information about customers and ensuring that this information is recorded on a database.

Sales representatives have a number of sales support tools at their disposal, including presentations (increasingly these are carried on laptops and tailored to the needs of each customer), trade shows, demonstrations, product samples and site visits. In addition, their activities are enhanced and reinforced by the other elements in the marketing communications mix such as direct marketing, advertising, sponsorship and public relations.

Personal selling enables firms to personalise communications. Each customer encounter delivers immediate feedback because, through a combination of verbal and non-verbal communication, sales representatives can gauge how well their information is being received, and can change the message if necessary.

Sales representatives are usually seen as a credible source of information and are able to respond to individual queries. Personal selling is dealt with in Chapter 13.

Factors influencing the composition of the marketing communications mix

The make-up of an organisation's marketing communications mix is influenced and ultimately determined by a number of factors (see Table 1.2).

Characteristics of the product

If a product is complex, expensive and rarely purchased by an organisation or an individual, personal selling may be necessary in order to secure a sale. Conversely, low-involvement, frequently purchased products do not present a high level of risk to the target audience. Therefore, messages can usually be delivered through mass media communications such as advertising.

Table 1.2 Factors influencing an organisation's choice of elements in the marketing communications mix

- Characteristics of the product
- A product's stage in the product life cycle
- Type of market in which it operates
- Level of control required
- Company policies
- Government and EU legislation
- Profile of senior management team
- Available budget
- Internal marketing team
- Marketing communications agency
- Competitive environment
- Economic environment

Stage in the product life cycle

According to the product life-cycle concept, product sales go through four stages: introduction, growth, maturity and decline.

1. At the introduction stage it is essential to make people aware of the product's existence and to persuade them to try the product. Advertising, publicity and sales promotions are important tools in achieving these objectives. Personal selling might be important if it is a complex product or if an organisation wants to persuade distributors to stock a product.
2. At the growth stage, assuming that awareness is at a high level, the organisation wants to build product loyalty. This is done through advertising and the establishment of database-driven loyalty programmes aimed at securing patronage.
3. At the maturity stage, users are familiar with the product and have greater choice as competitors establish themselves in the market. Reminder advertising is important and value-oriented sales promotions are used to beat the competition.
4. During the decline phase, sales promotions techniques are used to sustain sales levels.

Type of market

Fast-moving consumer goods (FMCG) manufacturers and distributors invest heavily in advertising and sales promotions. This is partly due to the fact that many of these products still enjoy mass appeal and are purchased by large segments of the population. Also, they depend on retailers to stock and sell their products. Sales promotions are used to build relationships with the retailers and to attract the end consumer's attention. In contrast, many manufacturers and sellers of industrial products have small customer bases. It is relatively straightforward for them to identify customers by name. This means that personal selling, direct marketing and attendance at trade shows are important elements of the marketing mix for business-to-business firms like Hilti, Kilsaran Concrete Products (KCP), Tegral, Capco and John Deere agricultural equipment. Advertising for these types of companies tends to be in specialist trade magazines that are aimed at specific business segments.

Level of control required

Some elements of the marketing communications mix are more easily controlled. When organisations want to be sure that the right message is communicated at the right time, advertising might be appropriate. In contrast, they cannot always guarantee that the desired message is communicated when using public relations and personal selling.

Company policies

Many organisations in Ireland are branches of multinational corporations (MNCs). It is very common for MNCs to adopt Europe-wide or worldwide marketing communications strategies. Therefore, many Irish branches of MNCs have little or no control over the marketing communications mix.

Government and EU legislation

Some organisations may want to employ certain elements of the marketing communications mix but are prohibited from doing so because of stringent legislation. As will be seen later in the book, the tobacco industry is severely constrained by legislation that has restricted marketing communications options. The alcohol industry is under increased scrutiny, and is likely to face greater restrictions, particularly in advertising and sponsorship.

Profile of senior management team

The size of the marketing communications budget is often influenced by the composition of the senior management team in an organisation. Some senior executives still consider marketing communications as a cost rather than an investment, thus making it difficult to persuade them to sanction adequate budgets.

Available budget

Even when organisations are predisposed to investing in marketing communications, the necessary funds may not be available. In reality, budget constraints often determine an organisation's options.

The internal marketing team

The expertise and career experiences of an organisation's marketing department are likely to influence the elements of the marketing communications mix that are utilised. Some organisations purposely recruit specialists who have worked in advertising agencies because they believe that they need to do more advertising. Many firms want individuals with experience in direct marketing in recognition of the fact that relationship marketing is so important.

An organisation's marketing communications agencies

The experience and core competences of an organisation's marketing communications agency or agencies are likely to influence the constitution of the marketing communications mix. Even though many advertising agencies are capable of providing services across all elements of the mix, it is often more lucrative for them to concentrate on advertising and media buying. This financial reality may influence their recommendations when dealing with clients.

The competitive environment

Many organisations utilise the same elements of the marketing communications mix as their competitors. For example, service providers in the mobile phone market, such as Vodafone and O^2, utilise similar elements of the mix. Traditionally, they have been heavily reliant on sales promotions and advertising, but the level of customer turnover (referred to in the industry as 'churn') suggests that relationship-building techniques may be more appropriate for the future.

The economic environment

In times of economic prosperity, more money is available for marketing communications. Expenditure on advertising rose sharply during the Celtic Tiger phase of the Irish economy, as did expenditure on high-profile sponsorship. Conversely, a downturn in the economy usually brings cutbacks in marketing communications budgets. Organisations turn to more accountable and cost-effective elements of the mix like sales promotions and direct marketing. Another symptom of an economic downturn is reduced consumer spending power. This makes consumers more receptive to cost-oriented promotions like sales promotions and loyalty schemes.

Many of these factors are revisited in Chapter 5, which examines marketing communications strategy formulation.

Integrated marketing communications

Figure 1.1 (page 8) introduced the main elements of the marketing communications mix. These should not be treated as stand-alone elements but should instead work together to communicate coherent, unified messages to target audiences. When this occurs, the objective of integrated marketing communications (IMC) has been achieved. The real strength of IMC lies in the fact that it starts with the needs of the target audience and views things from their perspective.

The American Association of Advertising Agencies (AAAA) defines IMC as 'a concept of marketing communications planning that recognises the added value of a comprehensive plan that evaluates the strategic roles of a variety of communications disciplines, e.g. general advertising, direct response, sales promotion and public relations – and combines these disciplines to provide clarity, consistency and maximum communication impact' (cited in Eagle and Kitchen, 2000).

Armstrong and Kotler (2003) are advocates of IMC and contend that it has a greater impact on sales than the implementation of unrelated elements of the marketing communications mix. This view highlights the economic rationale for implementing an integrated marketing communications mix and explains why the concept of IMC has caught the attention of many organisations.

In 1993, Schultz conducted extensive research into the IMC concept and put forward some definitions. He views IMC as the 'concept of marketing communications planning that recognised the added value of a comprehensive plan that evaluates the strategic role of a variety of communications disciplines ... and combines these disciplines to provide clarity, consistency and maximum communications impact'. Later that same year, he collaborated with Tannenbaum and Lauterborn to declare IMC as 'a new way of looking at the whole, where once we only saw parts such as advertising, public relations, sales promotion, purchasing, employee communications, and so forth. It's realigning communications to look at it the way the customer sees it – a flow of information from indistinguishable sources.'

Schultz argues that, 'it forces management to think about every way the customer comes in contact with the company, how the company communicates its positioning, the relative importance of each vehicle, and timing issues. It gives someone the responsibility – where none existed before – to unify the company's brand images and messages as they come through thousands of company activities. IMC will improve the company's ability to reach the right customers with the right messages at the right time and in the right place (cited in Armstrong and Kotler, 2003).

Clow and Baack (2002) present another definition, which in essence agrees with the previous ones. They see IMC as 'the co-ordination and integration of all marketing communication tools, avenues, and sources within a company into a seamless programme that maximises the impact on consumers and other end users at a minimal cost'.

Semenik (2002) succinctly defines IMC as 'the process of using promotional tools in a unified way so that a synergistic communications effect is created'.

The importance of integrated marketing communications is summarised in Table 1.3.

Table 1.3 The importance of integrated marketing communications

- **Synergy.** IMC creates synergy between the messages sent out by an organisation not only through marketing communications but also through the other elements of the marketing mix, product, place and price.
- **Forces organisations to view the marketing mix and the marketing communications mix from the target audience's perspective.** Target audiences do not view each element of an organisation's marketing communications mix in isolation. That is why it is confusing for them to receive radically different messages and images through various media. For instance, the sales representative's message should not conflict with messages contained in advertisments and direct mail.
- **Efficient.** IMC saves financial and human resources. It forces the marketing team and their agenies to think twice before creating and implementing different ideas for each element of the marketing communications mix.
- **The IMC 'champion'.** It motivates organisations to appoint someone to act in a unifying capacity. This person could be described as the 'champion' of the IMC concept and as someone capable of bringing together internal and external marketing communications specialists.

Factors contributing to the growth in IMC

There are a number of factors that have made organisations more receptive to integrated marketing communications (see Table 1.4 for a summary).

Table 1.4 Factors contributing to the rise in popularity of IMC

- The sum of all the elements of the marketing communications mix is more powerful than each one on its own
- Globalisation
- Desire to achieve cost efficiencies
- More frequent overlap between various elements of the promotions mix. In some cases, technology has been a contributing factor to this
- A shift in emphasis away from transaction marketing to relationship marketing
- Fragmentation of traditional media
- The arrival of the one-stop-shop marketing communications agency
- Intensification of competition in most markets
- Growing levels of clutter
- Cynicism towards traditional marketing communications techniques

The success of the sum of all elements of the marketing communications mix has the potential to be far greater than each element on its own. In order to realise this success, the elements must complement rather than contradict each other.

Many MNCs are advocates of the IMC concept. They recognise that consumers and business people travel more often and are exposed to international stimuli on an almost daily basis through the Internet, television, newspapers, magazines and radio. Where appropriate, it is preferable to communicate in a consistent manner across various markets.

Despite a buoyant economic environment in the 1990s, most organisations paid, and continue to pay attention to, achieving cost efficiencies. If a company approaches marketing communications in a piecemeal way, inefficiencies are bound to occur. For example, if a direct marketing campaign is designed and implemented in isolation from an advertising campaign, messages might be contradictory. Certain tasks might be duplicated. Rather than paying various agencies to come up with creative ideas for each element of the marketing communications mix, it is more cost effective and efficient that one good idea be implemented across several elements.

The various elements of the marketing communications mix are becoming less distinct. Many direct marketing campaigns incorporate sales promotions techniques; many television, radio and press advertisements contain direct marketing and sales promotions; public relations activity is often fuelled by the publicity gained from sponsorship programmes.

The emphasis in marketing has shifted from transactions to relationships. Rapid developments have resulted in the marriage of technology and marketing. Many organisations capitalise on this in order to build and maintain relationships with existing customers, and to target prospective customers.

Consumers and business customers demand greater choice in all areas of their lives. They cannot be communicated to *en masse*. Meanwhile, traditional media are fragmenting. Digital television has brought with it a wealth of choice and highly targeted channels. In Ireland, audiences enjoy a large choice of newspapers and magazines. They can choose from a large number of targeted radio stations. Consequently, organisations must work hard to co-ordinate their messages.

Many advertising agencies have adopted the one-stop-shop model. They no longer specialise in advertising, but provide expertise in direct marketing, sales promotions, public relations and sponsorship. While this is largely in response to the growth in interest in IMC, it has nevertheless helped to facilitate its acceptance. Leading Irish advertising agencies like McConnells, DDFH&B and Irish International, all promote their expertise in the various elements of the promotions mix.

Ireland's open economy makes it a competitive market place. This forces organisations to find ways of communicating with their target audiences in a clear, consistent manner.

One of the side-effects of increased competition is the clutter that bombards consumers and business people on a daily basis. A more integrated approach may improve the likelihood of standing out from the crowd. Inconsistent communications merely dilute the intended message or messages and leave the way clear for competitors to catch the target audience's attention.

By and large, target audiences are more tuned in to marketing communications techniques. Many people are cynical about the messages sent to them. At the very least, organisations must strive to ensure that they are not sending out conflicting messages, or this cynicism will increase.

The benefits of IMC

IMC brings many benefits to organisations that embrace the concept.

Cost savings

A more integrated approach to marketing communications can deliver cost savings. For instance, creativity – the ideas behind each element of the marketing communications mix – is very expensive. If an advertising agency comes up with a creative idea, there is no reason why it cannot be used in other elements of the mix. This means that an organisation is only paying once for creativity.

Less duplication of tasks

While many organisations believe that it is inadvisable to place all work with just one agency, it can also be argued that the use of too many agencies is inefficient. It takes up a lot of time working with a range of marketing communications agencies and can lead to a duplication of tasks. A commitment to IMC forces an organisation to review their agencies and to work with fewer. Policies should be implemented whereby the chosen agencies work together and commit to delivering integrated campaigns.

Greater impact

Heightened competition and increasing amounts of clutter have contributed to the growing interest in IMC. As differences between the physical characteristics of products become negligible, clear product positioning is essential for achieving competitive advantage. IMC can help an organisation in this.

Barriers to implementing IMC

The concept of IMC is very logical and makes sense to many organisations. Committing to it is an entirely different matter. This section examines some of the barriers typically encountered by organisations considering its use.

According to Fill (2002), committing to IMC usually requires immense organisational change. Change is rarely embraced without resistance from employees. Human nature means that if employees have been doing a job in a particular way for a long time, they find many reasons for not doing it the new way. Employees may fear that their job will no longer exist if the change is implemented. This may in fact be true in the case of IMC, because it means that many tasks are centralised and the need for some jobs may be eliminated. Sometimes organisations find it easier not to implement the change than to cope with employee resistance. However, this is a short-term remedy and does not benefit the organisation in the longer term.

Creative departments in advertising agencies tend to dislike the concept of IMC because there is a view that it can stifle creativity. They might argue that if they are constrained by rules and bureaucracy, they lack latitude with regard to coming up with new ideas. However, this does not have to be the case, and a good client/agency relationship will help ensure that this does not happen.

As mentioned above, an organisation committed to IMC centralises many of the tasks that were previously carried out in relatively autonomous units. Centralisation can deliver cost savings, but higher levels of bureaucracy can negate this benefit. The bureaucracy might be manifested in slower responses to competitive threats or longer approval times for campaigns.

When multinational corporations commit to IMC, local branches may worry that environmental differences, such as culture, economic and political conditions, are not taken into account. Local managers and their agencies may also resent the fact that all of the creative and strategic thinking is being done overseas. This is a particularly relevant issue in Ireland, where so many companies are subsidiaries or branches of MNCs. This can be addressed by involving subsidiaries in decision-making and seeking their opinions before the implementation of a campaign.

Fill (2002) highlights the contradictions that exist in many organisations. IMC requires a long-term outlook and can take time to deliver efficiencies. Marketing managers usually face the challenge of short-term financial targets. If these targets are to be fulfilled, they often require short-term tactical responses. Therefore, many organisations must address the way in which they set targets and reward the employees who achieve them.

Fill also contends that the traditional brand management structure in many organisations is not conducive to the easy introduction of IMC. Brand managers are used to having immense autonomy in relation to marketing communications. It is very common for them to select their own agencies and to implement campaigns without consulting other brand managers in the organisation. The way in which brand managers are remunerated means that they are competing with each other. IMC is difficult to implement with such a structure and entrenched culture in place.

Summary

Marketing communications is a management process that enables organisations to communicate with various audiences. It is the promotion element of the marketing mix and can be controlled by the organisation. Marketing communications enables firms to do many things, including inform, persuade, remind and reassure target audiences, and differentiate products and services from competitors' offerings. Marketing communications is executed through a number of tools. Collectively, they are known as the marketing communications mix or the promotions mix. The mix consists of advertising, public relations, sponsorship, sales promotions, direct marketing and personal selling.

Several factors influence the composition of a firm's marketing communications mix, including the characteristics of the product, its stage in the product life cycle, the type of market, the level of control required, a firm's policies, legislation, budget, and employees' experience.

Integrated marketing communications (IMC) is a concept that stresses the importance of transmitting consistent messages to target audiences, even if different elements of the marketing communications mix are utilised. IMC has the potential to bring cost savings and makes it easier for the target audience to interpret messages. There are a number of internal barriers that prevent its implementation in some firms, but the long-term benefits make it a concept worth pursuing.

Review questions

1. Define marketing communications and discuss its role.
2. Explain what is meant by the marketing communications mix and describe each element in the mix. Use examples to illustrate your answer.
3. Discuss the factors that influence the composition of an organisation's marketing communications mix.
4. What is integrated marketing communications? Discuss the reasons why it has attracted so much attention.
5. What barriers exist in firms that prevent the adoption of IMC? How do you think these barriers can be broken down?

References

Armstrong, Gary and Kotler, Philip, *Marketing: An Introduction* (Pearson Education, Inc., 2003).

Clow, Kenneth and Baack, Donald, *Integrated Advertising, Promotion and Marketing Communications* (Prentice-Hall, 2002).

De Pelsmacker, Patrick, Geuens, Maggie and Van den Bergh, Joeri, *Marketing Communications* (Pearson Education Limited, 2001).

Eagle, Lynne and Kitchen, Philip, 'IMC, Brand Communications, and Corporate Cultures: Client/Advertising Agency Co-ordination and Cohesion' (*European Journal of Marketing*, Vol. 34, No. 5/6, pp. 667–86, 2000).

Fill, Chris, *Marketing Communications: Contexts, Strategies and Applications* (Pearson Education Limited, 2002).

Gunning, Ellen, *Public Relations: A Practical Approach* (Gill & Macmillan, 2003).

Kotler, Philip, *Marketing Management: Analysis, Planning, Implementation and Control*, 8th edition (Englewood Cliffs, New Jersey: Prentice Hall International Editions, 1994).

Kotler, Philip, *Marketing Management*, 11th edition (Prentice Hall, 2003).

Pickton, David and Broderick, Amanda, *Integrated Marketing Communications* (Pearson Education Limited, 2001).

Schultz, D. E., 'Integrated Marketing Communications: Maybe Definition is in the Point of View' (*Marketing News*, 18 January 1993).

Semenik, Richard J., *Promotion and Integrated Marketing Communications* (South-Western, 2002).

2

COMMUNICATION THEORY

The aims and objectives of this chapter are:

- to explain what is meant by communication
- to examine the communications process
- to highlight the many forms of communication used in the process
- to understand the obstacles to and the challenges of effective communication
- to introduce the concept of semiotics
- to explain the basic theories of buyer behaviour
- to critically assess some of the more popular marketing communications models
- to understand the role of marketing communications in influencing individuals as they progress through the above processes.

What is communication?

The word 'communication' is used frequently at work, in leisure pursuits, and at home. However, despite its widespread use, it is often misunderstood and people assume that they are communicating when in fact they are not. Ask yourself how many times you think you have told somebody something, only to discover that they have not understood you. Similarly, in the more specialised sphere of marketing communications, many organisations assume that they are communicating effectively when, in fact, they are wasting money.

Communication
A two-way process that involves the exchange of messages between two or more parties.

So, what is communication? **Communication** is a two-way process that involves the exchange of messages between two or more parties. Furthermore, it is often intended that some sort of action or response will result from the communication. Individuals and organisations often overlook the two-way aspect of communication. There is a common misconception held by many organisations that if they send out a message, communication has taken place. This overlooks the importance of listening and understanding in communication – if the person that you intend communicating with does not listen to what you are trying to convey or does not understand the message, communication has not taken place. For organisations engaging in marketing communications, they must appreciate that, unless target audiences notice and understand their campaigns, money is being wasted.

Successful communication depends on a number of factors:

- **the relationship that exists between the sender(s) and the receiver(s) of the message(s)**. Personalised direct mail (direct mail that uses someone's name) tends to be more effective when targeted at people who already have some sort of relationship with the sender, as opposed to instances where the recipient does not already have a relationship with the sender. For example, if someone is already a customer of company X, the likelihood is that they will be more receptive to a piece of direct mail from that company than someone who is not and never has been a customer.

- **the type of message and the timing of its transmission**. If the timing of a radio advertisement for fast food coincides with a listener being hungry, it is more likely to have the desired effect on that person.

- **the environment in which the message is transmitted and received**. If someone is very involved in reading a report in a newspaper, they may not notice the presence of advertisements alongside the article.

- **the ability of both parties to understand each other and relate to one another**. One of the most difficult audiences to communicate with is the teenage market because teenagers develop and use their own language. This changes very quickly and terms that were once in vogue become dated within a short period of time.

Verbal and non-verbal aspects of communication play an integral part in bringing about understanding and will be explored later in this chapter.

The communication process

The communication process is best understood by examining Schramm's model (see Figure 2.1). It acknowledges one of the most fundamental aspects of communication – that both the sender and receiver of the message must be active participants in the process for communication to be deemed successful and effective. The nature of the feedback received allows the sender to evaluate whether or not the communication has been successful. Schramm's model also draws attention to the fact that receivers are not necessarily captive audiences when messages are transmitted because they are prone to distractions. Each of the components in the model is examined in detail below.

Figure 2.1 The communication process

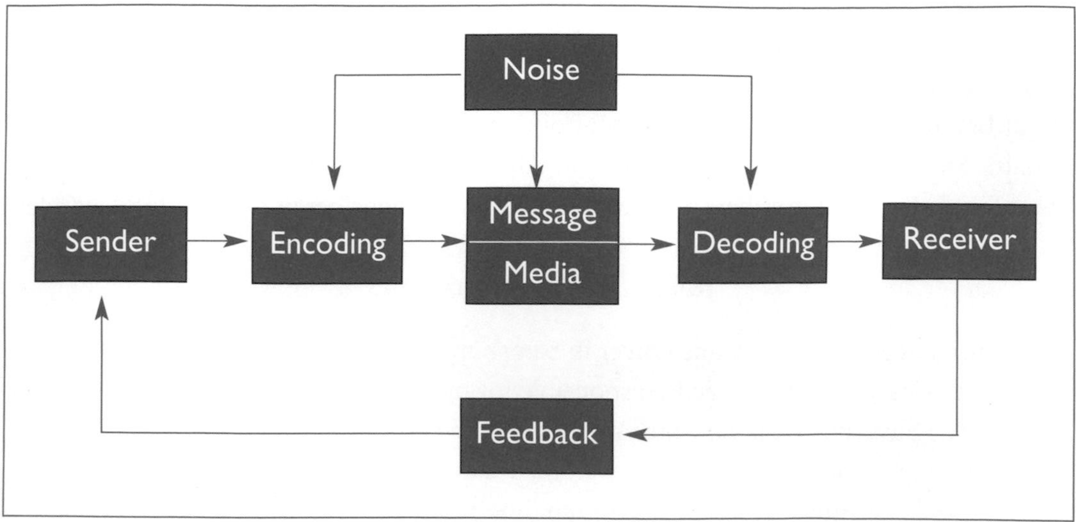

Source: Schramm (1955)

The sender

The sender is the person or organisation who recognises the need to communicate with another person or organisation. This may be due to the need to fulfil some or all of the following types of objectives:

- to launch a new product or service
- to reposition a brand or an organisation
- to remind customers about a company, brand or product
- to counter competitor activity
- to generate good publicity or to counter negative publicity
- to strengthen customer loyalty
- to relay important information.

For communication to be effective, it is necessary to find out as much as possible about the audience or receiver(s). In the context of marketing communications, this is often achieved by conducting market research. With regard to existing identifiable customers, information is often gathered by sales representatives or analysed using records held on customer databases. Loyalty programmes, such as those used by retailers like Tesco and Superquinn are used by many organisations to help build a more complete and incisive picture of their customers. This is dealt with in more detail in Chapter 13.

Depending on the content of the message and the situation in which it is communicated, it is very important that the sender or the person delivering the message displays some or all of the following characteristics.

Credibility

The sender's credibility is assessed in accordance with their expertise and trustworthiness. The definition of credibility depends on the nature of the message and the characteristics of the receiver(s) and the product or service in question. Companies sending out messages about branded sportswear and equipment often pay top athletes to communicate on their behalf. Similarly, celebrity chefs in the UK are employed by retailers and food manufacturers to endorse their brands because they are considered experts, for example:

> ### *Jamie lifts Sainsbury sales*
>
> The use of celebrity chef Jamie Oliver in Sainsbury's advertising was, according to the UK supermarket group, directly responsible for more than a quarter of its profits last year. The advertising for Sainsbury's generated an extra £1.12 billion [€1.76 billion] in turnover in less than two years from a campaign that cost £41 million. The supermarket estimated that, of its £535 million profit last year, £153 million could be attributed to the celebrity chef's involvement. The announcement was made after the Jamie Oliver campaign won an advertising effectiveness award from the Institute of Practitioners in Advertising in London in December 2002.
>
> Source: *The Irish Times*, 5 December 2002

Celebrities are often paid large sums of money for their involvement in marketing communications. However, the credibility of the message can be subsequently undermined by contradictory actions, such as their uninhibited use of competing brands.

Attractiveness

This does not necessarily mean that the sender or source of the message should be good-looking or pretty! Essentially, it means that the receiver should be able to relate to the sender and empathise with them. Older audiences might not listen to a 25-year-old trying to deliver a message about pensions, whereas a 20-something audience might respond very favourably to the same person. The use of ordinary, everyday people to deliver messages can prove effective. For example, since 2001, Flora's television, press and radio advertising has featured 'real' people relaying their personal experiences with Flora proactiv. It was felt that if those in the target audience saw people like themselves using the product and enjoying its benefits, they might decide to opt for it too (see Exhibit 2.1).

Power

There are situations when it is appropriate that the sender of a message should be seen to have power. Depending on the situation, the sender can exert either positive or negative power. Sales representatives often use positive power to close a sale or to retain customers. They might use expense accounts to entertain potential and existing customers, with a view to persuading them to commit to a purchase. This activity is seen as an integral part of relationship marketing and is examined in more detail in Chapter 15.

Individuals and organisations might exploit negative power when attempting to change behaviour. For this to be successful, the sender of the message must be seen to possess the power to punish the receiver(s). Radio and television advertisements advising television owners to pay their TV licence fees convey the consequences of non-payment – hefty fines and possible imprisonment. Through advertising, Revenue, the Irish organisation charged with responsibility for gathering tax revenue, attempts to persuade people to file their tax returns by particular deadlines. The penalties for late or non-compliance are clearly communicated in order to encourage the desired response.

Exhibit 2.1

Encoding

When the sender decides to communicate, careful attention must be given to getting the message across effectively. **Encoding** entails the application of words, signs, symbols, colour and sound to a message in order to get its meaning across. A key success factor at this stage is an in-depth understanding of the target audience. Care must be taken not to use jargon or technical language that the receiver will not understand. Some people may find certain imagery offensive or unappealing. It is not unusual for companies to place encoded messages in research in advance of their transmission so as to avoid costly errors. The objective of such research is to highlight, in advance of the launch of a marketing communications campaign, potential difficulties the target audience(s) might have with the particular words, signs, symbols, colours and sounds being used to communicate an organisation's message. As a consequence, some or all elements of the marketing communications mix may have to be adapted for transmission to different audiences.

Encoding
The application of words, signs, symbols, colour and sound to a message in order to get its meaning across.

Encoding often poses problems for international companies. They may assume that marketing communications programmes that succeeded in one country will automatically succeed in another country. However, symbols, colours, imagery and language do not always work across cultural boundaries.

Media

When the message has been encoded, it is transmitted to the receiver. This is done through a variety of personal and non-personal media:

- **non-personal media**
  - broadcast media (television, radio) – see Chapter 6
  - print media (newspapers, magazines, outdoor) – see Chapter 6
  - ambient media (media that surrounds the target audience, for example, packaging, shopping receipts, shopping bags – see Chapter 6
  - public relations – see Chapter 9
  - sponsorship – see Chapter 10
  - the Internet (categorised also as personal – this is explained in greater detail in Chapter 14)
- **personal media**
  - direct marketing media (mail, telephone, e-mail, fax) – see Chapter 12
  - sales representatives – see Chapter 13.

In addition to the media highlighted above, all staff and channel partners, such as agents and retailers, play an essential part in the delivery of messages. For example, when a technician arrives at a company to mend a piece of machinery, the way in which they communicate helps customers form an opinion about the technician's organisation.

Word of mouth is very important to many organisations, in particular those in the service sector. When a customer is satisfied with a product or service, they might recommend it to someone else. However, if they are dissatisfied, negative messages will be communicated. Organisations who take care to ensure that their product or service lives up to promises made in their marketing communications campaigns are in a better position to be able to positively influence word-of-mouth communications. Conversely, if a customer's experience of the company does not live up to expectations, word of mouth can have a damaging effect on the well-being of an organisation.

Finally, when selecting the most appropriate media, an organisation must take the following factors into account:

- **receiver's ability to gain access to particular media**. More than 1 million Irish people have access to the Internet. In contrast, almost everyone in Ireland has access to television and radio (almost 4 million people). If an organisation wants to communicate with a mass audience, television and radio might be appropriate.

- **receiver's desire to gain access to particular media**. Even when a significant proportion of the target audience has access to particular media, they might choose not to make use of it.
- **the ability of the media to deliver the message**. Some messages are communicated more effectively when visual cues are used. Radio is not suited to certain tasks. For example, cosmetics companies like to visibly demonstrate the benefits of using their products. Therefore, print or television media are more appropriate in these circumstances.
- **the type of message being transmitted**. For example, a sales representative might deliver complex information about a technical product. This gives the receiver the opportunity to ask questions and clarify areas of concern.

Decoding

The receiver carries out this part of the process and, presuming it reaches them, attempts to understand the message. He or she interprets the words, signs, symbols, colours and/or sounds that were used by the sender to articulate the message. Misunderstandings occur easily if the receiver interprets the message differently than intended by the sender. Receivers can be highly selective in their interpretation of messages and may take from communications only what they want to see or hear. This has been a problem for successive public health communications because target audiences can have 'it couldn't happen to me' or 'that doesn't apply to me' attitudes.

Effective communication is deemed to have taken place if the receiver decodes the message and gives it the same meaning as the sender gave it when encoding took place. Some of the visual and verbal aspects of communication and the meanings attached to them are explored in more detail later in this chapter.

Noise

Communication takes place in a noisy setting. People and organisations live and work in busy environments and distractions are the norm. As a result of noise, many messages never even reach the intended recipient(s).

Unfortunately, it is not unusual for the sender to create noise. This occurs when conflicting messages are communicated or when the organisation misunderstands the receiver's terms of reference and uses unfamiliar words, signs and symbols.

Sometimes the medium through which the message is transmitted experiences shortcomings in quality. Interference on broadcast media such as television and radio is not uncommon. This may cause the viewer or listener to switch channels or switch off. Print is not immune from quality-related distractions. Sometimes, printing presses that print newspapers and magazines produce poor-quality print. This weakens the message and may prevent successful message transmission.

Competitor activity is increasing and audiences are being bombarded with an ever-increasing number of messages, emanating from numerous sources. If a company's message is confusing or lacks impact, it may go unnoticed. Some competitors deliberately send out messages that are intended to ambush or take away from another company's message.

Other distractions are found in the receiver's immediate environment. For example, the receipt of a telephone call when an advertisement is being broadcast is a distraction.

Sensational headlines and stories in a newspaper may divert the reader's attention away from advertisements. Many advertisers had to resign themselves to the presence of significant 'noise' in the period immediately after the 11 September 2001 attacks.

Feedback

In order to evaluate whether or not effective communication has taken place, it is desirable that the sender receives feedback. The type of response issued by the receiver provides the sender with some level of feedback. In situations where the message has invited the receiver to do something, 'no response' is taken as feedback. While feedback of this nature is not very encouraging, it merits further investigation. Senders must identify reasons why the intended recipient has not responded. Research can be conducted to assess whether or not the message was understood, and whether or not it was sent via the most appropriate media. The sender must also judge whether or not the level of noise caused too many distractions. As explained above, noise levels are often outside the sender's control. However, it may be possible to devise inventive ways of minimising the likelihood of encountering noise levels the next time.

Direct and immediate responses are not always required when a message is transmitted, for example, public service information. Therefore, it may not be possible to gauge whether or not the message has been received and decoded correctly. In such instances, the sender should conduct research to find out whether or not the message has been received and understood.

Sales often provide the sender with a form of feedback. However, other factors must be taken into account when analysing sales levels in the period after marketing communications activity. Such factors include uncontrollable external environmental shocks and opportunities such as extreme weather conditions, traffic, industrial action, terrorism and economic change.

Messages transmitted through direct marketing media incorporate mechanisms that provide feedback to the sender. These include invitations to respond by telephone, mail and e-mail. Any responses received are directly attributed to the successful transmission of the message. Sales promotions response rates are measured by analysing uptake levels.

How many money-off coupons were redeemed? How many free gifts were ordered? How many 'buy one, get one free' packs were sold?

Personal selling makes it possible for the sender to actively encourage a response and to gather feedback. Sales representatives can judge whether or not their messages have been decoded correctly by listening carefully to the responses. If they are not getting their message across effectively, they can change it accordingly.

The ways that the effectiveness of marketing communications is measured are summarised in Table 2.1.

Table 2.1 Measuring marketing communications effectiveness

- Research to assess target audience's awareness and understanding of the message
- Identification of noise sources
- Sales levels
- Direct response rates e.g. number of calls made to free phone numbers, website visits
- Uptake of sales promotions e.g. coupons, gifts, etc.
- Feedback gathered by sales representatives

Semiotics and interpreting communications

Schramm's illustration of the communication process, as shown in Figure 2.1 (page 25), clearly depicts what Price (1997) refers to as 'the exchange of meaning between human agents'. Meaning is articulated in various forms and senders use a code to put a meaning on their messages.

Dyer (1982) describes **codes** as 'a set of rules or an interpretative device known to both transmitter and receiver, which assigns a certain meaning or content to a certain sign.' While Price (1998) concurs with this description, his definition of codes suggests that different cultures use different signs to communicate or use similar symbols to communicate differently than other cultures. He says that codes are 'a system which allows a particular culture to communicate through the use of signs'. Therefore, an understanding of the various interpretations placed on codes by people in different cultures is essential for any organisation implementing marketing communications programmes in more than one country. The use of colour is an important part of some elements of the marketing communications mix, and yet different colours convey different meanings in different cultures. For example, white represents purity and cleanliness in most western societies, whereas it signifies death in some Asian countries (Keegan and Green, 2000.).

Codes
A common set of rules or interpretative devices known to the sender and receiver of messages. They assign a specific meaning or content to a sign.

A wide range of signs is available to the sender – written and spoken, symbols and gestures. **Semiotics** involves the study and interpretation of the various signs, whether verbal, visual or both, used in communication. Ferdinand de Saussure is

Semiotics
The study and interpretation of various signs used in communication.

widely acknowledged as the founder of semiotics and he defined it as 'a science that studies the life of signs within society' (cited in Dyer, 1982). According to Wilkie (1990) symbols and signs perform two important functions:

- **They improve consumers' efficiency**. This function is best illustrated with reference to brands. In contemporary society, brand marks convey information to those who see them. When a consumer buys a product or service, an encounter with an already familiar brand mark can be compared to meeting an old acquaintance. As a result of marketing communications campaigns or previous experiences with the brand, the consumer can decide quickly whether or not they wish to continue the relationship. If they happily opt for the familiar brand, time does not have to be invested in analysing other less familiar brands.
- **They add to the enjoyment of consumers' activities.** Some brands instil confidence in the user and reduce uncertainty. Manufacturers of products that involve conspicuous consumption, such as clothing, cars and perfumes, invest heavily in brands. They know that if their consumers are confident in the brand, they will in turn feel better about themselves.

An understanding of semiotics is very important for the creative minds behind marketing communications. The symbolism used, particularly in advertising, is capable of conveying many important messages to the target audience. However, if inappropriate signs or symbols are used, the message can be undermined, misunderstood, cause offence or go unnoticed. Humans are visual beings and respond well to visual triggers. Through a lifetime of socialisation, certain signs acquire particular meanings in contemporary culture. Of course the use of symbolism to communicate has been in existence for many centuries and this fact is evident in the visual arts. For example, due to its prowess in the natural world, artists regularly use the lion to symbolise the state in paintings and sculptures.

Dyer (1982) contends that a range of visual symbols are used to convey meaning in marketing communications (see Table 2.2).

Table 2.2 Visual symbols used to convey meaning in marketing communications

Hair	Clothes
Body	Activity
Relative size	• Touch
Looks	• Body movement
Manner	• Positional communication
• Expression	Props and settings
• Eye contact	
• Pose	

Source: Adapted from Dyer (1982)

Hair

Depending on how it is arranged, hair can convey a wide variety of messages, from the sensible working woman to the rebellious youth to the sexy siren. The style in which the stars of advertisements wear their hair is no accident but is used to communicate a particular message.

Body

'Thin, fat, short, tall, clothed, partially clothed' – according to Dyer, all of these convey very different things to the intended recipient of the message. The decision to photograph top model Sophie Dahl in a provocative pose wearing nothing but diamonds to advertise the Yves Saint-Laurent perfume, Opium, was a deliberate tactic. It attracted high levels of media attention around the world and in December 2002 the offending advertisement was the centre of controversy in Ballina, Co. Mayo:

Ballina mayor says poster is offensive to women

A life-size advertisement poster of a nude supermodel has been removed from a shop window in Ballina, Co. Mayo, by order of the mayor. The poster of Sophie Dahl portrays the size-12 model lying on her back. It was on display in a pharmacy shop-front for three weeks but has been removed following complaints.

Ballina's mayor, Mr Ray Collins, said he objected to the poster as he deemed it offensive to women and suggestive in its pose. He was taking a stand because once this kind of thing started, you never knew where it would stop. 'I got complaints on this from a few women over the phone and some I met in the town. After it was removed, many were delighted but others said they were used to worse with page three girls in the paper every day. But my point is it is offensive to women and Christmas is not the time of year for it. It is women who do all the shopping, the cooking and the lot at Christmas. They have enough going on without having to be subjected to this kind of thing too.'

The mayor, an Independent councillor, asked why women were portrayed naked in everything from advertising to films on television and why men were not portrayed in the same way.

Mr Padraic Ward, proprietor of Ward's pharmacy on Pearse Street, Ballina, expressed surprise at the public reaction to the poster. 'When the mayor rang and complained, for the craic I put yellow luminous paper over the model's breast and wrote, "by order of the mayor". A huge amount had not even noticed the poster until then but after that, cars and trucks at the traffic junction up from the shop would be flashing their lights.'

He added that Yves Saint-Laurent, the company responsible for the poster, had difficulty getting pharmacies in the UK to display it, although it is regularly used in women's magazines. Six years ago, when the model in question was a size 16, nobody objected to a nude poster of her on display in his shop window then. 'I don't know where she has lost the weight from but I would still have no complaints about her at size 16.' Asked whether sales of the perfume had increased as a result, Mr Ward replied: 'Probably, but what I have really noticed is that the sale of Viagra has gone through the roof so obviously this has all had a very good effect on the men of Ballina.'

In a spirit of goodwill, Mr Ward agreed to remove the offending picture from his window and presented it to the mayor.

Source: *The Irish Times*, 19 December 2002

In contrast, in the 2002/3 print advertising campaign for Estée Lauder's perfume, 'Pleasures Intense', Catherine Zeta Jones wears a white nightdress, which exudes innocence and purity.

Actress Dawn French is the face of Terry's Chocolate Orange product line. She is perceived as an attractive woman with a fuller figure and appeals to the target audience. It is widely acknowledged that while she is attractive, she is also accessible and considered by many of the target audience as being 'one of us' because of her size.

Relative size

The relative size of one actor in an advertisement in relation to another conveys messages regarding hierarchy. Who is in charge? Who is the victim? Who is being cared for?

Looks

Controversially, many advertisements reinforce the ideal look for a particular point in time. This places immense pressure on target audiences to achieve 'the look', be it through excessive dieting or expenditure on expensive clothes and personal items, such as jewellery and cosmetics.

Manner

Dyer states that, 'manner indicates behaviour or emotion at any one time.' This is expressed through three codes of non-verbal communication:

- **Expression** conveys human states such as happiness, sadness, terror, despair, cool, love, delight and pleasure. These states transfer meaning to the message. The cosmetics company Rimmel chose the supermodel Kate Moss to revive their brand because she is considered to be the very embodiment of what it means to be 'cool'. Her manner in the advertisements exudes a 'coolness' that is then transferred to the Rimmel brand.

- The actor in an advertisement or a brochure can be instructed to look directly at the camera so as to make **eye contact** with the target audience. A widely used creative approach is to hide all features of a model's face, leaving only the eyes looking directly at the audience. In other instances the actor might be instructed to look at an object, which may be the product itself, or to completely shield the eyes with sunglasses, a hand, hair or a hat. A third approach for the actor might be to engage in what Dyer describes as a detached or distant gaze.

- According to Dyer, an actor's **pose** in an advertisement can be 'composed, relaxed, leisurely, passive, leaning, seductive, snuggling'. Since the 1970s, Cadbury's advertisements for Flake have featured attractive models in seductive poses in order to trigger certain feelings towards the brand.

Clothes

The clothes that people wear communicate a lot about a particular situation and can in turn convey certain messages to the intended audience, for example, formal, casual, sporty, seductive and party clothes. Sales representatives pay close attention to the messages conveyed by their clothing.

Activity

Dyer proposes three categories to deal with activity in advertising:

- **touch**. Depending on how it is done, touch can be used to convey sexual messages or to demonstrate the virtues of a product in a very practical way. For example, part of the controversy which resulted from the Opium advertisement featuring Sophie Dahl (see pages 33–4) was the fact that she was touching herself in a highly suggestive manner. In contrast, Black & Decker advertisements use touch in order to demonstrate the practical aspects of their power tools.

- **body movement**. In 1994, Guinness launched their classic television, cinema and poster campaign entitled 'Anticipation', which featured Joe McKinney dancing (Davies, 1998). The time taken to pour a pint of Guinness is very important to the quality of the final product. The frenetic movement of McKinney was used to demonstrate that this time should not be greeted impatiently, but savoured and enjoyed.

- **positional communication**. This is what Dyer describes as 'the relationships between actors and actors, and actors and objects.' Close-up shots signify intimacy while long shots are considered more remote.

Exhibit 2.2

Props and settings

These are things such as furniture (props), weather and colour (settings) and the product itself. Props are used to demonstrate the product's use (for example, Eircom's new generation digital home phones) and results of usage (shampoo advertising often demonstrates the benefits of using a particular brand in the guise of shining, healthy hair). Props also have a more functional role. For example, in 2002 a series of hard-hitting advertisements aimed at drivers and pedestrians were launched in a bid to reduce road deaths. A Renault Mégane car was used as a prop in one of these advertisements. The chief executive of Renault Ireland complained and argued that people might associate the Mégane with dangerous driving. He sought to prevent the advertisement being broadcast and would only allow the Mégane to be used if the brand name were distorted and unrecognisable.

As explained by Dyer, some props have been used so often that they have acquired 'symbolic value' – a meaning that goes way beyond their literal sense. For example, the umbrella is a widely used prop in insurance advertising and is immediately interpreted as meaning protection. Some well-known brands use the same prop in their advertising year in, year out. This aids instant recognition. For example, when people see an Old English Sheep Dog in advertisements, they think of Dulux paints. When they see an Irish redsetter, they might think of Bus Eireann. Polar bears are now synonymous with one of the world's most famous brands, Coca-Cola.

Buying behaviour

As shown in Figure 2.1 (page 25), a key player in the communications process is the receiver of the message. In order to communicate with the receiver, the sender must understand what makes the receiver tick and why they behave in the way they do. A thorough analysis of buying behaviour is beyond the remit of this text. However, some key concepts will be addressed. Marketing communications practitioners use these concepts to ensure that their messages are relevant to the target audience.

First of all, the difference between consumer buying behaviour and business buying behaviour is explained. **Consumer buying behaviour** involves buyers who purchase products and services for final consumption, for example, a teenager who buys a pair of trainers. It is non-commercial activity. **Business buying behaviour** refers to those buyers who purchase products and services for use in the production of other products and services that are sold or rented to others, for example, a bakery that purchases half a tonne of flour (Armstrong and Kotler, 2003). Both types of buyers are influenced and motivated by different factors (see Table 2.3).

Consumer buying behaviour
The behaviour shaping the purchase of products and services for final consumption.

Business buyer behaviour
The behaviour of buyers purchasing products and services for use in the production of other products and services that are sold or rented to others.

Organisations engaging in marketing communication must build a detailed profile of their target audiences, based on the categories outlined in Table 2.3. Since this book mainly concentrates on consumers, the factors influencing consumer buying behaviour will now be examined in greater detail. Those factors influencing business buying behaviour are more self-explanatory.

Factors influencing consumer buying behaviour

There are four main factors that influence consumer buying behaviour.

Cultural factors

Culture is deeply embedded in consumers because it represents a person's values, perceptions and behaviours. Culture is learned at an early age from family members and institutions such as schools, church and clubs. From the marketer's perspective, it is deeply embedded and cannot be changed in the short term. This is not to say that culture is static. Irish culture has changed dramatically since the 1980s and the church is much less influential than it was. Such shifts must be monitored by organisations so that their communications remain relevant.

Culture *represents a person's values, perceptions and behaviours.*

While people talk about 'Irish culture' or 'French culture', it is wrong to assume that everyone living in those countries shares the same culture. Greater mobility between countries has led to the emergence of subcultures in many countries. This is a relatively new phenomenon in Ireland, which until the 1990s was a monoculture, that is one culture was dominant. Immigration has led to the emergence of a number of subcultures that originate from a range of countries. Subcultures might also include minority religious groups. Care must be taken not to offend members of these subcultures. Many organisations specifically target some of their communications at subcultures.

Table 2.3 Factors influencing consumer and business buying behaviour

CONSUMER BUYING BEHAVIOUR	BUSINESS BUYING BEHAVIOUR
Cultural factors • Culture • Subculture • Social class	**Environmental factors** • Economic developments • Supply conditions • Technological change • Political and regulatory developments • Competitive developments • Culture and customs
Social factors • Reference groups • Family • Roles and status	**Organisational factors** • Objectives • Policies • Procedures • Organisational structure • Systems
Personal factors • Age and life-cycle stage • Occupation • Economic situation • Lifestyle	**Interpersonal factors** • Authority • Status • Empathy • Persuasiveness
Psychological factors • Motivation • Perception • Learning • Beliefs and attitudes	**Individual factors** • Age • Income • Education • Job position • Personality • Risk attitudes.

Source: Adapted from Armstrong and Kotler (2003)

Social class refers to the way in which a country's society is structured. In Ireland social class is primarily determined by occupation. This classification system utilises the ABC1C2D and E categories and is widely used, yet limited. Occupation used to be a very reliable indicator of spending power. However, the economic boom in the 1990s meant that some of the salaries of the occupations in the manual labour categories C2 and D overtook some of the occupations in ABC1. Therefore, organisations still use this system but augment it with other information on education, income and interests.

Social factors

Reference groups exert strong influence over consumer buying behaviour because many people have a very strong desire to belong. They try to fit in with people from various groups when they buy products or services and use them to vindicate their choices. These groups might consist of people with whom they spend considerable amounts of time, for example, school or work peers. Consumers often aspire to belong to certain unattainable groups. For example, Arnott's sponsorship of the Dublin Football team has proved very successful and sales of the Dublin jersey to fans were very high in 2002. While most fans will never actually play for Dublin, wearing the jersey enables them to belong in some small way.

Family members influence consumer buying behaviour. Children exert considerable pressure and influence on parents in a number of product categories including food, clothing and cars. Advertisers know this and often direct campaigns at children in the knowledge that they will influence their parents.

Roles and status influence buying behaviour. Someone's occupation and their resulting status in society play an important part in that person's buying behaviour. For example, many people believe that the car they drive, the clothes they wear and place they live should reflect their status in society.

Personal factors

Personal factors include straightforward descriptors such as age, occupation and economic situation. Age usually indicates a person's life-cycle stage. The life-cycle stage shows how purchasing patterns change as consumers go through different stages in their lives. Car manufacturers and financial institutions are just two industries that pay attention to this concept when marketing their products and services. For example, in an effort to retain customers for life, AIB Bank markets financial products that satisfy customers' different needs as they go through different life stages. These might include students, graduates, those living with a partner, married, married with young children, married with teenage or college-going children, married with children living away from home, retired, and widowed.

Activities, interests and opinions determine a person's lifestyle. Many marketers use databases to record information relating to customers' lifestyles. When individual customers are not known by name, marketers engage in market research to gain an insight into the target audience's lifestyle profile.

Psychological factors

Psychological factors are more difficult to quantify than cultural, social and personal factors. In an effort to understand the psychological factors influencing consumers, many organisations engage in in-depth market research. According to Armstrong and Kotler (2003), psychological factors can be further broken down into the following: motivation, perception, learning, and beliefs and attitudes.

Motivation

Motive
A pressing need that directs a person to satisfy the need.

Understanding the factors that motivate consumers is essential for marketing communications practitioners. Armstrong and Kotler define a **motive** as 'a need that is sufficiently pressing to direct the person to seek satisfaction of the need'. The work of two academics in particular are still applied in the marketing communications industry – Sigmund Freud and Abraham Maslow.

Freud's motivation theories are largely based on the premise that both conscious and unconscious forces motivate individuals. However, he was particularly interested in the conscious forces that motivate people's behaviour and believed that many of our actions may result from our life experiences. Advertisers, in particular brand advertisers, have tapped into this aspect of motivation. Some critics contend that they use it in a manipulative way. For example, someone buying a BMW car may argue that they are buying it for its superb engineering and reliability, whereas there might be a deeper motivation behind the decision. Perhaps they are buying it in order to create a particular self-image of success and status.

Maslow's motivation theory (as illustrated in Figure 2.2) is based on the premise that a hierarchy of needs motivates people.

The most basic needs, physiological and safety, must be satisfied before a person can

Figure 2.2 Maslow's hierarchy of needs

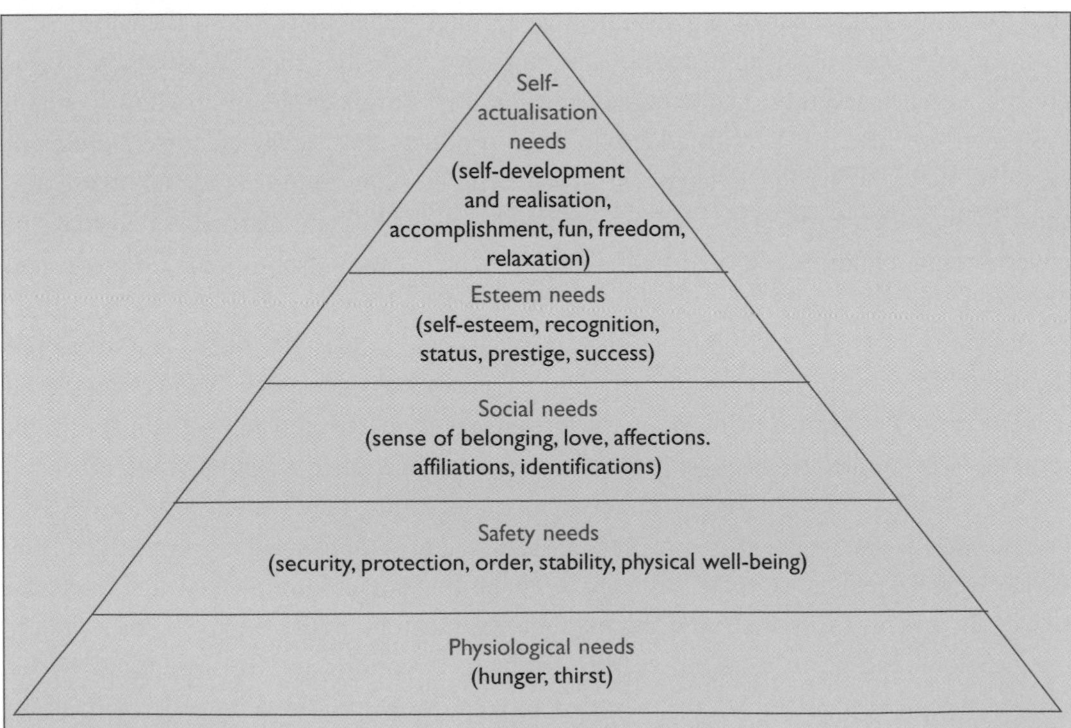

Source: Maslow (1954)

even think of satisfying needs that are more psychological than physical. However, organisations that deliver products and services must recognise that, while Maslow's hierarchy offers a logical approach to motivation, people move up and down the hierarchy due to changing circumstances. For example, a person might purchase a particular brand of soft drink in a bar in order to satisfy social needs (e.g. to generate a sense of belonging). In different circumstances, for example, a very hot day, the same person might purchase the same soft drink in order to satisfy a physiological need (e.g. thirst). Organisations must recognise that different circumstances create different needs. Consequently, different people are motivated by different needs, and the same person is motivated by different needs at different times.

Perception

Armstrong and Kotler (2003) define **perception** as 'the process by which people select, organise and interpret information to form a meaningful picture of the world'. This concept is important in marketing communications because different people perceive the same thing differently. This is caused by:

Perception *The process by which people select, organise and interpret information.*

- **selective attention**. As mentioned earlier in this chapter, one of the greatest communication challenges is getting noticed through high levels of noise or distractions. Therefore, people engage in selective attention and screen out messages that they do not consider relevant or that do not grab their attention. This means that the quality of the offer and the creativity used in marketing communications are important when attempting to combat the negative aspects of selective attention.

Selective attention *Screening out information.*

- **selective distortion**. According to Armstrong and Kotler, this is 'the tendency of people to interpret information in a way that will support what they already believe'. Therefore, if a person has already formed an opinion about something, they may not interpret a message in the way that it was intended. This presents difficulties for organisations held in low regard by target audiences. When they try to change their image, people may engage in selective distortion and focus on their formed opinions.

  Selective distortion can also be an advantage. Many people hold certain brands in high regard. When given messages about competing brands, they may not be able to look beyond a particular brand. This affords many brand leaders protection from competitor attacks.

Selective distortion *Interpreting information in a way that supports a person's existing beliefs.*

- **selective retention**. People only retain a certain amount of information. Therefore, they 'tend to retain information that supports their attitudes and beliefs' (Armstrong and Kotler, 2003). Once again, the level of creativity in marketing communications is an important tool for combating this problem.

Selective retention *Retention of information that supports a person's attitudes and beliefs.*

Messages delivered with impact and in a way that the target audience relates to are more likely to overcome the hurdle of selective retention.

Learning

Organisations find it useful to understand how people develop attitudes towards products and services. In other words, how do people learn? Connectionist learning theories contend that, 'associations can be made between messages or stimuli, and responses' (Smith, 1998). Marketing communications is used to send out messages in order to elicit a particular response. It is intended that the repetition of messages will lead to automatic responses. For example, Clarks means children's shoes; Flora means low cholesterol; Lidl means low prices. The connectionist theories work on the assumption that, if people respond to a stimulus, the nature of their experience reinforces their opinions. These opinions help shape future behaviour.

Beliefs and attitudes

Belief *Descriptive thought that a person holds about something.*

Experience and learning helps form beliefs and attitudes and these influence consumer buying behaviour. Armstrong and Kotler (2003) define a **belief** as 'a descriptive thought that a person holds about something'. Beliefs can be based on actual experience or research. People gather research about products and services from elements of the marketing mix (e.g. personal selling, publicity, advertising, etc.) and from friends, family and acquaintances (word of mouth). In situations where beliefs about a product or service are negative, corrective action must be taken to change the consumer's viewpoint.

Attitudes *Consistently favourable or unfavourable evaluations, feelings and tendencies towards an object or concept.*

According to Armstrong and Kotler, **attitudes** are 'a person's consistently favourable or unfavourable evaluations, feelings, and tendencies toward an object or idea'.

To create relevant, appealing and inoffensive marketing communications campaigns, marketers must understand their target audience's attitudes towards topics such as religion, politics, music, the environment, food and drink, and sport (particularly affiliations to particular clubs). Unlike beliefs, attitudes are more difficult to change. This perhaps explains why so many public health campaigns do not succeed. Many young people have very positive attitudes towards the use of so-called recreational drugs and do not respond to advertisements aimed at changing these attitudes.

The buyer decision process

In this section, various marketing communications models are presented. Many of them are based on buyer decision process models. Figure 2.3 shows both the consumer buyer decision process and the business buyer decision process.

Figure 2.3 Consumer and business buyer decision processes

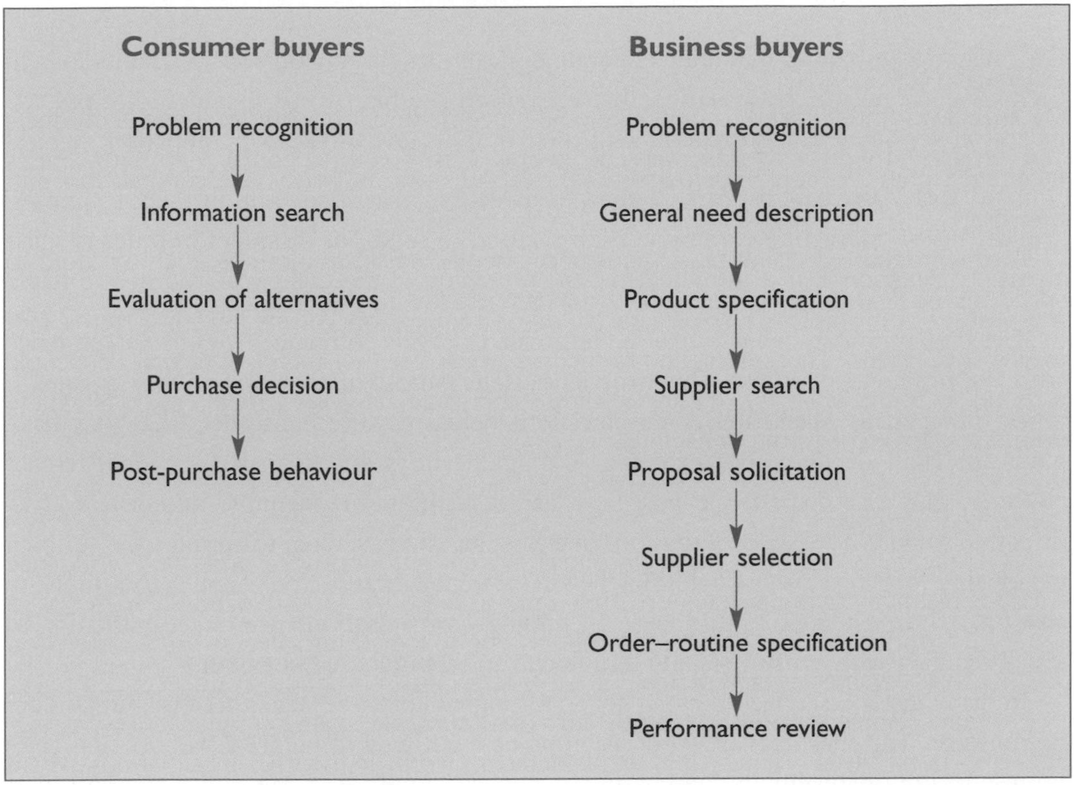

Consumer buyers	Business buyers
Problem recognition	Problem recognition
↓	↓
Information search	General need description
↓	↓
Evaluation of alternatives	Product specification
↓	↓
Purchase decision	Supplier search
↓	↓
Post-purchase behaviour	Proposal solicitation
	↓
	Supplier selection
	↓
	Order–routine specification
	↓
	Performance review

The consumer buyer decision process

The consumer decision process illustrated in Figure 2.3a is based on the assumption that people always behave in a rational way and go through a number of stages before finally deciding to purchase a product or service. For high-involvement items which involve a certain amount of risk, this is often the case. For example, if someone is purchasing a car, the wrong decision is costly in financial terms or it could undermine a person's status. Firms use marketing communications to influence the target audience's behaviour at each stage. In many circumstances, consumers do not identify needs for themselves, so organisations are more than happy to help them. For example, when Vodafone launched their picture messaging service 'live' in 2002, they used advertising to support it. Prior to this, the target audience did not know that they 'needed' the service.

At the information search stage, consumers rely on many sources:

- advertising
- the media (newspaper and magazine articles, television documentaries, radio programmes)
- sales representatives
- word of mouth

- direct mail
- the Internet.

If a consumer purchases in a retail environment, they might rely on sales assistants to help them evaluate all the information. In recognition of this, many organisations provide incentives for retail staff to recommend their product over that of a competitor. Typical incentives might include 'Sales person of the month' awards, prizes in a competition, and bonuses.

At the purchase decision stage, consumer-oriented sales promotions might be used to speed up the decision or to persuade a consumer to favour one product over another.

The post-purchase behaviour of a consumer is largely influenced by their experience with the product or service. This experience determines whether or not they engage in repeat purchasing. Marketing communications helps reassure consumers that they have made the right decision. For example, if someone buys an expensive branded item of clothing, they may experience post-purchase discomfort or cognitive dissonance. This discomfort might be reduced if the consumer sees an advertisement featuring a well-known personality wearing a piece of clothing bearing the same brand. Sponsorship and publicity also provide reassurance at this stage. Increasingly, organisations use direct marketing to stay in contact with consumers and to influence post-purchase behaviour.

In many instances, consumers do not go through all of these stages because humans are not rational. The consumer buyer decision process outlined in Figure 2.3a does not really represent low-involvement purchases or repeat purchases. Many low-involvement purchases do not cost a lot of money and do not merit extensive research. If the consumer makes the wrong decision, the financial loss is negligible and they need never purchase the product again. Some products are purchased on a daily or weekly basis, and the process is routine. The consumer simply moves straight from problem recognition to purchase decision. Finally, the issue of impulse purchasing is ignored in Figure 2.3a. Even if a consumer goes through the first three stages as depicted, a last-minute message may cause them to change their mind. This often occurs in the retail environment where attractive point-of-purchase offers from competing companies are displayed. These offers usually highlight attractive prices, features and free extras.

The business buyer decision process

As illustrated in Figure 2.3, there are more stages in the business buyer decision process. This is because the products and services purchased by business customers are often very expensive and directly or indirectly impact on the well-being of the organisation. In many cases, this contributes to a lengthy, drawn-out purchasing cycle so that the most appropriate decision is reached. There are usually more people involved in the purchasing decision and this adds to the complexity.

For high-value, strategically important purchases, the stages outlined are usually followed. In the early stages of problem definition, general need description and product specification, proactive sales representatives play a significant role. At the supplier search stage, advertising, the Internet, press releases in trade journals, trade shows, word of mouth, experience and personal selling are important influences. Sales promotion techniques, such as favourable prices, can be implemented at the latter stages in order to persuade the buyer to reach a final decision.

When a business buyer makes a routine purchase, they are unlikely to go through all of the stages shown in Figure 2.3. For example, if they reorder stationery, such as paper clips and photocopying paper, they will probably return to the previous supplier rather than search for the number of a new supplier. With regard to routine purchases, the purchasing task becomes one of routine reordering from a pre-approved panel of suppliers.

Marketing communications models

Buyer behaviour theory is central to many marketing communications models. These offer possible explanations as to why the receiver of marketing messages might behave in a particular way.

The AIDA model

The AIDA model represents **A**ttention, **I**nterest, **D**esire and **A**ction. Originally it was developed as a tool for salespeople and proposes that there are a number of stages that a salesperson must go through in order to achieve a sale. These stages are illustrated in Figure 2.4.

Figure 2.4 The AIDA model

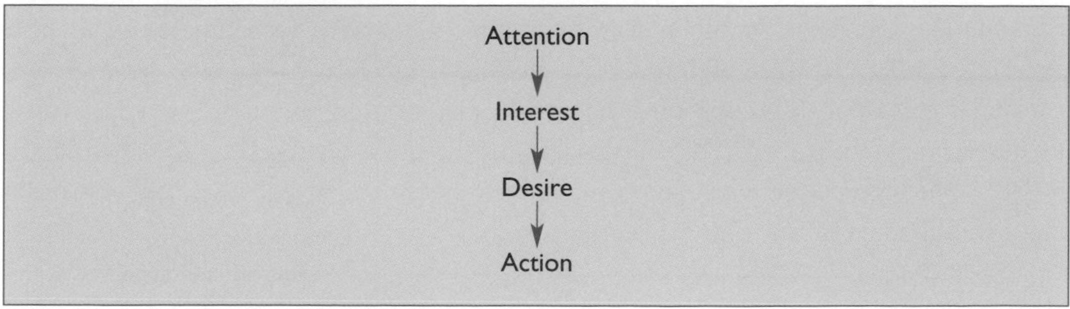

The 'hierarchy of effects' model

As far back as 1961, Lavidge and Steiner proposed that, while the ultimate function of advertising is to produce sales, it cannot be expected to trigger immediate purchases. Therefore advertising effectiveness should be measured in a long-term context. In reality, marketing managers are placed under immense pressure to deliver immediate results i.e. sales through advertising expenditure.

Lavidge and Steiner's 'hierarchy of effects' model proposes that a prospect typically moves through a number of stages before actually buying the advertised product or service. These stages are outlined in Figure 2.5 and appropriate marketing communications activities are suggested for each stage. Each stage is categorised as one of the following:

- **cognitive**. The consumer wants to discover what products are out there and adopts a learning state of mind. They are open to suggestions and information because this enables them to make decisions at a later stage.
- **affective**. Once a consumer has gathered information, emotional factors come into play. Organisations use marketing communications to differentiate their products by focusing on more emotive issues, for example, 'Buy this product and it will make you feel better' or 'Buy this product because it is much better than product Y.'
- **conative**. Even when consumers have positive feelings towards certain products, these must be harnessed and turned into action-oriented behaviour. Sales promotions are often used to elicit such action.

The 'hierarchy of effects' model is still used by marketing communications agencies and their clients to set objectives and evaluate the success or otherwise of campaigns.

Figure 2.5 The 'hierarchy of effects' model

Related behavioural dimension	Movement toward purchase	Advertising and promotion relevant to each step
Conative i.e. motivational	Purchase ↑ Conviction	Point-of-purchase Retail store ads Deals Last chance offers Price appeals Testimonials
Affective i.e. emotional/feeling states	↑ Preference ↑ Liking	Competitive ads Argumentative copy Image ads Status, glamour appeals
Cognitive i.e. intellectual, mental or rational states	↑ Knowledge ↑ Awareness	Announcements Descriptive copy Classified ads Slogans Jingles Sky writing Teaser campaigns

Source: Lavidge and Steiner (1961)

The 'consumer adoption process' model

Shortly after the emergence of the 'hierarchy of effects' model, Rogers (1962) devised the 'consumer adoption process' model (see Figure 2.6). It is based on the 'diffusion of innovations' model.

Figure 2.6 The 'consumer adoption process' model

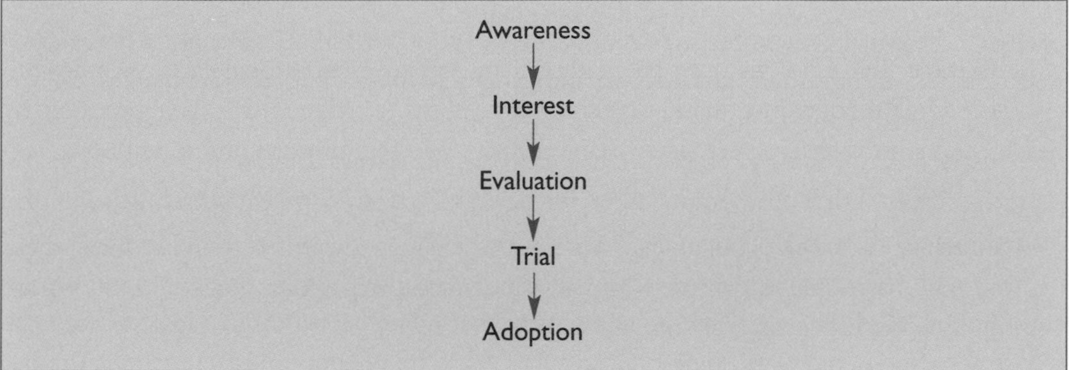

The information-processing model of advertising effects

In 1978, McGuire published his information-processing model of advertising effects (see Figure 2.7). Central to his findings was the assumption that the receiver of advertising messages is a rational being and likes processing information and solving problems.

Figure 2.7 The information-processing model of advertising effects

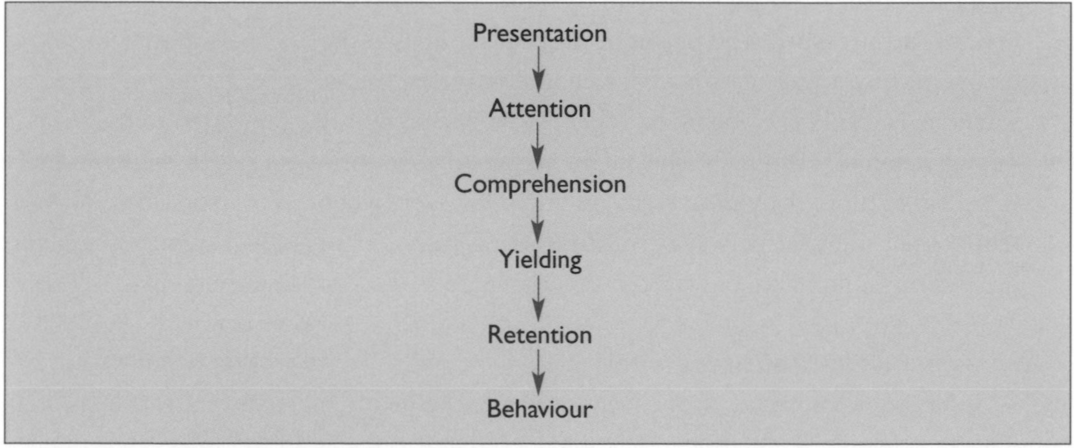

Critical assessment of hierarchical models of marketing communications

Each of the four models outlined above takes a hierarchical approach to the marketing communications challenge. They therefore support the basic consumer behaviour model which also takes a hierarchical approach. From a practical point of view, they recognise that different people in the target audience are at different stages in terms of their likelihood to purchase a product or service. This means that they require different marketing communications tactics. If someone is totally unaware of the existence of a particular product, a 'jingle-based' advertising campaign might be launched in order to raise awareness. For example, RTE used a jingle to build awareness and knowledge about its Telebingo programme. The words 'Telebingo Tuesday night' were repeated and set to a catchy tune that embedded itself in the target audience's mind. Where awareness and knowledge of a product is already high, marketing communications might be used to persuade the target audience to take action. It is common for FMCG manufacturers to work with retailers selling their products to implement point-of-purchase campaigns. When Yoplait launched their 'Everybody' product, they used advertising to raise awareness and then used in-store sales promotions to persuade the target audience to purchase the product. These sales promotions took the form of in-store product tastings and the distribution of money-off coupons.

The main shortcomings of the models lie in the fact that human beings are not logical and rational all of the time. The models assume that buyers go through a logical sequence before deciding to purchase something and that marketing communications can be used at each stage. They do not take into account the following situations:

- **impulse purchasing**. Buyers do not always feel it necessary to know everything about a product or service before actually purchasing it.
- **situation-induced purchasing**. If someone is faced with an unexpected situation, they may purchase a product or service without going through the sequence of events in the hierarchy. For example, if somebody is taken ill and requires over-the-counter medication, they may go directly to the purchase stage of the hierarchy.
- **peer-group pressure**. The power of the peer group and the salesperson in persuading people to buy a product or service should never be underestimated. For example, if someone is thinking of buying a DVD player, they might be committed to the idea of buying a Sony DVD player. This might be due to prior experience with Sony products which is reinforced by Sony's advertising. However, when the person goes into the retail outlet, the salesperson persuades them to buy a Philips DVD player by moving the person from a state of no prior knowledge to a purchase situation.

The dissonance/attribution model

In 1973, Ray took into account the fact that while the hierarchical approach is helpful, it is not appropriate in all situations. He contended that it is useful for products and services where the buyer is very involved in the purchasing process. If someone is likely to spend a large amount of money on something, they are more likely to take a rational approach to the purchase. Low-involvement, low-risk purchases do not require the same approach. Ray proposed the dissonance/attribution model. It states that in many purchasing situations people:

- do (i.e. purchase)
- feel (i.e. form an opinion about the product or service based on their experience of it)
- learn (i.e. decide whether or not they will buy the product or service again).

In these circumstances, marketing communications is used to reassure people after they have purchased the product or service that they have made the right decision.

Summary

To fully understand marketing communications, the word 'communications' was explored. Communication is a two-way process that involves the exchange of messages between two or more parties. It is often intended that some sort of action or response will result from the communication. Successful communication depends on the relationship that exists between the sender and receiver of the message. The type of message, its timing and the environment in which it is communicated are key success factors in communication.

Codes are used to send messages and senders should have an understanding of semiotics. This involves the study and interpretation of the various signs used in communication. Advertisers use a number of visual symbols to convey their messages including hair, looks, manner, activity, props and settings.

To communicate effectively, a thorough understanding of the target audience must be gained. Various factors influence consumer and business buying behaviour. If these are known, marketing communications messages will be more relevant.

Some theorists propose that consumers and business buyers go through a number of stages before reaching a purchase decision. However, it should be remembered that humans are not rational beings and do not always progress through a series of logical steps. Marketing communications is used in an effort to keep target audiences on track or to motivate them to change their minds.

Review questions

1. Illustrate the communications process and explain each component in detail. In your explanation, show how is it relevant to marketing communications theory.
2. Many organisations use actors, models and celebrities to convey their messages. What criteria should they fulfil? Use examples to illustrate your answer.
3. Explain how symbols and signs assist consumers.
4. What is semiotics?
5. What are the factors that influence consumer buying behaviour and business buying behaviour?
6. Critically assess the following marketing communications models:

a. the AIDA model
b. the 'hierarchy of effects' model
c. the 'consumer adoption process' model
d. the information-processing model of advertising effects.

Exercise

Select a television advertisement of your choice and, using Table 2.2 (page 32), analyse the signs (verbal, visual or both).

References

Armstrong, Gary and Kotler, Philip, *Marketing: An Introduction* (Pearson Education, Inc., 2003).

Davies, Jim, *The Book of Guinness Advertising* (Guinness Publishing Limited, 1998).

Dyer, Gillian, *Advertising as Communication* (Methuen, London, 1982).

Keegan, Warren J. and Green, Mark S., *Global Marketing*, 2nd edition (Prentice Hall, 2000).

Lavidge, R. J. and Steiner, G. A., 'A Model for Predictive Measurements of Advertising Effectiveness' (*Journal of Marketing*, pp. 59–62, October 1961).

Maslow, A., *Motivation and Personality* (Harper & Row, New York, 1954).

McGuire, William, J., 'An Information Processing Model of Advertising Effectiveness' in *Behavioural and Management Science in Marketing*, eds Davis, Harry, J. and Silk, Alvin J. (New York: Ronald Press, 1978).

Price, Stuart, *The A–Z of Media and Communications Handbook* (Hodder & Stoughton, 1997).

Price, Stuart, *Media Studies*, 2nd edition (Pearson Education, 1998).

Ray, Michael, L., 'Communication and the Hierarchy of Effects' in *New Models for Mass Communication Research*, ed. Clarke, P. (Sage Publications, 1973).

Rogers, Everett M., *Diffusion of Innovations* (New York: Free Press, 1962).

Schramm, Wilbur, *The Process and Effects of Mass Communications* (Urbana, Illinois: University of Illinois Press, 1955).

Smith, P. R., *Marketing Communications: An Integrated Approach*, 2nd edition (Kogan Page, 1998).

Wilkie, William L., *Consumer Behaviour*, 2nd edition (John Wiley & Sons, Inc., 1990).

3

CORPORATE IDENTITY

The aims and objectives of this chapter are:

- to explain corporate identity
- to examine the relevance of corporate identity to marketing communications
- to enable you to define corporate identity and differentiate between corporate identity and corporate image
- to help you identify the five main elements of corporate identity
- to recognise the three main types of corporate identity
- to examine the reasons why companies might change their corporate identity
- to explain the steps involved in creating and implementing a corporate identity programme
- to recognise the importance of corporate identity as the foundation for excellent marketing communications.

Introduction

Much confusion surrounds the term 'corporate identity'. It is all too frequently perceived as a mere logo and consequently, many contend that it belongs in the world of graphic design. This chapter demonstrates that corporate identity is far more than just a logo. It is the foundation upon which an organisation's products are created, its employees behaviours are shaped, and its marketing communications are created. It can help firms achieve consistency in their marketing communications and this can in turn support many of them in their move towards integrated marketing communications.

Exhibit 3.1a

In 1999, Telecom Eireann changed its name to Eircom and implemented the biggest corporate identity programme ever witnessed in

Ireland. It represented far more than a name and logo change. For Eircom, it heralded a new way of communicating with its publics and mirrored a strategy that is used by organisations throughout the world. The rapidly changing environment in which most organisations find themselves today necessitates the application of more creative marketing. Increased competition, fuelled by globalisation, makes it more difficult for organisations to stand out from the crowd. Consequently the ability to communicate successfully is a necessary prerequisite for survival. A well-nurtured corporate identity helps lay the foundations for excellent communications.

Exhibit 3.1b

Defining corporate identity

Olins (1979), one of the leading authors and practitioners in corporate identity, contends that 'corporate identity – real corporate identity that is – is about behaviour as much as appearance, and certainly about reality as much as symbolism.' Organisations can invest heavily in things like logos, buildings, packaging and advertising, but they will ultimately be judged by the actions of their staff and the performance of their products. Therefore, true corporate identity lies at the heart of an organisation and is articulated through its vision, mission and strategies.

Schmidt (1995) endorses this all-encompassing view of corporate identity and argues that it includes corporate culture, corporate behaviour, market conditions, strategy, products, services and communications as well as design. Therefore, corporate identity concerns every aspect of an organisation that causes people to form views and opinions about them.

Similarly, Balmer (2001) defines corporate identity as 'a summation of those tangible and intangible elements that make any corporate entity distinct. It is shaped by the actions of corporate founders and leaders, by tradition and the environment ... It is multidisciplinary in scope and is a melding of strategy, structure, communication and culture. It is manifested through multifarious communications channels encapsulating product and organisational performance, employee communication and behaviour, controlled communication and stakeholder and network discourse.' In this definition, the leader's role and influence in shaping corporate identity is highlighted.

Smith (1998) recognises corporate identity's role as a strategic asset, which can be invaluable in the achievement of an organisation's goals and objectives. In making this point, he compares it to tactical tools like advertising and public relations that can be changed on a daily basis. Conversely, corporate identity can be likened to a personality or, as Upshaw (1997) puts it, 'strategic DNA'. This emphasises just how difficult it is to change corporate identity. It is not simply a matter of designing a new logo. It necessitates a change in corporate culture and, therefore, a different way of doing things. In some instances the company may have to be restructured. Such changes take time and may need to be supported by intensive staff training.

As shown in Table 3.1, many aspects of corporate identity are difficult to control. For instance, the behaviour of staff is a key aspect of identity. If staff do not know how they are expected to behave or they lack training or expertise, their actual behaviour is likely to be very different to desired behaviour or that highlighted in positive advertising campaigns. Consequently, customers are often disappointed and form negative opinions about companies based on their experiences. Therefore, in many organisations, there is an undesirable gap between real and desired corporate identity.

Table 3.1 Key aspects of corporate identity

- Not just a logo
- Emanates from behaviour and reality as well as appearance
- Concerns tangible and intangible elements of an organisation
- Reflects and articulates corporate culture
- Concerns all parts of the organisation and is multidisciplinary in nature
- Must be led from the top

Conclusion: **desired** corporate identity does not always equal **actual** corporate identity.

Elements of identity

We saw above how corporate identity is made up of tangible and intangible elements. Now we can divide these elements into five main categories (Olins, 1989, van Riel *et al.*, 2001).

Products and services

Products and services provide clues to the target audience as to what kind of organisation is producing or providing them. For example, the computer company Apple manufactures products that are very different in appearance to those of their competitors because they pay a lot of attention to the outer appearance of their computer hardware. As a result, people perceive the company to be trendy and innovative at the cutting edge of design.

In the late 1990s, Marks & Spencer experienced a severe downturn in their fortunes. This was largely attributed to their clothing range that had become staid and old-fashioned. As a result, customers felt that Marks & Spencer was an out-of-touch company with little to offer younger shoppers. This was not the image that they wished to portray, but lack of attention to product design meant that the gap between their desired and actual image was widening. Following a collaboration with ex-Next chief executive, George Davies, they created the Per Una range of clothing. It is specifically aimed at women in their 20s and Marks & Spencer use it to send out a more contemporary message to an important market segment.

The product's image is strongly influenced by packaging and labelling. European Union (EU) legislation has ruled that member states must produce less packaging in an effort to reduce waste. Consumers too are more concerned about the volumes of packaging being generated. However, a cursory glance at Ireland's retail outlets reveals that in many cases a product's packaging forms an integral part of its personality and appeal.

When the snack, Pringles, was launched, the packaging was highly innovative for the snack food market and it was a major factor in the product's success.

The Irish retailer, Avoca, successfully markets a range of high-quality own-brand food products. The packaging is carefully chosen to portray the image of a home-made product containing natural, high-quality ingredients. The labelling articulates these attributes and the actual product inside lives up to the expectations, which have been raised. While labelling must be used by companies to meet legislative obligations, for example, to inform the product user of the pack's contents, expiry date, calorific values etc., the visual style and language used on the label say a lot about an organisation's identity.

Table 3.2 lists the main product elements of corporate identity.

Table 3.2 Product elements of corporate identity

- The product itself
- Packaging
- Labelling

Environments

Environments are the places where an organisation's products or services are made and/or sold. The physical environment is very important in the services sector because it contributes to the customer's overall experience. Does the building make a lasting impression and is this impression positive or negative?

In the business-to-business sector, the environment can be very important. This is why so many companies invest large sums of money in impressive corporate headquarters – AIB Bankcentre in Donnybrook, Dublin; R&A Bailey on the Naas Road, Dublin; Intel in Leixlip, Co. Kildare. The outward appearance of such buildings is used to help attract high-calibre staff, investors and important customers.

Charities and other not-for-profit organisations often take care not to create overly impressive environments because they do not want to suggest that they are diverting funds away from the central cause.

The buildings where fast-moving consumer goods are manufactured are of little importance to the end customer. However, the retail outlet where they are sold is important. That is why many branded goods organisations use limited or exclusive distribution strategies. Brown Thomas is one of Ireland's leading department stores in terms of quality and exclusivity. Some international cosmetic companies only sell their products in Ireland through Brown Thomas.

The Irish newspaper sector has undergone rapid change as a result of more intense competition at home and from the UK, the population's declining newspaper readership, and the advent of new media, such as the Internet. In response to these changes, the Independent Group invested in a state-of-the-art printing press on the Naas Road, on the outskirts of Dublin. The design of the building itself says something about the organisation and has become a landmark building. It says 'innovative, modern, and forward-thinking' to those who see it.

Many organisations pay close attention to internal and external signage. Signage makes it easier for people to find their way around and therefore can leave people with the impression of a well-organised, considerate company. For example, when customers enter a large department store, it is preferable that they find their own way around with the aid of clear and helpful signage, rather than asking staff for directions, thus diverting them from their main tasks.

Street furniture, such as benches, kiosks, waste-paper bins, can make an impression. Even though Eircom are in no way responsible for the damage inflicted on their pay-phone kiosks, they recognise that it is in their interests to rectify any damage done. Otherwise, people attempting to use their pay phones will have a frustrating experience and will be left with a bad impression of the company.

The way in which staff dress provides visual clues as to what sort of organisation they work for. Many organisations do not leave this aspect of their identity to chance. When staff interact directly with the public, it is common practice to provide uniforms. Ideally, uniforms should reinforce the tangible and intangible aspects of a company's corporate identity. Colours should be related to the corporate colours used in other elements of the corporate identity such as the logo, signage and leaflets. The style of the clothes should be functional and related to the tasks carried out by staff. Ideally, it should provide clues about the organisation's personality. Is it conservative, professional, fun, innovative or funky? Michael O'Leary, Chief Executive of Ryanair, famously embraces a casual style of dress in order to reinforce the company's low-cost image. However, cabin crew wear uniforms because it is important to communicate a sense of order in aeroplanes.

When uniforms are not compulsory, it is common practice to provide a written policy relating to dress code. When this is not done, new members of staff take the lead from other members of staff.

Table 3.3 shows the various types of environmental elements of corporate identity.

Table 3.3 Environmental elements of corporate identity

- Buildings
- Signage
- Display units
- Exhibition stands
- Street furniture e.g. rubbish bins, kiosks, seats
- Clothing

Communication

This involves all aspects of communication that an organisation undertakes with its various publics or audiences. It includes a wide range of items, many of which are shown in Table 3.4.

Table 3.4 Communication elements of corporate identity

- Advertising, direct marketing, sales promotion, public relations, sponsorship
- Trade shows
- Product brochures, annual reports, price lists
- Websites
- Instruction manuals
- Business cards
- Letterheads, complimentary slips, envelopes
- Quotations, invoices, receipts
- Warranties/guarantees
- Application forms
- Carrier bags
- Loyalty cards
- Vehicles
- Corporate gifts e.g. pens, golf balls, clothing

Organisations often design each of these items as stand-alone pieces of communication. This is usually inefficient and leads to confusion. Many organisations recognise the merit of designing each item as part of a communications suite. This helps to ensure that communication is coherent and consistent. This in turn helps key audiences cut through the clutter. It is important that each item is designed from the point of view of the target audience. For example, utility companies such as the ESB, an Bord Gais and Eircom traditionally designed customer bills to fit in with internal processes and procedures. This resulted in customer confusion and lack of understanding. This led to a rise in customer queries when bills were issued. These queries had to be answered and tied up customer service staff. By simplifying the layout and design of their bills, the likes of Eircom have reduced the number of queries they receive when bills are issued. This means that staff can be re-deployed into more productive areas, such as sales.

Exhibit 3.1c

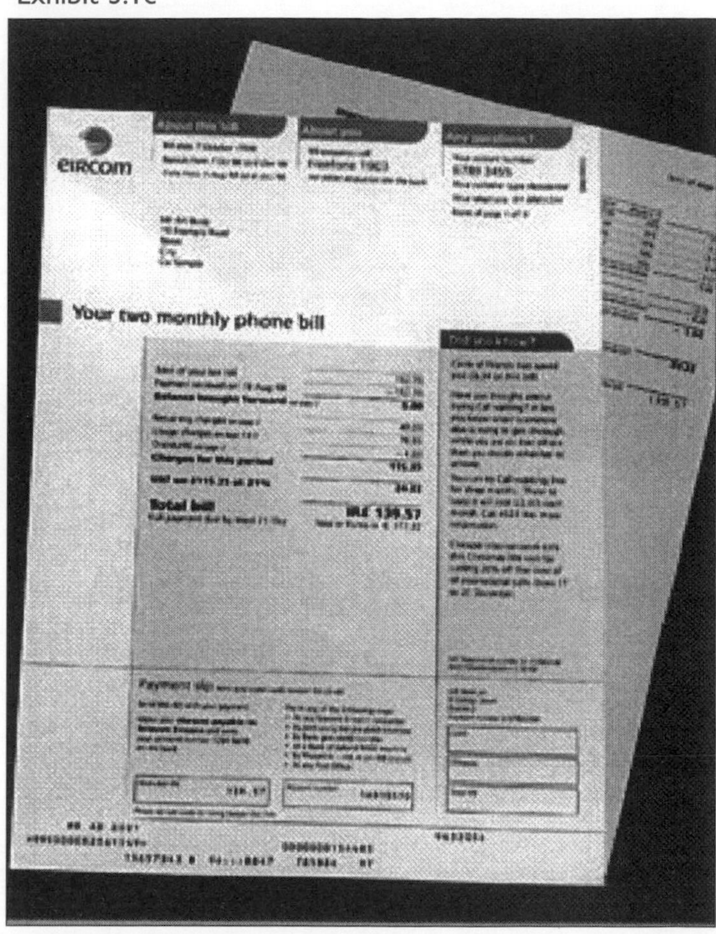
eircom

Your two monthly phone bill

Total bill

Basic items such as letterheads and envelopes say a lot about a company. For example, if an organisation states in its advertising that they are easily accessible, but omits to communicate contact information, it is sending out conflicting messages.

The type of paper stock used in printed communications such as stationery and brochures provides clues about the organisation. Ballinahinch Castle in Connemara is a high-quality hotel. Its promotional literature is printed on a heavy, quality paper, interspersed with transparent paper. This gives the reader the impression of luxury and quality. In contrast, charities, such as Concern, opt for cheap paper stocks to reassure target audiences that donations are not being 'wasted' on expensive materials. The environmental action group, Greenpeace, use recycled paper to reinforce their image as champions of the environment.

Corporate vehicles present opportunities for free billboard advertising.

Vehicle cleanliness and maintenance are particularly important in sectors where hygiene is of concern to customers. Food delivery vehicles should be clean when they arrive at customers' premises because people tend to form impressions about the contents of a vehicle based on the outer cleanliness.

Exhibit 3.2

Behaviour

Behaviour concerns the way people within the organisation treat each other and behave towards key audiences outside the organisation, such as customers, suppliers, distributors, media. Behaviour is the most difficult aspect of identity to control because it involves people. It can completely undermine or reinforce the other identity components. Organisations must recruit the right people, those who will be able to live up to the promises made in the communications, or alluded to in the symbols and environments.

The Eircom case study at the close of this chapter describes Eircom's core values – being professional, progressive and friendly. If Eircom staff do not live up to these promises, the gap between formal, planned communications and customers' actual experiences widens.

Symbols

Exhibit 3.3

These comprise logos or visual icons used to represent organisations. They are an efficient form of shorthand that enable an organisation's various audiences to instantly recognise them. Some organisations successfully use symbols in their logos. In time they no longer require their name to appear alongside them. One of the most prominent examples of this is Nike's 'swoosh' or 'tick'. The advantages are immense for a global company because it eliminates the need to translate or explain the name. Such an outcome is usually the result of heavy investment in activities such as advertising and sponsorship.

Exhibit 3.4

The Gaelic Athletic Association's (GAA) symbol is so well recognised that it does not need to be explained when it is seen by core market segments.

Some organisations take national symbols and incorporate them into their corporate identities. Irish Government departments, Ryanair and Guinness use the harp in their logos. The Government uses the harp to communicate authority and urgency and to ensure that target audiences receive their messages.

As highlighted by van Riel *et al.* (2001), perceptions and understanding of logos are strongly influenced by encounters people have with the organisation in question. Therefore, the other identity elements – products and services, environments, communication and behaviour – play a crucial part helping people interpret the meaning behind symbols. This is an important point because it means that in many cases the interpretations are not necessarily the ones organisations want people to have. It is not unusual for interpretations to be negative and damaging to the long-term success of an organisation. It is for this very reason that some organisations introduce a new logo and even a new name. Even when a company changes all of the other identity elements (products and services, environments, communication and behaviour), an unchanged logo may prevent people from recognising the change. This is one of the reasons Telecom Eireann changed its name to Eircom in 1999. This change was accompanied by a new symbol. Research informed them that a new name and logo was essential because internal and external audiences had very deeply held views and associations when they heard or saw the name Telecom Eireann. Therefore, the name change was intended to symbolise everything that was different about the newly privatised company and would be used to embed a new set of more positive interpretations in the minds of staff, customers, shareholders and competitors (for more details, see the case study at the close of this chapter).

Corporate image

In Table 3.1 (page 53), an important concept was presented. The desired corporate identity of an organisation does not always equal their actual corporate identity. It is necessary to introduce the concept of **corporate image**. According to Gray and Smeltzer (1985), corporate image 'is the

Corporate Image
The impression of the overall corporation held by various publics. Formed as a result of people's actual experiences with the organisation.

impression of the overall corporation held by various publics'. Building on the discussion to date on corporate identity, it can be argued that corporate image is formed as a result of people's actual experiences and ensuing perceptions of that organisation.

Table 3.5 illustrates the relationship between corporate identity and corporate image in the hypothetical case of a restaurant. When examining the example, it should be remembered that most organisations have a desired corporate identity. They aspire to produce products of a particular standard. They want to produce and/or sell them in certain environments. They want to communicate in a particular style. They want their staff to interact with each other, with customers, and with suppliers etc. in a manner which reinforces their communication style. They want the company logo to say something very specific and positive about the organisation.

Table 3.5 Corporate identity and corporate image – a comparison

Corporate identity – desired	Corporate identity – the reality	Corporate image
The product • Innovative, fusion-style cuisine • Fresh ingredients • Visually well presented • Value for money • Good choice of wine	**The product** • Bland, ordinary food • Frozen vegetables, dried herbs • Little care taken to make food look good • Very expensive • Many bottles out of stock	Customers left with the impression that the restaurant's food is very ordinary, not very wholesome, not very visually appealing and very expensive **Resulting image: low-quality, ordinary venue**
Environment • Well-lit, smoke-free dining room • Comfortable chairs • Sparkling, clean toilets • Clean, smart uniforms for staff	**Environment** • Gloomy setting, smoke wafting to table • Comfortable chairs • Toilets in need of cleaning • Staff badly dressed	Cleanliness is vital for any restaurant wishing to build a positive image **Resulting image: customers left with doubts about cleanliness and will give friends the bad news**
Communication • Advertised in local newspaper as an exciting venue with excellent food that won't break the bank • Smart printed menus containing lots of choice	**Communication** • Advertised in local newspaper as an exciting venue with excellent food that won't break the bank • Smart printed menus containing lots of choice	While the advertising tries to project a certain image, and the menus attempt to convey a certain level of quality, the actual experience is far removed from the promise. This serves to heighten the negative perceptions held by the customers.

Corporate identity – desired	Corporate identity – the reality	Corporate image
Behaviour • Friendly, attentive service • Knowledgeable staff who can explain the menu	**Behaviour** • Slow service, stressed staff • Staff lacking in knowledge about the menu	Many customers will be irritated by bad service and staff who are not capable of explaining the menu. **Resulting image: negative**
Symbols • Cutting-edge, well-designed logo which suggests that the food will be innovative	Symbols • Cutting-edge, well-designed logo which suggests that the food will be innovative	Like communication, symbols build up certain expectations. When the gap between the expectations and the actual experience is wide, the negative image is accentuated and the logo is associated with everything that is bad about the restaurant.

In the example of the restaurant, it is evident that the gap between the desired corporate identity and the reality is significant. In the real world, it would struggle to enjoy a positive corporate image and a negative one is more likely to stem from the its inability to live up to promises it has made through the controllable elements of its identity.

Organisations must not over-promise and they should not try to be something they are not until they have the ability to harmonise and deliver on all elements of their identity.

Types of identity

There are three main types of identity structures used by organisations (Olins, 1989, Schmitt *et al,* 1997). They are:

- **monolithic**. The organisation uses the one name and visual style in everything it does. This is easiest to manage when the business is not highly diversified, for example, Ryanair, Aer Lingus, Tesco Ireland.
- **endorsed**. The organisation has many activities and/or companies that it endorses with its name and identity. Examples include some car manufacturers, such as Opel Corsa, Opel Vectra; Ford Focus, Ford Fiesta; Fiat Brava, Fiat Punto.
- **branded**. One company may own an array of distinct brands, and in some cases the end consumer may not even be aware of that company. They are only familiar with individual brands. This is widely used in the FMCG sector. However, it is expensive to

support because each brand must be promoted heavily through advertising and promotion. Lever Brothers successfully employs this identity structure and have disguised the parentage of some of Ireland's most loved brands. Examples include Magnum, Surf, Comfort, Cif, Domestos and Organics.

Changing an organisation's corporate identity

In the preceding sections, it was emphasised that corporate identity is much more than just a logo. However, when an organisation decides to embark on a major change programme, the tangible aspects of identity are usually used to flag the change with key publics. In today's environment, there are many reasons why an organisation might decide to change its corporate identity.

Legislative change

Legislation may totally change an organisation's competitive landscape. Since the 1990s, previously state-owned telecommunication companies around Europe have gone from being protected monopolies in their home markets to being one of many players in a highly competitive sector. In order to cope with such radical upheaval, all aspects of their identities have had to change. Customers had very deeply rooted associations with the old symbols so, in many instances, new logos were designed so as to create a totally new set of positive associations.

Entry into new markets

One of the reasons behind Telecom Eireann's name change was its intent to develop its international presence. Research revealed that people outside Ireland had difficulties pronouncing 'Eireann' and in some cases confused it with 'Iran'.

Mergers and acquisitions

In 2001, Vodafone acquired Ireland's largest mobile network from Eircom. In 2002, Vodafone embarked on an extensive rebranding campaign. The visible aspect of this was communicated through advertising and retail outlets, but, within the organisation itself, staff had to be retrained to work and behave in the Vodafone way. Customers' expectations also changed because their service provider was now a global player as opposed to an Irish company.

In 2001, two of Ireland's financial services providers came together when Irish Life and Permanent acquired TSB Bank. They called themselves PermanentTSB.

Introduction of different products and services

Rapid technological change in the telecommunications sector left many service providers around the world with names that no longer suited their business propositions. There was a prevalence of the word 'telecom' or a derivative thereof in their names, but since the 1990s, most of these organisations are communications companies as opposed to mere telecommunications companies. This factor is just one of the reasons why Telecom Eireann became Eircom.

Outdated image

The museum sector in Ireland and the UK now uses marketing techniques in an effort to appeal to wider audiences and to compete with intense competition from other types of entertainment. In 1998, The Tate embarked on a project that would see it revitalise its identity. The name was changed to just 'Tate' and four brands were launched under this umbrella – Tate Britain, Tate Modern, Tate Liverpool and Tate St Ives. The way in which their product offering is presented has been revolutionised and much thought has gone into the environments. Consequently, a museum visit becomes a total experience where visitors can shop, eat, and view collections in an entertaining way.

According to Tate's identity consultant, Brian Boylan of Wolff Olins, 'it was an opportunity to de-institutionalise the gallery ... It respresents a different stance for art' (Marsh, 2000).

Creating a new identity

Creating a new identity requires a project management approach and is divided into four distinct work stages, as illustrated in Figure 3.1. Some consultants have the expertise to execute every stage, such as Ireland's leading brand and identity consultants, Enterprise IG. Some organisations prefer to use different consultants at different stages of the project. For example, they might use one consultant to complete the first stage and use their findings and recommendations to prepare a brief to invite consultants to tender for the creation and development stages. It is usual for a number of consultants and agencies to be involved at the launch and implementation stage. For instance, a PR agency could be given responsibility for certain aspects of the launch, such as the generation of maximum publicity. At the same time, an organisation's advertising agency might be involved in creating maximum awareness through advertising. A number of graphic design agencies might be selected to implement or apply the new identity across a range of items including brochures, signage, point-of-sale material and stationery.

Stage 1: Investigation and recommendation

This initial stage is very important in terms of determining what needs to be done when creating a new identity or in the case of an existing identity, assessing the extent of change that is required. In some cases, consultants recommend minor changes to corporate identity, while in others they may suggest radical change. Such decisions are not based on whims. They are based on research conducted on key audiences, such as employees, suppliers, distributors, customers and competitors. This research gives the consultant an insight into a number of issues:

- the desired corporate identity
- the actual corporate identity
- the corporate image.

Figure 3.1 Process for creating corporate identity

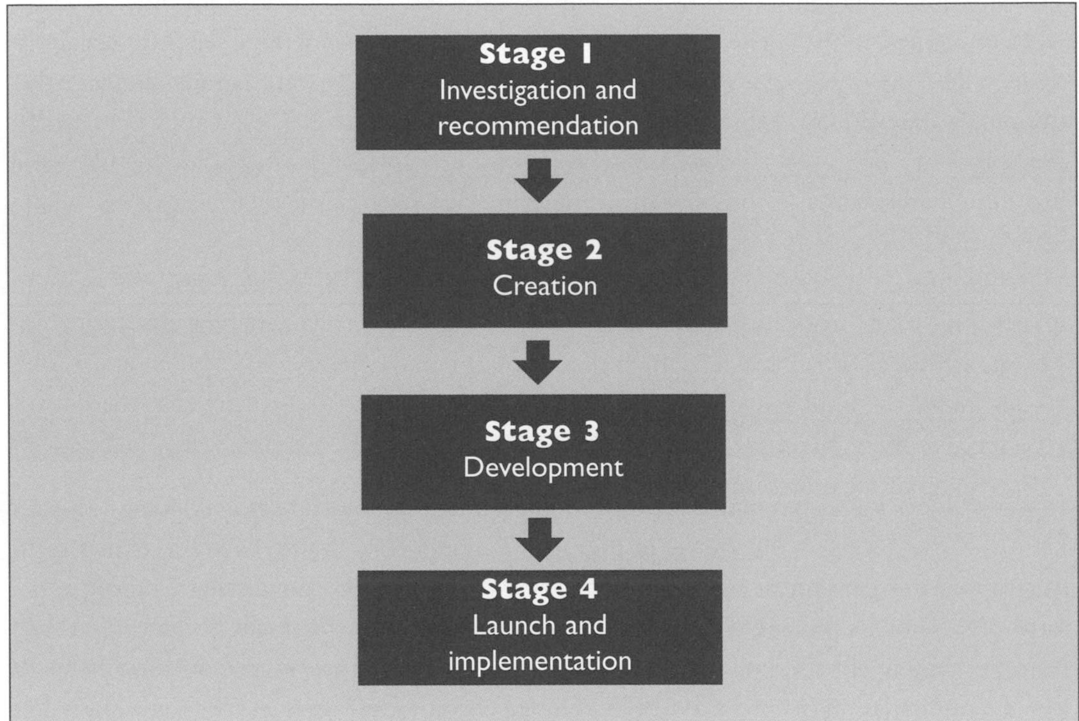

A complete audit is usually conducted of all tangible and intangible manifestations of the existing corporate identity. For example:

- Is there a consistent house style used in all printed communications?
- How well do the various elements of the promotions mix work together?
- How do employees treat each other?
- What sort of encounters do customers experience when they visit or contact the company?
- Is it easy for distributors to sell the company's products and services?
- Is it easy for visitors to find their way around a company's building?
- What sort of impression does the physical environment make?

The consultant gains an in-depth insight into the organisation's plans for the future. Goals and objectives, any planned mergers, new product developments are identified. The chief executive's vision must be explored. In fact, the involvement of the chief executive is vital in any identity change. Without the chief executive it inevitably becomes a cosmetic exercise and, while the organisation receives a new look, attitudes and behaviour remain unchanged. The consultant must conduct an audit of the organisation's competitors. This necessitates an examination of the tangible aspects of competitors' identities, in particular logos and communications material, because the visual aspect of a new identity must stand out from the competition.

Depending on the size of the organisation and its competitive environment, the investigation stage can take months to complete. At its conclusion, the consultant makes recommendations concerning:

- the name of the company – does it need to be changed?
- the company's logo – does it need to be changed?
- tangible aspects of the company's identity and the way in which it uses them
- the core values driving the identity – do they need to be reviewed? Core values guide employees as to the way in which they should behave. If staff enact them and if they are reflected in all tangible manifestations of the identity, it is likely that the desired identity will be the same as the actual identity (see the Eircom case study at the end of the chapter for more on this).
- the identity structure and its suitability – is it monolithic, endorsed or branded?

Another very important deliverable at this stage of the process is the brief for the creation stage of the project. Essentially, the brief is a set of instructions that is used, in this case, by the identity consultants, to create a new identity or to revamp an existing one. Two separate briefs may be required:

- a brief for renaming the company
- a design brief for creating a new logo.

The chief executive approves the recommendations and signs off the proposed brief or briefs. The briefs provide the criteria against which creative ideas are evaluated.

Stage 2: Creation

While some advertising agencies undertake the design of a new identity, most concede that the task is best done by identity specialists like the Irish-based Enterprise IG, and Wolff Olins from the UK. Both Irish Life and AIB Bank appointed Wolff Olins when they changed their identities in the 1990s. However, the level of expertise available in Ireland is strengthening. This means Irish consultants are appointed more often for large identity changeovers such as Eircom, Glanbia and PermanentTSB.

The brief, which is based on the information gathered in Stage 1, is used to kickstart the creative process. If a name has to be created, this must be done first and approved by the client before work on the visual aspects of the identity commences. Before finally selecting a new name, its suitability is usually researched. This means ensuring the following:

- that the proposed name can be legally protected in markets where it will be used. This involves finding out whether or not the name is already in use and, if it is, whether or not it is legally protected by another organisation
- that the name does not have embarrassing or inappropriate meanings in domestic and foreign markets.

When the name is approved, design work commences and graphic designers create ways of rendering, i.e. visually representing, the name:

- What sort of typeface should they use?
- Should each letter be upper case or lower case or a combination of both?
- Should there be a symbol? If so, what should it be?

Three options are usually presented to the client for discussion. They are roughly applied to stationery, a brochure, a picture of a vehicle (if applicable) and a press advertisement to make it easier for the chief executive and others to envisage how the proposed logos might look in a real-life situation. At this stage it is important to show how the proposed designs look when placed alongside the competitors' logos. Ideally, by the end of this process, one design is selected for further development. However, this does not always happen, and it is not unusual for two of the design options to be selected for further development.

Stage 3: Development

The development stage is exactly as the name suggests. The chosen option or options from Stage 2 are taken and developed in much greater detail. While in Stage 2 the identity was roughly applied to key items of communication, the applications are further refined. Close attention is given to the following:

- the logotype i.e. the way in which the name is rendered
- the selection of corporate colours
- animation and the way in which the logo might respond to animation. This is an important consideration if it is going to be used in television advertising and website applications
- further development of the new identity when applied to tangible items.

Stage 4: Launch and implementation

This stage helps determine whether or not the new identity will be noticed and accepted by key publics. The benefits of the change must be clearly communicated to those who will be affected by it.

> When Irish Life and Permanent and TSB Bank merged in 2002, they kept key publics informed as to what was happening and what it meant. For example, account holders received a letter from Harry Lorton, Chief Executive, informing them of the change. An accompanying leaflet explained how the merger would benefit the customer in terms of an extended branch network, longer opening hours, a 24-hour banking facility, an extensive national ATM network, new products, financial advice and faster processing of transactions.
>
> Taken from *Embarking on a New Journey*, (PermanentTSB, 2002)

For an identity launch to be successful, staff must be told about it first. Ideally, they should have been involved in the first three stages (see the Eircom case study), but if this has not occurred, they must be informed in detail about the changes before anyone else. They must be told what it means in terms of the way they go about their daily tasks and in terms of what customers will expect of them. Key publics who must be informed of identity change are outlined in Table 3.6 and ways of communicating the change are suggested.

Arising out of much of the activity outlined above, many organisations employ the services of a PR agency to generate positive publicity about the identity change. Photographers attend launch events and the photographs are submitted to relevant newspapers and magazines. PR agencies often invite journalists to attend launch events, with the objective of securing news coverage about the change on television, radio and in the press.

Corporate identity and marketing communications

Many marketing communications textbooks include corporate identity as one of the elements in the promotions mix. However, as this chapter shows, corporate identity is an all-embracing concept that has many facets. It is a strategic tool that influences and shapes all elements of the marketing mix. As previously illustrated, gaps between the desired and real corporate identity make it difficult to realise a positive corporate image with target audiences. This in turn makes it difficult to retain customers, thus making the long-term survival of an organisation more challenging. Therefore, it is no coincidence that many organisations pay more attention to the business of ensuring that their desired and actual corporate identities are identical. They see it as an investment in their long-term viability and utilise it to improve customer service, product design, distribution outlets and marketing communications.

How does investing in corporate identity help improve marketing communications?

Table 3.6 Communicating change to key audiences

Audience	Communicating change
Staff	• Party/function hosted by chief executive • Distribution of information pack that includes samples of new stationery, forms, brochures, advertising • Debriefing meetings with departmental manager • Ongoing training to explain core values and new work practices • Internal newsletter (paper or online version) • Screensavers • Gifts like tee-shirts, umbrellas, mouse mats
Distributors, partners, suppliers	• Party/function hosted by chief executive • Information pack (as above) • Regional roadshows – go and visit these people • Training • Newsletter • Corporate gifts
High-net-worth customers	• Party/function hosted by chief executive • Information packs • Visit from key account manager • Corporate gifts
Customers (other)	• Direct mail • Advertising • Competitions • Establishment of a customer helpline

Essentially it serves as a foundation which allows organisations to make more of their promotions mix. A well-managed corporate identity pays dividends in terms of effectiveness and efficiency:

- **recognition**. Existing and potential customers become familiar with the style and tone of all communications.
- **speedier response to market needs**. Instead of reinventing the wheel every time a new piece of communication is required, standard templates are already in place. A **template** is used as a guide, and can be very effective for printed communications. Templates might specify a particular typeface, layouts, and colour.

- **economies of scale in print and production**. Organisations that look after their corporate identity are likely to appoint an approved panel of suppliers. Only suppliers on this panel are appointed to work on projects involving tangible manifestations of the identity, such as the production of brochures, stationery, signage, advertising, etc. Better prices can be negotiated when using a panel of approved suppliers on a regular basis.
- **review and improvement**. Like with like can be compared and used to measure communications effectiveness i.e. what impact is the piece of communication having on the target audience? Does it achieve its communications objectives? The onus is placed on the supplier to maintain standards and non-compliance may lead to their removal from the panel of approved suppliers.
- **improved internal communications**. A consistent house style gives staff a sense of belonging and helps them 'live' the core values.
- **protection of a valuable asset**. Corporate identity is an asset and requires constant protection and management.

There are a number of internal procedures that organisations should put in place in order to enjoy the benefits described above.

- **panels of approved suppliers**. Supplier panels should be appointed. Depending on an organisation's needs, they might consist of advertising agencies, direct marketing agencies, PR agencies, sales promotions agencies, web designers, printers and design consultancies. Without panels in place, variations tend to creep into marketing communications.
- **identity manual**. An identity manual should be produced. It contains rules and guidelines governing the use and application of the corporate identity. Many identity manuals are published in electronic form, which makes them easier to use and update. All panel members should be issued with a copy of the manual.
- **internal procedures for working with suppliers**. Procedures for working with suppliers should be established and distributed to staff.
- **identity advisory group**. An identity advisory group should be appointed. The membership of this group should comprise key employees like the chief executive, the head of marketing and the head of procurement (i.e. purchasing). They should meet on a monthly basis to review all new manifestations of the identity, for example, brochures, advertisements, point-of-sale material, etc. Discrepancies and deviations from identity guidelines are caught early and are less likely to take hold.
- **identity working group**. An identity working group should be established and given responsibility for implementing the identity. This group works directly with approved

suppliers and endeavours to ensure that all communications comply with guidelines in the identity manual.

When selecting approved suppliers for the panels described above, organisations should apply selection criteria to help them evaluate their suitability. Typically, these criteria might include the following:

- the supplier's ability to demonstrate an in-depth knowledge of the organisation's industry sector
- project management skills
- possession of relevant core skills, for example, design, creativity, advertising, print buying, etc.
- pricing structures and payment terms
- tax clearance certificates (necessary for a supplier working with a government-funded organisation)
- quality assurance systems
- professional indemnity insurance
- terms and conditions of business
- business credit rating.

Summary

Corporate identity is a strategic asset. In essence, it encapsulates an organisation's personality and is articulated through tangible and intangible aspects. These are products and services, environments, communication, behaviour and symbols.

Corporate image is the impression of the overall organisation held by various audiences. This impression is usually based on someone's experience of the organisation. While most organisations have in mind a desired corporate identity that they want to articulate, the 'real' corporate identity does not always live up to this. This then gives the organisation a poor corporate image.

There are three types of corporate identity. A monolithic identity is when an organisation uses one name and visual style with all of its activities. An endorsed identity is when an organisation visibly endorses its various activities and brands with its name. A branded identity is when each distinct product is given its own brand name and visual identity. The parent company is not necessarily identified.

A number of factors might cause an organisation to review or change their corporate identity. These factors include legislative change, a decision to enter new markets, mergers and acquisitions, the introduction of new products and services, or an outdated image.

The creation of a new corporate identity requires a systematic approach and is best approached using a four-stage model that involves investigation; creation; development; and launch and implementation.

Corporate identity can improve marketing communications. It helps an organisation's various audiences instantly recognise products and communications. From the organisation's perspective it facilitates speedier response to market needs and can lead to economies of scale in print and production. An organisation should introduce internal procedures, particularly the appointment of a panel of approved suppliers and an identity manual.

Review questions

1. Clearly distinguish between desired identity and real or actual identity.
2. What is corporate image?
3. Identify reasons why an organisation might decide to review its corporate identity.
4. Explain what is meant by monolithic identity, endorsed identity and branded identity. Provide an example of each.
5. Prescribe a process for creating a new identity.
6. Discuss how corporate identity might make an organisation's marketing communications activity more effective and efficient.
7. Recommend and describe the internal procedures, which might be put in place in order to ensure that marketing communications activity benefits from corporate identity.

Exercise

Select an organisation of your choice. Using Table 3.5 (page 60–61), critically assess its actual or real corporate identity. Interview an employee of that organisation so that you can describe its desired corporate identity. Is the real identity the same as the desired identity? If not, what recommendations would you make to close the gap?

References

Balmer, John, M. T., 'Corporate Identity, Corporate Branding and Corporate Marketing: Seeing Through the Fog' (*European Journal of Marketing*, Vol. 35, No. 3/4, pp. 248–91, 2001).

Gray, Edmund R. and Smeltzer, Larry R., 'Corporate Image: An Integral Part of Strategy' (*Sloan Management Review*, pp. 73–8, summer 1985).

Marsh, Harriet, 'How the Tate modernised its brand' (*Marketing*, p. 19, 25 May 2000).

Olins, Wally, 'What Corporate Identity Means' (*Management Today*, pp. 80–85, April 1979).

Olins, Wally, *Corporate Identity: Making Business Strategy Visible through Design* (Thames and Hudson, 1989).

Schmidt, K., *The Quest for Corporate Identity* (Cassell, 1995).

Schmitt, Bernd and Simonson, Alex, *Marketing Aesthetics: The Strategic Management of Brands, Identity, and Image* (New York: The Free Press, 1997).

Smith, P. R., *Marketing Communications: An Integrated Approach*, 2nd edition (Kogan Page, 1998).

Upshaw, Lynn, B., 'Transferable Truths of Brand Identity' (*Design Management Journal*, pp. 9–14, Winter 1997).

Van Riel, Cees B.M. and van den Ban, Anouschka, 'The Added Value of Corporate Logos' (*European Journal of Marketing*, Vol. 35, No. 3/4, pp. 428–40, 2001).

Case study

Ringing in the changes for Eircom

In 1998, Eircom, then known as Telecom Eireann, embarked on the most comprehensive corporate identity change programme ever carried out by an Irish company. They employed the services of identity consultants, The Identity Business (now known as Enterprise IG).

From the start, it was intended to be far more than a change of name and logo. A constant backdrop to the project was Telecom Eireann's imminent privatisation and growing competition. Deregulation in the telecommunications industry heralded the arrival of intense competition and brought with it raised customer expectations.

Extensive research into perceptions of the Telecom Eireann identity with customers, staff and partners in Ireland and abroad revealed a number of key issues, among them:

- It was perceived as a state-owned company, which brought with it many negative connotations.
- The visual image was seen as 'dated and conservative'. Staff felt that their identity was so dated that it was working against them as they engaged in new work practices. They felt that customers still saw them as the 'old' company enjoying monopoly status.

The findings showed that swift action was required, and so Telecom Eireann agreed to a radical change process as opposed to an evolutionary approach. An evolutionary identity change could take years to implement, but the new competitive environment did not afford the company the luxury of time. However, it would not have been possible to implement radical change without the full support and involvement of staff. Gerry O'Sullivan, Corporate Relations Director at the time, said of the involvement of all staff that, 'the idea was to internalise the concept behind the change. The process we followed resulted in staff feeling more confident in the end result.' This process consisted of initial interviews with a selection of staff across the company, staff workshops to ascertain their views on the proposed change, and the publication of three brochures that informed staff about the final changes.

Core values

At the workshops, staff used the findings of the research to assist them in identifying the core values that would be an integral part of the new identity's foundations. Three values underpinning the revitalised organisation were chosen by staff. Their involvement at this stage made it more likely they would take ownership of them and live up to them. Eircom's core values are to be:

- professional
- progressive
- friendly.

These values were intended to serve as a 'roadmap' for staff so that their behaviour would bring the new identity to life. The intention was that customers would come to associate the new identity with positive words like 'professional', 'progressive 'and 'friendly'. The values also serve as guidelines for Eircom's suppliers. For example, advertising agencies are asked to create campaigns that reflect Eircom's core values.

A new look

The visual elements of the new identity were the name, logotype, symbol, colours and typeface.

A radical approach to the identity process involved the creation of a new name. The decision-making process was influenced by a number of factors:

- The word 'Eircom' provided a link with the previous name and its positive associations.
- As an international company, the new name had to be capable of travelling abroad without presenting pronunciation or translation problems.

The final outcome was 'Eircom', which was not already being used by any other organisations in Ireland or abroad. It retains a certain amount of Irishness, which is important in terms of positioning the company, particularly in Ireland. And it also makes reference to the fact that the company is no longer just operating in the telecommunications sector but is in the wider world of communications.

The logotype (the style in which the name is rendered) is simple and modern. The use of a lower case 'e' and higher case 'R' is suggestive both of the company's Irish origins and of friendliness.

In an unprecedented move in Ireland, a specialist typeface designer was commissioned to create a unique typeface for use in Eircom's advertising and sales materials. This further contributes to the Eircom 'look', thus further differentiating the company from a growing number of competitors. Other companies in Ireland are restricted to using typefaces that others can access (common examples of typefaces are Courier, Times New Roman, Comic MS, etc.)

The Identity Business designed a symbol to be incorporated in the logo. It symbolises the world but not in the way that we are used to seeing it represented. It is being reshaped by communications and provides people with access to a borderless world of communications. It also suggests movement and dynamism and was designed to afford Eircom maximum visibility in the newly deregulated world of communications.

The corporate colours chosen were blue and terracotta. The blue provides a link with the past while the terracotta is a new colour, which was chosen for its 'vibrancy and warmth'. Together, the colours were designed to stand out from the competition.

One brand, many services

Eircom is the provider of hundreds of products and services. Prior to the identity review, more than 200 product and service names were in existence. For customers, this was often confusing because, as far as they were concerned, they were buying a range of services from one company, when the multitude of names suggested that they were dealing with many companies. A decision was made to take the 'masterbrand' approach. This means that Eircom still provides many products and services but they all reside under the one brand.

Launching the new identity

A radical identity change means that an immediate makeover should take place. This means that all remnants of the old identity are replaced as soon as possible. When the new identity was launched in May 1998, Eircom allocated a budget of €8.25 million to the changeover. Just over €1 million of that was spent on a high-profile, intensive, three-week advertising campaign. The remainder of the budget was spent rebranding the likes of 4,600 vehicles, 4,500 telephone kiosks and signage.

According to a BMR/IMS Customer Barometer, 99 per cent of those surveyed 'were able to state, or recognised, the new name within one week of the public launch date'.

This case study was cited in *The GDBA Design Effectiveness Awards: Award Winners* (The Identity Business, summer 2000).

Sources

Adworld.ie, *Eircom – the creation of Telecom Eireann's new identity* (6 April 2001).
Eircom, *Building Eircom Together* (1999).
Eircom, *A New Look for a New Millennium* (1999).
Euromonitor (October 2002).

4

KEY PLAYERS IN THE MARKETING COMMUNICATIONS INDUSTRY

The aims and objectives are to help you:

- to identify the key players in the marketing communications industry
- to describe the main components in a marketing communications brief
- to explain how a marketing communications agency works
- to distinguish between various roles in marketing communications agencies
- to understand how firms select marketing communications agencies
- to describe how agencies are paid for their work
- to prescribe best practice for managing agency/client relationships
- to understand some of the external forces and regulatory bodies impacting on the marketing communications industry in Ireland.

Introduction

In Chapter 2, the communications process in Figure 2.1 (page 25) demonstrated how messages are transmitted from one party to another through particular media. However, this approach does not in any way convey the number of parties usually involved in creating, producing and implementing these messages.

As illustrated in Figure 4.1, marketing communications activity starts with an organisation that has a particular communications problem or opportunity, for example, the need to advise customers about a batch of contaminated food or inform target audiences about a new product or service. The organisation establishes marketing communications objectives and formulates a strategy that will achieve these objectives (These are examined in detail in Chapter 5). When the strategy is agreed, the marketing communications problem or opportunity and all related material are articulated in a brief. Essentially, a brief is a written set of instructions and information used by an agency to solve a marketing communications problem. Depending on the nature of the strategy, variations of the brief are given to one or more external agencies, for example, an advertising agency and a direct marketing agency. In response to the brief, the agencies devise solutions that solve the marketing communications problem or opportunity. The sales function in many firms plays an important part in fulfilling marketing communications objectives and should be fully integrated with all other marketing communications activity.

In reality, marketing communications activity does not always follow the path shown in Figure 4.1. However, it does provide a starting point and other variables are highlighted throughout this chapter.

Figure 4.1 Overview of key players in the marketing communications industry

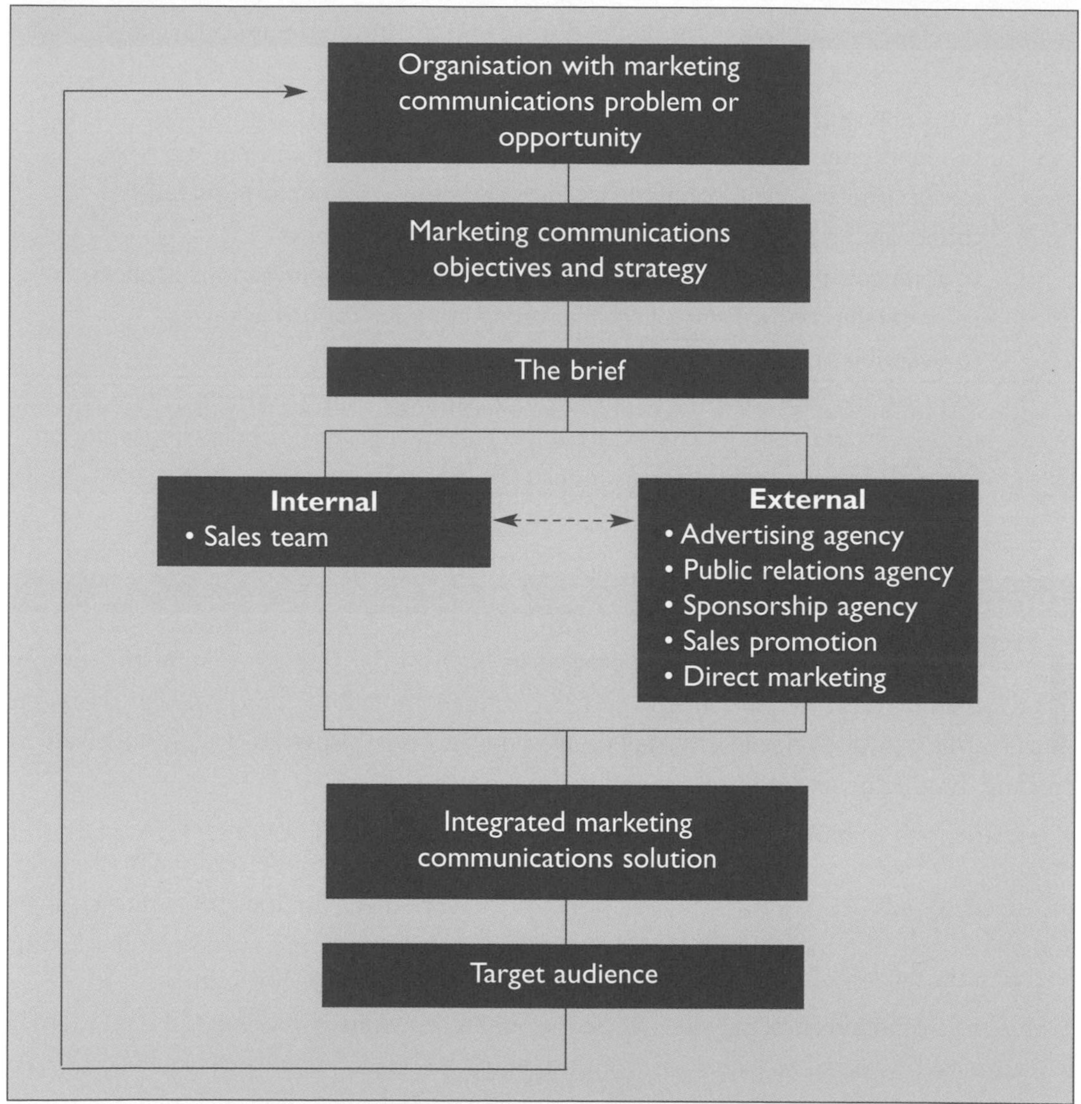

The marketing communications brief

The **marketing communications brief** is a written document that forms the basis of any marketing communications campaign. The initial brief is usually written by the client organisation and is distributed to one or more marketing communications agencies. If the brief does not contain enough information, the agency might work with the client to refine it and ensure that it is comprehensive. Firms use briefs to introduce their business and provide background information during the agency selection phase. In an agency/client relationship, they are just as important. However, as a relationship grows and the agency learns more about the client, there is less emphasis on company information in the brief. Different types of marketing communications agencies require different information, but there are certain pieces of information that should always be included in any marketing communications brief. These are, according to the Institute of Public Administration (1997):

Marketing communications brief
Written document that forms the basis of any marketing communications campaign.

- company and department details
- the nature of the business
- a description of existing business environment
- the company's present business situation (strengths, weaknesses, market share, position, image, competition)
- the corporate and marketing objectives (where the firm wants to be)
- the business strategy (how the firm intends getting from where they are to where they want to be)
- details of previous marketing communications activity
- marketing communications objectives
- the specific problem to be solved
- desired consumer responses
- description of target markets, their characteristics, behaviour and lifestyle
- description of the product – features, advantages, customer benefits
- key dates
- restrictions or limitations, for example, corporate guidelines
- budget
- who makes the final decisions
- who the agency should report to – contact names, telephone, fax, e-mail
- the role of market research before, during and after campaign
- how the campaign effectiveness will be measured
- any other relevant information.

The client usually provides a brief and then the agency transfers the information into a standard brief format, as illustrated in Figure 4.2.

An advertising brief usually refers to media, for example, a client may want to use outdoor advertising or may not want to use television advertising. This should be stated within the brief. A sales promotion brief includes details about the environment in which sales promotion takes place. A direct marketing brief usually includes details about the client's database of potential and existing customers. Due to the growing importance of integrated marketing communications, briefs should provide information about other marketing communications activity.

The brief should be ratified by the client and the agency and the client should understand that if any part of the brief changes once work begins, additional costs might be incurred. Both parties use the brief to evaluate the agency's output.

Figure 4.2 Agency brief

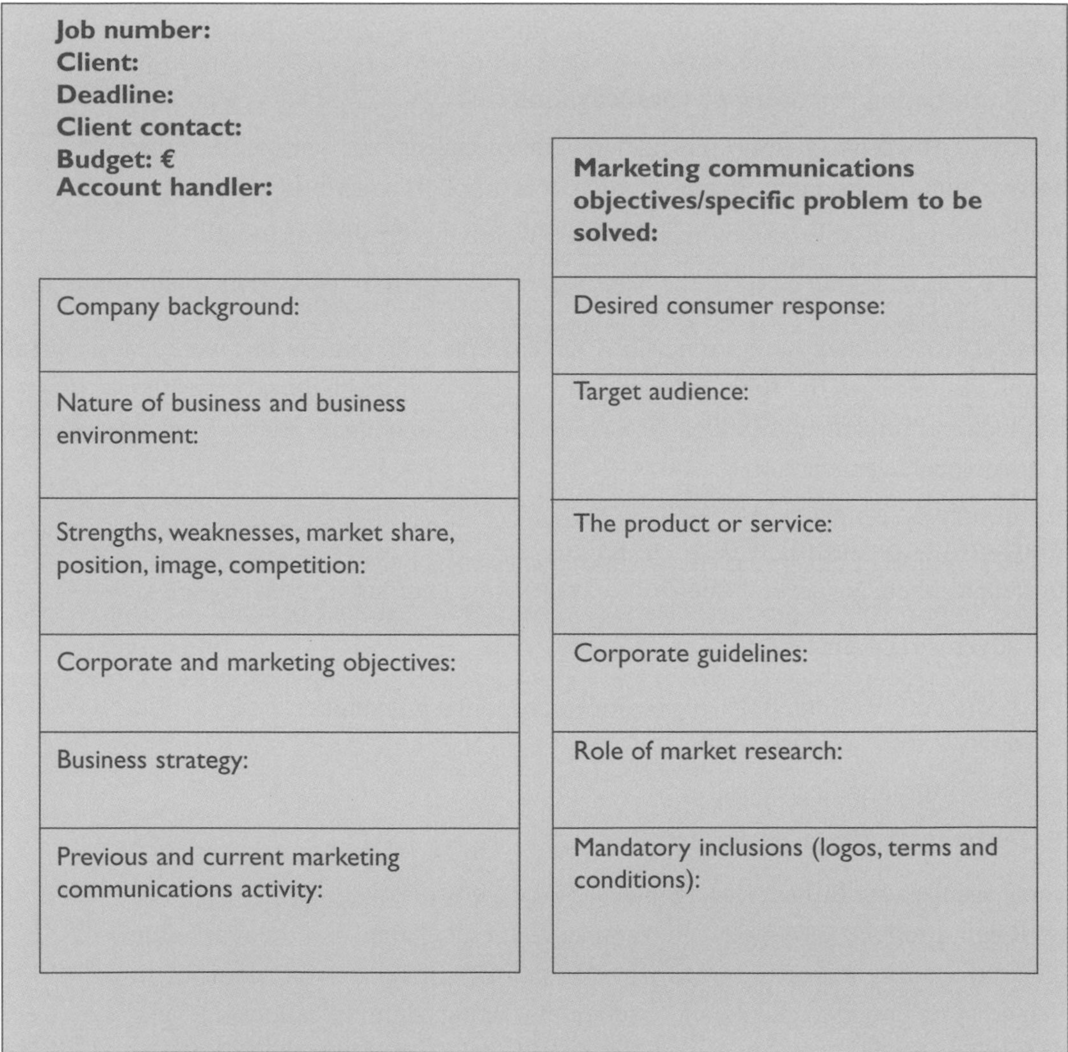

Job number:
Client:
Deadline:
Client contact:
Budget: €
Account handler:

Company background:	**Marketing communications objectives/specific problem to be solved:**
Nature of business and business environment:	Desired consumer response:
Strengths, weaknesses, market share, position, image, competition:	Target audience:
Corporate and marketing objectives:	The product or service:
Business strategy:	Corporate guidelines:
Previous and current marketing communications activity:	Role of market research:
	Mandatory inclusions (logos, terms and conditions):

Key players in the marketing communications industry

Figure 4.1 (page 76) shows that marketing communications starts with an organisation that has a marketing communications problem or opportunity. Without this group there would be no marketing communications industry. They control the budgets and decide whether or not to employ the services of an agency or agencies. Figure 4.1 also shows how internal resources are used to execute part or all of a marketing communications strategy, for example, the sales team.

This chapter focuses on a firm's relationship with external agencies in marketing communications. Therefore, from this point on, the firm is referred to as the **client**. This term is used to describe firms that engage the services of marketing communications agencies.

Client
Term used when referring to firms that engage the services of marketing communications agencies.

The Irish marketing communications industry comprises many firms with various skills and expertise in the design, production and implementation of marketing communications campaigns. Agencies vary in terms of what they can do, but when they do not have the necessary skills in-house, they usually have access to **third-party suppliers**. These are specialists not employed by an agency on a permanent basis. Third-party suppliers might be individuals working on their own, for example, photographers, or they might be companies, for example, printers and model agencies. Herein lies one of the reasons why clients use agencies. Even if agencies do not have the capability to carry out particular tasks, they have strong links with people who can do the work. Most clients simply do not have the time, expertise, knowledge or third-party relationships to design, produce and implement marketing communications campaigns. In effect, agencies assume a project management role.

Third-party suppliers
Specialists not employed by an agency on a permanent basis.

Marketing communications agencies

In Ireland, there are several categories of marketing communications agencies:

- advertising agencies
- public relations agencies
- sponsorship agencies
- sales promotion agencies
- direct marketing agencies.

Some agencies are **full-service agencies**. These are firms that have the expertise to design, produce and implement campaigns for all elements of the marketing communications mix. The growth in the number of full-service agencies in Ireland is attributed to clients' allocation of marketing communications budgets. According to Nula Bermingham of McConnells Advertising Agency (30 March 2001), some observers in the UK and US advertising industries estimate that 50 per cent of agency revenue comes from below-the-line activity. **Below-the-line** promotions are non-media-based promotions. This means that their message is

Full-service agency
An agency able to design, produce and implement all elements of the marketing communications mix.

Below-the-line
Promotions that are non-media-based.

Above-the-line *Marketing communications activity that is media-based.*

not transmitted through broadcast, print or outdoor media. Below-the-line activity includes direct mail, telemarketing and sales promotions. **Above-the-line** activity comprises media-based activity, such as television and newspaper advertising (see Chapter 6). A full-service agency provides services for clients that utilise all elements of the marketing communications mix. Some argue that it helps ensure that all work is fully integrated. Also, it is more efficient for the client to work with fewer agencies. Most of Ireland's top advertising agencies describe themselves as full-service agencies (see Table 4.1).

Table 4.1 Ireland's leading advertising agencies 2001/2

Agency	Type	Billings	Affiliation
Irish International	Full-service	€74 million	BBDO Worldwide
McConnells Advertising Ltd	Full-service	€73 million	Irish-owned; alliance with Lowe Lintas
DDFH&B	Full-service	N/A	JWT
McCann Erikson	Full-service	€38 million	McCann Erickson
Owens DDB	Advertising and marketing	€33 million	DDB Worldwide
QMP D'Arcy	Full-service	€30.5 million	D'Arcy World Wide
Ogilvy & Mather	Brand communications	N/A	Ogilvy & Mather
Des O'Meara & Partners	Full service	€20 million	Irish-owned but linked to Publicis
Helme Partnership	Advertising, PR, CRM	€20 million	PR@The Helme
AFA Advertising	Full-service	€19 million	Irish-owned

Source: *MAPS Directory 2002/2003*

Billings *Level of media expenditure handled by an agency on behalf of its clients, expressed in monetary value.*

Table 4.1 shows (where available) the billings for each agency. **Billings** refer to the level of media expenditure handled by an agency on behalf of its clients, for example, the amount of money clients spent buying television and radio time and newspaper, magazine and outdoor space. The table also highlights each agency's affiliation. This refers to any links an agency has with another agency. In some cases, affiliation means ownership, while in others it simply highlights network partners who introduce one another to business opportunities. The agency landscape changes frequently, which means that Table 4.1 only provides a picture of the advertising industry at a particular point in time. For example, in February 2003, AFA and Des O'Meara & Partners merged in a move that gives them more clout in the Irish market. They have prevented yet another take-over bid from a global network.

The phases in a marketing communications campaign

Marketing communications campaigns go through three main phases – creation and design, production, and implementation.

Creation and design

During this stage, the marketing communications agency comes up with ideas that solve the problems posed in the brief and that will achieve the marketing communications objectives. Market research agencies play a role during this phase. Some clients and their agencies conduct research with the target audience to try and find out which ideas are likely to be the most successful. This is common practice in advertising and is dealt with in more detail in Chapter 9.

Irish clients that are part of international or global corporations do not always require the creation and design services of Irish marketing communications agencies. Instead, the Irish office often uses ideas that are created outside Ireland and calls on their Irish agencies to advise them on local differences that might exist in the Irish market. Once again, market research might be conducted to ensure that an internationally devised sponsorship programme, advertisement, direct mail shot or sales promotion works in the Irish market.

Production

The production stage involves taking the idea and turning it into the message that will be sent to the target audience. Most marketing communications agencies use third-party suppliers during the production phase. Some of these are outlined in Table 4.2.

Implementation

The implementation phase is all about transmitting the finished message to the target audience. Some of the players at this phase include media organisations, for example, TV3, JCDecaux (outdoor advertising company), the *Star*, and Today FM. Many direct marketing messages are transmitted by post, over the Internet and by telephone. Therefore, key players include An Post, Internet Service Providers (ISPs) such as Ireland on-line and Eircom, and telemarketing agencies.

Many sales promotion and direct marketing campaigns invite the target audience to make contact with the client. Therefore, the client must be able to respond and third parties are often employed to fulfil their promises, for example, to post the free gift that featured in a promotion.

Market research companies play a role during the implementation phase. They are often appointed to conduct research to assist in evaluating a marketing communications campaign.

Table 4.2 Services used in the production of advertisements

- **Stylists:** decide what the visual elements in advertisements should look like, for example, a model's hairstyle and clothes, the contents of a room, props
- **Make-up artists**
- **Model agencies:** have a portfolio of models and agencies and their clients select the most appropriate one for their advertisement, for example, child models, models with good legs
- **Photographers**
- **Illustrators**
- **Library shots**: it is not always necessary to take photographs for print advertisements because suitable images might already exist. The right to use these images is purchased and the price charged is usually based on the number of people likely to see the image
- **Freelance art directors and copywriters**
- **Music composers**
- **Musicians**
- **Spell checkers and proof readers**
- **Typesetters**
- **Reprographics:** companies that turn material into a format that can be printed
- **Film directors**
- **Actors and voice-over artists**
- **Studio and editing suites** for television and radio advertisements
- **Printers**
- **Sign makers**
- **List brokers**
- **Packaging companies**
- **Display equipment manufacturers**
- **Merchandisers** (e.g. corporate gifts, balloons etc.)

Organisational structures in marketing communications agencies

__Account__ Term used to describe an agency's customer.

__Account handler__ serves as the interface between the client and the agency.

Most Irish marketing communications agencies adopt a similar basic structure that is called an account management or client services structure (see Figure 4.3). Each customer in an agency is known as an **account** and one person in the agency or a team is given responsibility for managing each account. They are known as **account handlers** and serve as the interface between the client and the agency. In advertising agencies, account handlers are a cost centre. This means that the client is not directly billed for the work carried out by the account handlers. Instead, they add value to the agency's other activities and ensure that the client's needs are fully understood and that their marketing communications objectives are fulfilled. In public relations agencies, account handlers carry out most of the work, for example, writing press releases and advising the client on crisis management.

Account handlers build relationships with their clients to cultivate repeat and ongoing business. This role requires interpersonal skills because account handlers often have to critically assess their colleagues' work in the best interests of the client. They must also defend the agency's work if necessary when presented to clients.

Figure 4.3 The basic account management/client services structure in marketing communications agencies

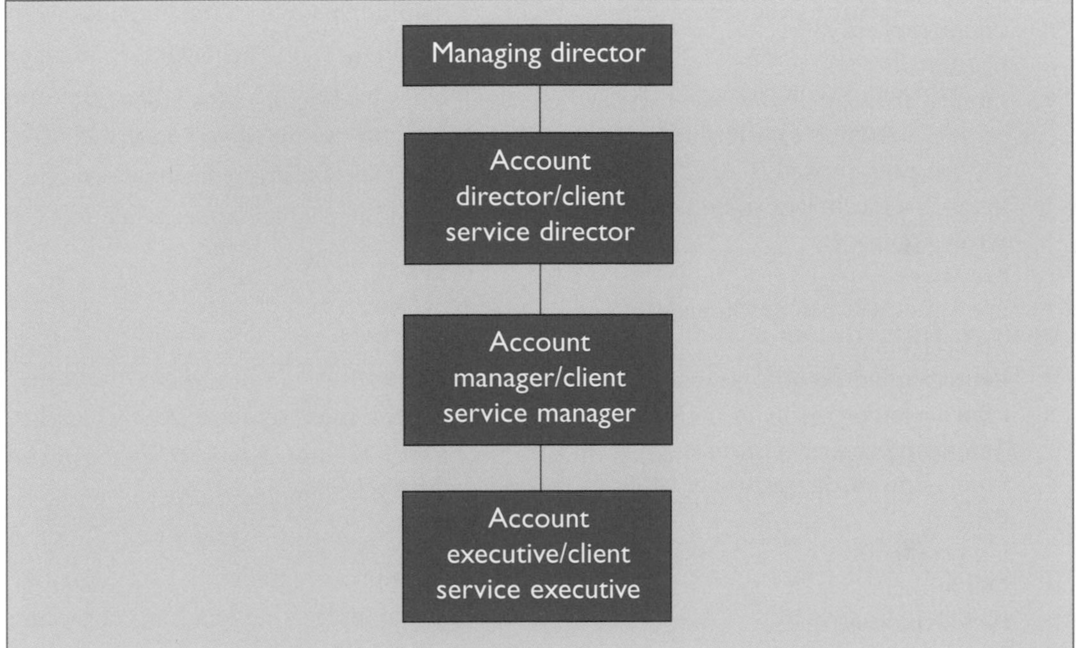

__Account director__ usually leads the client services team, and holds ultimate responsibility for the profitability of each account.

While the structure in most agencies is relatively flat, a hierarchy of roles exists in client services. An **account director** usually leads each team. They hold responsibility for the profitability of each account under their charge. They work closely with clients to help formulate the brief, and they are responsible for strategic issues relating to each account. They are also the overall guardians of quality. An account director's input is particularly important when an account first arrives with an agency and they work hard to develop the account in terms of revenue. They are not usually involved in the day-to-day operational issues of an account. Instead, they are key players in an agency's search for new business and they assess how much effort should go into new business development as opposed to existing client service. Their assessment is influenced by several factors, including the prestige of a potential piece of business, the long-term value of the new business, and the agency's ability to handle the business.

Account manager *ensures the client's needs are satisfied and that all work is successfully executed by the required deadline and within budget. A project management role.*

Account managers report directly to an account director. Usually, they are quite senior personnel and might manage one or more account executives. Their role is to ensure that a client's needs are satisfied and that all work is successfully executed by the required deadline and within budget. The account manager's role is, in effect, a project management role. Therefore, excellent organisational skills are required, as well as an ability to handle very busy periods of activity. Like account directors, account managers need excellent interpersonal skills, since much of their day-to-day activity requires them to represent the conflicting positions of the agency and the client.

Account executive *Most junior person in the client services team. Involved in day-to-day activity.*

Account executives tend to be the most junior people in the client services department. They report directly to one or more account managers. In smaller marketing communications agencies, the structure may be flatter than the one illustrated in Figure 4.3. In such cases it is not unusual for the account executive to report directly to an account director. The account executive is often considered a 'runner' and they are responsible for chasing internal and external people, so as to ensure that schedules are adhered to and deadlines are met.

Agency/client contact

In many cases the hierarchy illustrated in Figure 4.3 determines which account handler liaises with which person in the client organisation. As the most senior account handler, the account director usually maintains direct contact with the most senior person in the client organisation. In small firms, that person might be the managing director, while in larger organisations, the chief executive officer (CEO) or managing director has limited involvement with marketing communications agencies, preferring to delegate responsibility to a senior marketing executive, for example, the head of corporate communications or the marketing director. Therefore, the account director and their opposite number in the client organisation are more concerned with strategic marketing communications matters.

In FMCG firms, the primary point of contact between the agency and the client tends to be between the account manager and the brand manager. However, due to the quickening pace of globalisation, and the subsequent centralisation of corporate decision-making in many global FMCG firms, the role of many Irish brand managers is one of implementation as opposed to strategic decision-making. This means that marketing communications strategy is decided outside Ireland.

Contact between the client and agency account executives usually concerns day-to-day matters. The agency's contact in these circumstances is usually with an assistant brand manager or a marketing executive. As account executives become more experienced, they liaise directly with brand managers and marketing managers.

When a new marketing communications campaign is presented to the client, it is usual for both parties to send many representatives. On the client side, the CEO and the marketing director/communications director almost certainly attend, as do other key managers. In some situations, senior executives representing other functions might also attend, for example, the human resources manager, the purchasing manager or the finance director. On the agency side, the account director and account manager with responsibility for the client will be at key presentations. When presenting creative work, a senior creative person often attends. Clients often like this side of the business and enjoy meeting the creative brain behind a campaign. In the case of an advertising campaign presentation, a senior media person from the agency usually attends.

For meetings concerning day-to-day matters, it is more usual for one or two account handlers to meet with one or two representatives from the client organisation.

Roles and functions in advertising agencies

Figure 4.3 showed the client services structure that lies at the heart of most marketing communications agencies. In some cases, it more or less represents the entire organisation structure, except for the inclusion of finance and administration functions. However, in advertising agencies there are other areas of expertise represented by separate functions. Figure 4.4 illustrates the organisational structure in a typical Irish advertising agency.

Figure 4.4 The organisational structure in an Irish advertising agency

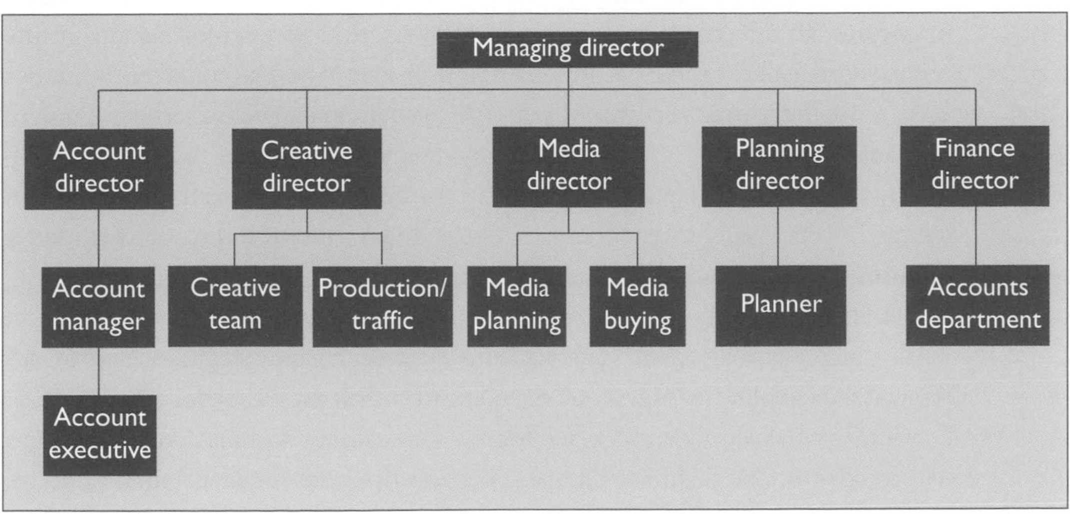

The creative department is sometimes considered the engine of an advertising agency because it generates and executes the ideas behind an advertising campaign. Overall responsibility for the creative department lies with the creative director who is usually a member of the agency's board. In large agencies, there might be two creative directors, one from each of the core creative disciplines, art direction and copywriting (see below). In circumstances where there is only one creative director, that person has an in-depth understanding of both disciplines and assumes the dual roles of mentor and director. This person usually possesses superb leadership qualities and can motivate their team. In some large Irish advertising agencies, this team might consist of more than 20 people, all organised into smaller creative teams of two people. A creative team consists of an art director and a copywriter. The **art director** is responsible for the visual appeal of an advertisement and usually has an art- or design-based qualification. The **copywriter** is responsible for the words in the headlines, subheadings and the main body copy contained in advertisements. These two people work together on a long-term basis and due to the close nature of their relationship, the division of tasks is not necessarily adhered to. For example, it is not unusual for an art director to come up with a headline or for a copywriter to think of a strong visual idea. A good creative team is an asset to an agency and its client and, as a team, may be headhunted by competitors.

Art director *Responsible for the visual appeal of an advertisement.*

Copywriter *writes the words contained in advertisements.*

When the client approves the creative idea and the creative team finalises the idea, the art director works with experts in the production department to produce the finished advertisement. The complexity of the task, the internal resources, and the budget determine the level of work involved.

Most agencies employ a **traffic manager** who is part of the creative department. This person co-ordinates each stage in the production of an advertisement and ensures that it is completed on time. It is their responsibility to ensure that advertisements are sent to the selected media on time and in the correct format, for example, to the *Star* newspaper. The traffic manager fulfils a very important role because there are usually several advertisements in production at any one time.

Traffic manager *co-ordinates each stage in the production stage of an advertisement and ensures that it is completed on time.*

There are two main job specifications in the media department – media planners and media buyers. As the name suggests, the main responsibility of the **media planner** is the production of a media plan. To do this, the media planner liaises with the relevant account handler and compiles a media brief. This sets out in writing exactly what the client wants to achieve by advertising and provides information about the target audience, the product and the budget. It is also helpful for the planner to be told as early as possible what the actual campaign will look or sound like. This is particularly important if the planner wants to recommend print media because some publications may not be able to reproduce certain creative techniques to the desired quality level.

Media planner *produces a media plan to help fulfil the client's advertising objectives.*

The term **media buyer** is very descriptive. This person deals directly with the various media organisations and negotiates the best possible prices for their clients.

Media buyer *deals directly with media organisations and negotiates the best possible prices for clients.*

Much of the revenue generated in Irish advertising agencies is derived from media buying. This is because many clients are part of international organisations and their advertising is created by agencies in other countries. However, many of these clients still require the services of Irish media buyers to place their advertisements in the most effective media. Media buying has come under increased client scrutiny and buyers must work very closely with media planners to ensure that the client derives optimal performance from the media budget.

Planner *represents the consumer's perspective. Experienced in qualitative research. Develops the advertising brief.*

Figure 4.4 includes a planning department. The people who work in this department are called **planners**. They represent the consumer's perspective. For example, they might conduct qualitative research to help paint a better picture of the client's target audience. They then use the research results to develop the advertising brief which is approved by the client and executed by the creative team and the media department. Therefore, the planner's work often makes advertising better. They should remain involved throughout the creative process to ensure that the advertising brief is properly interpreted and executed. To do this, they need to adopt a questioning role with the creative team. This serves to enhance, develop and refine their work. The planner's criticisms should be objective and from the target audience's point of view. This often makes it easier for the creative team to accept any criticisms. However, this is not always possible and conflict between the planner and the creative team can occur. Planners must be inquisitive by nature and this manifests itself in an ability to question every idea. 'Will this advertising work?' 'Will the idea appeal to the target audience?' 'Does it fulfil the advertising brief that the client approved?'

Not all Irish advertising agencies have a separate planning department but they all have some level of expertise in the discipline. Planners serve many important functions and, like account handlers, most of their work does not generate specific income. However, it should add significant value to the work done by an agency.

Roles and functions in PR and sponsorship agencies

PR and sponsorship agencies tend to adhere to the basic account management structure illustrated in Figure 4.3 (page 83). Some agencies might employ a designer to design materials such as promotional literature and signage. Generally, the design function is outsourced.

Roles and functions in sales promotion agencies

Sales promotion agencies usually adopt the account management and creative team structure, similar to that used in advertising and direct marketing agencies (see Figure 4.5). The main difference is the inclusion of a merchandising department. Merchandisers ensure that the sales promotions are delivered to the target audience, for example, on-street distribution of coupons, in-store tastings, the erection of point-of-purchase displays in retail stores. Some sales promotions are delivered in print media, for example, in magazines. In these situations, the sales promotion agency might work with the client's media buyer to ensure that the most appropriate media are used.

Figure 4.5 The organisational structure in an Irish sales promotion agency

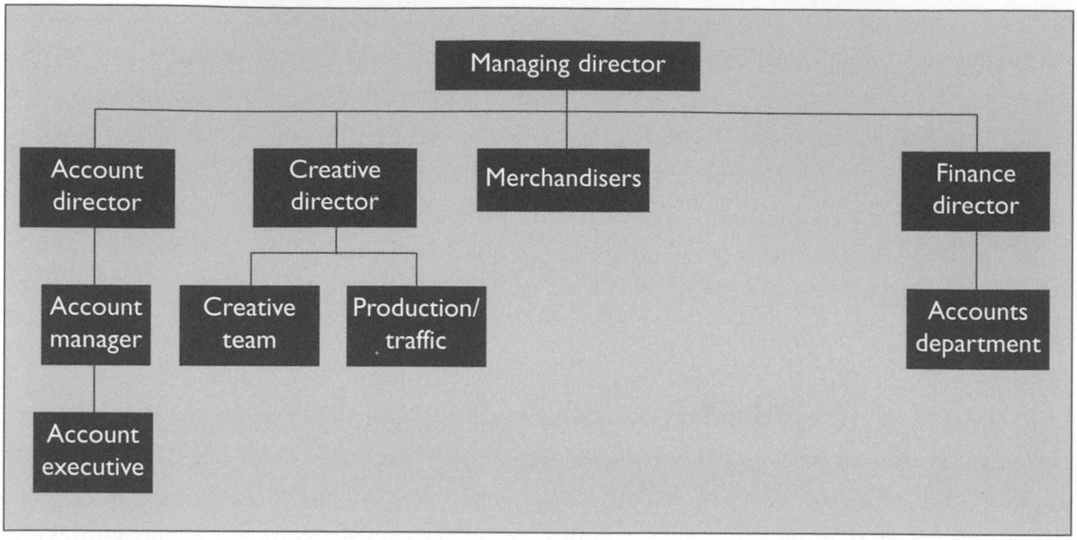

Managing director

Account director

Creative director

Merchandisers

Finance director

Account manager

Creative team

Production/ traffic

Accounts department

Account executive

Roles and functions in direct marketing agencies

The typical structure in a direct marketing agency is illustrated in Figure 4.6. In many ways, the structure is similar to that of the advertising and sales promotion agencies. The account management structure is used and the creative department in a direct marketing agency plays an important role. The creative team consists of a copywriter and an art director, although the creative skills required in direct marketing are different to those required in an advertising agency. The main difference is that the direct marketing copywriter and art director must write and design so as to motivate the target audience to respond immediately and make contact with the client organisation. Instead of media planners and buyers, the direct marketing agency might have a list broker and a database

Figure 4.6 The organisational structure in an Irish direct marketing agency

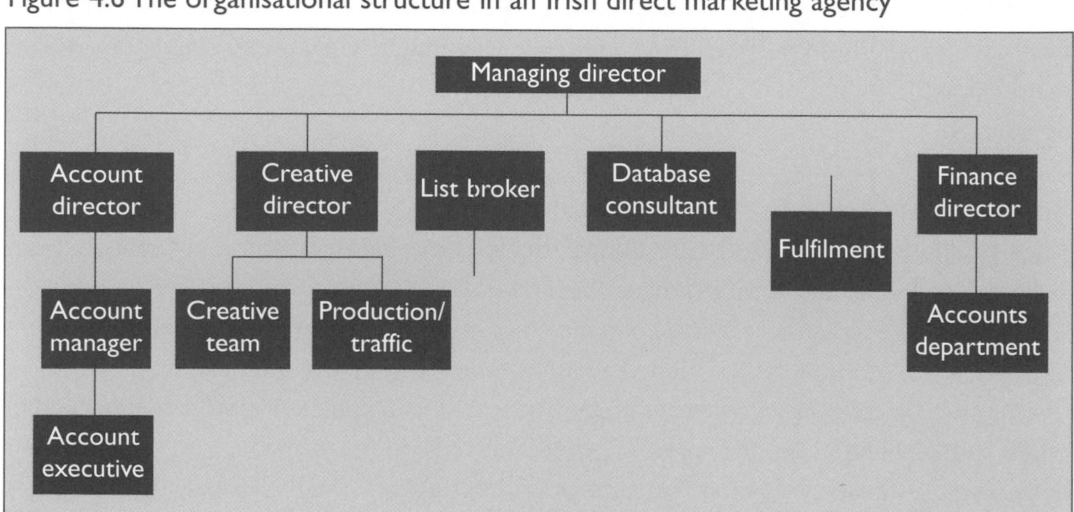

consultant because direct marketing messages are transmitted directly to the target audience in many cases. A direct marketing agency might also employ an individual or team in the fulfilment area. Their function is to ensure that the client's promise to the target audience is kept when responses are generated.

Agency selection

For many organisations, marketing communications expenditure represents a significant proportion of their overall budget. Therefore, agency selection is an important procedure that requires care and attention. The selection process (see Figure 4.7) can be daunting for firms with little experience in marketing communications and so they might commission the services of an independent advisor to manage the process for them. Most firms appoint agencies with a view to using their services for a number of years.

Participating in the selection process is time-consuming for agencies too. However, if they are successful, the investment can be recouped. For unsuccessful agencies, the investment in time and money must be written off.

Not all firms have complete control over the agency selection process. Managers working in the Irish subsidiary of a multinational company may have to use the Irish partners of the company's international marketing communications agencies.

Other organisations without complete control over the process include state-owned companies (for example, Enterprise Ireland and Aer Lingus), government departments, and government agencies (for example, the Irish Aviation Authority). Under EU legislation, they must operate an open tender process and must publish invitations to tender for marketing communications in an EU journal. Initially, many Irish agencies feared that this would leave them open to more competition from agencies outside Ireland, especially since technology such as high-speed ISDN telecommunications lines, e-mail and videoconferencing, has made it possible to conduct agency/client relationships in different countries. However, the nature of this relationship is still one that many clients prefer to conduct in close proximity.

Agency selection arises for a number of reasons:

- a new set of circumstances that did not previously require the services of an agency
- dissatisfaction with current agency or agencies
- satisfied with existing agency or agencies but with them a long time
- change of personnel in the client or agency.

If selection arises as a result of any of the last three reasons, Ward (2000) stresses that it is important to keep the existing agency informed. This keeps them interested in current projects and prevents the relationship from turning sour.

The Institute of Advertising Practitioners in Ireland (IAPI) and the Association of Advertisers in Ireland (AAI) published a set of guidelines on the Internet to assist organisations select agencies. While the guidelines are aimed at advertising agency selection, they can be applied when selecting other types of marketing communications agencies.

Identification of agency type

An organisation must spend time deciding what type of agency is best suited to their needs. As we saw earlier, there are full-service agencies that are capable of providing solutions in all elements of the marketing communications mix. However, some firms prefer to use a mix of agencies. When identifying agency types, firms refer to business magazines and journals, advertising and marketing press, the Media Advertising Promotions Sponsorship (MAPS) directory, colleagues, contacts in other firms, and industry associations like the Marketing Institute, Association of Advertisers in Ireland (AAI), The Institute of Advertising Practitioners in Ireland (IAPI) and the Irish Direct Marketing Association (IDMA).

The Irish business community is close-knit. This means that referrals from business colleagues are a particularly important source of information for many firms.

Figure 4.7 Guidelines for selecting agencies

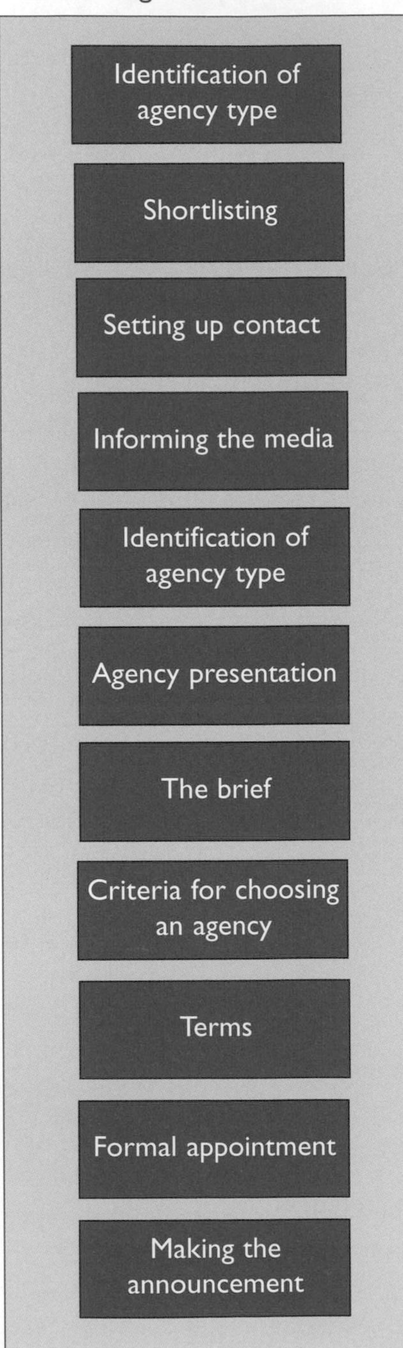

Shortlisting

When selecting any type of marketing communications agency, it is best to compile a shortlist. If a firm already has an agency, it should be included on the shortlist. Under these circumstances, the agency is referred to as the incumbent. The AAI and IAPI recommend that the shortlist is limited to four or five agencies. Any more than this is likely to result in a confusing and time-consuming process.

A number of criteria are used when selecting agencies for inclusion on the shortlist:

- agency statistics, for example, billings, expertise, ownership
- list of current clients

- range of services
- specialist services
- examples of recent work
- production capability – some agencies do not have the expertise in-house to be able to transform ideas into the finished piece of communication
- the opinions of existing clients
- market experience – some agencies may be experts in devising marketing communications programmes for particular market sectors such as the financial services sector or the charity sector
- the quality of the agency's own promotional material
- data from magazines, journals, newspapers
- awards, for example, PR Awards for Excellence, Advertising Effectiveness Awards, Direct Marketing Awards.

Setting up contact

All agencies on the shortlist are contacted, usually in writing, and informed that they are on the shortlist. This correspondence includes information about the firm and the type of selection process that will follow. At this stage, an agency may decide that they do not want to pitch for the firm's business. This decision may be due to a number of factors, for example, conflict of interests and pressure of work.

Informing the media

Firms usually inform the media if agency appointments are under review, particularly if it is a high-profile account or worth a lot of money. All parties should be made aware of these press releases and their content, for example:

> Green Isle has put the Donegal Catch account out to pitch. Four agencies have been invited to bid for the business including Bates, CDP, Dimension and Youngs. The incumbent agency, DDFH&B, will not be pitching.
>
> Source: *The Irish Times*, 8 February 2001

Agency presentations

The IAPI and the AAI suggest three types of presentations that can be used to select an agency:

- **credentials presentations**. A credentials presentation offers agencies the opportunity to showcase their agency in front of the potential client and to go through the equivalent of their curriculum vitae. Areas covered include the agency's philosophy, working methods, staff experience and qualifications, range of services, existing clients, and examples of work. Agencies should be given at least two to three weeks to prepare for this type of presentation.

- **strategic proposals**. Agencies are given a brief and invited to respond with a strategic document that focuses on addressing the issues pertinent to the marketing communications strategy. Agencies should be given at least three to four weeks to prepare for this type of presentation.
- **creative projects**. The presentation of creative work is referred to as a creative pitch. It responds to a detailed brief. From an agency perspective it is an important speculative investment and gives them an opportunity to make an impact. However, it is costly and time-consuming. The IAPI and AAI state that there must be a clear understanding between both parties of the complexity, extent and cost of the work involved. In some instances, the client contributes to the cost of the creative pitch. The contribution should be agreed in advance and should be the same for all shortlisted agencies. Any plans, materials and ideas presented by the agency are their property, and may not be used without written consent.

The brief

The brief should follow the guidelines outlined in Figure 4.2 (page 78). Guidelines governing the use of the firm's corporate identity elements should accompany the brief, for example, the logo, corporate colours or typefaces.

Criteria for choosing an agency

The IAPI and AAI identify a number of criteria that assist a firm's objective evaluation of each agency on the shortlist:

- the agency's ability to understand their business
- the agency's commitment to the project
- the agency's cost consciousness
- agreement on goals and objectives
- the independence of the agency's views
- the opinions of existing clients
- the quality of the agency's personnel
- the quality of the agency's proposals
- the range of the agency's services.

Another important consideration is the 'chemistry' between the two parties. Before selecting an agency, the firm should ask, 'Will we be able to work with this agency and get on with their main contacts?' If the answer is no, this places an immediate strain on the relationship that may contribute to long-term problems.

Terms

Once an agency is chosen, both parties enter detailed discussions on the terms of the contract. These discussions cover a number of important issues, such as, methods of remuneration, the timing of payments, third-party supplier mark-ups, and copyright ownership.

Formal agreement

Once the terms of the contract have been negotiated, a formal agreement or contract between the two parties is drawn up and signed.

Making the announcement

The IAPI and AAI suggest that no more than 30 days should elapse between the final presentation and announcement of the decision. Before the announcement is made, all unsuccessful agencies are notified. If requested, the firm should make itself available to provide constructive feedback to the unsuccessful agencies. The pitching process is costly and time-consuming, so if an agency is unsuccessful, it is important that they are given the opportunity to learn from the experience so that they can address any weaknesses.

Agency remuneration

Marketing communications agencies are paid or remunerated for their services in a variety of ways. **Remuneration** methods usually depend on the types of services provided by the agency.

Remuneration
The way in which an agency's work is valued and paid for by the client.

Media commission

This is the most common way of remunerating agencies that engage in above-the-line activity. The media buyer purchases advertising time or space directly from the various media organisations on behalf on an agency's clients. Due to the levels of business placed with the various media organisations, the agency receives a commission, usually 15 per cent. The agency usually receives a further discount for early payment of invoices. Table 4.3 illustrates how media commission might operate. It takes a very simplistic view of the commission-based remuneration because when advertising agencies buy a lot of time or space from a particular media organisation, they rarely pay the list price. Instead they qualify for bulk discounts and are able to pass these on to high-net-worth clients.

Even though this method of remuneration is widely used, it has been widely criticised by clients for a number of reasons. Firstly, it may encourage advertising agencies to prescribe above-the-line solutions for their clients' marketing communications problems when an alternative element of the marketing communications mix might be more appropriate. Secondly, if media price inflation occurs, agency commission automatically increases without any corresponding increase in the amount of effort. Finally, clients vary in terms of the demands they place on advertising agencies. Therefore, media commission remuneration does not always adequately compensate an agency working for a particularly demanding client.

Some clients offer performance-related bonuses to their advertising agencies. The bonuses relate directly to media performance and are in addition to the standard commission. They are calculated using media audits to assess an agency's ability to negotiate rates with the various media. Experienced advertisers like Procter & Gamble, Lever Brothers, Diageo and Mars all use this method.

Table 4.3 Media commission

A Transaction between agency and *Irish Examiner*	
Full-page colour ad in *Irish Examiner*	€15,120.00*
Less 15% commission	€ 2,268.00
Invoice to agency from *Irish Examiner*	€ 12,852.00
Less 2% discount for early payment	€ 257.04
Total paid to *Irish Examiner* by agency	€ 12,594.96
B Transaction between agency and client	
Invoice to client from agency	€ 14,862.96
(less 2% for early payment of invoice)	
Media commission retained by agency	€ 2,268.00

*This price is based on figures quoted in the *MAPS Directory 2002/2003*.

Results-based payment

As a result of growing client dissatisfaction with media commission-based remuneration, the idea of results-based payment is gradually being introduced by some of the more powerful clients. It advocates a partnership approach and if the client's performance improves as a result of an advertising agency's work, the agency shares in the profits. However, if the client's performance deteriorates, so too does the agency's remuneration level. Procter & Gamble and Orange caused a stir when they announced that they were going to pay their advertising agencies on the basis of their own sales performance:

Advertisers balk at sales-based payment

Procter & Gamble, the world's biggest advertiser, has announced it is going to pay its advertising agencies on the basis of sales performance. The decision is a major shock to an industry used to being paid on commission. The new results-based system is being seen as a serious reality check, especially for creative departments. Procter & Gamble spends more than €2.79 billion annually advertising its extensive portfolio of brands, many of which are household names, including Pampers, Tide and Sunny Delight. Of that, €380 million commission is paid to its four advertising agencies. Under the new arrangement, which Procter & Gamble says its agencies fully support, payment will be in the form of a flat percentage of revenue from the company's brands. The move is being seen as a reaction to Procter & Gamble's modest recent sales figures. The group is now looking for results for its mammoth advertising spend. The runaway success of Sunny Delight also fuelled the company's move. The sugary drink with 'the citrus taste' is one of the most successful new brands of the decade. Saatchi & Saatchi spent almost €11.5 million marketing Sunny Delight which brought in more than €200 million of sales.

Procter & Gamble business in Ireland is divided between Youngs, DDFH&B and Grey Mediacom. According to Mr Steve Shanahan at DDFH&B, his agency has yet to hear anything officially from its client about the new payment system but he is doubtful how it could be implemented in practice. Mr John Fanning, managing director at McConnells, is similarly sceptical. 'A sales-based performance system would be too difficult to measure,' he says, 'simply because sales are affected by several variables over which the advertising agency has no control, such as distribution, production and even being de-listed by a retailer.' He further suggests the issue of control arises again over the creative output of an advertising agency. Clients currently have ultimate say on creative output but that would have to change in a sales-performance-based relationship. According to Mr Fanning most advertising agency clients conduct performance audits at the end of each year anyway, so agencies are used to performance reviews. These are always conducted by the company's marketing department and cover a broad range of categories. It would not be unusual for an agency to lose an account after a bad review. 'If you don't perform, you're fired,' says Mr Fanning succinctly.

Ms Frances Marsh, managing director at Universal McCann, is equally doubtful about the implementation of such a performance-based payment system, not least because large international accounts cost so much to service and no agency would be in a position to take on such an account without some guarantee of a certain level of payment. She does like the notion of the close relationship between agency and client but points out that no other professional would agree to be remunerated on that basis. 'A client would never dream of setting up a pay-per-results system with their accountant or solicitor,' she says, 'so I don't see why advertising agencies should accept it.'

Source: *The Irish Times*, 23 September 1999

Naturally, advertisers want to account for their expenditure on advertising. However, as shown above, a results-based system is not without flaws. The strongest argument against the system stems from the fact that advertising and the other elements of the marketing communications mix are just one element of the marketing mix. An advertising agency might create a flawless advertising campaign while at the same time the client's distribution strategy might be seriously flawed. In these situations, sales might actually decrease and the advertising agency's income would suffer accordingly.

Fees

Remuneration might be in the form of pre-agreed fees between the agency and the client. Fees are usually agreed at the start of the client/agency relationship and then at the start of each financial year. They are based on predicted levels of agency activity on behalf of the client. The fee structure is built into the business contract and is usually invoiced on a monthly basis. Third-party costs are not usually included in the negotiated fee. Instead, they are invoiced as and when they occur. However, the business contract usually states clearly how the agency calculates third-party fees. Usually, the agency recoups the full third-party cost and adds a percentage to cover handling costs. For example, if an agency incurs photography costs of €3,000 on behalf of a client, they might invoice the client for €3,000 plus 6 per cent. This brings the total amount invoiced to €3,180 plus VAT.

This type of remuneration is common in public relations agencies because some firms like to employ PR experts on a year-round basis.

Fee-based remuneration may be risky for agencies if they are not familiar with the client and the types of demands likely to be placed on them. Clients may take advantage of the situation and extract so much work from the agency that the account becomes unprofitable. Conversely, clients should ensure that the agency is providing value for money. Therefore, it is very important that the scope of work is clearly defined and contained within a contract.

Project-based remuneration

Some firms avail of agencies' services on a project basis and pay them for each individual project. This is a common form of remuneration in PR agencies, direct marketing agencies, sales promotion agencies and sponsorship agencies. The costs associated with each individual project are calculated and invoiced on a stand-alone basis. In establishing a price for each project, an agency takes a number of factors into consideration:

- the amount of work carried out in-house, that is, the amount of work carried out by agency staff
- the number of staff hours required to devise and execute a campaign
- the number of subcontractors and suppliers required, for example, photographers, printers, models

- whether print work is purchased on behalf of the client or whether print consultancy is provided to the client.

When clients first come to agencies with a marketing communications problem or opportunity, some agencies might charge a very competitive price for the project. This is done to encourage the client to use the agency again. However, this is a risky strategy because when a client gets used to paying a particular price for work, they may subsequently not be prepared to pay a higher price.

Some advertising agencies are remunerated on a project basis, particularly for creative and production work. Part of the reason for this is the growing trend for clients to use one agency for creative work and to employ the services of a media specialist to purchase media space and time.

When fees and project-based remuneration are used, it is advisable for the agency and client to sign an agreement in advance of any work being done. The types of issues that are taken into consideration when finalising agreements are outlined in Table 4.4.

Table 4.4 Agency checklist when finalising an agreement with a client

- Obtain written agreement as to what the agency is going to do for the client.
- Seek clarification on any aspects of the brief that are ambiguous or unclear.
- Agree date for completion of work.
- Ensure that the client knows and understands the limits of the agency's responsibilities.
- Agree in advance whether or not the agency will be given credit for the work.
- Clarify limits (where necessary) on the use of the agency's work, for example, if a photograph is taken and used in a press advertisement, can it be used in an outdoor advertisement? If so, should the client pay more for the photograph?
- Agree a price with the client for each stage of the project.
- Agree terms of payment and include provision to charge interest on late payments.
- Ensure that the client understands that they will be charged for any additional work that results from changes to the initial brief.
- In the event of a dispute, under what country's laws is the agreement interpreted?

Source: Adapted from Jebb (1996)

Fees and project-based remuneration

Many agencies are remunerated by a combination of fees and project-based remuneration. Fees are negotiated at the beginning of the year and any work done outside the terms of the fee agreement is charged on a per-project basis. For example, a PR agency might be remunerated with a retainer fee. Unforeseen problems or opportunities might arise during the year and they create additional work. Therefore, they are invoiced over and above the fees.

Table 4.5 demonstrates that results-based remuneration is already used to reward advertising agencies and will soon be used to reward other types of agencies.

Table 4.5 Remuneration of marketing communications agencies

	Media commission	Results-based	Fees	Project-based	Fees and project-based
Advertising agency		✔	✔	✔	✔
PR agency		✔	✔	✔	✔
Sponsorship agency		✔	✔	✔	✔
Sales promotion agency		✔	✔	✔	✔
Direct marketing agency		✔	✔	✔	✔

Managing agency/client relationships

According to Ward (2000), most agency/client relationships last a number of years, a few last for decades, and a growing number fall apart relatively quickly. He suggests that one of the reasons behind the growing failure rates is the reluctance of clients to commit to agencies as partners. Also, many clients are open to the advances of new, exciting agencies that promise to revitalise their marketing communications. Marketing communications agencies work in a people business. Assuming that most agencies are capable of providing a certain level of service, the best agency/client relationships 'are those where there is a common agreement on goals, a strong personal chemistry at all levels, plenty of give and take and, above all, success. As soon as any one of these elements is missing or in doubt, then, like a marriage, there is bound to be a questioning of whether one really is in the right bed.'

One of the most important ingredients in any agency/client relationships is honesty. For example, no client likes to be told that a direct mail shot will be mailed out late or that a brochure will not be ready until after the deadline. However, if the agency keeps the client informed from the start and demonstrates that they are working hard to rectify the situation, the client's dissatisfaction may diminish and the relationship may strengthen. If the agency lies and covers up mistakes, the repercussions may be severe and may threaten the relationship.

Both parties should be open with each other. If the client is unhappy about something, they should tell the relevant account handler rather than hope that the agency detects the problem for themselves. The sooner this is done, the sooner the problem can be solved. Otherwise, it festers and causes long-term problems. The agency can demonstrate its commitment to the client by taking heed of the complaint and putting it right. If, however, the problem is ignored, the client has real grounds for concern.

Many agencies put in place a formal review process. The client is invited to critically assess all aspects of the agency's performance and service offering. This usually takes place at least once a year, and many agencies provide more regular review opportunities, for example, upon completion of each job. The annual review is usually attended by the most senior contacts from both the client and agency organisations. Key aspects of the agency's performance are reviewed, for example, ability to achieve marketing communications objectives, level of service, creativity, value for money, quality of work and ability to meet deadlines. The problem with this type of review forum is that it calls on the client to be honest, even if the truth is not palatable. The nature of the agency/client relationship means that friendships are forged and this sometimes makes it awkward for the client to tell the whole truth. This has prompted many agencies and clients to use more impartial review procedures. Clients might employ the services of an independent industry expert to review their marketing communications agencies. Agencies might employ the services of a market research agency to conduct in-depth interviews with their clients. Clients are more likely to open up to people if they do not have a close relationship with them.

Regulation of the advertising industry

The Irish advertising and sales promotion industries are regulated by the Advertising Standards Authority for Ireland (ASAI). It is an independent self-regulatory body that was established and financed by the advertising industry. It is 'committed in the public interest to promoting the highest standards of advertising and sales promotion'. Self-regulation means the adoption by the advertising industry of standards drawn up by and on behalf of all advertising interests. It involves the enforcement of those standards through the commitment and co-operation of advertisers, agencies and media. The objective is to ensure that all commercial advertisements and promotions are 'legal, decent, honest and truthful' (www.asai.ie). The standards are contained in the Code of Advertising Standards. This applies to all advertisements that promote the sale of a product or service and these are known as commercial advertisements and sales promotions. Non-commercial advertisements, such as those expressing an advertiser's position or opinion, are not subject to the Code.

When members of the general public object to commercial advertisements, they can register their complaints with the ASAI. The ASAI undertakes to investigate complaints free of charge. These investigations are published, complete with the names of the advertisers and their agencies. Here is an example:

ASAI Complaints Bulletin, 2001 edition

Product	Toilet tissue
Advertiser	SCA Hygiene Products
Agency	Publicis & Fallon London Limited
Medium	Television

Complaint

A television commercial for Velvet Toilet Tissue was the subject of objections. The commercial showed a series of naked bottoms which were described with words such as 'cuddly' or 'firm'. The strap-line used was 'love your bum.' Many of the complainants considered the commercial offensive and distasteful. Others were concerned that the commercial had been shown in the early evening when their children were watching television.

Response

The advertisers said that when developing the campaign they had taken the utmost care to ensure that the commercial would avoid causing unnecessary offence to consumers. They appreciated that nudity could be a contentious issue with a minority of people and had done everything possible in production and media placement terms to avoid offence. They gave details of the research that had been undertaken before the concept was fully developed and they had considered the learnings from consumers' reactions when producing the final commercial. They also ensured that they complied with the UK ASA [Advertising Standards Authority] Code of Practice and the commercial was presented to both the ASA in the UK and to the ASAI for pre-vetting. They considered they had produced a gentle commercial that was relevant to the product and in no way alluded to sexual gratification. The commercial was not run during children's programmes.

Conclusion

Complaint not upheld. The Code of Advertising Standards requires that an advertisement should contain nothing that is likely to cause grave or widespread offence and advertisers should take account of public sensitivities in the preparation and publication of advertisements. They should not use offensive or provocative copy or images merely to attract attention. The Committee did not consider that the use of nudity was done in a provocative, offensive or sexually suggestive manner and considered that it had a relevance to the product being advertised. The Committee decided that the commercial was not in breach of the Code.

Source: www.asai.ie/newsletter

If an advertisement or sales promotion breaks the rules, the advertiser must withdraw it or amend it. Non-compliance results in the refusal of the media to publish the advertisement.

Some advertisers avail of the ASAI's pre-publication vetting service. This enables them to seek confidential advice on a proposed advertisement or sales promotion free of charge. While the advice does not have to be adhered to, it may help the advertiser avoid damaging complaints that might ultimately lead to the withdrawal or amendment of the communication.

ASAI Complaints Bulletin, 2001 edition

Product	Pharmaceutical product – nicotine patch
Advertiser	Pharmacia Consumer Healthcare
Medium	Television

Complaint

An advertisement for a nicotine replacement patch was the subject of an objection by a medical doctor. The advertisement for a Nicorette Patch was described as the only patch designed just for waking hours and made the claim 'you're twice as likely to succeed with Nicorette daytime-only patch.' The complainant said that his understanding of the peer-reviewed data is that one is much more likely to succeed if one uses nicotine replacement therapy as opposed to not using nicotine replacement therapy. However, he had not seen any data that suggested that one type of patch was superior to another and he felt that the advertisement suggested that this product was superior to its competitors. He also believed that some heavy smokers benefit from waking up with some nicotine in their system to beat the morning cravings.

Response

The advertisers who were the holders of the product licence for Nicorette Patch explained that the patches are designed to be worn for approximately 16 hours, that is, applied in the morning and removed before bedtime. They said that the claim to be twice as likely to succeed with Nicorette daytime-only patch was a well-documented clinically proven fact that all the commercially available forms of nicotine replacement therapy increase long-term quit rates (of smoking) approximately 1.5–2-fold compared to placebo regardless of setting. They said that this was the basis of the advertising claims. They said that nowhere in the advertisement was the effectiveness of the Nicorette Patch to other nicotine patches compared. The claim only related to the effectiveness of the Nicorette Patch compared to the use of nothing at all.

Conclusion

Complaint upheld. The Code of Advertising Standards stipulates that advertisements should not mislead by ambiguity or otherwise, that any comparisons made should be fair and should be so designed that there is no likelihood of a consumer being misled and that claims about health products and treatments should be backed up by substantiation including the results of practical trials on human subjects. The Committee noted the advertiser's reference to research relating to the relative effectiveness of various nicotine replacement therapies.

The Committee considered that the principal issue arising under the Code was whether or not the advertiser claimed that their product was better than other similar products and, if so, whether the claim had been substantiated.

The full script of the commercial read as follows: 'While you're asleep your cravings don't bother you. So try Nicorette Patch, the only patch designed just for waking hours. Beat cigarettes one at a time. You're twice as likely to succeed with Nicorette daytime-only patch.'

The advertisement carried two advertising claims. The first was essentially that it was the only patch designed just for waking hours. The second was that you're twice as likely to succeed with the Nicorette daytime-only patch.

The Committee considered that if the advertisers' contention based on research that all commercially available forms of nicotine replacements have similar success rates had been made known in the advertisement, then the statement, 'You're twice as likely to succeed with Nicorette daytime-only patch,' would clearly relate to the benefit of nicotine replacement therapy and would not be implying any comparison with other products similar to the one advertised.

However, as consumers would not be aware of the relative merits of one patch against another, the advertisement could be interpreted by consumers as being a 2-fold claim to favourably differentiate the product from others, firstly, by stating its uniqueness as a daytime patch and, secondly, by claiming to be twice as successful.

In these circumstances the complaint was upheld and the Committee recommended that in future advertising the basis of the claims should be expressed more clearly.

Source: www.asai.ie/newsletter

The ASAI Code covers a wide range of issues including the advertising and promotion of alcoholic drinks. Here is an extract showing the principles contained in the Code's General Rules:

2.1 All advertisements should be legal, decent, honest and truthful.

2.2 All advertisements should be prepared with a sense of responsibility to consumers and to society.

2.3 All advertisements should respect the principles of fair competition generally accepted in business.

2.4 The Code is applied in the spirit as well as in the letter.

2.5 An advertisement should not bring advertising into disrepute.

2.6 Primary responsibility for observing the Code rests with advertisers. Others involved in the preparation and publication of advertisements such as agencies and media also accept an obligation to abide by the Code.

2.7 Any unreasonable delay in responding to the ASAI's enquiries may be considered a breach of the Code.

2.8 The Authority will observe requests to treat any confidential material supplied in strict confidence unless the Courts or an official agency acting within its statutory powers compel its disclosure.

Source: www.asai.ie/codes

The General Rules also deal with issues such as safety, prices, free offers, the availability of products, comparisons, and imitation.

The ASAI is a founder member of the European Advertising Standards Alliance (EASA). This was established in recognition of the fact that growing numbers of advertisements are pan-European or global, as opposed to being made in and aimed at national markets. If the ASAI receives a complaint about an advertisement that was published in another member country, it is referred to the appropriate national regulatory body.

External forces impacting on the Irish marketing communications industry

Throughout the rest of this book reference will be made to trends that are impacting on the marketing communications industry. The remainder of this chapter highlights a number of important relevant issues.

EU harmonisation of marketing communications laws

As reported by Curtis (2000), a number of areas have been or will be effected by the EU harmonisation of marketing communications laws:

- the planned introduction of laws banning the use of free gifts and competitions in sales promotion
- Sweden's desire to persuade the EU to follow its lead and ban television advertising to children under the age of twelve (see below)
- the ban on all tobacco advertising and promotion across Europe by 2006 (as shown in the case study in Chapter 5, this ban is already in place in Ireland)
- the relaxation of laws that currently limit patient access to information about medicines. The pharmaceutical industry confines marketing spend to trade advertising and sales promotions (*Sunday Times*, 23 February 2003).

Children's health first casualty of these TV ads

New research from Britain claims some ads could be damaging children's health. The study, which was carried out by the British retailing group Co-op, found that 99 per cent of the food products advertised during children's television are potentially unhealthy and it accuses junk food manufacturers of using cynical psychological ploys to get children hooked on their products during critical stages of their development. This undermines parental authority and breaches government recommendations on healthy eating, it claims.

Irish children watch more advertisements than most of their European counterparts. On average they are exposed to 20,000 a year. While no commercial breaks are shown on RTE during programmes for pre-school children, all other children's TV is interrupted by adverts twice an hour, although they must be shown 20 minutes apart. Although there are no regulations on the type of food advertised during children's television, the marketing of toys and games is controlled. Adverts must not be misleading when it comes to the size and scale of the product and must present it in as realistic a manner as possible. Noise or special effects must be kept to a minimum and the price must always be clearly advertised. However, most Irish children also have access to British television channels which soon could be showing more ads for junk foods than they currently do. Previous studies show that children watch three to four times more adverts for fizzy drinks and fatty foods than adults. Junk food ads account for up to three quarters of food ads screened at children's peak viewing times. As advertisers increasingly target young consumers, there are conflicting views about the effects. Current research suggests that most children understand the difference between television programmes and commercials by the time they are eight. Although children are perceived as naïve and impressionable, a study from the University of Exeter found that children's advertising literacy begins from the age of four and that by seven they have usually developed a good understanding of the function of advertising. As junk food ads become more pervasive, parents are becoming increasingly annoyed by them and feel they are being blackmailed into buying foods which are bad for their children. The new study showed that seven out of ten children asked their parents to buy what they saw advertised. Fifty per cent refused to take no for an answer, while 77 per cent of parents said they wanted to see a ban on adverts targeting children.

Concerns about the ethics of advertising to children have caused other European countries to take tough action. In 1991, Sweden introduced legislation to ban television advertisements that 'purposefully' attract the attention of children under the age of twelve. Norway and Greece have followed suit. Spain has banned adverts for what it calls 'war toys' and Denmark, Italy and Poland are currently considering stricter controls.

Source: *Irish Independent*, 8 July 2000

Promotion of alcohol

The alcohol industry has come under increased scrutiny in Ireland, as the number of alcohol-fuelled, violent attacks on young males grows. According to research carried out by the National Alcohol Policy Unit in the Department of Health, annual consumption rates of pure alcohol in Ireland have risen from 8 litres per person in 1990 to 11.4 litres per person in 2001. Moves are afoot to diminish the alcohol industry's stranglehold on sports sponsorship and advertising and promotions activity is being watched closely.

New restrictions planned on alcohol advertising for young

Tough new laws to restrict advertising for young people are being considered by the Department of Health. This follows Cabinet approval for the establishment of an inter-departmental committee to look at an overall approach for dealing with alcohol as a social problem, based on the Task Force Report on Alcohol. A separate Department of Health committee will draw up proposals specifically aimed at advertising. Many of the proposals are already in the voluntary advertising standards code, according to the Minister for Health, Mr Martin, who last night confirmed the establishment of the committee. The department will look at placing health warnings on all drink advertising and banning alcohol advertising in cinemas for films for under-18s as well as the banning of low-cost selling by discounts and vouchers, such as apply in colleges. Consideration will be given to imposing a compulsory watershed for television advertising, banning advertising and promotions in public areas where there are children, such as outside schools and banning alcohol-related sponsorship of events aimed at under-18s. There could be a total ban on the advertising of spirits. The proposals are listed in EU Council recommendations and the department wants to put some of those EU recommendations into national legislation.

Further proposals being considered for legislation include a ban on the portrayal of drinking as a challenge, or of it being depicted as brave, daring or implying social, sexual or sporting success. Advertising should not be linked with violence or high-risk activities. The committee would look at limiting the content of adverts so that their design or promotion does not appeal to children or adolescents.

Source: *The Irish Times*, 23 January 2003

Clients and agencies

The number of internationally-owned clients will continue to grow. This means that decisions concerning agency selection will be made outside Ireland and marketing communications agencies will win and lose clients through no fault of their own. Many marketing communications agencies have been preparing themselves for this by aligning themselves with international networks.

Summary

Marketing communications agencies are key players in the marketing communications industry. However, many more individuals and firms are involved in the creation, production and implementation of marketing communications campaigns.

Most marketing communications agencies adopt a basic account management structure. Other roles and functions are added to the structure, depending on the nature of the service that is provided.

Agency selection is best approached using a well-planned process. Recommendations from colleagues and peers are valuable when reaching a final decision.

Agency remuneration is under increasing scrutiny as clients seek greater accountability from their agencies. Four main methods were described – media commission (advertising agencies only), results-based payment, fees and project-based remuneration.

Agency/client relationships can only survive in the long-term if they are built on trust and honesty on both sides. Like any relationship, it requires work and the people involved must get on with each other.

The marketing communications industry continues to be affected by changes in the Irish and international environments.

Useful websites

www.aai.ie	The Association of Advertisers in Ireland
www.iapi.ie	The Institute of Advertising Practitioners in Ireland
www.asai.ie	The Advertising Standards Authority for Ireland

Review questions

1. Describe the essential ingredients that should be present in a marketing communications brief.
2. Describe in detail the key players in the marketing communications industry.
3. Compare and contrast the various organisational structures found in the marketing communications industry.
4. Prescribe a framework for any firm selecting a marketing communications agency.
5. Critically assess the various methods used to remunerate marketing communications agencies.
6. Agency/client relationships are like marriages. Some are good. Some are bad. Discuss.

References

Curtis, James, 'Should these ads be banned?', *Marketing*, 23 March 2000.

Institute of Public Administration, *Marketing Communications*, (Institute of Public Administration, Ireland, 1997).

Jebb, David, *Best Practice in Business Relations* (Design Business Association, November 1996).

Ward, John, *Using and choosing an advertising agency: an insider's view* (WARC, 2000).

Case study

Jameson Irish Whiskey

The Jameson brand enjoyed considerable success in world markets in the 1990s, and by 2003 it was still the biggest Irish whiskey brand in sales terms, having been the fastest growing spirit brand in the world in 1996 (*Drinks International*, 7 February 1997). The brand's success was due to a combination of factors including growth in the demand for premium whiskies, increased penetration in a number of markets and the positioning approach adopted by Irish Distillers Ltd in international markets. By 2003, however, the market for whiskey was changing. Consumption had begun to decline in the home market as a result of increased competition from other spirits and in international markets a number of challenges had to be overcome.

In late 2002, the marketing department of Irish Distillers was considering its options. The advertising account for Jameson had been put out to tender and a new advertising agency had been selected. How should the positioning of Jameson evolve? How should the company react to the changes that were taking place in the market? What implications would this have for the new advertising agency?

Company history

The Jameson brand originated in 1780 when John Jameson secured a licence to establish a distillery. The company remained an independent entity until the 1960s, when it merged with John Power Ltd and the Cork Distillery Company to form Irish Distillers Ltd. In 1988, the French firm, Pernod Ricard, acquired Irish Distillers Ltd; they occupy third place in the global drinks market, with annual turnover of €4.8 billion. In addition to Jameson, Pernod Ricard market a number of other brands that have significant sales in international markets (Table CS4.1).

Table CS4.1 Leading Pernod Ricard spirit brands 2002, sales of 9-litre cases (12 x 75cl bottles)

Brand	Cases (million)	Annual growth (%)
Ricard	6.5	–2.9
Seagram Gin	3.2	–0.4
Chivas Regal	2.8	–9.1
Pastis	2.0	–2.6
Havana Club	1.7	+11.6
Clan Campbell	1.6	–0.9
Jameson	1.5	+6.6
Amaro Ramazzotti	1.1	+14.3
Martell	1.0	–10.5
Wild Turkey	0.7	–5.4
Glenlivet	0.4	+2.3

Pernod Ricard operates as a federation, with a small HQ in Paris that lets its local subsidiaries get on with production and formulating marketing plans. The acquisition of Irish Distillers was significant for the Jameson brand as Pernod Ricard decided it was a brand it wished to develop in international markets. Consequently a considerable marketing effort was devoted to Jameson, including the development of markets in Europe, the Far East and in the United States.

In 2002, 1.5 million cases (12 x 75cl bottles) of Jameson were sold, an increase of 6.6 per cent on 2001. In 1988 the year Pernod Ricard took over, Jameson sold 400,000 cases. Jameson accounts for over half the estimated 2.7 million cases of Irish whiskey produced annually, with the other Irish Distiller's whiskey brands, Paddy's, Bushmills and Power's accounting for another 900,000 cases.

Table CS4.2 Percentage volume sales of spirits by sector, by country, 2001

	W	B/C	WS	R	T	L	OS
Austria	7.1	21.7	11.2	17.4	2.0	27.5	13.1
Belgium	29.9	8.6	8.6	4.7	1.5	15.5	31.2
Denmark	9.6	2.1	14.0	4.1	1.2	19.4	49.7
Finland	7.3	9.5	9.5	61.8	3.3	0.2	8.0
France	34.5	1.8	3.7	5.8	0.4	9.3	44.6
Germany	7.2	26.3	9.1	6.5	0.4	18.5	32.1
Greece	38.9	7.6	12.3	3.8	1.9	9.0	26.6
Ireland	38.7	2.8	44.8	8.6	0.2	4.9	–
Italy	13.4	9.6	9.5	2.6	0.9	32.5	31.5
Netherlands	15.0	4.7	1.9	4.1	0.7	23.3	50.3
Norway	12.2	25.5	35.3	1.1	0.6	12.6	12.8
Portugal	39.8	7.5	19.1	14.4	0.2	6.6	12.4
Spain	44.5	14.1	14.5	7.1	0.2	9.3	10.3
Sweden	36.5	3.3	51.5	1.6	0.5	5.1	1.5
Switzerland	18.1	6.8	9.6	5.1	0.6	37.5	22.2
Turkey	4.5	0.3	4.1	0.4	0.1	1.5	89.1
United Kingdom	39.4	7.7	31.9	6.7	0.2	4.5	9.6

Key W = whiskey
B/C = brandy/cognac
WS = white apirits (vodka, gin)
R = rum
T = tequila and mezcal
L = liqueurs
OS = other spirits

Source: Euromonitor

In addition to its Irish whiskey brands, Pernod Ricard also owns a number of Scotch Whisky brands including Chivas Regal, Clan Campbell and Glenlivet.

In marketing whiskies, distillers tend to place significant emphasis on the nature of the production process, the length of maturation and the quality of the oak casks used to age the product. Whiskey connoisseurs pride themselves on their ability to distinguish different brands on the basis of taste, and a significant market has been established in premium-priced mature whiskey as a result.

In addition to the standard Jameson whiskey, a number of more mature whiskies are marketed under the Jameson name. Jameson Limited Edition is a 15-year-old whiskey, while Jameson 1780 is matured for 12 years. Jameson Gold is a similarly aged whiskey that differs in that it is aged in a combination of seasoned oak casks. These brands tend to appeal to whiskey connoisseurs and command premium prices.

THE EUROPEAN WHISKEY MARKET

According to Euromonitor (2002), volume sales of whiskey in 2001 accounted for particularly high shares of total sales in a number of European markets. Share was highest in Spain at 44.5 per cent but it was also prominent in many other national markets as Table CS4.2 indicates.

Table CS4.3 Litres per capita consumption of spirits, by country, 1997–2001

	1997	1998	1999	2000	2001
France	7.8	7.6	7.4	7.4	7.5
Spain	7.2	7.2	7.2	7.2	7.2
Germany	6.1	6.0	5.8	5.7	5.5
Finland	5.1	5.1	5.1	5.3	5.4
Greece	5.3	5.3	5.3	5.3	5.4
Ireland	4.1	4.2	4.5	4.8	5.1
Netherlands	5.1	5.0	5.0	4.9	4.9
United Kingdom	3.5	3.4	3.4	3.5	3.5
Austria	3.4	3.4	3.3	3.2	3.2
Denmark	2.7	2.7	2.7	2.7	2.7
Sweden	2.7	2.6	2.7	2.7	2.7
Belgium	2.7	2.6	2.6	2.6	2.6
Italy	2.6	2.7	2.6	2.6	2.6
Switzerland	2.2	2.2	2.5	2.5	2.5
Norway	2.3	2.2	2.3	2.3	2.3
Portugal	2.0	2.0	2.1	2.1	2.2
Turkey	1.2	1.3	1.2	1.2	1.2
Others	3.3	3.3	3.3	3.2	3.2
Regional average	4.5	4.4	4.3	4.3	4.3

Source: Euromonitor

Performance in 2001 varied. The growing popularity of premium whiskey brands saw sales consolidated in Spain, Portugal, Greece and France, but the share held by whiskey was under threat in established markets, such as the United Kingdom and Ireland, primarily by the fast-growing white spirits market.

Volume consumption of spirits in Ireland increased by 1 litre per capita over the period 1997–2001, as Table CS4.3 indicates. According to Euromonitor this was because more young working adults were 'inclined to have a good time on a permanent basis'.

Per capita expenditure on spirits in Ireland was the world's highest in 2001, reaching US$252.1 as Table CS4.4 indicates.

Table CS4.4 US$ per capita expenditure on spirits, by country, 1997–2001

	1997	1998	1999	2000	2001
Ireland	238.0	242.6	252.4	228.0	252.1
France	274.6	265.9	250.6	205.3	213.5
United Kingdom	185.4	178.0	176.0	166.2	159.8
Finland	173.6	175.0	170.0	142.4	152.0
Spain	134.3	142.4	142.6	120.2	128.7
Greece	160.9	154.1	151.2	129.9	128.2
Norway	150.2	138.4	140.2	126.6	124.0
Sweden	132.9	130.0	132.7	123.0	110.3
Denmark	131.7	129.7	126.5	109.1	105.4
Netherlands	109.5	108.9	105.9	85.3	86.5
Switzerland	107.8	107.1	103.6	84.5	80.9
Austria	92.1	88.9	85.2	68.6	72.3
Portugal	72.1	72.5	72.3	61.5	66.6
Germany	83.7	82.2	76.4	61.1	60.8
Italy	61.8	62.4	60.3	49.3	51.0
Belgium	62.5	61.0	57.9	46.9	48.4
Turkey	15.2	16.0	15.5	15.7	15.9
Others	85.4	82.5	80.0	73.3	72.9
Regional average	121.1	119.0	115.0	98.2	99.5

Source: Euromonitor

INTERNATIONAL ADVERTISING – THE 'RUSH HOUR' EFFECT

The success of Jameson on international markets was due to several factors, not least because of the advertising campaign developed by the Dublin-based agency, McConnells.

Since 1998, Jameson has been advertised in Ireland and in most international markets using an advertising campaign entitled 'Rush Hour'. This came about as part of a global marketing strategy when it was decided to adopt an advertising campaign that would reflect the brand's international success. The advertising was to feature stylish young people in fashionable locations enjoying Jameson in an oasis of calm surrounded by a streaming rush of others in a hurry (IAPI, Advertising Effectiveness Case Study). The importance of people finding time to enjoy themselves with friends was to be emphasised, as was the presentation of the product as a dynamic and stylish international spirit for men and women (in itself, unusual in the whiskey market). The advertising was designed for use on television, magazines and poster sites. In the

United States, for example, the Rush Hour adverts appeared in magazines such as *Rolling Stone*, *Maxim*, *Men's Journal*, *Playboy* and *Golf Digest*.

The first locations chosen were Berlin, New York, Tokyo and Rome (see example in Appendix 4.1). This was extended to include Los Angeles and Chicago and these were used in markets all over Europe, the United States, the Far East and Australia. In 2001, McConnells created two New York executions entitled 'Rush Hour Soho' and 'Rush Hour Grand Central Station' for use in US media. In 2002, the campaign was adapted for television, three commercials were produced, the themes being that Jameson could be mixed with cola or cranberry juice or used in a Jameson whiskey-sour cocktail (a combination of Jameson, sugar and lemon juice). Regulations on the advertising of alcohol in the Irish Republic prohibited the use of radio and television for spirits (see Appendix 4.2). There were no such restrictions in the United Kingdom, and IDL screened television adverts on Ulster Television (UTV).

The Rush Hour campaign won an IAPI advertising effectiveness award for McConnells in 2002. The campaign was judged to have been successful in breaking the older more conservative values associated with whiskey and with recruiting younger drinkers in the 25–35-year-old category. In qualitative research conducted by Behaviour and Attitudes in 2002, the Rush Hour campaign was seen to be 'motivating and engaging', communicating successfully the core image values of the brand, sophistication, cosmopolitanism, warmth and camaraderie. The fact that Jameson had already become an international brand helped its position considerably in the Irish market.

In addition to the United States and France, most of the growth in demand for Jameson in recent years has come from the Mediterranean markets of Spain, Portugal, Italy and Greece. The Rush Hour campaign has not been used in France and Spain, however. In France, regulations regarding the advertising of alcohol meant that it could not be used, as advertisements cannot feature people drinking or cannot feature people and alcoholic drinks in the same picture.

Sponsorship is quite a common method of marketing communication among whiskey producers. Brands such as Johnnie Walker and Suntory are associated with international golf competitions, the Famous Grouse is sponsor of Scotland's international rugby team and the Black and White brand is associated with a 'pub of the year' competition.

Visitor centres

In the early 1990s, Irish Distillers opened a visitor centre at the Midleton Distillery. This received over 200,000 visitors per year. It was marketed as a tourist attraction and provided visitors with displays and audio-visual presentations that explained how whiskey was made and offered a chance to taste the products. A similar centre was opened at Smithfield in Dublin on the site of the original Jameson distillery and by 2002 it was attracting over 400,000 visitors per year.

Competition

The main source of competition to Jameson on international markets was Scotland. There were 28 distilleries in Scotland producing a large number of brands.

Scottish whisky (note the Scottish spelling of 'whisky', without the 'e'), or 'Scotch', is sold in over 200 countries, in 2001 shipments were worth Stg£2,295 million. Sales to the European Union (excluding the UK) accounted for 40 per cent of shipments. The largest single market for Scotch whisky, in value terms, is Spain followed closely by the United States, as Figure CS4.1 illustrates.

Figure CS4.1 Top 10 export markets for Scotch

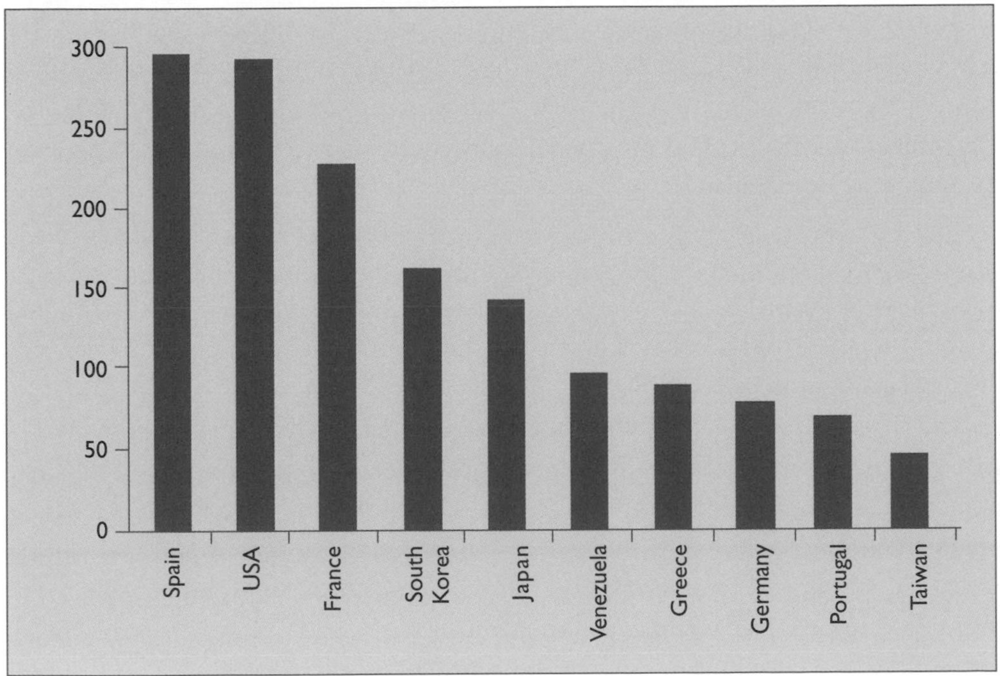

To be termed a Scotch whisky, the spirit must mature in oak casks in Scotland for at least three years. The majority of Scotch whisky is consumed in blended form, this means that a combination of grain-distilled whisky is blended with malt distilled whisky. In Scotland it is common for whisky blenders to assemble 30 or 40 different malt whiskies from different distilleries and blend them with one or two grain whiskies. Grain whiskies are produced mainly from corn using a quicker column distillation process than conventional barley malts.

A growing segment of the market is single malts, these can only be the product of one distillery. Single malts account for 5 per cent of world whisky sales. There are several single malt brands, the most significant in sales terms is Glenfiddich, which is the largest-selling single malt scotch in the world (see illustrations in Appendix 4.4). It is produced by William Grant & Sons Ltd, an independent distillery. The best-selling single malt in Scotland is the brand Glenmorangie.

Consumption tastes vary in different parts of the world. In Britain, whiskey is usually consumed with a little water, in Spain it is typically consumed with cola or club lemon, while in Japan a lot of ice and water is used.

Scotch whisky differs from Irish in that the unmalted barley is usually dried over peat fires, the smoke from the peat penetrates the barley giving Scotch whiskies a distinctive smoky taste. Irish whiskey is produced from barley that is dried in closed ovens, so there is no contact with smoke. In addition, Scotch whisky is usually distilled twice whereas most Irish whiskey is distilled three times. This triple distillation increases the purity and smoothness of the whiskey.

Scotch whisky dominates the world market, with an estimated share of 48 per cent of all whisky sold. Canadian whisky has 13 per cent of the global market while Bourbon (United States) has 12 per cent. Irish whiskey has 2 per cent of world sales. The remaining 25 per cent is accounted for by countries such as Japan, Korea, India, Australia and New Zealand.

Global competitors

In addition to Pernod Ricard, two large companies, Diageo and Allied Domecq, tend to dominate the world whiskey market. The three companies account for 57 per cent of global whiskey sales.

The Diageo Group own a number of whisky brands including two of the world's best-selling whiskies, Johnnie Walker and J&B. Diageo have categorised all their brands, including whisky, into three groups. 'Global priority brands' refers to those brands that are critical to Diageo's global market presence. This would include the Baileys liqueur brand, for example. The whisky brands, J&B and Johnnie Walker, fall into this category. The Johnnie Walker brand is the world's biggest Scotch whisky brand. It sells 11 million cases annually, while J&B sells 6.3 million cases. 'Local priority brands' are those that do not have a global presence but are important in local markets, thus the Buchanan's brand is important in Latin America and Bells is important in Britain. 'Management brands' are those that are not critical growth drivers for the company and will not be significant value creators in the future – the Vat 69 brand is included in this category.

Allied Domecq owns several whiskey brands, including the Irish brand Tullamore Dew. This has an estimated share of 5 per cent of Irish whiskey exports to the United States. The company's leading Scotch brand is Ballantines, which holds the number one or two position in 18 European markets. In addition, Allied Domecq have four other Scotch brands, Laphroaig (a single malt), Teacher's (the number three blended whisky in the UK), Glendronach (a single malt) and Scapa (a 12 year old malt). Allied Domecq owns one Spanish brand called DYC, which is the number two brand in Spain and a brand called Imperial, which is distilled in Korea and is market leader there.

The other Scottish distillers include some large companies like the Edrington Group (which owns the Cutty Sark and Famous Grouse brands) and some small independent distillers such as Glenmorangie which specialises in single malts.

Competition from other spirits

Traditionally, whiskey was the dominant spirit in the Irish market. However, in the late 1990s, this position was challenged and sales of vodka increased dramatically.

Vodka's share of Ireland's spirit market has grown since 1998, when the Red Bull brand was launched on the market. This became a popular mixer for vodka and despite the fact that sales of Red Bull have declined in recent years, consumption of vodka has remained high. By 2001, consumption of white spirits (principally vodka and gin) increased to 44.8 per cent of total spirit consumption (see Table CS4.2, page 109). Euromonitor predicts that this growth in consumption will continue in Ireland (and in the United Kingdom) primarily through the increasing appeal of heavily advertised premium brands which carry desirable lifestyle associations.

Many spirits producers have launched vodka pre-mixes, so called because they contain vodka and various fruit juice flavours that are pre-packaged, usually in bottles. Popular brands include Smirnoff Ice and Boru Black. Initially these brands were sweet-tasting and were aimed at the 18–24-year-old female market. Positioning placed a strong emphasis on the club scene. Producers have, however, sought to extend the appeal of these pre-mixes, and the Smirnoff Black Ice brand, launched in 2002 was aimed at the younger male and female consumer (*Sunday Business Post*, 17 November 2002). This product is citrus-flavoured and not as sweet as the Smirnoff Ice product.

The growth in the consumption of spirits in Ireland benefited producers. However, there was considerable public debate about the social side-effects of this increased consumption. There was a general increase in public order offences and assaults in 1998–2002 and many argued that these were related to the over-consumption of alcohol. In 2001, legislation had provided for longer opening hours for pubs, there had also been a trend towards larger 'super-pubs', and it was argued that this resulted in consumers drinking more. Health experts warned about the risks associated with the over-consumption of alcohol and there were calls for more restrictions on the advertising of alcoholic products.

Significant trends in the whiskey market

As they surveyed the market, Irish Distillers' management highlighted a number of issues that were significant:

- vodka's increasing share of the spirit market in Ireland and in the United Kingdom
- the continued importance of the French, Spanish and Greek markets
- declining spirit sales in the United Kingdom (consumption dropped by 22 per cent between 1990 and 1999)
- potential growth in new EU member states
- growth in demand for Irish whiskey
- a move towards premium whiskies generally.

Scottish whisky distillers were already limbering up for battle. Determined to downplay its 'tweed and tartan' image, many of the producers of Scotch were determined to appeal to a new generation of drinkers. The big three producers all had the financial resources and distribution networks to develop new markets and keep their (mainly Scotch) whiskey brands in top position. Inevitably the consolidation that had taken place in the global whiskey industry meant that many smaller brands would find the market extremely competitive. Jameson was in a good position and had achieved significant growth – but would this growth be sustained?

Market forecast

According to Euromonitor, whiskey is expected to continue to drive growth in France, Spain, Austria, the Netherlands, Portugal and Turkey in the period 2001–2006. Premium whiskey brands are already well established and extremely popular in countries such as France and Spain, but can also be expected to rise in importance in less-developed whiskey markets such as Turkey, as leading brands become similarly valued for their perceived status-enhancing kudos.

The Scottish Whisky Association, a representative body for distillers, predicted volume growth of 1.8 per cent per annum between 2002 and 2007.

Many whisky distillers in Scotland were pinning their hopes on the development of growing markets in Asia and on the enlargement of the EU. It was hoped that when tariffs come down in the new applicant states that sales will go up, as was the case in Spain in the 1980s (*Time Europe*, 25 November 2002).

The future

For Jameson the challenge would be to build on the existing position. Research in consumer perceptions had shown that the Jameson brand was perceived to be 'stylish, international and sophisticated'. How could this be built on so that the word 'unique' was added? The brand certainly had the credentials in terms of heritage, quality and a premium whiskey image, but this would need to be clearly differentiated in a market where there was likely to be increased competitive pressure. In addition, the success of vodka brands among younger consumers suggested that market growth was highest in product categories that were associated with club culture. Was this something that should be considered by Jameson? In considering its options, the marketing department knew that the positioning of Jameson would have to bear in mind the essential difference of the Jameson brand and would have to focus on the markets where whiskey consumption was at its highest.

This case study was developed by Donal Rogan as a basis for class discussion rather than to illustrate either the effective or ineffective handling of a business situation. The author acknowledges the assistance received from Irish Distillers Ltd in researching this case. The case study was runner-up in the Marketing Institute of Ireland/Irish Marketing Teachers Association Case Study Competition in 2003.

REFERENCES

Islay, Chris, 'Whisky Business', *Time Europe*, 25 November 2002.

Institute of Advertising Practitioners in Ireland, Advertising Effectiveness Awards, 'Jameson: The Rush Hour Effect', 2002.

McGuane, Elizabeth, 'Smirnoff to woo males with Black Ice', *Sunday Business Post*, 17 November 2002.

Mulcahy, Nick, 'Jameson Mixes in the Big League', *Business Plus*, March 2003.

USEFUL WEBSITES

www.jameson.ie
www.scotch-whisky.org.uk
www.diageo.com
www.allieddomecq.com

Appendix 4.1: Rush Hour advertisement

Exhibit 4.1

Appendix 4.2: Advertising Standards – alcoholic drinks

6.1 Advertisements for alcoholic drinks (i.e. those that exceed 1.2 per cent alcohol by volume) should be socially responsible and should not exploit the young or the immature. They should neither encourage excessive drinking nor present abstinence or moderation in a negative way. Under broadcasting regulatory requirements, the advertising of spirit-based alcoholic drinks (i.e. whiskey, gin, vodka, brandy, etc.) is not permitted on radio or television broadcasting services.

Social dimension

6.2 An advertisement may refer to the social dimension or refreshing attributes of a drink but

- a. should not imply that it can improve physical performance,
- b. should not imply that drinking can contribute to social or business success or distinction or that those who do not drink are less likely to be acceptable or successful than those who do,
- c. should not suggest that any drink can contribute towards sexual success or make the

drinker more attractive to the opposite sex by word or association,

d. should not portray drinking as a challenge, nor should it be suggested that those who drink are brave or daring,

e. should not link in any way the consumption of alcohol to aggressive or anti-social behaviour.

6.3 Advertisements should not suggest that a product can mask the effects of alcohol in tests on drivers; advertisements for breath-testing devices should include a prominent warning on the dangers of drinking and driving.

Young people

6.4 Advertisements should not be directed at minors (those under 18 years of age) or in any way encourage them to start drinking. Accordingly:

a. Anyone depicted in an alcohol advertisement should be over 25 and should appear to be over 25.

b. Treatments that are likely to appeal to minors should not be used. Advertisements should not feature characters (real or fictitious), motifs, colours or styles that are likely to appeal particularly to minors in a way that would encourage them to drink.

c. Alcohol advertising should not be placed in media primarily intended for minors. Advertisers should take account of the age profile so that advertisements are communicated, so far as possible, to adults.

Health and safety

6.5 In the interests of health and safety:

a. Advertisements should not encourage immoderate drinking or regular solitary drinking and abstinence or moderation should not be presented in a negative light. Buying of large rounds should not be depicted or implied.

b. Advertisements should not claim that alcohol has therapeutic qualities or that it is a stimulant, a sedative or a means of resolving personal conflict.

c. Advertisers should ensure that low alcohol drinks (i.e. those that contain 1.2 per cent alcohol by volume or less) are not promoted in a way that encourages inappropriate consumption.

d. Advertisements should not depict any association with activities or locations where drinking alcohol would be unsafe or unwise. In particular, advertisements should not associate the consumption of alcohol with operating machinery, driving, any activity relating to water or heights, or any other occupation that requires concentration in order to be done safely.

e. Factual information can be given about the alcoholic strength of a particular drink but it should not be the principal theme of any advertisement. Drinks should not be promoted as being more or less intoxicating or presented as preferable because of their higher or lower alcohol content.

Source: Advertising Standards Authority of Ireland

Appendix 4.3 Jameson advertising – Spain

Exhibits 4.2, 4.3 and 4.4

Appendix 4.4 Glenfiddich advertising

Exhibit 4.5

5

PLANNING FOR MARKETING COMMUNICATIONS

The aims and objectives of this chapter are:

- to prescribe a process that can be used when planning marketing communications
- to examine each stage of the process in detail.

Introduction

Few businesses succeed in the long term without engaging in proper planning. Some may argue that an increasingly volatile business environment calls for a more fluid approach to doing business. However, most would concede that planning is still a necessary and ultimately rewarding exercise. Marketing communications activity is no exception and can benefit from a measured and organised approach to its creation, design and implementation. Subsequent chapters refer to planning again and focus on activities relevant to individual elements of the promotions mix. In this chapter, the overall approach to marketing communications planning is examined.

The difference between strategy and planning

In Chapter 1, the concept of integrated marketing communications was introduced. We saw how important it is for each element of the marketing communications mix to fully complement the other. Unless proper planning takes place, this will not occur. Even when marketing communications planning does take place, this in itself is no guarantee of success. Close alignment with other organisational plans, strategies and activities is imperative, as shown later in this chapter.

Before examining what is involved in the marketing communications planning process, it is necessary to define strategy and planning and thus highlight the differences between the two.

Strategy acts as a roadmap for an organisation, whereas planning is concerned with the detail of the strategy and making it happen. Fill (2002) explains these two terms in the context of marketing communications. He states that 'strategy is about the direction, approach and implementation of an organisation's desired marketing communications whereas **planning** is usually about the formalisation of the strategy and ideas, into a manageable sequence of activities that are linked, coherent and capable of being implemented in the light of the resources that are available.'

Strategy *concerns the direction, approach and implementation of marketing communication.*

Planning *The formalisation of strategy into a manageable sequence of linked activities.*

Building on these definitions, he goes on, stating that a 'marketing communications plan is concerned with the development and managerial processes involved in the articulation of an organisation's marketing communication strategy.'

Marketing communications planning – key ingredients

Good planning involves a number of sequential steps, all related to one another. The steps involved in marketing communications planning are illustrated in Figure 5.1.

Figure 5.1 Marketing communications planning process

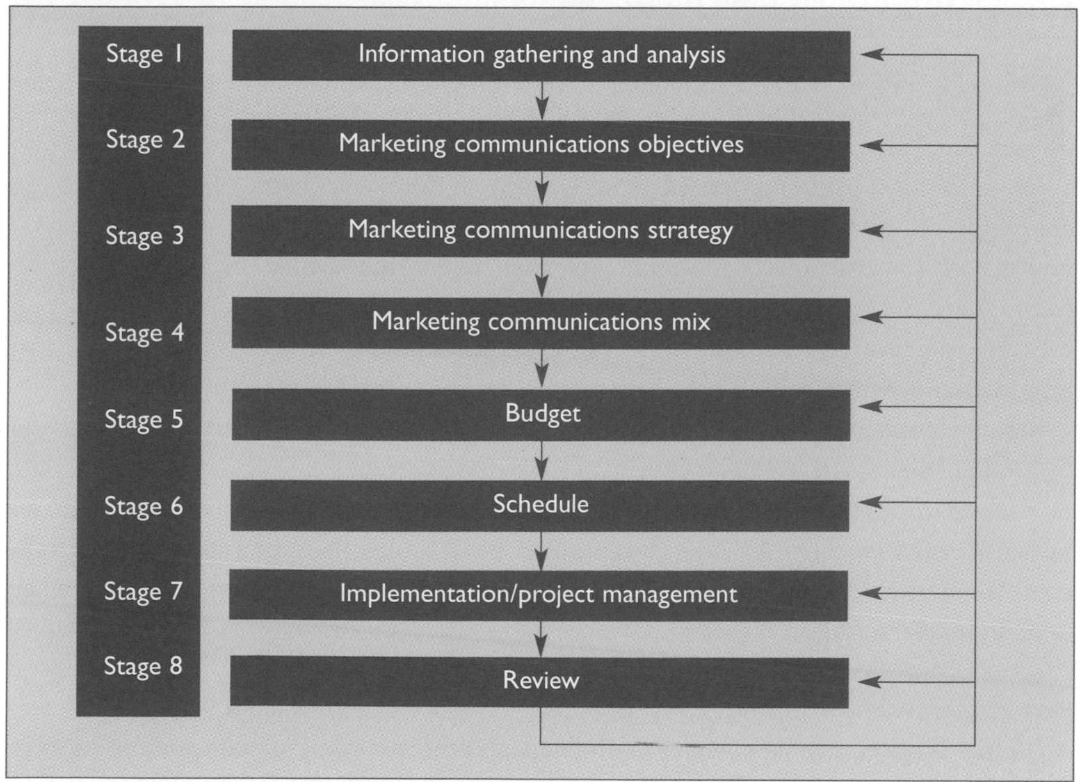

Before taking a detailed look at the plan itself, one question in particular should be answered. Who devises the marketing communications plan? While marketing communications agencies are often invited by their clients to provide input into the plan, they should not be given responsibility for writing it. This responsibility lies with the client organisation. Agencies are motivated by different and often conflicting goals to their clients. This means that they may lack objectivity when it comes to putting together marketing communications plans. Inappropriate plans favouring an agency's core disciplines and most profitable activities may emerge, leaving the clients with unsolved problems. For example, media buying is a very profitable activity for many advertising agencies. The more media time or space they purchase on behalf of clients, the more revenue they accrue. Therefore an agency might recommend to their client that they plan for a high level of media-based activity, such as newspaper and television advertising, when in fact a mix of public relations, sponsorship and direct marketing might be more suited to the particular communications problem or opportunity.

To guard against this, each organisation must take responsibility for devising their own marketing communications plans. However, it is advantageous and advisable to consult with a range of experts in the field of marketing communications when putting together the most appropriate plan.

Stage 1: Information gathering and analysis

When engaging in corporate and marketing planning, organisations usually compile information about key internal issues and relevant external opportunities and threats. This information provides an essential backdrop to those involved in the marketing communications planning process and is used to form the basis of any **marketing communications brief**. The marketing communications brief is a document containing information, instructions and guidelines that direct the formation of a marketing communications campaign (this is explored in detail in Chapter 4). The utilisation of existing information minimises the duplication of effort. In cases where essential information does not exist, it may have to be generated through research.

Both external and internal data are essential to the formation of a meaningful marketing communications plan. A full analysis of current and potential customers is mandatory. As we can see throughout this book, excellent marketing communications is dependent on an in-depth understanding of the target audience. Table 5.1 outlines the type of information concerning the external environment, which should be known and understood by decision-makers.

The external environment

A comprehensive analysis of the opportunities and threats facing any organisation serves to paint a realistic picture of the type of environment in which a marketing communications campaign aims to excel. Environmental research should unearth data relating to the following.

Table 5.1 External environment

- Economic trends
- Changes in the natural environment
- Technological trends
- Demographic trends
- Social and cultural trends
- Political and legislative changes
- Competitor analysis

Economic trends

Economic well-being affects consumer and business confidence and influences responses towards an organisation's marketing communications activity. Important economic indicators include inflation rates, interest rates, levels of disposable income, numbers of new car registrations, unemployment and investment. In Ireland, investment levels from abroad are an important barometer of the health of the economy.

Changes in the natural environment

The trials and tribulations of the natural environment are rarely out of the news. Growing consumer awareness and concern about the negative impact of economic activity on the environment cannot be ignored. Organisations must understand the implications of their actions on the natural environment and how the public is likely to react. Some companies incur the wrath of consumers because their way of doing business is seen as harmful to the natural environment. There has been a backlash against companies who distribute large quantities of direct mail because there is a perception among consumers that this necessitates the destruction of large swathes of forest.

Many organisations recognise that by being seen to be concerned about the environment in the way that they conduct business, consumers may have less to complain about. However, legislators in Ireland and the EU in particular believe that a *laissez-faire* approach to environmental protection no longer suffices. Many activities are legislated against and this constrains organisations in terms of what they can and cannot do when it comes to marketing. This in turn influences the type of messages that they send out through their marketing communications.

Technological trends

Rapid improvements in technology have touched the lives of most people in developed countries. In many instances technology has been harnessed to bring organisations closer to their suppliers, distributors and customers. It has the potential to revolutionise marketing communications and evidence of this can be seen already in many elements of the marketing communications mix, especially sales promotions and direct marketing.

Failure to keep up with these developments places organisations at a competitive disadvantage. It was already highlighted in Chapter 1 that retailers are becoming more powerful. One reason for this is their close proximity to the end customer. Through sophisticated loyalty schemes, retailers have strengthened their relationships with end consumers, while manufacturers and brand owners are distanced from the end consumer. Some manufacturers are fighting back and, where practicable, they are either eliminating the retailer from the distribution chain or building direct relationships with the end customer. Technological developments enable them to do this.

Demographic trends

Demographics concern the study of populations and provide marketers with a wealth of information about their target audiences. Typically, in relation to consumers, marketers are interested in data on variables such as age, gender, geographic location, occupation, marital status, birth rates, religion and nationality. Business-to-business marketers also require demographic information about their target audiences. This might include the size of the business, geographic location, number of employees and main activity. The Central Statistics Office is an excellent source of demographic information because it is responsible for census administration and analysis. However, many organisations gather this information themselves through marketing research. Demographic data is essential to marketing communications activity. As we saw in Chapter 2, the sender of a message must know the characteristics of the receiver.

Social and cultural trends

The composition of a population is quantified as outlined under demographic trends above. However, in order to build a more in-depth profile of its target audiences, an organisation really needs to understand the implications of the various 'labels' attached to them. More in-depth information about the target audience's interests and beliefs enables an organisation to create relevant, appealing marketing communications. They must also find out more about key influences on the lives of the target audience. Ireland's population is very diverse. Many Irish people have lived abroad for a number of years before returning to their native country. A growing number of people from other European, African and Asian countries are migrating to Ireland and bringing with them a diverse range of cultural influences. Every day, the Irish population is exposed to news, music and television programmes that originated outside Ireland.

Political and legislative change

Legislative changes can have a profound effect on organisations. Much of the legislation governing Irish organisations comes from the EU. Changes can open up a previously closed or sheltered market. For example, the European telecommunications and aviation sectors have changed dramatically as a result of legislation.

Legislative changes might necessitate changes in manufacturing, distribution, and marketing strategies. The tobacco industry is one example of a sector where draconian measures have severely curtailed its marketing communications options and this is highlighted below. Data protection legislation has been introduced to police the use of company databases and to protect consumers from unsolicited approaches through the post, by e-mail and by phone. This impacts on organisations that rely on direct marketing.

Legislation, the tobacco industry and marketing communications

This excerpt is taken from a case study, which was written and prepared by Amanda Finnegan as part of her Degree at the Institute of Technology, Tallaght in 2002.

ADVERTISING

- **Television advertising** ended in 1974 due to binding contracts with broadcasting companies.
- **Radio advertising** ended by voluntary agreement in 1976.
- **Cinema advertising** ended in 1979.
- **Poster and billboard advertising** ended as a result of legislation in 1980.
- **Bus advertising** ended following legislation in 1980.
- **Shop-front advertising** ended following legislation in 1987.
- **Press advertising** ended in 2001.
- **Packaging**. The EU directive on labelling (which mandates rotating health warnings and the listing of tar and nicotine contents on the package) has been implemented into Irish law. The current regulations stipulate that the front of the pack should state 'Tobacco seriously damages health. Irish Government Warning.' The back of the pack must carry, by rotation, five of the following eight health warnings (the first two being mandatory): 'Smoking causes cancer;' 'Smoking causes heart disease;' 'Smokers die younger;' 'Smoking kills;' 'Smoking when pregnant harms your baby;' 'Stopping smoking reduces the risk of serious disease;' 'Don't smoke if you want to stay healthy;' or 'Smoking causes fatal diseases.' A proposed EU directive requires that the size of health warnings be increased to at least 30 per cent of the front and 40 per cent of the back of packs, and more where two or more languages are involved. The warnings would be in black type on a white background, surrounded by a black border. The law requires tobacco companies to disclose details of additives to tobacco products and their purpose and plan to ban descriptors such as 'light' and 'mild', as they are considered misleading.

ON-PACK PROMOTIONS

Direct marketing in the form of leaflets or literature targeted directly at the consumer is completely prohibited. Tobacco companies may not produce any literature or promotional material that advertises the product or promotes it in any way.

The Internet

Advertising and promotion is prohibited on the Internet. The tobacco industry may not use e-mail to target consumers. However, there are no boundaries in electronic communication. Anybody in any part of the world can create their own website and place it on the Internet for any individual to access. Therefore it is difficult to monitor the advertising and promotion of tobacco products on the Internet. The EU is trying to prevent it through the harmonisation of European law in relation to the tobacco industry.

Sales promotion

Sales promotion has been almost completely prohibited since the enforcement of the Tobacco Act of 1978. This Act prohibits use of coupons, vouchers, trading stamps, tokens or gifts. Sampling of actual cigarettes has been banned for over 50 years. Branded items seen like pens and lighters are prohibited for both retailers and consumers under the regulations of the new Public Health (Tobacco) Bill. Branded non-tobacco goods e.g. Rothmans Jackets or Camel Clothing are illegal, although some retailers still sell these goods in Ireland.

Advertising at point of sale is now prohibited under the new laws and no tobacco brands may be displayed in the open anymore. The retailer may have a sign in the outlet informing customers that cigarettes are for sale but these signs cannot contain imagery of the cigarettes.

Delivery vans are permitted to have the name of the company and the type of products sold displayed on the van. Gallahers have their corporate logo and name printed on the sides of their delivery vans. However, PJ Carrolls stopped labelling their vans for security reasons.

Personal selling

Sales representatives cannot push tobacco products in the form of trade incentives. This has been illegal since 1978. They cannot influence product positioning as point-of-sale displays are prohibited.

Vending machines

Vending machines cannot convey imagery of particular brands or advertise any tobacco product. Instead they often carry advertisements for other products, such as alcoholic products. The only place where the brand name can be displayed and the brand colours conveyed is the deckels on the machine which are placed beside the option buttons differentiating one brand from another.

SPONSORSHIP

Sports sponsorship has become increasingly important to the tobacco industry as other promotional options have been outlawed. The tobacco industry spends tens of millions of euros a year sponsoring sports around the world, mainly on high-profile exciting sports – particularly motor sport – which receive a lot of television coverage.

Formula 1 motor racing is the sport most closely associated with tobacco sponsorship. Tobacco sponsorship accounted for around two-thirds of the sponsorship of the sport up to 1999. In 1999, the tobacco industry invested around US$250 million (€230 million) in Formula 1 teams. The FIA, Formula 1's governing body, has voluntarily undertaken to end tobacco sponsorship by 2006. As a result, the prevalence of tobacco sponsorship, while still extremely high, is beginning to fall.

Some people fear that a withdrawal of tobacco sponsorship will harm sports, which are currently heavily sponsored by cigarette brands. However, evidence suggests that this is not necessarily the case (two of the world's biggest sporting events, the Olympic Games and the football World Cup have not suffered financially).

Tobacco companies still sponsor many British sporting events. In 2001, Gallahers sponsored a number of sports events including golf (Benson & Hedges International Open), snooker (Benson & Hedges Masters Tournament), cricket (Benson & Hedges Cup) and rugby League (Silk Cut Challenge Cup). Imperial sponsors several snooker events, including the Embassy World Championship and the Regal Welsh Open.

Competitor analysis

All organisations must find out as much as possible about their current and potential competitors. Current competitors are usually relatively straightforward to identify and monitor, although failure to look beyond the obvious can lead to nasty surprises and the arrival of unexpected competitors. These predators might attack with substitute products or may make themselves available through new distribution channels. Therefore, an understanding of the barriers to market entry is very helpful when identifying likely competitors. Previously impervious barriers can be removed at the stroke of a legislator's pen, thus clearing a path for the arrival of new competitors. Organisations in EU member states frequently face new competitors as a result of EU deregulation.

When current and potential competitors have been identified, an organisation must find out as much as possible about them – their market share, positioning, mission statements, strengths and weaknesses, likely reaction to competitor activity, resource bases.

Internal strengths and weaknesses

Just as an in-depth knowledge of the external environment is necessary, so too is a detailed analysis of an organisation's own strengths and weaknesses (see Table 5.2). Ideally, this should be carried out at least once a year. The results can be used to inform those working on the marketing communications plan which product and organisational attributes should be emphasised and which negative aspects and perceptions should be redressed.

Table 5.2 Internal environment

- Corporate objectives and strategy
- Resources
- Marketing objectives and strategy
- The product or service
- Brand values
- Distribution

Mission statement *Statement of a company's fundamental purpose and focus, and how it will add value for customers and other key audiences. Informs staff as to what is important.*

Corporate objectives and strategy

All objective- and strategy-setting activity in an organisation should stem from the overall corporate objectives and strategy. In turn, the foundation for these is the organisation's mission statement. According to Wood (2003), a **mission statement** is a 'statement of the company's fundamental purpose, its focus, and how it will add value for customers and other stakeholders'. Therefore it sets the tone for the organisation and informs staff and stakeholders what is important. The mission statement is sometimes referred to as the 'vision'. Vodafone's vision is 'to be the world's mobile communications leader – enriching customers' lives, and helping individuals, businesses and communities to be more connected in a mobile world' (Vodafone, 22 February 2002).

Everything that an organisation does should be in harmony with its mission statement and should reinforce its values.

An organisation's marketing objectives and strategy should be derived from the corporate objectives and strategy, and these in turn should shape the marketing communications objectives and strategy.

Resources

An analysis of the organisation's financial and human resources must be conducted. For example, if customer service is a weakness, a marketing communications campaign should not make promises that the organisation cannot live up to. Take another situation where a campaign looks for a response from the target audience. Regardless of whether the responses are made by telephone, mail or e-mail, can they be handled by staff within the organisation or are the services of an external, specialist agency required?

Marketing objectives and strategy

As illustrated in Figure 5.2, the marketing objectives and strategy must be considered when putting together a marketing communications plan. If the organisation has stated that it wants to be a low-cost producer and is pursuing a direct distribution strategy, then the marketing communications objectives and strategy should support this. In such a situation, a marketing communications objective might be to persuade 20 per cent of the target audience to make direct contact with the organisation. The marketing communications strategy in this case would probably involve some sort of direct response advertising and telemarketing activity (marketing communications objectives are examined under Stage 2 of the process).

Figure 5.2 Corporate objectives and strategy and marketing communications

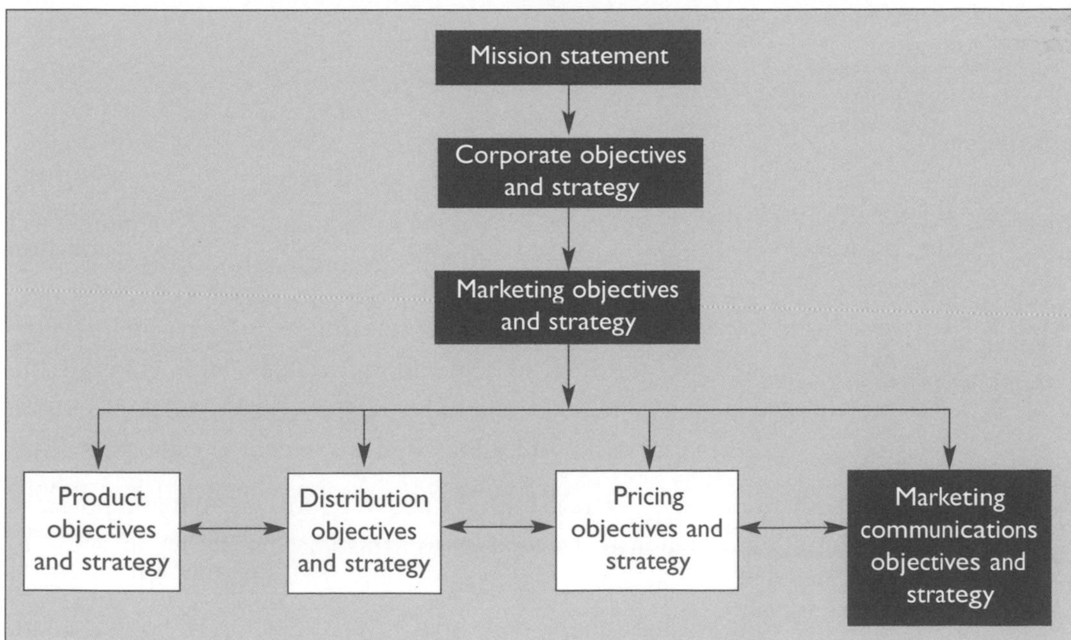

Products or services

The nature of the products and services in question and their stage in the product life cycle should be taken into account when planning for marketing communications. The objectives and strategy relating to a new consumer product differ from those relating to a well-established industrial product.

Brand values

All major, successful brands have very clear, well-defined brand values. These inform and direct marketing communications activity. For example, AIB Bank's brand values are to be 'dependable, engaging and pioneering'. Depending on who they are communicating with, at least one of these brand values must be portrayed. For example, when AIB Bank communicates with staff, it is important to reinforce the 'dependable' value and to motivate staff so that they will behave in a professional manner. When the bank communicates with customers, it wants to reassure them that the bank is dependable and can be trusted with their money.

According to Vodafone (22 February 2002), their vision can only be realised if employees commit to their corporate or brand values. They refer to these as 'passions'. Their four passions are:

- Passion for customers
- Passion for our people
- Passion for the world around us
- Passion for results.

Distribution

The method of distribution used by an organisation must be taken into account. If the product is sold direct to the customer, the marketing communications strategy will probably use personal selling and direct marketing. If the organisation sells an FMCG product through major retailers, the marketing communications strategy is more likely to involve a mix of personal selling (to the retailers), advertising, sponsorship and sales promotions (to the retailers and the end consumers).

Customer analysis

As already stated, organisations must learn as much as possible about current and potential customers. This allows segmentation to take place and this enables the organisation to transmit the most appropriate messages to each of the segments. In the case of organisations communicating to consumer markets, they must find out the following about current and potential customers:

- their needs, wants, attitudes, behaviour
- their buyer readiness stage – from need recognition to purchase
- their influences
- their purchasing criteria
- their stage in the life cycle, for example, single, married with no children; married with young children; retired, etc.
- their lifestyle
- their age, income, occupation, marital status, nationality
- their preferred place and/or method of purchase.

When organisations communicate in the business-to-business sector, they require the following information about current and potential customers:

- their needs, wants, attitudes, behaviour
- the identity and profile of each individual in the decision-making unit
- their buyer readiness stage
- their purchasing criteria
- a profile of the customer's business – size, location, resources, purchasing policies, nature of business.

The more an organisation knows about their target audience, the more relevant and effective their marketing communications campaigns are likely to be.

Stage 2: Marketing communications objectives

According to Wood (2003), **goals** are 'longer-term performance targets for an organisation or a particular unit', while he describes **objectives** as short-term targets 'that support the achievement of an organisation's or unit's goals'. Therefore, **marketing communications objectives** provide direction for those charged with designing, implementing and evaluating marketing communications strategy.

Goals *Long-term performance targets.*

Objectives *Short-term targets that support the achievement of goals.*

Marketing communications objectives *provide direction for the marketing communications strategy.*

Marketing communications objectives clearly specify the targets that need to be achieved following the implementation of the communications strategy. The benefits of objective-setting in marketing communications are:

- It facilitates communication between those working on a marketing communications strategy within the organisation itself and between key contact people in the organisation and their various agencies. It means that all parties know exactly what they are working towards.
- It forms the basis of a more objective approach to evaluating the work of those involved in the marketing communications process. For example, if a direct marketing agency presents ideas to the client and states clearly how they will help them achieve their objectives, the client can judge the work on that basis. In the absence of clearly defined objectives, the evaluation of ideas can become a highly subjective process, with personal likes and dislikes forming the basis of acceptance or rejection.
- Without objectives the success or otherwise of a campaign cannot be measured when it has been implemented.

Types of marketing communications objectives

Smith (1998) and Belch and Belch (1999) tell us there are two types of marketing communications objectives:

- sales- or marketing-oriented objectives
- communications objectives.

Regardless of the orientation, objectives should always emanate from and relate to the organisation's overall marketing plan and strategy.

Sales- and marketing-oriented objectives

Sales- or marketing-oriented objectives *set targets in terms of quantifiable results as measured against sales, market share, distribution achievements and customer contacts.*

Sales- and marketing-oriented objectives set targets for marketing communications programmes in terms of quantifiable results as measured against sales, market share, distribution achievements and customer contacts. Examples of sales- and marketing-oriented objectives are:

- to increase the number of people visiting retail outlet A from 1,000 customers to 2,000 per week. The volume of people visiting retailers is referred to as 'store traffic'. Power City's advertising suggests that they pursue this type of objective.
- to add 500 new names to the company database
- to increase market share from 3 to 8 per cent within a six-month period
- to secure 12 new agents in the Cork region in the first quarter of the year
- to sell 100,000 units of a new product within 12 months of the launch date
- to increase sales of an existing product X by 5 per cent.

In today's competitive environment, senior management teams place far greater demands on staff in terms of accountability. They want to see exactly what they are getting for their money. That is why many organisations favour the use of sales- and marketing-oriented objectives in marketing communications. They are quantifiable and the strategies used either deliver the required results or they don't. Rightly or wrongly, failure to meet these objectives is often attributed to a defective marketing communications strategy.

Is it always appropriate to reach conclusions with regard to a campaign's success or failure, as measured against sales- and marketing-oriented objectives? Clearly, marketing communications techniques can be used to achieve the types of objectives outlined above. For example, if a company wants to add names to its database, it might encourage people to telephone its customer care line by using attention-grabbing advertisements featuring the free phone number. The requisite number of contacts might be received or exceeded. However, failure to attract the target number of contacts might not necessarily be attributable to the quality of the advertising. An external shock, such as extreme weather conditions, may have occurred and distracted the target audience. Or the telephone system may have been inadequate to cope with the reaction to the advertisement, thus causing people to give up trying to get through to the telephone number. Unless all of the external factors are explored, failure to achieve the objective may be put down to poor advertising.

Therein lies an essential point. When sales- and marketing-oriented objectives are not reached or are exceeded, all other factors likely to affect their achievement must be analysed before declaring a marketing communications programme a success or failure:

- **What external factors may have contributed to the results?** (e.g. competitor activity, adverse weather conditions, government policy, terrorism)
- **Were all other essential elements of the marketing mix in place?** (e.g. distribution, pricing policy, the product itself)
- **How did the behaviour of customer contact staff contribute to the results?** (e.g. were they rude, or very helpful?)

When to use sales- and marketing-oriented objectives

While sales- and marketing-oriented objectives should not be used to shape all marketing communications activity, there are certain situations when their use is appropriate:

- **sales promotions**. Ideally sales promotions are used as short-term tactical responses to specific situations. They aim to encourage action-oriented responses from the target audience. In turn, these responses can be measured – for example, the number of coupons that were redeemed, the number of 'two for the price of one' packs that were sold, the number of people who sampled a new product, the number of people who entered a competition.
- **generating in-store traffic**. As mentioned earlier, retailers use marketing communications to increase store traffic and the results of a campaign are plain to see.
- **direct marketing**. Direct marketing delivers results that can be directly attributed to the activity used, for example, the number of people who responded to a mail shot, the number of people who purchased a product as a result of telemarketing.
- **the launch of a new product**. When launching a new product, it is important to generate awareness and achieve sales targets. Therefore, sales- and marketing-oriented objectives should be identified and tackled using marketing communications.

Communications objectives

Communications objectives are more complex than sales- and marketing-oriented objectives because performance against them can prove much more difficult to measure. Communications objectives set targets for a marketing communications programme in terms of creating a good impression on the target audience so as to move them further up the hierarchy of effects model (see Chapter 2). This model contends that people move through a number of stages before they actually buy a product or service. In order to ensure that they do actually reach that stage, marketing communications techniques are used in different ways at different stages. There are five stages in the model:

***Communications objectives** set targets for a marketing communications programme in terms of creating a good impression and to move the target audience further up the hierarchy of effects model.*

- awareness
- knowledge
- liking

- preference
- conviction, purchase or action.

At the first three stages of this model, communications objectives might be used. Here are some examples of communications objectives:

- to reposition the *Cork Examiner* as a nationwide newspaper
- to launch Vodafone 'live' and generate 100 per cent awareness among 15–34-year-olds
- to position Eircom as the best service company in Ireland by 2003.

As can be seen from the above examples, the challenge with communications objectives stems from the fact that the results are not as tangible as those arising from sales- and marketing-oriented objectives. How can an organisation determine whether or not they have successfully repositioned a brand, achieved awareness or positioned a brand in a certain way? It can be done but it necessitates investment in research before, during and after marketing communications activity.

Research prior to the launch of a campaign is necessary in order to elicit the views, feelings and opinions of the target audience. The results serve as a benchmark against which any changes can be measured. During and after a campaign, research is conducted to assess the success or otherwise of the campaign. It is also important to design the research questionnaires in such a way that they will find out whether or not changes in attitudes are directly attributable to the campaign itself or to other factors such as the product, price levels, distribution channels, customer service levels or external events.

Perhaps this explains why communications objectives are less popular in some organisations than the more quantifiable sales- and marketing-oriented objectives. Research is expensive and, to do it properly, it must be conducted regularly.

Another reason why some organisations dislike using communications objectives is because results are often less instantaneous. Take one of the examples used above – 'to position Eircom as the best service company in Ireland by 2003'. Desired positioning is rarely achieved overnight and often takes years, not months. However, most organisations set financial objectives that must be achieved within a much shorter time frame. Many brand managers work towards monthly and quarterly sales targets. This makes them favour sales- and marketing-oriented goals as opposed to communications-oriented goals.

As far back as 1961, an advertising practitioner, Russell Colley, proposed a model for setting advertising objectives and measuring the results. It was called Defining Advertising Goals for Measured Advertising Results and is referred to by the acronym Dagmar. It is based on a hierarchical communications process:

- awareness
- comprehension
- conviction

- action.

Colley emphasised the importance of a good objective when engaging in advertising and said that good communications objectives should display certain characteristics. They should:

- be specific and measurable
- have a well-defined target audience
- include a prior statement of the degree of change required.
- state a specific time period within which the advertising activity should occur.

While it is acknowledged that Colley's approach helped shift the emphasis away from sales-oriented objectives, he has not been without his critics. The main criticisms are:

- Implementation of Dagmar requires expenditure on research in order to come up with a statement of the degree of change required. Some organisations simply do not have the resources necessary for such research, while others see such expenditure as a waste of money. The question remains, however, when setting communications-oriented objectives, can an organisation afford not to conduct research?
- Due to the imposition of restrictions and constraints, creativity may be inhibited. However, this argument holds less credence now, as creativity is often evaluated in terms of its commercial effectiveness.
- Advocates of sales-oriented objectives believe that Dagmar does not deliver tangible returns in the form of sales.
- Dagmar is based on a hierarchical communications process and, as we saw in Chapter 2, this approach is flawed. The models assume that consumers always go through a logical sequence before finally deciding to purchase a product and, of course, this is not true.

Sales- and marketing-oriented objectives, or communications objectives – which way is better?

For best results, a combination of the two should be considered. While there tends to be far greater emphasis on short-term achievements, few companies can afford to ignore their long-term prospects. Therefore, if an organisation concentrates exclusively on achieving sales-oriented objectives, its longer-term success may be jeopardised. Successful brand managers use sales- and marketing-oriented objectives to achieve short-term objectives but they also set communications objectives to nurture and develop their brand. For example, Coca-Cola invests heavily in advertising to ensure that the brand remains the number one choice of its target audience in the long term. This approach has proved central to its longevity. However, the company also uses the marketing communications mix to achieve sales-oriented objectives. For example, they might implement a sales promotion campaign that offers consumers the opportunity of purchasing two 1-litre bottles of Coca-Cola for the price of one.

Communications-oriented objectives might be more appropriate in the early stages of the hierarchy of effects model. Meanwhile, the use of sales-oriented objectives might be more appropriate towards the latter stages of the model in order to encourage action. For example, in order to persuade somebody to commit to a particular product or service, sales promotions techniques might be used. As seen earlier, objectives relating to sales promotions can be set in quantifiable terms.

Stage 3: Marketing communications strategy

When an organisation has set targets and articulated them in the form of objectives, it maps out how it intends achieving these objectives. Smith (1998) identifies a number of components that are essential to the formation of an effective marketing communications strategy:

- **segmentation**. The grouping of people and organisations into segments reflecting their distinct needs
- **targeting**. Focusing on one or more of the segments identified
- **positioning**. The position that an organisation's products or services occupy in the minds of its target segment(s). Is it the cheapest, the highest quality, the most innovative, the trendiest, the safest, the most reliable when compared to the competitors' offerings?
- **objectives**. As discussed in the previous section. At all times, the objective or objectives must be considered.
- **integration**. All elements of the promotions mix should work together.
- **tools**. Which elements of the marketing communications mix are best suited to reaching the target audience and achieving the objectives?

Push strategy
The use of marketing techniques aimed at an organisation's channels.

Once the target audience is identified and segmented for communications purposes, a good starting point is to make decisions regarding the use of a push or pull strategy or a combination of the two. A **push strategy** entails the use of marketing communications techniques aimed at an organisation's distribution channels. Channels include sales representatives, agents, brokers, wholesalers and retailers. Organisations use push-oriented marketing communications strategies to persuade channel members to accept and actively promote their products. Examples of push-oriented activities include competitions to reward the salesperson of the year and contributions towards advertising spend for retailers. These techniques are examined in more detail in Chapter 11.

A **pull strategy** aims to create demand among end users. By and large, retailers have become more powerful. This has forced FMCG manufacturers to work much harder to sustain demand for their products. They do this by implementing marketing communications programmes that motivate the end consumer to actively seek their products. Brand advertising, sponsorship and consumer-oriented sales promotions are just some of the techniques deployed in a pull-oriented marketing strategy.

Pull strategy *Marketing techniques intent on creating end-user demand.*

Many organisations use a combination of the two approaches. They ensure that channel members sell and stock their products and that the end consumer actively demands those same products from the distributor. However, a growing number of organisations have eliminated distributors and sell their products and services directly to the end customer. Dell Computers, Ryanair and Aer Lingus are all exponents of the pull strategy.

When its strategy is formulated, an organisation can set about making it happen.

Stage 4: Marketing communications mix

In an ideal world, the marketing communications mix would be selected before the budget is set. Why is this? As we have already seen, the marketing communications objectives state what the company wants to achieve and the strategy outlines how it hopes to achieve the objectives. Once the 'how' is known, the most appropriate marketing communications mix is chosen. Only then is it possible to estimate the costs associated with the most appropriate marketing communications mix. On this basis the required budget is requested.

In reality, many organisations set the budget in advance of this stage. This means that the marketing communications mix is often formulated within inadequate budgetary constraints. For the moment, however, let us assume that best practice is adhered to and that the planning of the marketing communications mix is done in advance of budget formulation.

Determining the best mix of marketing communications elements depends on a number of factors, which have been explored in the previous stages:

- the target audience
- the nature of the product
- overall corporate and marketing objectives
- the marketing communications objectives
- the nature of the external environment and internal factors
- the marketing communications strategy.

Figure 5.3 proposes a grid that might assist at this stage of the planning process. It illustrates how information relating to a fictional product helps inform decisions about the most appropriate marketing communications mix.

Figure 5.3 Choosing the most appropriate marketing communications mix

Factors influencing the marketing communications mix

NATURE OF PRODUCT
- New, flavoured mineral water
- Low-calorie, natural ingredients only
- 'Green' packaging

TARGET AUDIENCE

Trade
- Large retailers e.g. Tesco, Dunnes
- Newsagents
- Sports clubs

Consumer
- Male and female
- 18–35-year-olds
- Mainly urban
- Play hard, work hard

EXTERNAL ENVIRONMENT
- Intense competition from major national and international soft drinks brands
- Cultural shift to concern for health
- Growing concern for the environment

INTERNAL FACTORS
- Very experienced marketing capability
- Available funds for marketing activity
- No database of potential customers
- Poor distribution network

CORPORATE OBJECTIVES
- To be the number one soft drinks manufacturer in Ireland

MARKETING OBJECTIVES
- To achieve 10% market share one year from launch
- To secure 350 distribution outlets in six months
- To position brand as the healthiest soft drink on the market

MARKETING COMMUNICATIONS OBJECTIVES
- To achieve 30% brand awareness
- To secure distribution with three large food retailers
- To ensure that 100,000 consumers sample the product in a three-month period.
- To sell 300,000 units within six months

Advertising	Trade magazines, TV, cinema, outdoor, magazines
PR	Trade and consumer magazines
Sponsorship	Well-known sports figure
Sales promotions	Push (trade) Pull (consumers)
Direct marketing	Trade only
Personal selling	Trade only

Stage 5: Budget

Proper budgeting requires that an organisation knows what it is trying to achieve (objectives) and how it will achieve its objectives (strategy). As already stated, many organisations set budgets before they do anything else. This means objectives and strategy are set retrospectively. In many instances this can be attributed to a management mindset that views marketing communications as an expense that cannot be recouped. Setting the budget in advance of objectives is referred to as a top-down approach to budgeting and contrasts sharply with the more strategic build-up approach. Both of these approaches are now examined.

Top-down approach to budgeting

The top-down approach to budgeting is shown in Table 5.3. This is the approach taken when senior management determines the level of funding that will be set aside for marketing communications activity. The main drawback of taking approach is that the budget is not always based on a sound rationale. There are four techniques in the top-down approach.

Table 5.3 Top-down approach to budgeting

Affordability technique
- Funding on the basis of what a company can afford
- Common in SMEs
- Marketing communications seen as an expense
- Budget fluctuation from year to year
- Ignores opportunities and threats
- Tendency for reduction in recession

Percentage of sales technique
- Based on a fixed percentage of previous year's sales or projected sales
- Relatively simple to calculate
- Widely used method
- May not take into account corporate goals and objectives
- Not always suited to long-term planning

Arbitrary technique
- *Ad hoc* approach
- Dependent on the whims of senior management
- Can result in the allocation of over-generous amounts
- Budget may fluctuate significantly from year to year
- Makes long-term, strategic planning difficult

Competitive parity technique
- Bases budget on that of the competition
- Prevents advertising warfare
- Assumes that the competition is right
- May lack relevance to company-specific issues

The affordability technique

Management allocates an amount that it can afford to marketing communications expenditure, once all other costs and investments have been taken into account. This technique is very common in many small and medium-sized enterprises (SMEs). There are two main reasons for this. Firstly, they do not usually have large amounts of funding available. Secondly, they tend to consider expenditure on marketing communications to be an expense rather than an investment.

From the point of view of those responsible for implementing the marketing communications budget, planning can prove difficult because the allocated budget might fluctuate significantly from year to year.

Since this technique is based on what a company can afford, it does not take into account external opportunities and threats. Consequently, it does not facilitate the use of marketing communications to take advantage of opportunities or to counter threats.

Finally, in times of recession, the marketing communications budget is likely to be reduced because the organisation believes that it can no longer afford the funding.

The percentage of sales technique

This technique is widely used by many organisations. Its popularity can be attributed to the fact that it is relatively straightforward to calculate. The budget amount is calculated on the basis of a percentage of either the previous year's actual sales or the projected sales for the coming year. The examples in Table 5.4 illustrate this.

Table 5.4 Percentage of sales technique

Example 1	
Previous year's actual sales	€1,000,000
Percentage used to calculate budget	5%
Marketing communications budget	€50,000
Example 2	
Projected sales	€2,000,000
Percentage used to calculate budget	5%
Marketing communications budget	€100,000

Source: Adapted from Smith (1998)

However, the examples also illustrate a fundamental flaw with the percentage of sales budgeting technique. If an organisation bases budget calculations on actual sales of €1,000,000 as shown in Example 1, but is aiming to achieve sales of €2,000,000 in the forthcoming year, budget allocation only amounts to €50,000. Meanwhile, if a competitor uses projected sales to allocate their budget, and is similarly aiming to achieve €2,000,000 worth of sales, its marketing communications budget will be €100,000. This gives the second organisation a competitive advantage.

While organisations using projected sales in their calculations recognise that expenditure helps achieve objectives, those basing their calculations on the previous year's sales do not take objectives into account. Therefore, they do not tend to consider long-term planning issues and external factors.

The arbitrary technique

As its name suggests, the arbitrary technique to budgeting is an *ad hoc* approach that is largely based on the whims of those in charge of the purse-strings. This is not to suggest that the budget allocated is always small. For example, the senior manager responsible for budget allocation may decide that they want to commit significant funds to marketing communications. However, while marketing communications planners might welcome the allocation of a generous budget, this might encourage spending for the sake of it. Unless the appropriate planning and analysis has preceded budget allocation, generous budgets are likely to result in waste.

Another downside of the arbitrary technique is that while funding might be generous one year, there might be little or no funding the following year. This does not facilitate ongoing planning and makes the job of implementing relevant and strategic marketing communications programmes very difficult.

Competitive parity technique

Organisations using this technique determine their marketing communications budget by mirroring that of their main competitor or by following the norm of their industry. While this technique prevents advertising warfare, it does have some major weaknesses. It assumes that the competition is doing the right thing, when they might be pursuing a relatively weak, unplanned marketing communications strategy. Also, the competition might have a different set of goals and objectives that must be addressed in a particular way. This way may not be appropriate for any other organisation.

Build-up approach to budgeting

In Figure 5.1 (page 123), the marketing communications planning process shows clearly that the budget should only be set after the marketing communications objectives and strategy have been identified and the marketing communications mix decided upon. This approach to budgeting means that it is more likely to assist in the achievement of long-term goals and objectives. Marketing communications agencies are important at this stage because they advise the client as to the likely cost of the proposed marketing communication strategy. While adherence to this technique should mean that sufficient funds are invested in marketing communications, it also ensures that unnecessary funds are not allocated. It might mean that the budget varies from year to year but as long as it is directly related to each year's goals and objectives, this should not present difficulties. For example, when Telecom Eireann changed its name to Eircom in 1999, more than €1 million was allocated to advertising and promotions (*The Irish Times*, 7 September 1999). This budget was allocated to build awareness within a very short timeframe and would not be necessary every year.

Stage 6: The schedule

When the budget is approved, it is advisable to put together a schedule. This indicates when each element of the marketing communications mix will be implemented. This stage is important to achieving integrated marketing communications. It is particularly necessary when a wide range of internal employees and external agencies are involved in implementation. Smith (1998) recommends the use of a Gantt chart for this particular task. This displays the activities, timing and corresponding budget in a straightforward, user-friendly manner. Table 5.5 shows a schedule for the launch of a fictional new product.

Table 5.5 Schedule for the launch of new product X

	J	F	M	A	M	J	J	A	S	O	N	D
Advertising												
• TV			✔	✔					✔	✔		
• Press						✔	✔	✔				
• Outdoor (teaser campaign)		✔	✔									
Public relations												
• Press release			✔									
• Publicity				✔								
Sponsorship				✔	✔	✔	✔	✔	✔	✔		
Sales promotion												
• Trade incentives	✔	✔	✔									
• Coupons						✔	✔	✔				
• In-store tastings												
Direct marketing								✔	✔	✔	✔	✔

Stage 7: Implementation and project management

This stage of the planning process necessitates taking each element of the marketing communications mix and putting in place an action plan to make it happen. Project management skills are necessary to ensure that the overall schedule, as explained in Stage 6, is adhered to. Attention to detail and adherence to tight schedules are key success factors. Once again, Gantt charts are used to plan the execution of each element of the marketing communications mix. Everybody involved in each individual project must be kept fully informed about the schedule. It is usual for daily or weekly project review meetings to be held. The regularity of these meetings depends on the complexity of the project and the particular stage it is at.

Stage 8: Review

Each of the chapters dealing with specific elements of the marketing communications mix refers to review and evaluation. Was the campaign successful? Did it achieve its objectives? What could have been done better?

Unless the marketing communications plan undergoes rigorous review and evaluation, an organisation has no way of judging whether or not their investment has been effective. Qualitative and quantitative research should be used at this stage. Qualitative research gives marketers an insight into the respondent's mind. Participants in qualitative research engage in detailed interviews on their own or in focus groups. The types of issues covered in these interviews might include:

- Did the advertising motivate them?
- What is their opinion on an organisation's sponsorship programme?
- What is their attitude towards the product as a result of the campaign?

Quantitative research involves the collection of large amounts of statistical data that can be analysed. Quantitative research is conducted through structured questionnaires and measures behaviour, attitudes, opinions and respondent characteristics. This type of research is used to measure advertising effectiveness:

Quantitative research
The collection and analysis of large amounts of statistical data.

- How many people saw or heard the advertisement?
- Where did they see or hear it?
- What did they do as a result of it?

Without post-campaign review, an organisation cannot improve or learn:

- What did the campaign do well?
- What did it do badly?
- Did it succeed in bringing the target audience from a state of ignorance to a commitment to purchase?

Investment in marketing communications can be justified if the results are measured against clear and specific objectives. Therefore, while it may be tempting for organisations to move on to the next project when one is complete, they should invest time and money in looking back and reviewing each completed project. Only then will the sense of investing in marketing communications become clear to marketers and non-marketers alike. Specific review techniques relating to each element of the marketing communications mix are examined in their respective chapters.

Summary

Marketing communications strategy serves as a roadmap to those involved in marketing communications activity. A marketing communications plan formalises the strategy into a sequence of linked activities. Marketing communications planning is an eight-stage process, which commences with information gathering and analysis. All stages are directly influenced by an organisation's corporate and marketing strategy.

Marketing communications objectives articulate what an organisation wants to achieve. They must be specific so that the strategy's success can be measured against them. There are two main types of marketing communications objectives: sales- and marketing-oriented objectives; and communications-oriented objectives.

The marketing communications strategy maps out how the organisation intends achieving its objectives and takes into consideration the target audience and the product's position. The strategy determines whether a push or pull approach is required and these decisions influence the composition of the marketing communications mix. Once this has been decided, the budget is agreed. A strategy-driven budget suggests a build-up approach to budgeting. The budget often drives the marketing communications mix options – this is a top-down approach to budgeting. Once the budget is agreed, the marketing communications mix can be implemented. Marketing research should be conducted when the plan is implemented, so as to find out how effective the campaign was.

Review questions

1. Who do you think should take responsibility for marketing communications planning? Give reasons for your answer.
2. Stage one of the marketing communications planning process involves information gathering and analysis. Describe the type of information gathered at this stage.
3. Discuss the role of corporate objectives and marketing objectives in the marketing communications planning process.
4. Critically assess the difference between sales- and marketing-oriented objectives and communications-oriented objectives.
5. Compare and contrast push and pull strategies. In your answer you should clearly state who each is aimed at.

6. Critically assess the top-down and build-up approaches to budgeting.
7. Discuss why the review stage of the marketing communications planning process is so important.

Exercise

Select a company of your choice and set up an interview with the person responsible for marketing communications planning. Find out how they plan for marketing communications and use Figure 5.1 (page 123) to assess their process. What do they do particularly well? Would you recommend any changes in their approach?

References

Belch, George E. and Belch, Michael, A. *Advertising and Promotion: An Integrated Marketing Communications Perspective*, 4th edition (Irwin McGraw-Hill, 1999).

Colley, R. *Defining Advertising Goals for Measured Advertising Results* (New York: Association of National Advertisers, 1961).

Fill, Chris, *Marketing Communications: Contexts, Strategies and Applications* (Pearson Education Limited, 2002).

Smith, P. R., *Marketing Communications: An Integrated Approach*, 2nd edition (Kogan Page Limited, 1998).

Wood, Marian Burk, *The Marketing Plan: A Handbook* (Prentice Hall, 2003).

6

MEDIA OPTIONS

The main aim of this chapter is:

- to critically evaluate the main media options available to advertisers, which involves, in particular, an examination of:
  - broadcast media
  - print media
  - outdoor media
  - ambient media
  - cinema
  - directories.

Introduction

This chapter takes a close-up look at each of the traditional media options from an Irish perspective. Therefore, some of the more significant trends and challenges that look likely to shape the future of the Irish media industry are highlighted. While the Internet continues to attract some advertisers, it will be examined separately in Chapter 8.

An overview of Irish advertising expenditure

The IAPI undertakes regular research into advertising expenditure (Adspend) across all Irish advertising media. A year-end report is published each year and the findings in the 2002 review painted the picture of a buoyant advertising industry. In particular, television, radio, cinema and outdoor experienced increased activity. Overall, advertising spend increased from €1.02 billion in 2001 to €1.03 billion in 2002 (see Table 6.1). However, as cautioned in the report, the increases in 2002 probably reflected the intense activity that accompanied the World Cup, the General Election and the launch of Vodafone and O2, and were unlikely to be sustained.

Table 6.1 Advertising expenditure across all media in 2001 and 2002

	2001 (€ million)	2002 (€ million)
National press	492	489
Regional press	102	138
Magazines (consumer)	17	22
Magazines (business)	2.5	2
Television	196.5	207
National radio	38	45
Local radio	16	20
Outdoor	86	98
Cinema	5	9

Source: IAPI (2003)

Broadcast media

Broadcast media consists of television and radio. Like so many aspects of the business world, broadcast media ownership, in particular, television, has become increasingly internationalised. As we will see later in this chapter, the previously dominant national providers around Europe are facing increased levels of competition when it comes to selling their media slots. This situation is similarly evident in Ireland.

Television

According to the Media Advertising Promotions Sponsorship (MAPS) directory (AAI, 2002), 3.751 million Irish people had access to television in 2001, that is practically the entire population. 1.271 million homes were able to receive the national broadcaster, RTE, while 963,000 homes were able to watch multi-channel TV through the likes of NTL, Chorus and Sky Digital (see Table 6.2).

Table 6.2 Television ownership and access to channels in Ireland (September to December, 2001)

Total number of homes	1,293,000
RTE TV homes	1,271,000
Multi-channel TV homes	963,000
Total population	3,787,000
TV population	3,751,000
Percentage of population with access to TV	99

Statistics like these make it impossible for advertisers to ignore television, and its ability to bring their messages into the homes of the majority of the Irish population. However, television advertisers are faced with many challenges.

The pros and cons of television

From an advertiser's perspective there are a number of advantages and disadvantages associated with television (see Table 6.3). These must be taken into consideration when deciding whether or not television is appropriate.

Table 6.3 The advantages and disadvantages of television as an advertising medium

Advantages
Potentially high impact
Capable of delivering mass audiences
Relatively low CPM
Growing opportunities for targeting
Disadvantages
High production costs
Viewer receptivity being challenged
Short life of messages

Advantages of television

- **Impact**. Television makes an impression on two human senses – sight and sound. Properly executed, television advertisements are capable of grabbing the viewers' attention. Some advertisers do this by attempting to entertain viewers. Television enables advertisers to demonstrate their products and services in a realistic manner. Sellers of fitness equipment use television to show their products in use.

  The visual aspect of television is highly advantageous for firms in the services sector because it is a good way of making their offerings more tangible. For example, the financial services sector uses television to show target audiences what they can do with financial products. They might show someone driving away in a new car or going on holiday.

- **Mass coverage**. The statistics outlined in Table 6.2 (page 149) highlight the relevance of television in most Irish people's lives. Therefore, advertisements broadcast on television have the potential to reach a large number of people. However, this also means that television is not very selective because the advertisements reach many people outside the advertiser's target audience.

- **Relatively low cost per person reached**. Television advertising has a reputation for being expensive. It is true that production costs are prohibitively high for some companies. However, the **cost per thousand (CPM)** is relatively low. The letter 'M' is the Roman numeral for 1,000 and, in some literature, the M is replaced by a T for the English word 'thousand'.

CPM provides a measure of media efficiency and is calculated on the basis of the cost of buying media space and the number of people viewing or reading that medium. It is calculated as follows (Belch and Belch, 1999):

$$\text{CPM} = \frac{\text{Cost of ad space (absolute cost)}}{\text{Circulation/viewers/listeners}} \times 1{,}000$$

For example, if an advertiser buys a 30-second slot with RTE for €9,000 and expects 500,000 viewers to be exposed to the advertisement, the CPM is:

$$\frac{€9000}{500{,}000} \times 1000 = €18$$

This compares very favourably with the postage costs of a direct mail shot aimed at 1,000 people. Working on the assumption that each letter costs 48 cents to post, postage costs alone amount to €410. However, a mail shot is likely be more targeted and relevant to those who receive it, whereas a television advertisement usually reaches people who have no interest in the message.

- **Targeting**. Traditionally television was categorised as the ultimate mass media. The popularity of cable and satellite television and, consequently, the growing number of households who enjoy multi-channel viewing, means that better targeting is possible for television advertisers. Special-interest channels are available to cable and satellite subscribers in increasing numbers. This means that advertisers have a number of alternatives over and above the mainstream channels like RTE and TV3. Examples include Sky Sports, Eurosport, MTV Artsworld, The History Channel and National Geographic.

Disadvantages of television

- **High production costs**. While the CPM of television advertising is relatively low, production costs are high. This is why many firms simply cannot afford to advertise on television. Many of the advertisements seen on Irish television were developed and produced by multinational corporations. They have the necessary funds to pay for advertisement production and they can enjoy economies of scale by broadcasting one version in several countries.
- **Viewer receptivity**. In order to avoid television advertisements, viewers have to make a concerted effort. For example, they have to physically leave the room, change channels, or do something else. This means that television advertisers are increasingly concerned by the levels of noise and clutter affecting the media:

- Multi-channel viewing has heightened the amount of 'channel hopping' that occurs. Remote controls have assisted this phenomenon.
- Busy consumer lifestyles make many people more selective in their viewing. Viewers can record programmes and watch them in their own time. More importantly, this gives them the power to fast forward through commercial breaks.
- Clutter on television is substantial. Advertisers not only have to compete with other advertisements but they have to contend with messages about forthcoming attractions on particular channels. This makes it more difficult for advertisers to get themselves noticed and remembered.
- Technological developments have led to the development of powerful software called TiVo. It has been embraced by the likes of Philips and Sony and they are using the software as a central platform for their TiVo machines. It is designed to sit between a person's television and their cable box, satellite receiver and/or aerial and is described as a personal assistant that enables people to record and watch programmes at their own leisure. This facility is already available through video recorders but TiVo offers additional features (www.tivofaq.com):

  1. Television buffering gives the viewer the power to pause and rewind television programmes as they are being transmitted.
  2. It allows viewers to watch a recorded programme while recording another at the same time.
  3. Viewers can store recordings.

  The worrying aspect of TiVo from an advertiser's perspective is its ability to screen out advertisements. For obvious reasons, it is this aspect of the technology that is being monitored by advertisers.

- **Messages have a short life**. With newspaper or magazine advertising, the reader can return to an advertisement in their own time. In the case of television advertising, this is not likely or possible (unless the viewer records the commercial breaks). Therefore, creativity and production quality has to work hard to ensure that an advertisement makes a lasting impression on the viewer.

Measuring television audiences

As with any media, advertisers demand detailed information about audiences. They need to know how many people are watching particular programmes and they need a profile of these people i.e. age, sex, occupation and where they live. Nielsen Media Research, part of the international research agency AC Nielsen, gathers this information in Ireland. They are responsible for Television Audience Measurement which aims to measure the size of television audiences and to ascertain their characteristics. This information enables various networks to compile ratings. Favourable ratings allow them to justify their cost structures – the higher the rating, the higher the price of a television slot.

Every year Nielsen conducts an establishment survey of 3,500 households. Participants are asked questions about themselves (age, sex and occupation) and about their television equipment. Many of these participants are then invited to join a panel. Those who accept and go on the panel have a people meter installed in their home. All household members over the age of four are assigned a button on the people meter's remote control and a unique log-in code that they must use every time they change channel. The people meter is connected to the telephone line and between 03.00 and 06.00 Nielsen download the information relating to each household member's television viewing for that day.

The people meters monitor ten specific channels – RTE1, Network 2, TV3, BBC1, BBC2, ITV, Channel 4, E4, Sky One and Sky News. All other channels watched by the household are monitored under a category called 'other.' In 2002, the most watched programmes by adults on RTE1, Network2 and TV3 were *The Roy Keane Interview* (697,000), *Sunday Game Live* (406,000) and *Coronation Street* (389,000) (AC Nielsen, cited on www.medialive.ie).

Some digital channels take a more direct approach to finding out information about their viewers. They employ interactive devices that invite viewers to become more involved in their programmes. For example, Sky News regularly run polls whereby viewers can respond by pressing the interactive button on the satellite remote control.

Radio

Just over 2.6 million Irish adults listen to the radio everyday and it reaches 89 per cent of all consumers each day. These listeners are represented by a broad spectrum of the population. For example, 91 per cent of 15–19-year-olds, 87 per cent of over-55-year-olds and 90 per cent of students listen to the radio every day (Independent Radio Sales, 2001). In Ireland, radio offers a lot of choice to advertisers and listeners. There are four national radio stations – RTE Radio 1, 2FM, Today FM and Lyric FM. Independent local radio stations are very important to advertisers and radio listeners and there are more than 25 of these stations. With the liberalisation of the radio market, this figure is set to expand. There are also a number of pirate radio stations who remain outside the legitimate radio sector but continue to attract a large number of young listeners.

The pros and cons of radio advertising

Radio remains a popular choice with many Irish advertisers. However, there are a number of advantages and disadvantages that should be considered before including radio in a media plan (see Table 6.4 for a summary).

Table 6.4 The advantages and disadvantages of radio as an advertising medium

Advantages
- Relatively inexpensive
- Geographical segmentation
- Selectivity
- Widespread access to radio among population

Disadvantages
- High levels of noise and clutter
- Short life of a radio advertisement

Advantages of radio

- **Relatively inexpensive**. When compared to television advertising, radio advertising is relatively inexpensive. A contributory reason for this is that production costs are quite low because it is not a visual form of advertising. Therefore, the main costs incurred in creating and producing radio advertisements typically include copywriting, voice-overs, special effect sounds, music composition or rental, and recording.

  Time slots are relatively inexpensive when compared to television. For example, local radio stations offer 30 second slots for as little as €12.69 with Tipperary Mid West FM and as much as €160 for 96/103 FM in Cork. National radio consists of RTE Radio 1, 2FM, Lyric FM and Today FM and they can charge up to €1,714 for a prime time slot. In relation to radio, a prime time slot on RTE Radio 1 is between 07.25 and 09.00 (*MAPS Directory*, 2002). These rates are significantly less than quoted television rates.

- **Selective**. The radio sector in Ireland enables advertisers to be quite selective in terms of the audiences they can reach. Liberalisation of radio broadcasting has led to a significant increase in the number of radio stations. Some of these cater for specific interest groups, for example, Lyric FM is a classical music station. Radio stations broadcast programmes aimed at different target audiences. The national broadcaster, RTE, has a mix of programmes on RTE Radio 1 that enable advertisers to target different market segments. According to the *MAPS Directory* (2002), the Joint National Listenership Research poll of 2001, done in conjunction with MRBI, found that housewives tune in to RTE Radio 1 most often between the hours of 07.30 and 14.45. This is important information for advertisers wanting to communicate with this segment.

  Radio personalities are important to radio stations in terms of their 'pulling power'. If they cannot attract large audiences, their employer, the radio station finds it more difficult to attract advertisers.

- **Geographical segmentation**. This is possible with radio due to the large number of local radio stations in Ireland. Dublin alone has four local stations – FM104, 98FM, Lite FM and Spin FM. Each of the remaining 25 counties either has its own county radio station or is served by stations aimed at listeners in a few counties. For example, LMFM serves counties Louth and Meath, while Midlands Radio 3 is aimed at listeners in Laois, Offaly and Westmeath. Local companies can advertise on the radio without wasting unnecessary resources on advertising nationwide.
- **Access to radio**. Access to radio is very high and while many people listen to the radio at home, it is not unusual for people to listen to the radio at work. Commuters tune in to the radio on their way to work, school and college. Radio enjoys a captive audience on many of Ireland's congested roads.

Disadvantages of radio

- **High levels of noise and clutter**. Even though most people have easy access to radio, it has to compete with high levels of noise and clutter. Noise levels are high because many people do something while listening to the radio, which means that they do not give it their undivided attention. Advertisers also have to cope with increasing clutter as they try to compete with other advertisements. Since they can only use sound to grab attention, the creative challenge is immense. The existence of more sophisticated radios has heightened this challenge. A high incidence of radios that give listeners the ability to pre-set and store the frequencies of a number of radio stations, means channel hopping occurs among radio listeners when commercial breaks are transmitted. This is often done to avoid advertisements.
- **Short life of a radio advertisement**. Like television advertising, the life of a radio advertisement is short. Once it has been transmitted, it is gone. This too presents challenges for the creators of radio advertisements.

Measuring radio audiences

Radio listenership is monitored and measured through the JNLR (Joint National Listenership Research) programme. According to O'Donoghue and Harper (1995) its management committee comprises representatives from a number of organisations. They are RTE, the IRTC (the Independent Radio and Television Commission), the IAPI (the Institute for Advertising Practitioners in Ireland, and the AAI (the Association of Advertisers in Ireland). The IRTC is responsible for issuing franchises to local and community radio stations.

Listenership data is gathered through personal interviews with a sample of 6,500 people each year. The interviewees are asked whether or not they have listened to all the legal stations broadcasting in their area on the day prior to the interview. When they have listed the relevant stations, they are shown a list of programmes that were broadcast on those stations the day before the interview. Radio stations utilise the findings from this research to establish prices for air time and they even advertise and publicise their listenership figures extensively in the national media.

Print media

Print media comprises national and regional newspapers, and magazines. Traditionally, Irish people have had a very high newspaper readership. Both national and local newspapers are popular. However, the print media landscape in Ireland is changing due to a number of environmental factors:

- The Irish population still reads newspapers. However, this readership is not as strong as it was. The decline is attributed to:
  - busy lifestyles leaving people with less time to read newspapers
  - other media that are easily accessible for news, for example, 24-hour news on television through Sky News and Aertel, and through various websites, and on the hour news on the radio
  - the instantaneous nature of news dissemination – news is relayed as it happens through the media described above. Newspapers are considered static and are sometimes perceived as carriers of old news.
- The newspaper market is highly competitive. Irish people are able to purchase British dailies and Sunday papers. Ironically, they are often cheaper than their Irish counterparts.
- Both the Independent Media Group, which publishes the likes of the *Irish Independent* and the *Sunday Independent*, and *The Irish Times* invested in state-of-the-art printing presses which allow them to produce high-quality, colour newspapers and magazine supplements for their own titles. They also print newspapers and magazines for rival titles.
- Globalisation in the media sector gives greater power to a smaller number of groups. Rupert Murdoch and Tony O'Reilly are two so-called 'media moguls' who own newspapers all over the world. Rupert Murdoch's dominance is further strengthened through his ownership of Sky.

Types of print advertisements

There are a number of options open to advertisers in terms of the types of advertisements they place in magazines and newspapers:

- **display advertisements** (for example, Exhibit 6.1). The advertiser's advertising agency designs the advertisement and sends it to the publication in the required format. The design might be relatively straightforward in that it might just be in black and white, or it might involve colour photographic imagery.
- **classified advertisements** (for example, Exhibit 6.2). As the name suggests, these advertisements are classified and usually appear under certain categories. This makes it easier for the reader to find what they are looking for. They are widely used in national and local newspapers by businesses and consumers, and they are prevalent in the areas of births and deaths, cars, holidays, employment, pets for sale, and furniture. The advertiser does not have any input into the style of the advertisement since the advertisements are usually printed in the newspaper's own style.

Carry on in France behind your wife's back!

Our great value 5 day and 9 day short break fares cover car and up to 4 adults with 2 nights aboard ship. €4 handling fee may apply. **20% off for over 55s.**

5 DAY BREAK Travel up to 25 May	9 DAY BREAK Travel up to 10 June
€229 return	€339 return

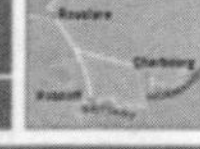

Book On-Line www.irishferries.com
LoCall 1890 31 31 31 N.I. Freephone 0800 018 22 11
or see your travel agent.

Exhibit 6.1

OFFICE STAFF

CONFIDENT OFFICE Person used to dealing with people, good telephone manner ess. With working knowledge of computers. Dublin 12 area. CV'S to Fax **01 - 4080640**, e-mail **charola@iol.ie**

FULL TIME BOOK-KEEPER required for two prominent licenced premises in Dublin city area. Knowledge of book-keeping, payroll software and spreadsheets necessary. A minimum of 3 years practical experience required. Salary €30K. Replies to Howlin O'Rourke & Co. 328, North Circular Road Dublin 7.

SECRETARY regd. Experience in MS Office, Word and Excel required. Send CV to Nicholas ODwyer International, E4 Nutgrove Business Park, Dublin 14 or Fax CV to **296 4015**

★ **TRAINEE ADMINISTRATORS x 5** Financial company based in Eastpoint Business Park require enthusiastic Trainee Administrators will at least 6 months office based experience. Six month contracts available with immediate start for the right candidates. Salary €17,200 Contact oonagh.o'connor@reed.ie **Phone 670 4466**

PHARMACEUTICAL

HICKEY'S PHARMACY
MAIN STREET,
NEWBRIDGE,
CO. KILDARE.
We will soon be re-opening in our newly refurbished store.
We are now recruiting for the following positions:-
Sales Assistants (full time, part time and seasonal
Experience is an advantage but not essential
Apply with C.V. to:
Carmel O'Leary at above address.
Please state clearly the position you wish to apply for.
Closing date for applications is Friday, December 6.

EXCITING POSITION available for an experienced Pharmacy Assistant in a new city centre pharmacy. Ph: **085 1430979**

EXP'D PHARMACY TECHNICIAN req'd for Stillorgan area. Excellent terms and conditions. Ph: Evelyn at **01 288 2113**

EXP. F/T O.T.C. Sales Assistant

SITUATIONS VACANT

COMPLEX MANAGER req'd. Must have Bar/Management skills. Computer knowledge desirable but not ess. Please reply in writing with refs and CV to Home Sec., c/o 15 Grangepark Rd., Raheny, Dublin 5.

COUNTER ASSISTANT req'd for butcher's shop in Finglas. Outgoing personality req'd. No experience necessary. Training provided. Ph: **836 1572.**

COURIER OWNER DRIVERS required immediate start. Contact **4607878.**

CUSTOMER Service Administrator req. for Telecommunications Company in the Dublin 12 area. Email CV to **keith@sierra.ie**

DRIVER REQUIRED part-time, early starts, D licence, Newbridge area. Contact James **086 3808766**

DRIVER/STOREPERSON req'd. Must have full clean C Licence. Leinster area only. Phone Hugh **087 2595518**

DRIVERS REQ. for Airport Car Rental Co. **086 8071399**

DRIVERS REQUIRED, Four Star Pizza, Walkinstown. Please call to shop for application forms between 5/10p.m.

DRIVING INSTRUCTOR training courses (Certified) with Irish School of Motoring, Ireland's nationwide driving school. Also Franchise opportunities now available. Bookings Tel: **01-874 6677**

ELECTRICIAN qualified / senior trade with safe pass. Full drivers licence. Greater dublin area. Fax CV **01 - 6245318** or e-mail **connorelectric@eircom.net**

EXP'D COUNTER & Alterations staff req'd for dry cleaners in Clontarf, D.3. Tel. **087 8811624**

EXP. TRUCK DRIVER req for Deliveries to Dublin City and County area. Full Clean Licence req. Attractive conditions of employment. For further details Call. **087-9583395.**

EXPERIENCE SECOND FIX Joiners req immed. to work in the Dublin area for shop fitting company.Ph **668 0615** 9-5pm.

EXPERIENCED JCB DRIVERS required, Dublin area. Tel: **087-2680700**

FIRE YOUR BOSS! Work from home, unlimited income, No exp. nec. **www.eurfree.com.**

FULL-TIME/PART-TIME DELI Assistants required. No evening or weekends. Immed. start. Phone **086 6004410.**

HACKETTS BOOKMAKERS are

Exhibit 6.2

- **inserts**. These are produced by the advertiser and supplied for distribution with the newspaper or magazine. The advertiser can give instructions for them to be distributed nationwide or to certain geographical areas. The computer manufacturer, Dell, regularly uses this form of advertising.

The pros and cons of newspaper advertising

Newspaper advertising is well established among advertisers. However, before committing to its inclusion in a media plan, the advantages and disadvantages must be considered (Table 6.5).

Table 6.5 The advantages and disadvantages of newspapers as an advertising medium

Advantages
- Readers can read newspapers at their own pace
- Allows advertisers to pursue national, regional and lifestyle segmentation
- Relatively low CPM
- Can lend credibility to the advertiser
- Multiple readership
- Theme of ads can be very current
- Enables advertiser to convey a lot of information

Disadvantages
- Short shelf life
- High levels of clutter and noise
- Concerns about print quality
- As a purely visual medium, it can be difficult to capture the reader's attention

Advantages of newspaper advertising

- **Readers can set their own pace**. Compared to television and radio, newspapers are considered less intrusive as readers can read through them at their own pace. This presents advantages and disadvantages for advertisers. It means that readers can take as much time as they want to examine advertisements that interest them. However, advertisers cannot do anything to prevent the reader skipping over certain pages.

- **Relatively low cost per thousand**. The CPM of newspapers is relatively low when compared to television advertising. While €21,384 may sound like a lot of money for a full-page advertisement in *The Irish Times*, its readership is 305,000. This means that the CPM is just over €70.

- **Opportunities for national, regional and lifestyle segmentation**. Newspapers allow advertisers to pursue national and regional segmentation. National coverage is achieved through the likes of the *Irish Independent*, *The Irish Times*, the *Star* and the *Irish Examiner*. Meanwhile, weekly regional newspapers enable advertisers to target their messages on a geographical basis. Examples of these include *Bray People*, *The Corkman*, *Derry People* and *Donegal News*, the *Guardian* in Enniscorthy and Gorey, the *Liffey Champion*, and the *Nenagh Guardian* (*MAPS Directory*, 2002).

Many newspapers publish supplements that appeal to particular lifestyles, hobbies and interests. For example, property, business, sports, and entertainment supplements are published by leading newspapers. The inclusion of magazines is common in weekend editions of newspapers. These might include regular features on topics such as travel, gardening, eating out, health and beauty. Therefore, supplements and features give many advertisers the opportunity to target their newspaper advertising more effectively.

- **Advertiser credibility**. Some newspapers lend credibility to the advertiser because if a newspaper's readers respect its editorial content and impartiality, advertisements may benefit.
- **Multiple readership**. It is very common for newspapers to enjoy multiple readership. This means that people other than the person who bought the paper often read them.
- **Theme of advertisements can be current**. Unlike television and magazine advertising, newspaper advertising allows advertisers to place advertisements that are current. There are two main reasons for this. The lead-time for booking a space and supplying the final copy is relatively short. Depending on whether the advertisement is black and white or colour, the lead-time can be as little as 24 hours. This is important to firms who operate in a volatile environment because they need to be able to change the content of their advertisements.

  The time and expense associated with creating and producing a newspaper advertisement are much less than creating and producing a television advertisement.
- **Advertisements can convey a lot of information**. Newspapers enable the advertiser to include a lot of information in their advertisements. For example, Dell often include technical information in their advertisements. If someone is interested in purchasing a computer, they are quite likely to read the information provided before making enquiries.

Disadvantages of newspaper advertising

- **Short life of newspapers**. As mentioned earlier, the ready availability of global news stories through television, radio and the Internet often renders newspaper out of date. This can even occur before the newspaper appears on the news stands and further precipitates the short life of a newspaper.
- **High levels of clutter and noise**. Like so many mainstream media, clutter and noise levels are high in newspapers. Apart from the large number of advertisements, there

are other distractions within newspapers vying for the attention of the reader. These include headlines that are trying to get the reader to read an article, and photographs. Busy lifestyles make it difficult for readers to give newspapers their undivided attention.

- **Concerns about print quality**. Historically, print quality was quite poor and in some cases, unacceptable to advertisers. Until quite recently, it was not possible for newspapers to publish colour advertisements. However, some newspaper groups have invested heavily in improving their print capabilities. This move was intended to satisfy readers and to attract advertising revenue. While this type of investment has improved matters, the fact remains that excellent print quality is difficult to achieve on newsprint paper and perfection cannot always be guaranteed.
- **Visual-only media**. Since newspapers are a purely visual media, it can prove difficult to grab the reader's attention. In contrast, television appeals to two senses, sight and sound.

The pros and cons of advertising in magazines

Visit any newsagents and you will see an array of magazines for sale, most of which are produced outside Ireland. However, some advertisers, for example, those operating in a business-to-business environment, confine their advertising to magazines. For others, magazines form an important part of the media mix. Regardless, they must weigh up the advantages and disadvantages of magazine advertising (Table 6.6) before including it in the mix.

Table 6.6 The advantages and disadvantages of magazines as an advertising medium

Advantages

- The range of magazines available offers segmentation opportunities
- Long shelf life
- Scope for creativity
- Excellent print quality
- Multiple readership
- Suited to the carriage of sales promotions
- Often read **for** their advertising

Disadvantages

- Long lead-times
- High levels of clutter

Advantages of magazine advertising

- **Segmentation opportunities**. The range of business and consumer magazines available is immense. Many of the publications sold in Ireland are written and produced abroad, and they cater for a diverse range of interests, from cooking to running, business to photography, fashion and health to gardening. In addition, a wide range of magazines and journals are aimed at people working in specific sectors of the economy. For example, *Irish Architect* is the official journal of the Royal Institute of the Architects of Ireland and is read by architects, main contractors, engineers and local authorities (*MAPS Directory*, 2002). Therefore, a significant advantage of advertising in magazines is the potential for segmentation. While circulation figures for some magazines are low, the advertisements are more precisely targeted, thus resulting in less waste.

- **Long shelf life**. When people buy magazines they often keep them and refer back to them. This means that unlike newspapers, magazines enjoy a long shelf life. Consequently, this means that the advertisements in magazines have a longer life.
- **Scope for creativity**. There tends to be greater scope for creativity with magazines than with newspapers. Advertisements can occupy an entire page and spread to the outside edges. This is known as **bleed**. This option creates greater impact. Newspapers do not offer this possibility because the printing methods used do not print text or images right up to the edge of the page. Some magazines have the production capability to offer **gatefolds**. This is where the size of a page is extended and folded back on itself. Cosmetic companies often use this technique to distribute 'scratch and sniff' samples of their perfumes. Gatefolds are an effective creative technique in that they help arouse the reader's curiosity and cause them to stay with the advertisement for longer.
- **Excellent print quality**. In most instances, the reproduction or print quality of magazines is excellent. For advertisers who attach great importance to their brand image, this is a major advantage. Take a look through some magazines and observe the types of advertisements contained in them. In consumer-oriented magazines, the advertisements tend to be very glossy and eye-catching.
- **Multiple readership**. It has already been mentioned that each newspaper is often read by more than one person. Magazines enjoy multiple readership to a greater degree. Many consumer magazines are placed in hairdressers and waiting rooms and this means that many people read them. In the case of business-to-business magazines, such as *Business and Finance*, it is common practice for one copy to be circulated among a number of employees.
- **Sales promotion suitability**. Magazines are suited to sales promotions. Cosmetic companies often use magazines to carry perfume samples. Magazines are also used to distribute trial-size versions of food and cosmetic products, and toy manufacturers use children's magazines to provide free gifts.
- **Magazines are often read for their advertising**. People rarely purchase newspapers

for their advertisements. However, some specialist magazines provide excellent information and associated advertising for people wanting to buy particular products and services. Therefore, people often read the magazines for the advertising. For example, *Amateur Photographer* is a magazine that is imported from the UK and is read by keen photographers. Much of the magazine is taken up with advertisements and they are one of the primary purchase reasons.

Disadvantages of magazine advertising

- **Long lead-time**. There is a long lead-time associated with the placement of advertisements in magazines. This means that the space has to be booked well before the advertisement actually appears. Depending on the publication, this can mean months. For companies operating in a volatile environment, magazine advertising may not be appropriate because a more flexible medium is preferable. It also means that advertisements cannot make reference to or take advantage of current, unforeseen events.
- **High levels of clutter**. Successful magazines attract large numbers of advertisements. This means that some magazines experience high levels of clutter.

Magazine and newspaper circulation

Primary circulation
The number of individuals who receive a publication through subscription or store purchase.

Secondary readership
Takes into account everyone who reads a publication.

Circulation means 'the number of individuals who receive a publication through either subscription or store purchase' (Belch and Belch, 1999).

This is called **primary circulation** and forms the basis of the rates charged for advertising space. We have seen that newspapers and magazines are not just read by those who buy them. Therefore, publications take into account the multiple readers and calculate a figure called **secondary readership**. This is almost always greater than the primary circulation figure. However, it is generally accepted that the primary circulation figure is more important. These people are likely to be more committed to the publication because they have taken the trouble to buy it or subscribe to it.

Circulation and readership figures are used to sell advertising space and so it is important that advertisers can trust in them. The Audit Bureau of Circulations (ABC) is a system used in many countries, including Ireland. An independent body carries out audits in order to certify that the circulation figures stated by a publication are valid. Many publications do not have an ABC certification because it is not mandatory. Instead, they provide uncertified figures to potential advertisers. Consequently, some advertisers prefer not to advertise with publications that do not carry ABC certification. The circulation figures of the more established publications are not immune from controversy, as we will see in this next extract:

Agencies still sceptical despite Indo defence of 'bulk sales' circulation

When is a newspaper sale not a newspaper sale? The circulation of *Ireland on Sunday*, owned by Associated Newspapers, was up a staggering 185 per cent for the second half of 2002. But this increase, extremely large by the standards of the newspaper industry, did not seem to have greatly damaged the *Sunday Independent*, believed by most to be *Ireland on Sunday*'s main rival. Strange, said many observers in the advertising world.

The *Sunday Independent* claimed an average circulation of 305,182, a 1.4 per cent drop, but hardly a massive plunge considering the rise of *Ireland on Sunday*.

All of this made agencies scratch their collective heads, until they discovered that only 90 per cent of the *Sunday Independent*'s circulation were paid sales, known in the trade as 'actively purchased' sales. Over at the *Evening Herald* the figure was lower at 85 per cent.

The remaining 10 per cent of the Sunday paper's circulation was made up of 25,738 one-off bulk sales and 5,572 regular bulk sales, while the *Irish Independent* included 14,500 one-off bulk sales and 6,665 regular bulk sales in its overall circulation.

Bulk sales are essentially free giveaways of the paper to the consumer, although third parties who distribute them – for example, hotels – normally pay a discounted price to the newspaper group. The widespread use of this practice prompted Goodbody Stockbrokers to question Independent's figures. Goodbody analyst Mr Neil Clifford said the decline in actively purchased newspapers might have an impact on advertising revenues at Independent. 'Readers that actively purchase their newspaper are more valuable to advertisers,' he said.

Mr Liam McDonald of All Ireland Media, the biggest press advertising spenders in the State, said yesterday: 'It is clearly of concern, particularly the proportion of bulks and the way they have been increasing in recent times. There is a big difference between the man who puts his hand in his pocket and pays for a paper and the man who is just handed a paper. Research shows that somebody who pays for a paper has more affinity with that paper.'

Mr Richard Law of the agency MediaVest, also raised concerns. 'With greater competition in the market for circulation and ad revenue, it is no surprise that titles seem to be adopting a more aggressive stance, either by looking at ways to massage circulations or by pointing the finger at others' circulation practices,' he said. 'Some instances of bulking/lesser rate sales can be perfectly acceptable. For instance, if Independent offered an incentive to its readers to also buy the *Sunday Independent* at a reduced subscription price, that is just sound marketing. The fact, however, that certain issues of the *Sunday Independent* seem to have such high levels of bulking, when we all know there is increased competition from titles such as *Ireland on Sunday*, is something that needs explanation as we will not pay for unwanted circulation,' he added. Asked how agencies treat bulk sales, he said: 'Each agency's view is different. My view is that some level of bulking/promotional work is fine, but that this looks too much like artificial propping up of headline figures. It is up to each agency how they deal with it.'

However, Independent has strongly defended the use of bulk sales or giveaways. Mr Barry Brennan, group marketing manager at Independent, says there is a lot of hype around the issue. 'It is inaccurate to say we have begun pursuing these sales since July. We have been involved in sales programmes to vital reader sectors for many years.' Asked about why the numbers appeared to be rising, he said: 'This is simply the first year the ABC has reclassified these figures from discounted papers to regular multiple bulks,' he said. He said the bulk sales went to airlines, hotels, industry and primary and secondary schools. He said they were part of legitimate marketing campaigns to get these groups to sample Independent papers and nothing to do with panicking in the face of new competition. In a reference that must surely be aimed at *Ireland on Sunday*, he said: 'Indeed, it is worth asking if a consumer who spends one hour on a flight reading the *Sunday Independent* is more or less valuable to advertisers than a consumer purchasing a newspaper for a free CD.' He strongly rejected the charge that Independent was dumping the titles on the market. 'These papers are not dumped, but are actively used in key channels, adding to the strong readerships we achieve.'

Source: *The Irish Times*, 6 March 2003

Determinants of print media advertising prices

A number of criteria are taken into account when setting print media advertising prices. These are made available to advertisers on rate cards. **Rate cards** contain information about a media vehicle's prices, publication times, readership and circulation, deadlines for receipt of advertisements, technical specifications and key contact details. Some rate cards also contain audience profiles (see Appendix 6.1 for an example of a rate card).

Some of the terms that typically appear on rate cards are:

- **circulation and readership levels**
- **size of the advertisement**. There is particular terminology associated with size:
  - **newspaper advertisement sizes**

    full page
    half page

SCC (single-column centimetre) – display advertisements (with the exception of those that occupy full, double or half pages) are measured and costed in terms of the number of columns that they occupy
per line – mainly for classified advertisements

- **magazine advertisement sizes**

  DPS (double-page spread)
  half DPS (half double-page spread)
  full page
  half page
  quarter page

- **colour**. Some newspapers can print full-colour images, while others might only be able to add one or two colours. Most magazines print full colour. Typically, colour options are specified and priced according to whether they are:

  black and white, usually referred to as mono
  full colour
  one spot colour
  two spot colours

- **position of the advertisement**

  OBC (outside back cover)
  IFC (inside front cover)
  IBC (inside back cover)
  bleed page (see earlier explanation, page 161)

- **the inclusion of photographic material in the advertisement**
- **discounts for bulk buying**. When advertisers commit to place several advertisements with a publication over a certain period of time, their media buyer usually negotiates discounted rates.

Outdoor media

As its name suggests, outdoor media involves the use of outdoor locations for advertising. In 2002, the biggest spenders on outdoor advertising in Ireland (26 counties only) were Guinness, Bulmers, Vodafone, Budweiser and Coca-Cola (www.medialive.ie).

The most common types of outdoor locations are:

- **billboards**. These are erected at sites around the country. These sites are owned by a number of outdoor media specialists, such as JCDecaux and Viacom, and they rent the space to advertisers for different rates. Rates are largely determined by the size of the site and, in some cases, the location is taken into account. The size is determined by the number of printed sheets required to cover the billboard site and ranges from '4-sheet' to '96-sheet'.

- **public transport**. Vehicle sites in stations (some public transport advertising comes under the category of ambient advertising and is explored later in this chapter).
- **mobile billboards**. These billboards are mounted on vehicles that are driven around the required areas.

Recently, more innovative approaches have been devised to grab the attention of passers-by. The building boom of the 1990s in Ireland prompted advertisers to capitalise on the widespread presence of scaffolding and cranes. Prominent building developments became sites for advertising. However, this type of activity is threatened by increasingly stringent planning laws.

Until recently, outdoor advertising suffered from an image problem, but improved printing techniques led to a parallel improvement in the production quality of the posters used in outdoor advertising. Also, as traffic congestion gets worse, car and public transport commuters have more time to look at outdoor advertising.

Technology has enabled outdoor advertisers to achieve greater impact through the use of three dimensional (3D) displays such as electronic billboards. For example, Bulmers use these at Christmas time. They feature apple orchards with lights adorning the trees. Rather than portraying this through a standard poster, an electronic billboard enables Bulmers to use real lights in the advertisement. This approach is very effective in the dark.

The pros and cons of outdoor advertising

As we saw at the beginning of the chapter, expenditure on outdoor advertising grew from €86 million in 2001 to €98 million in 2002 (IAPI, 2003). These figures emphasise its importance in the media mix. However, as with the other media options, the advantages and disadvantages (Table 6.7) must be considered before using outdoor advertising.

Advantages of outdoor advertising

- **Wide coverage in specific areas**. Outdoor advertising allows advertisers to achieve wide coverage in specific areas. Advertisers can achieve national coverage with a campaign or they can locate their advertisements in specific geographical areas.

- **Ability to make an impact**. When excellent creativity is combined with the large size of outdoor advertisements, they have the ability to make an impact and be noticed. Pretty Polly tights and Triumph's Wonder Bra outdoor campaigns are famous examples of advertisements that generated a lot of publicity in newspapers and on television. Consequently, outdoor advertising's ability to make an impact often appeals to organisations launching new brands.

- **High levels of repetition**. Outdoor advertisements give advertisers the opportunity to achieve high levels of repetition. Target audiences may be exposed to a particular advertisement several times every day as they travel to and from work, school, college, the shops etc.

Table 6.7 The advantages and disadvantages of outdoor advertising

Advantages
• Wide coverage in specific areas
• Ability to make an impact
• High levels of repetition
•
Disadvantages
• High levels of wastage
• Over-exposure of audience to advertisements during a campaign
• Short exposure time
• Increasingly difficult to obtain planning permission for sites

Disadvantages of outdoor advertising

- **High levels of wastage**. Due to its indiscriminate nature, people not included in the target audience are exposed to the communication. This means that there is quite a high level of wastage associated with outdoor advertising.

- **Over-exposure of audience to advertisements**. While outdoor advertising facilitates high levels of repetition, it means that many people become over-exposed to the outdoor sites and their advertisements and fail to take notice of them after a while.

- **Short exposure time**. Despite the level of congestion on Irish roads, exposure time is short and this necessitates the creation of succinct advertising. Take a look at some billboard advertisements and observe how they are composed – the number of words, the importance of visual elements, the size of the text.

- **Planning permission issues**. In Ireland and many European countries, there is growing dissatisfaction among environmental pressure groups against outdoor advertising. Many people consider them unsightly, and detrimental to the physical well-being and appearance of Irish cities and the countryside. The main outdoor contractors have planning permission for their sites but it is becoming increasingly difficult to acquire planning permission for new sites. Since 1992, planning permission has been granted for just ten new 48-sheet sites, on condition that some contentious sites were removed (*Sunday Times*, 16 February 2003). The use of scaffolding as a temporary site for outdoor advertisements has already been mentioned. Dublin

> Corporation allows this as long as the sites are temporary. Posters that permanently cover buildings and block windows and doors are not permitted by Dublin Corporation (*Sunday Business Post*, 6 April 2000).

In a business environment that seeks greater accountability, pressure is on outdoor contractors to prove the medium's effectiveness. This next extract illustrates how in 2002 JCDecaux set out to do this with a piece of research that attracted some publicity:

Out of the blue

In August 2002, one of Ireland's main outdoor contractors, JCDecaux embarked on a high-profile piece of research by utilising one hundred of its billboard sites to launch a fictitious bank. The posters were an eye-catching blue and carried the straightforward proposition – *Bleu – Banking will never be the same again*.

In January 2002, JCDecaux Airport, the company's division that specialises in airport advertising, and the British Airports Authority had already run the same campaign in all four terminals at Heathrow Airport. Interviews among passengers were conducted and total brand awareness of *Bleu* after one month was 31 per cent, which represents 1.3 million passengers. The same percentage were able to remember the slogan, while 8 per cent recalled it spontaneously.

JCDecaux were unable to admit to the fictitious nature of the brand until the research was complete. This meant that they had to contend with a large number of calls from banks, especially those involved in Internet banking.

Sources: Coffey, Aine, 'Sacre bleu, brand new banking or new brand banking', *The Sunday Tribune*, 18 August 2002; Harrison, Bernice, 'Banks and ad agencies duped by test campaign', *The Irish Times*, 22 August 2002

Meanwhile, some outdoor advertisers are using text messages from mobile phones as a way of measuring response levels to outdoor posters:

Text responses linked to posters

Here's another way of measuring responses to outdoor posters: text messages from mobile phones. Developed by William Charlwood, founder and chief executive of the UK company RSVPi, the technique has been used by Ford in billboard advertising for its Fusion model. Investment house Jupiter is following suit.

Potential customers are invited to text a codeword – 'fusion' in Ford's case – to a phone number printed on the poster. The codeword goes to RSVPi, which sends a message inviting the respondent to submit their e-mail address. Those who do so receive Ford's marketing information, sent directly to their personal computer. So two purposes are fulfilled: a measure of how many people have seen the poster and an indication of likely customers.

Source: *Financial Times*, 11 November 2002

Ambient advertising

Ambient advertising *surrounds the target audience.*

The dictionary definition of 'ambient' is 'surrounding'. This captures the essence of the term '**ambient advertising**', which is, quite literally, designed to surround the target audience. 'Ambient advertising makes the message become part of the surrounding environment in which the consumer operates' (Blythe, 2000). It relies on surprise tactics in order to grab the target audience's attention because it communicates messages in unexpected circumstances. According to Poster Management Limited, ambient advertising spend in 2001 rose by 27 per cent to €19.8 million (*The Irish Times*, 29 August 2002).

While many of the techniques used in ambient advertising could also be described as outdoor advertising, they tend to go further. Ambient advertising methods include:

- **tickets**. Bus, train, airline and concert tickets are used to communicate messages.
- **street furniture**. This means litter bins, telephone kiosks, benches, bus shelters, etc.
- **taxis** (fully wrapped, see below)
- **petrol nozzles**. For example, Peugeot places advertisements for its cars on petrol nozzles.
- **supermarket and airport trolleys**
- **beer mats**
- **transport vehicles**. While this can be categorised as outdoor advertising, a single advertiser can cover an entire double-decker bus with a message. This is known as a full wrap. The public refers to these buses as the advertiser's bus, for example, the Vodafone bus.

  Radio stations give some of their employees cars that are totally covered in the name, frequency, logo and colours of the station. For example, 98FM, FM104 and SpinFM use this technique. Public awareness is heightened when the vehicles are seen on the roads.

- **doors of public toilets**. For example, Liffey Valley Shopping Centre advertises the availability of Liffey Valley gift vouchers on the inside of public toilet doors.
- **FashionSites**. These are A4 poster panels in ladies fitting rooms nation wide. They are aimed at females aged 18–40 in the ABC1 category (www.medialive.ie)

- **carrier bags**. Carrier bags include retailers' bags but a recent development is the Mediabag. Mediabags carry advertisements on take-away sandwich bags distributed in Dublin. The profile of the Mediabag consumer is males and females aged 18–35 in the ABC1 category (www.medialive.ie)
- **inflatables**. Inflatables are giant 3D representations of products or images associated with particular brands. For example, the tiger is synonymous with the Esso brand. Giant inflatable tigers are often placed on the roofs of Esso petrol stations in order to attract customers.
- **aerial vehicles**. Small aircraft or blimps, for example, carrying messages are quite common at public outdoor events.
- **pay-and-display parking tickets**.

Ambient advertising is most effective when it is positioned in the vicinity of the point of purchase. It can precipitate impulse purchases or speed up the decision-making process. It is also an effective way of launching a new product or of heralding the revitalisation of a brand. Vodafone's predecessor, Eircell, used bus wraps and employee vehicles to generate awareness. This approach was also adopted by Vodafone as part of their rebranding exercise.

Cinema

When video recorders became commonplace in people's homes, many experts predicted the end of cinema. What these experts failed to take into account is the fact that cinemas are more than mere conduits for movies. They are a night out and provide entertainment. Cinema has thrived and its resurgence has been fuelled by massive investment in the sector. Multiplexes provide immense choice to cinema-goers and their close proximity to car parks, shopping centres and restaurants makes them very convenient. According to Fry (2000), these factors lead to an increase in the number of planned and impulse visits. In 1999, 22 per cent of all Irish adults had visited the cinema within a month of research carried out for JNRR. This figure was further broken down by age group – 28 per cent of 15–19-year-olds, 24 per cent of 20–24-year-olds and 27 per cent of 25–34-year-olds (*MAPS Directory*, 2002).

Carlton Screen Advertising sells the advertising space for 97 per cent of Ireland's 319 cinemas. Between 1990 and 2001 cinema admissions grew 112 per cent and the number of screens increased by 88 per cent (*Sunday Times*, 1 December 2002).

The pros and cons of cinema advertising

While cinema is growing in popularity with advertisers, the advantages of this medium should be examined in conjunction with the disadvantages (Table 6.8).

Table 6.8 The advantages and disadvantages of cinema as an advertising medium

Advantages
• Enables advertisers to achieve rapid awareness at key points of the year
• Can create an impact because of its environment
• Focused targeting opportunities
• Less distractions and clutter
Disadvantages
• Advertisements irritate some cinema-goers
• Easy to avoid cinema advertising

Advantages of cinema advertising

- **Awareness building at key points of the year**. According to Fry, cinema advertising enables advertisers to achieve rapid awareness at key points of the year. For example, at Christmas time many family-oriented movies are released and this is exploited by advertisers when they opt for cinema advertising.
- **Impact**. Due to the size of the screen and the sound quality in most cinemas, it is easier to make an impact on the audience than with television advertising.
- **Focused targeting opportunities**. Advertisers are able to target their advertisements quite precisely at specific age groups and, in some instances, specific genders. Movies make audiences self-select and put themselves into certain groups when they decide what to attend.
- **Less distractions and clutter**. Unlike some of the other media discussed earlier in the chapter, cinemas provide a largely distraction-free and clutter-free environment. Some people consider the advertisements to be part of the overall entertainment.

Disadvantages of cinema advertising

- **Irritation**. Some people are irritated by the advertisements and may even see them as an intrusion.
- **Easy to avoid**. Some cinema-goers may purposely avoid the advertisements before the movie. This is an area of some contention between the advertisers and the sellers of cinema advertising space. Attendance helps determine the price of cinema advertising. However, even if a cinema enjoys 100 per cent attendance, this does not mean that everyone has seen the advertisements.

Directory advertising

Directory advertising *Advertiser pays to have information published in a directory.*

There is another form of advertising that is widely used by many companies and that is **directory advertising**. This is where an advertiser pays to have information about their company published in a particular directory. The information in directories is presented in categories and subcategories and these make it easy for the user to find what they are looking for. Depending on the advertiser's business, their entry appears under one or more relevant categories.

Perhaps the most prominent example in the directory category is the *Golden Pages*. It is distributed to every household and business with a landline telephone. There is also a wide array of directories available for the business-to-business sector. Some of these are distributed free of charge, while others are available for sale. Examples of business-to-business directories include *Kompass*, *the IPA* [Institute of Public Administration] *Yearbook and Diary* and the *Marketing Institute of Ireland Diary*.

Directories are very popular with people when they want to buy a product or service but are not familiar with any suppliers. Therefore, these directories perform an important function at the information-gathering stage of the buying decision process which we looked at in Chapter 2. However, the Internet helps fulfil this role for many people. This has led many publishers to launch their directories online.

Directories tend to be a relatively low-cost medium and, while they are utilised by large advertisers as part of an integrated marketing communications programme, they are accessible to small companies that may not be able to advertise in the more expensive media.

Most directories are intended to last a year but in that time, a certain amount of the information becomes outdated. For example, if a company goes through an unanticipated change in ownership or change in location, the information in the directory becomes inaccurate. Technology helps some directory publishers to address this issue as they publish directories online or on CD-ROM. However, many directory users, particularly in the consumer market, still prefer to use a paper copy.

Another drawback with directories is the long lead-time for receipt of entries. This means that advertisers must be able to predict their details for the year ahead to the best of their ability.

Summary

The main advertising media used in Ireland are national and regional newspapers, consumer and business magazines, television, national and local radio, outdoor and cinema. Cinema and outdoor advertising continue to grow at rapid rates.

Broadcast media comprise television and radio and both are widely accessible to almost everyone in Ireland. Television audiences are fragmenting with the growing popularity of digital television. Similarly, radio audiences have far greater choice as the Irish radio regulators continue to offer more licenses.

The Irish newspaper readership habit is not as strong as it used to be. While many advertisers continue to use press, advertising expenditure in national press declined between 2001 and 2002. However, new titles continue to launch and the British press groups still view the Irish market with interest.

Concerns about the validity of published readership figures for newspapers and magazines continue and must be resolved in order to restore confidence in print media.

As advertisers continue their search for new and exciting ways of reaching target audiences, outdoor and ambient advertising are enjoying popularity. They are considered harder to avoid and aim to surround the target audience.

Cinema's growing popularity with advertisers coincides with the Irish public's enthusiasm for going to see movies in custom-built cinema multiplexes. It offers good targeting opportunities.

Directory advertising is still popular with organisations targeting consumer and business markets. Technology has helped many publishers overcome the static nature of directories and has made them more flexible.

Useful websites

- www.iapi.ie — Institute of Advertising Practitioners in Ireland
- www.aai.ie — Association of Advertisers in Ireland
- www.acnielsen.com — A research company that compiles information about television audiences
- www.medialive.ie — This website contains statistics about various media.

Review questions

1. Discuss the advantages and disadvantages of the following as advertising media:
   - television
   - radio
   - print
   - outdoor
   - ambient
   - cinema
   - directory.
2. Explain the differences between primary circulation and secondary readership.

Exercises

1. Using the *MAPS Directory* or the website www.medialive.ie, compare the CPM of a full-page advertisement in the *Sunday Independent*, the *Sunday Times*, the *Sunday Tribune* and the *News of the World*.
2. Select a product or service of your choice and make recommendations as to which

media would be most appropriate when launching it to a new target audience. Give reasons for your choice(s).

3. In this chapter, a number of ambient advertising methods were identified. Give three specific examples of ambient advertising that you have observed and comment on each one.

References

Association of Advertisers in Ireland, *MAPS Directory*, 2002/03 (AAI, 2002).

Belch, George, E. and Belch, Michael, A. *Advertising and Promotion: An Integrated Marketing Communications Perspective*, 4th edition (Irwin McGraw-Hill, 1999).

Blythe, Jim, *Marketing Communications* (Pearson Education Limited, 2000).

Fry, Andy, 'Fresh views on the big screen' (*Marketing*, 5 October 2000).

Independent Radio Sales, *Radio Works, Turn It On*, (IRS, 2001).

Institute of Advertising Practitioners in Ireland, *Adspend – Year-end report 2002* (IAPI, 2003).

O'Donoghue, Aine and Harper, Tom, 'Media research in Ireland', in (eds) Meenaghan, Tony and O'Sullivan, Paul, *Marketing Communications in Ireland* (Oak Tree Press, 1995).

Appendix 6.1

Irish Independent rate card

Affiliation: *Sunday Independent & Evening Herald* Independent House, 90 Middle Abbey Street, Dublin 1

Tel: 01 705 5333. Fax: 01 705 5555

Website: www.independent.ie

Frequency: Daily – morning (weekend magazine: every Saturday)

Agency commission: on application

Format: Broadsheet (Weekend Magazine: Full colour, 372 x 290mm)

Single copy: €1.30

Rate effective date: January 2002 (Rates exclude VAT)

Mechanical data: technical specifications (mono and colour are available on our website: www.unison.ie/adspec)

Copy requirements: Day prior to publication date

Cancellation requirements: 48 hours prior to publication date

Weekend magazine copy requirements: Monday 10 a.m. before publication date

Readership: 595,000

Circulation: 170,055

Key contact(s): Group Advertisement Director: Joe Webb; Advertisement Manager: Tom Rafferty

Source: *MAPS Directory* (2002/2003)

Table A6.1

Mono	**€**
Full page	22,450
Half page	11,225
SCC	57.70
Financial SCC	67.35
Colour	
Full page	28,390
Half page	14,195
SCC	75.25
Special positions	
Front semi-solus	3,037
Classified	
Appointments SCC	61.50
Legal notices per line	11.45
Legal notices SCC	56
Lineage	8.10
Motor page SCC	42.25
Personal notices per line	16.50
Personal notices SCC	57.70
Property – regional SCC	42.25
Guaranteed positions	+20% (neg)
Weekend magazine	
DPS	18,400
Full page	9,240
OBC	11,880
Page 2–page 5	10,560
TV listings (series 3 for 2)	920

7

MEDIA STRATEGY AND PLANNING

The aims and objectives of this chapter are:

- to explain media planning and its role in marketing communications
- to emphasise the relevance of analysis as a prerequisite to effective media planning
- to introduce the key terminology associated with media planning
- to explain the concepts used by media planners when devising and evaluating media plans
- to present a framework for assessing the possible effects of various media on advertisements.

What is media planning?

Some of the media available to advertisers were examined in detail in Chapter 6 – television, radio, print, outdoor, cinema and ambient. These are known as **above-the-line media**. This means that the media buyer buys space or time from the media owner on behalf of the advertiser. The buyer invoices the advertiser for an amount that covers the cost of the media plus a commission (see Chapter 4). Other media include the Internet, mail, telephone and personal selling. All of these are dealt with elsewhere in the book. This chapter focuses on above-the-line advertising media.

Above-the-line media
Paid for by advertisers on a commission basis. The media buyer invoices the advertiser for an amount that covers the cost of the media.

Media planning
Involves the identification and selection of media that are best suited to the delivery of an advertisers' message.

In Chapter 2, Figure 2.1 (page 25) outlines the communications process. It shows how messages are transmitted to the intended recipient through channels referred to as the media. This chapter examines the reasons behind advertisers' and agencies' choice of media through which their advertising messages are communicated.

Before proceeding, media planning must be defined. **Media planning** is a process that involves the identification and selection of media that are best suited to the delivery of an advertiser's message to a particular target audience in a cost-effective manner. Therefore the **media plan** documents the decisions made during the media planning process. Specialists known as media planners are responsible for media planning. Meanwhile, media buyers implement the media plan and buy media time or space on behalf of the advertiser. As explained in Chapter 4, media planners and buyers are part of an advertising agency's media department. This is usually an important profit centre. Increasingly, however, the media departments of advertising agencies are competing with media specialists that are part of global networks, thus allowing them to offer advertisers the benefit of significant purchasing power. While some advertisers bring the media planning and buying functions in-house, most Irish advertisers employ the services of an advertising agency or a specialist media agency.

Media plan *documents the decisions made during the media planning process.*

Figure 7.1 Media planning in relation to the marketing plan

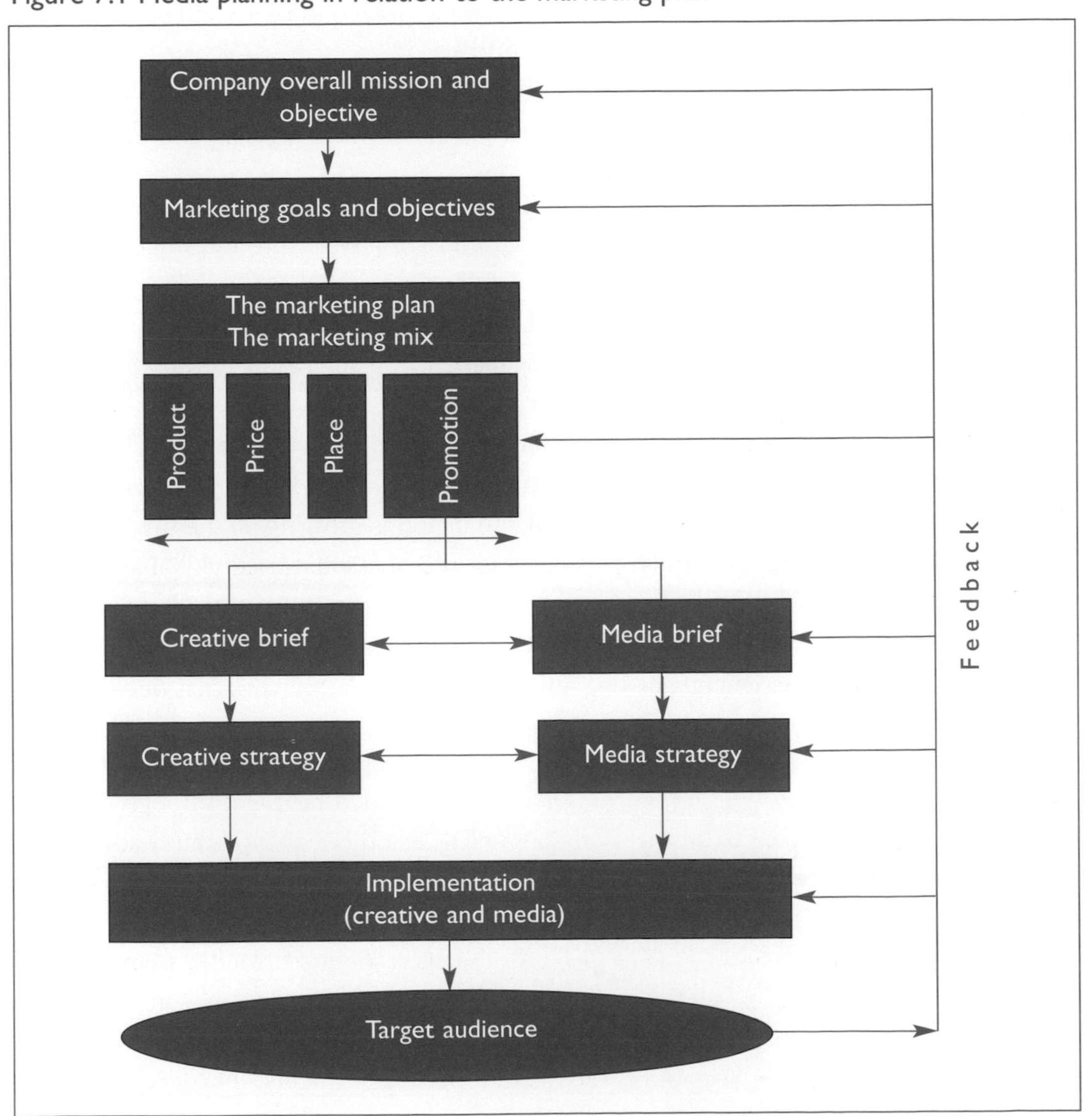

Media brief *contains information, which enables the media planner to devise a media plan.*

Good media planning can only be carried out if a clear and concise media brief exists. The **media brief** contains information from the advertiser that enables the media planner to devise a media plan. Ultimately, the brief determines the quality of the media plan. It is also worth noting that high-quality creative advertising is less likely to succeed or realise its full potential if the media plan is based on a flawed media brief. As illustrated in Figure 7.1, the advertiser's overall marketing plan should clearly state the company's marketing objectives. When these are in place, plans can be devised for each element of the marketing mix. This includes the marketing communications component. If this sequence of planning is adhered to, the media brief and the ensuing media plan should fit in with the marketing communications plan and indeed plans relating to all of the other elements of the marketing mix.

External forces impacting on media planning

Like so many aspects of marketing communications, media planning has undergone a significant amount of change. This is attributed to a number of factors (summarised in Table 7.1):

- **Advertisers** want to see measurable results from their advertising and want the media to add value.
- **The advent and growing acceptance of digital and cable television** has led to a proliferation in the number of television channels. Never before has there been so much choice available for viewers and advertisers.
- **Greater selection of media**. In an attempt to deliver results, media owners are constantly seeking new media through which they can deliver the advertisers' messages. Consequently, the range of available media is growing all the time.
- **Globalisation** has led to a much greater incidence of standardised global advertising campaigns. This has not only impacted on the creative component of advertising, but has convinced advertisers to take a global view when it comes to media planning. This in turn has led to the emergence of a few specialist media agencies that devise media plans intended for pan-European or global transmission or circulation. These specialists enjoy much greater purchasing power than the media departments of local advertising agencies.

Table 7.1 External forces impacting on media planning

External forces
• Advertisers' demand for greater media accountability
• The growing popularity of digital and cable television
• Growth in the range of available media options
• Globalisation and the trend towards standardised advertising campaigns

Media planning – the terminology

At this point, it may be helpful to introduce a number of key concepts that are taken into consideration and referred to during the media planning process.

- '**Media vehicle**' is the term used to describe a specific television or radio programme, magazine or newspaper. For example, *Hot Press* magazine and the *Gerry Ryan Show* on 2FM are examples of media vehicles.
- '**Reach**' refers to the total number of people in a target audience who are exposed to a media vehicle at least once during a specific time period. This figure is usually expressed as a percentage of the estimated target audience size.
- '**Frequency**' refers to the number of times a member of the target audience is exposed to a media vehicle during a specific time period. While target audiences might be exposed to particular media vehicles and the advertisements carried by them, they may not necessarily notice the advertisements. For example, a member of an advertiser's target audience might watch *EastEnders* on RTE1 on a particular night. This does not necessarily mean that the person will see the advertisements targeted at them because the level of distractions during commercial breaks can be very high – the viewer might change channel, prepare a snack or make a telephone call.
- '**Opportunity to see**' (OTS) and (in the case of radio) '**opportunity to hear**' (OTH) are sometimes used instead of the term 'frequency'. Both terms take the likelihood of distractions into account. OTS and OTH refer to the number of opportunities a person had to see or hear an advertisement within a certain time frame. In contrast, frequency, deals with the number of times an individual is actually exposed to a media vehicle. The conclusion that can be drawn from the comparison between frequency and OTS/OTH is that frequency is almost always greater than OTS and OTH.
- **Gross rating points** (GRPs). Advertisers use data on reach and frequency in order to quantify the relationship between reach and frequency. By multiplying reach by frequency, a measure called gross rating points is arrived at. For example, if a television programme is seen at least once by 40 per cent of the target audience and is broadcast 15 times in a certain period, the GRP is calculated as follows:

40 (reach) x 15 (frequency) = 600

However, GRPs do not measure effectiveness. They do not indicate whether or not a high GRP rating is due to high frequency figures and low reach. Therefore, GRPs do not take into account waste and possible inefficiencies in the media plan.

Media vehicle *Specific programme, magazine or newspaper*

Reach *The total number of people in a target audience exposed to a media vehicle at least once in a specific time period.*

Frequency *The number of times a member of the target audience is exposed to a media vehicle during a specific time period.*

Opportunity to see (OTS) *and* ***opportunity to hear (OTH)*** *The number of opportunities a person has to see or hear an advertisement within a certain timeframe.*

Gross rating points *equals reach multiplied by frequency.*

Effective reach
The number of people in the target audience who become aware of an advertisement within a specific time period.

Effective frequency
The number of times a member of the target audience needs to be exposed to an advertisement within a specific time period in order to be effective.

Duplicated reach
When a person is exposed, more than once, to an advertisement that is carried in a range of media vehicles.

Advertisers demand accountability from their media spend. In this regard, much criticism has been levelled against reach and frequency measures. This has motivated media planners to find ways of measuring effective reach and frequency.

- **Effective reach** is the number of people in the target audience who become aware of an advertisement within a specific time period. Remember, the earlier definition described reach as 'the total number of people in a target audience who are exposed to the media vehicle at least once during a specific time period'.
- **Effective frequency** is the number of times a member of the target audience needs to be exposed to an advertisement within a specific time period in order to be effective. Much research has been carried out in this area. It is generally accepted that if a person is exposed to an advertisement on at least three occasions, the effectiveness of each exposure increases. However, if someone is exposed to the same advertisement more than ten times, it ceases to be an effective allocation of media budget (Belch and Belch, 1998).
- **Duplicated reach**. Advertisers often use a range of media vehicles to deliver an advertisement to the target audience. This inevitably leads to what is described as duplicated reach. This is when the same person is exposed, more than once, to an advertisement that is carried in a range of media vehicles. For example, if an advertisement is placed in the *Irish Independent* and *The RTE Guide*, some members of the target audience will be exposed to it in both publications. This is not always a bad thing, as long as frequency does not exceed a certain level. This level is dependent on a number of factors that are explored later in this chapter (page 186).

The media planning process

The media planning process entails decision-making in a number of related areas – the selection of general and specific media, and when and how often they should be used. These decisions are made in response to the media brief, which in turn is derived from the advertising brief. The key deliverables at the end of the process are a media plan and an accompanying schedule (Figure 7.2).

Stage 1: Analysis and the media brief

The advertising brief forms the basis of the media brief. The media planner uses it to carry out a full analysis of the factors that are most likely to influence media decisions:

- the target audience
- the marketing and advertising objectives
- the product

Figure 7.2 Media planning process

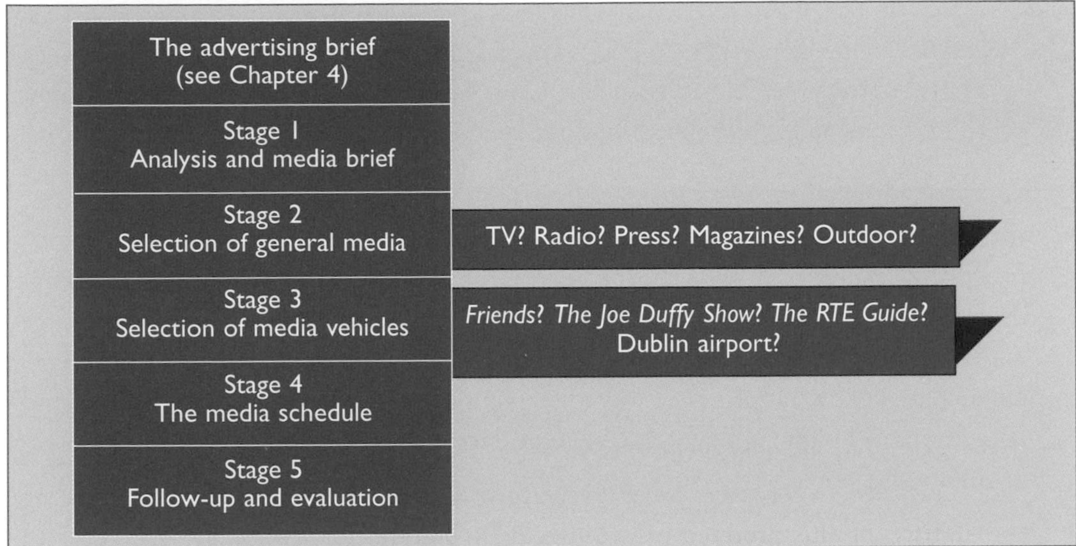

- purchasing habits, including the purchasing cycle; for example, the purchasing cycle for many food products takes place over a short time period
- available budget
- competitors
- the marketing environment. This incorporates economic, social, cultural, and legislative considerations.

Media objectives *serve as criteria against which general and specific media options are evaluated.*

At this stage, **media objectives** are set. These serve as criteria against which general and specific media options can be evaluated. They also provide measures against which the success or otherwise of the actual media used can be measured. Therefore, media objectives are no different from any other types of objectives in that they must be specific. Examples of media objectives when launching a new car to women aged 25–34 might be:

- to reach 70 per cent of the target audience at least three times over a four-month period
- to concentrate media spend in November, December, January and February, in order to ensure a presence is established in the run-up to the main car-buying phase, as well as during the phase.

Stage 2: Selection of general media

During the second stage of the media planning process, the media planner selects the general media through which the advertiser's message is most likely to be transmitted successfully. At this stage specific media vehicles are not considered but the planner recommends media that are likely to be the most effective in terms of reach and frequency. There are a number of factors that should be considered (summarised in Table 7.2):

Table 7.2 Factors influencing the selection of general media

• Media habits of target audience • Nature of product or service • Characteristics of media options • Cost of various media

- **the media habits of the target audience**. In the first stage of the media planning process, a detailed analysis of the target audience will have been conducted. From this, the media planner can deduce which media are most likely to reach the target audience. For example, if an advertisement is aimed at men and women aged 25–34, cinema might be an appropriate way of reaching them. However, if the target audience is aged over 45, radio or newspapers would probably be more effective (see Chapter 6 for more on this).
- **the nature of the product or service**. If a product or service is very complex, specialist print media may be appropriate, for example, *Technology Ireland*. In contrast, if an advertiser wants to create a brand image, without saying much about the actual product, television and cinema are desirable because they can make use of visual and aural effects.

  When it is important to show a good representation of the product, a visual medium is a good option, for example, newspapers, magazines, television, cinema and outdoor.
- **the characteristics of the media options and their ability to help meet objectives**. In the previous chapter, the advantages and disadvantages of the various media were discussed. These factors must be borne in mind when putting together a media plan.
- **the cost of the various media**. Available budget is a very important consideration and it can prevent the advertiser from implementing the most appropriate media plan. However, in the real world, costs must be taken into account. The cheapest media are not necessarily the best because less-expensive media may not be capable of reaching an advertiser's target audience. For example, if an advertiser wants to reach children under the age of ten, television is more appropriate than radio. It is also far more expensive. However, the advertiser in this case must question the wisdom of using radio if it does not reach the target audience.

Stage 3: Selection of media vehicles

When the media planner has decided on the most appropriate media, decisions can be made about specific media vehicles. Once again, a very detailed knowledge of the target audience is necessary. This time, their habits regarding specific media must be explored. To this end, the owners of the individual media vehicles should be able to furnish the media specialist with detailed information regarding their readers', viewers' or listeners' profiles. Look back at Chapter 6 to see how this is done. Other factors that must be considered are covered in detail in that chapter:

- cost – absolute and per thousand
- circulation (for printed media)
- coverage (for broadcast media)
- JNLR, JNRR and Nielsen
- geographical coverage
- reputation and credibility of the vehicle
- ability to do justice to the creative approach. For example, up to the mid- to late 1990s, most Irish newspaper titles were unable to guarantee a high standard of print reproduction. For advertisers wishing to portray a high-quality image, this made them less willing to advertise in newspapers. Heavy investment in sophisticated printing presses has marked a vast improvement in the quality and scope of newspaper production.

Stage 4: The media schedule

When the specific media vehicles have been chosen, a media schedule is compiled. The purpose of the media schedule is to establish exactly **when** and **how often** an advertisement should be placed in the specific media. Budgetary constraints have a bearing on these decisions, but where possible, the schedule should be driven by the campaign and media objectives.

There is still considerable debate about media scheduling and views vary across the industry. Recently, much of the debate has focused on recency. This concept is based on the premise that consumers buy products when they are ready to do so and that advertising should be scheduled to reflect this (Ephron, 1997; Jones, 1995; Reichel and Wood, 1997) According to Ephron and Heath (2001) recency is based on three ideas:

- **receptivity**. Advertising works best when the target audience is in the market to buy a product.
- **propinquity**. Advertising is most effective if scheduled when the target audience is close to purchase.
- **near-random distribution**. With the exception of seasonal products, such as cranberry sauce at Christmas, it is impossible to predict which consumers are ready to purchase.

Taking these three ideas into consideration, the objective for many advertisers should be to reach as many different potential purchasers as possible over as long a time period as possible.

According to Burnett and Moriarty (1998), the media planner must consider the following when compiling the media schedule:

- the number of opportunities to see or hear, that are created by the media schedule
- the profile of the audience that is exposed to the advertisements
- whether or not one media vehicle generates more impact than another (this point is examined in more detail under media factors on page 181–2).

Belch and Belch (1998) contend that three main factors should be taken into account when determining frequency levels (summarised in Table 7.3):

Marketing factors

- **Brand-related issues**. In relation to established brands, the bigger their market share and the stronger the loyalty levels, the less frequency is required. However high frequency is necessary for new brands.
- **Purchase and usage cycles**. Products with short purchase cycles, that is frequently used products, such as non-durables, require higher frequency so as to maintain a strong position in the buyer's mind.
- **Competition**. If an advertiser operates in a very competitive market place that produces high levels of advertising, high frequency is required.
- **Target group**. If the target audience is capable of retaining messages and information, lower frequency levels may suffice. Of course, creative execution should strive to make advertisements memorable, thus helping to reduce the frequency levels required.

Message or creative factors

- **Message complexity**. The more complex the message that is being communicated, the greater the need for frequency.
- **Message uniqueness**. If a message is strong and stands out, lower levels of frequency are more likely to suffice.
- **New versus existing campaigns**. New campaigns require more repetition in order to get the message across.
- **Image versus product messages**. Image building requires higher frequency levels than straightforward product selling.
- **Message variation**. If an advertisement communicates just one message, it requires less repetition. Conversely, if a number of messages are communicated in an

advertisement, it is more likely to require higher frequency.

- **Wearout**. The more an advertisement is transmitted, the greater the likelihood of wearout. This occurs when the target audience no longer notices the advertisement.

Media factors

- **Clutter**. Some media transmit a lot of advertising, thus necessitating higher frequency levels so as to ensure that the advertisement is noticed. For example, many television channels broadcast a lot of advertising and this makes it difficult for advertisers to be noticed.
- **The editorial environment**. If an advertisement is relevant to the editorial environment, it is more likely to be noticed. Therefore, it does not need to be repeated as often. For example, the editorial content in the magazine *Wild Ireland* is concerned with Ireland's wildlife. Since its readers are predisposed towards the editorial content, they may also be more likely to notice relevant advertisements.
- **Attentiveness**. Some media are more capable than others of grabbing and holding attention. In such cases, there is a greater likelihood of advertisements being noticed. This means that less frequency is required. Cinema is a medium capable of getting attention because there are fewer distractions when compared with media like television and radio.
- **Repeat exposures**. The nature of certain media means that once an advertisement has been transmitted, it will not be seen or heard again unless it is transmitted again. Radio is an example of such a medium, while monthly magazines present good opportunities for repeat exposures. Therefore, advertisements placed in media with low probabilities of repeat exposures may require higher frequency.

Apart from the number of times that a member of the target audience is exposed to a media vehicle (i.e. frequency), the media planner must make decisions regarding the timing of each exposure. Should they be spread out over a relatively long period of time? Should they be scheduled close together over a short period of time? Should there be a concentrated period of high-frequency exposures, followed by a period of low-frequency exposures? Budgetary constraints, product or brand considerations, levels of competition, target audience characteristics, and media factors all influence scheduling. When examining the scheduling patterns below, it is important to take recency factors, as discussed earlier, into account.

Scheduling patterns

There are three main scheduling patterns used by advertisers. They are flighting, continuous and pulsing.

Table 7.3 Factors determining required frequency levels

	Low frequency	High frequency
Marketing factors		
• Large market share	✔	
• Strong brand loyalty	✔	
• New brand		✔
• Short purchase cycle		✔
• Long purchase cycle	✔	
• Non-durable products		✔
• Large number of competitors		✔
• Target audience with good retention	✔	
Message/creative factors		
• Complex message		✔
• Simple message	✔	
• Unique message	✔	
• New campaign		✔
• Existing campaign	✔	
• Image advertising		✔
• Selling advertising	✔	
• Single message ad	✔	
• Multi-message ad		✔
Media factors		
• High clutter		✔
• Compatible editorial environment	✔	
• Good attention holding properties	✔	

Source: Adapted from Belch and Belch, Figure 10.22 (1998)

Flighting pattern

These entail intense periods of media activity during short time periods (see Figure 7.3). They are ideally suited to products or services that are not in demand all year round. Producers and retailers of seasonal products, such as cranberry sauce at Christmas and suntan lotion in summer, might use a flighting pattern because it is inappropriate to advertise all year round.

A flighting pattern may be used to solve time-specific marketing problems or opportunities. Revenue, the Irish organisation responsible for taxation, advertises at certain times of the year to coincide with important deadlines for taxpayers.

However, use of the flighting approach may give competitors the opportunity to target customers during periods of advertising inactivity.

Figure 7.3 Flighting pattern

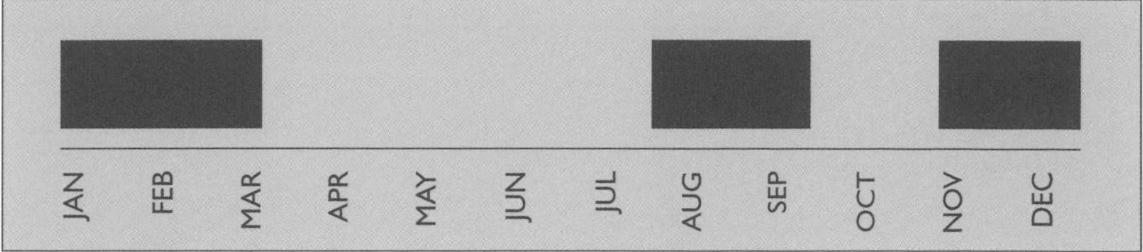

Continuous pattern

This involves a steady level of media expenditure throughout the year (see Figure 7.4). Companies selling products with a long purchase cycle may take this approach. At the other extreme, it may be appropriate for suppliers of emergency services to take this approach. For example, plumbers and electricians might spend a little throughout the year in local newspapers. The aim is to ensure that when someone needs a plumber or an electrician, their name will be the obvious choice. Manufacturers of products that are well known and possibly reaching the end of the product life cycle are advertised continuously.

Figure 7.4 Continuous pattern

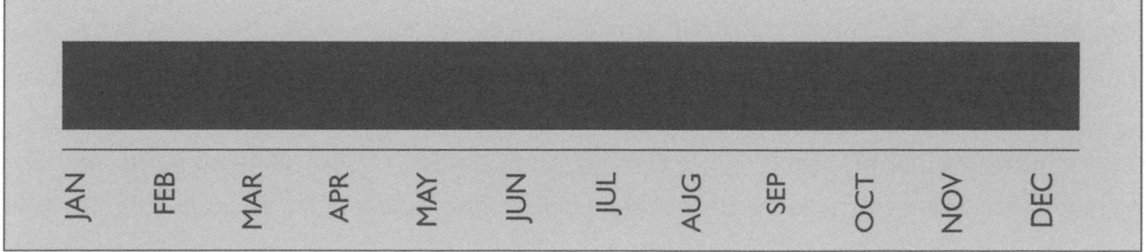

Pulsing pattern

A pulsing pattern is a combination of the flighting and continuous patterns (see Figure 7.5) and is widely used by many advertisers. Intense periods of activity alternate with steady, sustained levels of advertising. It keeps the product or service in the minds of the target audience and guards against competitors taking advantage of inactivity. Banks and car manufacturers might use the pulsing approach. For example, at certain times of the year, banks spend heavily on advertising in order to take advantage of seasonal spending patterns. Car loans are promoted in the run-up to the introduction of the new car-registration period, while pension advertising coincides with key tax dates. At other times of the year, banks reduce levels of advertising but continue to do a certain amount in order maintain market share. Similarly, cars are heavily advertised in Ireland at the end and beginning of each calendar year because the year's new registration number is launched in

January. Well-known FMCG advertisers often use this approach in order to maintain awareness levels throughout the year and to encourage purchases at certain times of the year.

Figure 7.5 Pulsing pattern

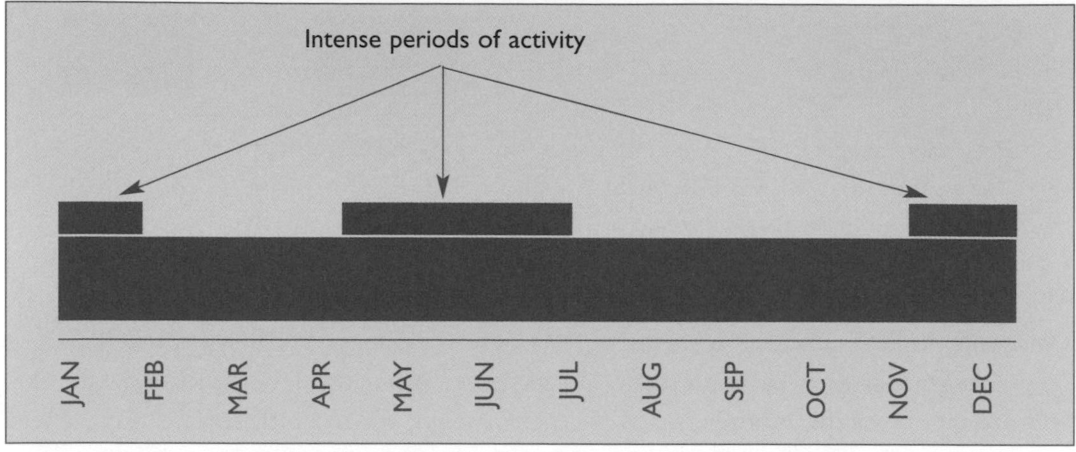

Stage 5: Follow-up and evaluation

An important stage in any plan is its follow-up and evaluation. Media planning is no exception. Following the implementation of any media plan, media planners and buyers should engage in qualitative and quantitative research. The results of this research may help form future decisions. Owners of the various media vehicles are important partners in quantitative research. They should be able to furnish media specialists with the type of information outlined in Table 7.4 It also highlights industry sources of this information. While the media owners themselves conduct their own research, independent research is more likely to present an unbiased picture.

Many advertisers carry out research themselves, particularly among new customers. For example, it is not unusual for advertisers to instruct customer-contact personnel to ask buyers how they heard about the product, service or organisation itself. If it was through advertising, they are asked to specify the source.

Qualitative research might also be conducted by independent bodies, media owners, advertisers and media specialists. The purpose of this is to gain a deeper insight into the media habits of target audiences and to ascertain whether or not media spend is effective.

Summary

Media planning involves the identification and selection of media that are best suited to the delivery of an advertiser's message. Media planners and buyers usually carry it out in advertising agencies or specialist media agencies. Media planning should be driven by the

Table 7.4 Quantitative research into media habits

Television • How many people watched each programme? • Who were they? (profile – age, sex, occupation, etc.) Source: Nielsen.
Radio • How many people listened to a radio station and when did they listen? • Where did they listen? (e.g. car, work, home) • Who listened to the radio? (profile) Source: JNLR.
Newspapers • How many people read a particular newspaper? • Did they buy it themselves? • Who read the newspaper? (profile) Source: JNRR
Magazines • How many people read a particular magazine? • Who are they? (profile) • Are they subscribers? or do they borrow the magazine from someone else? • Do they receive it free of charge from the publication itself? Source: ABC.
Cinema • How many people went to the cinema? • Who were they? (profile) • What did they go to see? • How frequently do they go? Source: EDI Nielsen and Carlton Screen Advertising

advertiser's overall marketing goals and objectives and should fit with all elements of the marketing mix.

Media planning is undergoing significant change as a result of external forces, such as demand for media accountability, the spread of digital and cable television, the growth in the number of media options, and the rise in the number of global advertising campaigns.

Media planning entails decision-making in a number of related areas. Effective media planning is built on an information-rich media brief, which clearly sets out the media objectives. Once these have been agreed, the remaining stages can be carried out.

The selection of general media is influenced by the media habits of the target audience, the nature of the product or service, the characteristics of the media options and the cost of the various media.

Media scheduling is a complex and as yet unresolved area of debate. However, practitioners and academics agree that frequency levels should not be finalised without taking three broad factors into account – marketing factors, message or creative factors and media factors.

When a media plan has been implemented, its effectiveness should be evaluated. This is usually done in conjunction with independent agencies and the media owners. For best effect, a combination of qualitative and quantitative research should be conducted.

Review questions

1. With regard to media planning, which comes first, the media plan or the marketing plan? Give reasons for your answer.
2. Media planning operates in a turbulent environment. Discuss.
3. Explain the key differences between reach and effective reach; frequency, effective frequency and opportunity to see or hear.
4. Discuss the disadvantages associated with the use of GRPs in media planning.
5. Prescribe a framework that could be used to determine frequency.
6. Compare and contrast flighting, continuous and pulsing frequency patterns. In each case, give one example of an organisation that adopts that particular approach.
7. Explain how media planners and media buyers evaluate media plans.

Exercise

You have been invited to put together a media plan for a company of your choice. Your media budget is €1,000,000 and you can consider any of the main media categories – television, radio, newspapers, magazines, outdoor, cinema and ambient. In putting together your plan, you must adhere to the media planning process outlined in Figure 7.2 (page 181). To assist you with Stages 3 and 4, you should refer to the *MAPS Directory 2003/2004* or www.mediactive.ie.

References

Belch, George, E. and Belch, Michael, *Advertising and Promotion: An Integrated Marketing Communications Perspective*, 4th edition (McGraw-Hill International Editions, 1998).

Burnett, John and Moriarty, Sandra, *Introduction to Marketing Communications: An Integrated Approach* (Prentice-Hall, Inc., 1998).

Ephron, Erwin, 'Recency theory', *Admap* (February 1997).

Ephron, Erwin and Heath, Melissa, 'Once may not be enough, but it's the best we can do', *Admap* (November 2001).

Fill, Chris, *Marketing Communications: Contexts, Strategies and Applications*, 3rd edition (Pearson Education Limited, 2002).

Jones, John Philip, *When Ads Work: New Proof that Advertising Triggers Sales*' (Lexington Books, New York, 1995).

Reichel, W. and Wood, L. 'Recency in media planning redefined', *Journal of Advertising Research* (July/August 1997).

8

ADVERTISING

The aims and objectives of this chapter are:

- to explain the role of advertising
- to differentiate between the different types of advertising
- to define creativity in an advertising context
- to gain an insight into the process behind creating, developing and making advertisements
- to distinguish between emotional and rational advertising appeals
- to explore various advertising styles
- to propose a framework for recognising good advertising
- to outline the role of marketing research in advertising.

What is advertising?

Advertising is a non-personal form of mass communication that utilises mass media. Mass media comprises TV, radio, newspapers, magazines, outdoor, catalogues and directories (see Chapter 6 for more on mass media). The organisation that uses advertising is known as the advertiser and pays to have its messages transmitted through one or all of the aforementioned mass media. This means that the advertiser controls **what** is communicated about the organisation and **when** and **where** the message is transmitted.

Being a non-personal form of mass communication means that the target audience cannot be addressed by name and that the message is standardised. Some argue that this puts advertising at a disadvantage when compared to database-driven elements of the marketing communications mix. However, it is very effective when an organisation wants to reach a large number of people at a relatively low cost. Also, as the names and contact details of the target audience may not be available or known to the advertiser, this makes advertising a viable option.

The role of advertising

Advertising is used for a number of reasons and these are captured by Brierley (1995) and summarised in Table 8.1.

Table 8.1 Role of advertising

- To increase the sales of a product or the usage rates of a service
- To improve corporate image
- To change people's attitudes and behaviour
- To address generic issues
- To reassure consumers
- To remind loyal consumers to buy an advertiser's products or services
- To generate awareness
- To encourage trial of new products
- To encourage users of rival brands to switch

Source: Adapted from Brierley (1995)

- **to increase the sales of a product or the usage rates of a service**. For example, Eircom frequently promotes its services on Bank Holidays and uses the lure of competitive rates to encourage customers to telephone friends and relations living abroad.
- **to improve corporate image**. Advertising might be used by organisations to improve their image if they have been involved in adverse publicity. For example, the petroleum company Shell was involved in high-profile environmental disasters in the 1990s. Consequently, they now invest heavily in advertising in order to promote their positive attitude towards the environment.
- **to change attitudes and behaviour**. Advertising is used to change attitudes towards harmful activities such as drink-driving, speeding, smoking, casual sex and drug-taking.

  Commercial organisations use advertising for this purpose. For example, in the 1980s, BT (British Telecom) ran their widely acclaimed 'Ology' campaign featuring the actress Maureen Lipman. The aim of the campaign was 'to encourage people to understand the value of a phone call in an inter-family relationship, i.e. phone your mother' (Robinson, 2000). A change in attitudes led to increased phone usage by many customers.
- **to address generic issues**. When an entire industry is threatened or has an important message to communicate, its composite companies might join forces under the auspices of one body in order to get their point across through advertising.

  For example, the 'Feile Bia' programme is co-ordinated by Bord Bia (the Irish Food Board) and run in conjunction with the Restaurants Association of Ireland and the Irish Hotels Federation. The Irish farming community also supports the initiative. Individual participants in the programme include many Irish hotels and restaurants. In signing up to this programme, they are telling customers and suppliers that they are committed to using products from recognised quality assurance schemes and/or high-quality local produce. In order to make consumers aware of the initiative, Bord Bia ran radio and press advertisements. It is hoped that, as a result of the campaign, consumers will support the Feile Bia Programme and actively seek out participating hotels and restaurants.

- **to reassure consumers**. When somebody buys a product or avails of a service, they may experience post-purchase discomfort. In particular, this might occur if the purchase is expensive or highly visible to others. In such circumstances advertising can be used quite literally to reduce discomfort and reassure the customer that they made the right decision.

- **to remind loyal consumers to buy an advertiser's products or services**. Using advertising in this way is why successful brands like Coca-Cola and Nike remain successful. They make sure that their consumers do not forget about them and migrate to competing brands.

- **to generate awareness**. Before someone buys a new product or tries a new service, they need to be aware that it exists. Since many media are seen, read or heard by a large number of people, advertising is an ideal vehicle for generating awareness of a new product or service.

  In their pre-Christmas 2002 onslaught, Vodafone secured high levels of awareness for their new service 'Live!' which allows the user to avail of many features, including the facility to send and receive full-colour pictures. The use of high-profile global sports personalities like David Beckham and Michael Schumacher helped achieve high levels of awareness quickly.

- **to encourage trial of new products**. This task becomes more necessary when there is a limited time span for using the product. Seasonal products and products strongly influenced by fads and fashion need to encourage trial within a short time period. Also when products are launched in an already crowded market place, it is essential to encourage trial. When launching a new FMCG product, advertising is often used in conjunction with sales promotions.

- **to encourage users of rival brands to switch**. While deregulation often results in market expansion, new arrivals usually target the incumbent's customer base. When the Irish health insurance market was deregulated in the 1990s, British-based BUPA entered the market. Their customer base now consists of lapsed VHI customers and previous non-users of private health insurance.

Types of advertising

We have seen that advertising has many functions. This has led to the emergence of many types of advertising, which Wells *et al.* (1998) categorise as follows (summarised in Table 8.2):

Table 8.2 Types of advertising

- Brand advertising
- Political advertising
- Directory advertising
- Direct response advertising
- Business to business advertising
- Institutional or corporate advertising
- Public service advertising

Source: Adapted from Wells *et al.* (1998)

Brand advertising

The aim of brand advertising is to develop a personality for the brand. Evocative imagery and language is used and after an advertising campaign, this should enter the consumer's mind when they think about the brand. Brand advertising often sells a lifestyle image and promises the consumer that if they buy the brand, they too can enjoy this lifestyle.

Exhibit 8.1

Retail advertising

Retail advertising usually concentrates on increasing retail traffic and informing target audiences about their product ranges, prices, special offers, opening hours and location. Retailers use advertising to position themselves as the best at something specific. For example, DID Electrical (Exhibit 8.2) highlights competitive prices, product range or opening hours.

Political advertising

Politicians have discovered the power of advertising and, since the 1990s, the wealthier political parties in Ireland have followed the lead of their UK counterparts. In the run-up to any general election or by-election, they advertise on billboards and in the press. As in any advertising, care must be taken not to make promises that cannot be kept!

Directory advertising

Directory advertising is used to reach consumer and business audiences. The *Golden Pages* is an example of a widely used directory targeted at business and consumer markets alike, while the *IPA Yearbook and Diary* is used by a range of advertisers in order to reach business customers.

Direct response advertising

Direct response advertising is used across a range of media including television, radio, mail, telephone, radio and the Internet. Its objectives are action-oriented and set out to elicit a response from the target audience. For example, charities often use direct response advertising as a way of securing donations (Exhibit 8.3).

Exhibit 8.2

Exhibit 8.3

IRAQ CRISIS APPEAL

Image reproduced with kind permission of Alliance 2015 Alliance 2015

Devastating wars and twelve years of sanctions have brought the Iraqi people to their knees. One million children under five are chronically malnourished and extremely susceptible to disease.

Now war is pounding Iraq again. For the Iraqi people it will mean further suffering. Hundreds of thousands could lose their homes, leaving them exposed and vulnerable. Sadly, it is always women and children who suffer the most.

Concern has been monitoring this emergency for months. Now we are urgently appealing for funds to help pay for our response.

Place of registration Dublin, Ireland. Registered number 39647. Registered Charity No. CHY5745. www.concern.net

Call 1850 410 510 or cut the coupon to make a donation today.

I will give €30☐ €50☐ €100☐ €250☐ *(Please make your cheque payable to Concern)*
OR debit my Mastercard/Visa/Amex/Laser card:

Card No. Expiry Date /

Signature Today's Date / /

Title Initials Surname

Address

Email

Tel No. Mobile No.

Call 1850 410 510 now OR return the coupon to:
Concern, Camden Street, FREEPOST, Dublin 2 www.concern.net ERAD03-05/002

Place of registration Dublin, Ireland. Registered number 39647. Registered Charity No. CHY5745.

CONCERN
WE'RE IN THIS TOGETHER

Business-to-business advertising

Business-to-business advertising is aimed at distributors, purchasers, professionals and any commercial businesses. It tends to be transmitted through targeted media vehicles rather than mass media vehicles, such as the magazines *Business and Finance* and *Technology Ireland*.

Institutional or corporate advertising

This type of advertising does not communicate about a specific product or service. It aims to enhance an organisation's corporate identity and communicate its core values to the target audience, thereby leaving the target audience with a positive view of the overall organisation (Exhibit 8.4).

Exhibit 8.4

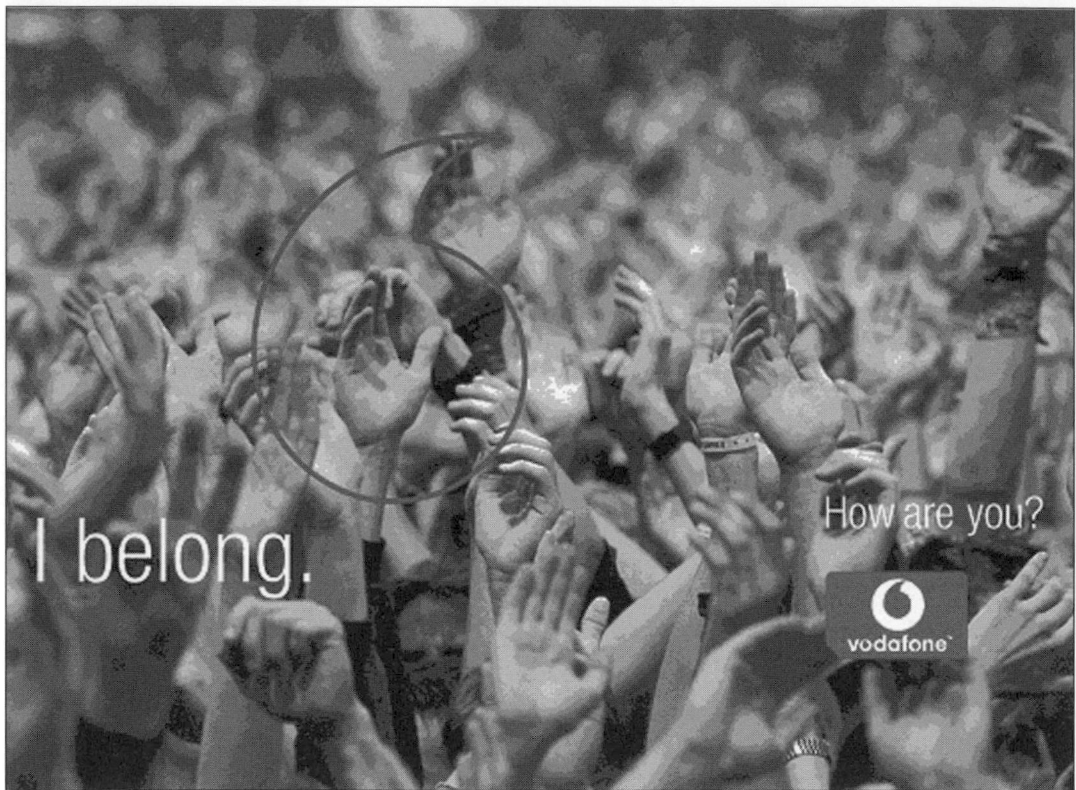

Public service advertising

Public service advertising is used to communicate on behalf of good causes such as road safety, drink-driving, safe sex, anti-smoking, and environmental awareness. In order to cover the costs of creating, producing and transmitting the advertisements, the backing of a major profit-making organisation is often sought. For example, AXA Insurance backed the recent National Safety Council's road safety campaign (Exhibit 8.5).

Exhibit 8.5

Advertising and creativity

Creativity is all about being inventive and imaginative. It is a word that is often used when discussing advertising. However, if an advertisement is not creative, as per the above definition, does this mean that it is doomed to failure? Similarly, if an advertisement is very creative, does this automatically mean that it will be effective? Evidence shows that the answer to both of these questions is no. For decades, the advertising industry has awarded the creativity of those who create advertisements without taking into account whether or not the advertising objectives were achieved. However, at a time when clients are demanding greater return on their advertising spend, this situation has changed. Increasingly, advertising effectiveness is taken into account when judging creativity as borne out by the industry's Advertising Effectiveness Awards. The judges take an advertisement's commercial success into account when judging creativity. Therefore, an excellent idea must also perform against the advertising objectives.

Belch and Belch (1998) define advertising creativity as 'the ability to generate fresh, unique, and appropriate ideas that can be used as solutions to communications problems'. Creative teams should not simply aim to come up with fresh and unique ideas that win awards. They must always take into account who the advertisement is aimed at (i.e. appropriateness) and whether or not it sets out to achieve the campaign's objectives. If it meets these challenges, then the resulting advertising may deserve to be labelled 'creative'.

Creating, developing and implementing advertising ideas

This section examines the process involved in creating and making advertising. Figure 8.1 outlines the stages involved in making an advertisement from the start. These tasks are primarily the responsibility of the creative department and should only be started on receipt of a comprehensive creative brief.

Figure 8.1 Creating, developing and making advertising: an overview

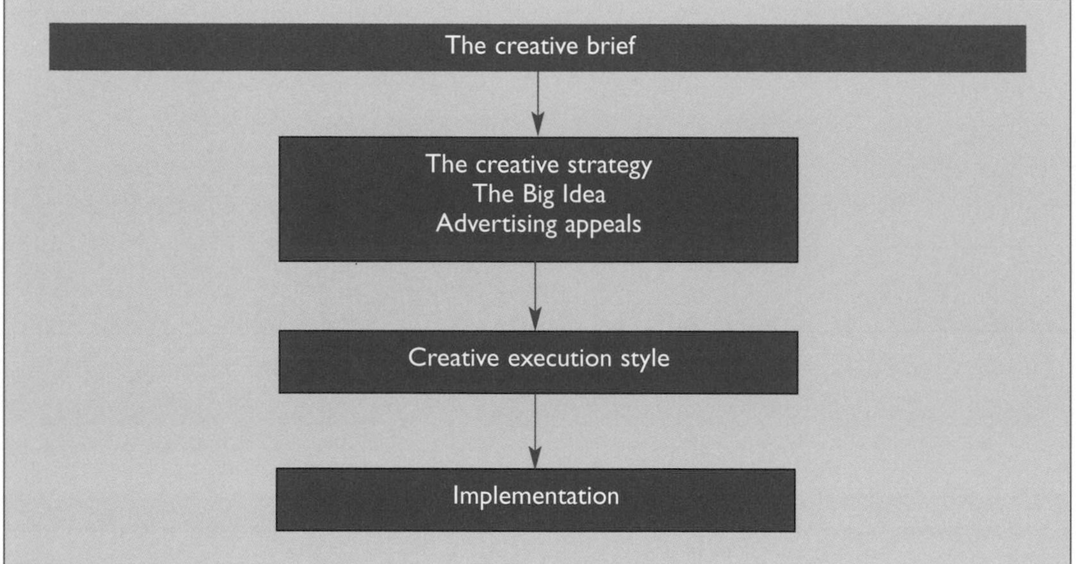

The creative brief

Creative brief *Written document containing background information that helps the creative team execute their task.*

The **creative brief** is a written document that informs the creative team of their task. It provides them with the necessary background information that will help realise the advertising objectives. Experienced clients often write their own creative briefs. Alternatively, account handlers might write the brief, following in-depth discussions with the client. Some advertising agencies invite their planners to provide significant input into the formulation of the brief because they view things from the perspective of the consumer (see Chapter 4 for further insights into advertising agencies and how they work).

The content of the creative brief varies from client to client and from campaign to campaign. However, there are a number of headings that are usually present in creative briefs.

Background information

This covers information about the company, the product or service, the threat or opportunity being addressed through advertising, the business environment, the competition and any previous advertising activity.

Advertising objectives

The setting of advertising objectives is essential so that the success or otherwise of the advertisement can be evaluated. Like all good objectives, advertising objectives must be specific, measurable, aspirational but achievable, and time-specific. Examples of advertising objectives are:

- to launch a new brand of cat food and to achieve 80 per cent awareness among cat owners aged 35–70 within a three-month time frame
- to increase store traffic in Supermarket X by 20 per cent on Mondays, Tuesdays and Wednesdays in the months of January, February and March.

The target audience

Effective advertising that enables the advertiser to achieve its objectives depends on having meaningful consumer insights. Information about the target audience should go beyond mere demographics and should inform the creative team about the mind of the target audience. It is not enough to know the target audience's age profile, typical occupations and geographical location. Intimate knowledge of its lifestyle, motivations, likes and dislikes is a necessary prerequisite to effective advertising. If this information does not exist, research may have to be conducted.

Current target audience attitudes

Relevant research concerning the attitudes of the target audience towards the company and its products provides vital clues when embarking on the creative process. For example, negative attitudes may have to be addressed, as demonstrated by Iarnrod Eireann when they acknowledge that, even though their service is far from perfect, they are working hard to put this right.

Values, identity and personality

In Chapter 3 corporate identity was explored in detail and values were discussed. When creating advertising, the creative team must be fully informed of these issues so that the corporate and/or brand identity is reinforced and developed. For example, Vodafone's advertising must capture its core values or passions. These are:

- Passion for customers
- Passion for people
- Passion for the world around us
- Passion for results.

This develops the brand's personality.

The main proposition

The Big Idea *The foundation of an advertising campaign.*

This informs the creative team of the key consumer benefits derived from the organisation's offer. The description of this might provide creative triggers that can be incorporated into the **Big Idea** behind the advertising. The Big Idea is explained later in this chapter (see page 205).

Source of credibility

What information is available that lends credibility to the main proposition? This might be available in the form of scientific evidence, testimonials (i.e. endorsements from satisfied customers), favourable comparisons with competitors, and company expertise.

The role of advertising

The creative team needs to know what other elements of the marketing communications mix are being used and how. The role of the other elements of the marketing mix (price, product and place) must also be known. All of this information helps clarify advertising's role.

Exhibit 8.6

Desired target audience action

Is the advertising a call to action or is it simply being used to raise awareness or change attitudes? (See Exhibit 8.6.)

Restrictions/mandatory inclusions

Some advertisers have corporate guidelines that help shape the appearance of communications material. For example, many organisations use the same typeface in all printed communications, and advertising is no exception (see section on visual components). Some advertisers are legally obliged to include certain information in their advertisements. For example, financial institutions, diet products manufacturers and pharmaceutical companies are closely monitored by outside regulatory bodies and are required to include certain information in their advertising. This information is known as a **mandatory inclusion**. Other mandatory inclusions specified by advertisers themselves might include their logo and contact details.

Key dates

Does the advertising have to coincide with a key date such as an anniversary, a product launch, an external event or a public holiday?

Budget

While the budget should not preclude the creative team from coming up with the most appropriate advertising solution, the reality is that it often does matter. If budgets are limited, television advertising may not be worth considering.

The creative strategy

The creative strategy details how the advertising objectives will be realised. Creativity lies at the heart of creative strategy and must be nurtured and encouraged in advertising agencies. Certain conditions are conducive to the creation of great advertising and these are found in the most creative advertising agencies. They recognise that inventive, imaginative and effective ideas are more likely to emerge when the process proposed by Young (1975) and outlined in Figure 8.2 is followed.

Figure 8.2 The creative process

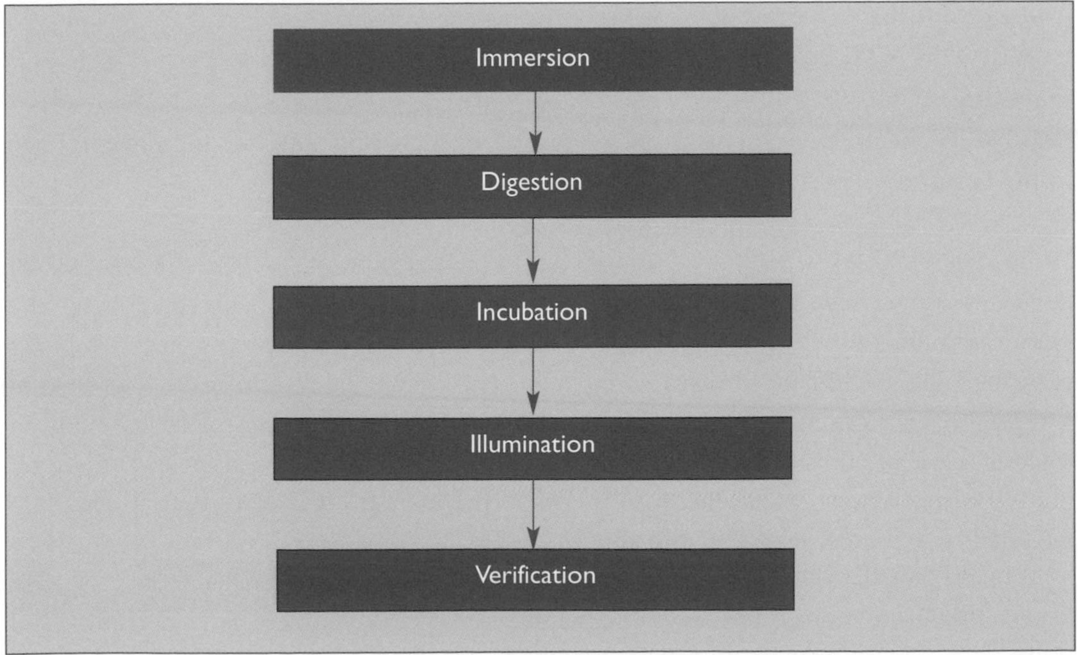

Immersion

This stage of the process sees the creative team quite literally immersing itself in the problem or opportunity in question. This entails the collection and analysis of all the relevant information. If team members are unfamiliar with the product or service, they usually experience it first hand in order to see what it is like to actually use. In-depth knowledge of the target audience is gleaned and the creative team must get inside the heads of the target audience. What sort of music do they listen to? What do they do in their free time? Where do they go on holidays? What sort of clothes do they wear? What do they read? What are their political views? While much of this information might already be contained in the advertising brief, the creative team might actually spend time with the target audience in order to gain better insights.

Digestion

When the first stage is complete, the creative team must digest all of the information, think about it and become very familiar and comfortable with it.

Incubation

The creative team stops consciously thinking about the problem and allows the subconscious to do the work. Great ideas often come to those who walk away from working directly on the problem or opportunity in question. Many creative departments provide facilities for their teams to unwind and engage in activities unconnected with work. The incubation stage might take place outside the confines of the agency. This means that a great idea might come to somebody when they are at home or taking part in a leisure pursuit.

Illumination

Possible solutions begin to emerge as a result of the gathering, analysis and musing done in the first three stages.

Verification

Each idea is reviewed by considering whether or not it is capable of solving the communications problem or opportunity. Usually, three likely contenders emerge and are presented to the client for further investigation. This might entail seeking out the views of a representative sample of the target audience through focus groups. The feasibility of turning ideas into finished advertisements is also considered. This is particularly important for television advertisements because the daily production costs of filming a television advertisement are between €50,000 and €100,000.

For the creative process to occur, the onus is on advertising agencies to give creative teams the time and space to really immerse themselves in a problem or opportunity, and to take time away from it so as to allow the subconscious to take hold. Realistic deadlines should be set and clients should never expect to see creative, effective advertising ideas too quickly. The most important components of creative strategy, the Big Idea and the advertising appeals are now examined in detail.

Developing the Big Idea

In the course of the creative process, a number of ideas are likely to emerge. Through a process of elimination and verification, the Big Idea should emerge. The Big Idea is the foundation of any advertising campaign and once this has been decided upon, the development and execution of the campaign can follow. Examples of some well-known Big Ideas include catch phrases like Tesco's 'Every little helps', Nike's 'Just do it', Carlsberg's 'Probably the best lager in the world', Vodafone's 'How are you?' and The National Lottery's 'It could be you/It could be them/him/her.'

Metaphors are also used as the basis for Big Ideas. Examples include the Andrex puppy and the Dulux dog. The Dulux dog was first used in 1961 and has featured in 28 campaigns over 32 years. The Andrex puppies have been used since 1972 (Robinson, 2000). These Big Ideas provide the platform on which certain advertising campaigns have been based for years and, in some instances, for decades.

Exhibit 8.7

Creative teams use several approaches when searching for the Big Idea. Ogilvy (1983) said that if the following five questions could be answered with a 'yes' when reviewing possible Big Ideas, then the likelihood is that it has immense potential:

- Did it make me gasp when I first saw it?
- Do I wish I had thought of it myself?
- Is it unique?
- Does it fit the strategy to perfection?
- Could it be used for 30 years?

While these questions should always be answered, any of the following approaches are also used when searching for the Big Idea:

The Unique Selling Proposition (USP) (Reeves, 1961)

When mass advertising first emerged, the USP was at the heart of many Big Ideas. Reeves identified three characteristics of the USP:

- Each advertisement must make a proposition to the consumer. Not just words, not just product puffery, not just show-window advertising. Each advertisement must say to each reader, 'Buy this product and you will get this benefit.'
- The proposition must be one that the competition either cannot or does not offer. It must be unique either in the brand or the claim.
- The proposition must be strong enough to move the mass millions, i.e. pull over new customers to your brand.

Duracell batteries use this approach in their advertising. They maintain that their batteries outlast those of their competitors. In order to get this message across, they show toy rabbits, being run on Duracell batteries, competing against toy rabbits run on competitors' batteries. At the end of the advertisement, the only rabbit still moving is the one propelled by Duracell batteries.

Exhibit 8.8

The USP approach was easier to achieve in the 1960s and 1970s when competition was less intense. At that time, many products really did have a competitive advantage. In today's competitive environment, the physical appearance and performance of many competing products is very similar. Unique propositions are difficult to identify. Even if the advertiser and its advertising agency succeed in identifying a USP, they must question whether or not it is sustainable in the long term. If not, it should not form the basis of an advertising campaign because it can only enjoy a short life span. Also, in using this approach, advertisers must ensure that any claims they are making can be substantiated. Otherwise, they may be found guilty of misleading advertising and this may result in negative publicity.

Brand image (Ogilvy, 1983)

As stated above, the physical difference between products and brands is very difficult to discern in many instances. This has made the USP approach more difficult to pursue and has given rise to the pursuit of a distinct brand image as a key differentiator. Underpinning this approach is the belief that brand image equates to personality and that 'every advertisement should be thought of as a contribution to the brand image. It follows that your advertising should consistently project the same image, year after year. This is difficult to achieve as forces are always at work to change the advertising – like a new agency, or a new Marketing Director who wants to make his mark' (Ogilvy, 1983).

Guardians of the world's leading brands embrace this approach when it comes to finding the big advertising idea. It is widely used in areas such as clothing, financial services, cars, FMCGs and perfumes. The more visible the consumption process is to others, the more concerned the consumer is likely to be about the brand image. Smirnoff Ice quickly found a foothold in a crowded market place by bringing the brand's personality to the fore. Its 'As clear as your conscience' campaign captures the imagination of their target audience and persuades them to choose Smirnoff Ice over the many alternatives. In so doing, the consumers embrace the brand's personality and perhaps, albeit subconsciously, hope that by drinking Smirnoff Ice they will assume some of the brand's characteristics.

Similarly, Renault used brand image advertising to successfully launch the Renault Clio in the early 1990s. The hugely popular 'Papa/Nicole' campaign featured characters 'who had to reflect the car's 'personality' – the small car with big-car refinement'. The advertisements were designed so 'that nearly all potential buyers of the car would identify with someone in the stories – young females with Nicole, men and older people with Papa. Even if they didn't directly identify with one of the characters, everyone could aspire to the relaxed, Provençal lifestyle which, despite our [the UK's] historical anti-Frenchness, was sure to be an attractive proposition' (Robinson, 2000). These advertisements were also highly successful in Ireland.

The Levi 501s advertising campaign in the 1980s, as described below, illustrates how powerful the brand image approach can be if the Big Idea is found and harnessed to good effect. This series of advertisements gave Levi 501s a personality and appealed to the target audience's emotional side.

Levi 501s – Launderette 1985

The opening bars of Marvin Gaye's hit 'I Heard It Through The Grapevine' are among the most evocative in television advertising history. For a whole generation, at least, those first few moody seconds only bring one image to mind – that of model Nick Kamen walking into a launderette. The ad might not have been set in the 1980s (more likely a mythical 1950s), but for many those first few seconds can evoke memories of an entire decade.

Kamen's 'launderette' was shown for the first time on Boxing Day 1985. Thought up by John Hegarty and Barbara Noakes of Bartle Bogle Hegarty, the ad campaign was designed to try and save Levi's flagging fortunes; the company was under attack from all sorts of other fashionable brands. In short, Levi's (which had been going since the 1850s) were becoming the sort of jeans worn by people's dads.

Research showed that the intended target audience for Levi's 501s – 15–19-year-olds – saw the United States of the 1950s and 60s as a cool time and place in history. James Dean, Elvis Presley and Sam Cooke all belonged to this mythical, wondrous world. Unless the ad agencies came up with something new, the alternative was going with the American campaign for 501s, which was all about how well the jeans fitted in the United States of Ronald Reagan. The image seemed the opposite of MTV and European chic.

So, director Roger Lyons was given the go-ahead to film an ad that showed drop-dead-gorgeous model Nick Kamen stripping down to his boxer shorts, while flustered women and bemused elders looked on, and then sitting and waiting while his jeans were in the wash. All this and Marvin Gaye thrown in too.

'Grapevine' was the first of four Levi's-related songs to all make the Top Ten, a feat that made advertisers realise that choosing the right music was of paramount importance because it really could help push a product on TV. They call it 'integrated marketing' – and it meant a single in the charts and an ad on the box simultaneously, as well as the '501' logo alongside the artist's name on the record sleeve in every record shop in Britain.

Sales of 501s shot up by an incredible 800 per cent in the wake of the ad, which eventually had to be taken off the air because the company couldn't produce enough jeans to meet the new demand. By 1987 sales of Levi's jeans were reported to be 20 times what they had been just three years earlier. 'The ad said: "Wear Levi's jeans and you'll be a rebel without a cause,"' says psychologist Dr David Lewis. 'You'll be able to alienate older people – who young people despise anyway – and you can be cool.'

Source: Robinson, 2000

Positioning (Ries and Trout, 1981)

This approach uses advertising's Big Idea to position the product or service in a particular place in the consumer's mind. Products or services can be positioned in terms of their attributes. These include safety, comfort, economy and sensitivity. For example, Volvo and, more recently, Renault have built their big advertising ideas around safety as an attribute. Their aim is to position their cars as the safest cars on the road in the minds of their target audiences.

Other positioning platforms include price (Ryanair, 'The low fares airline'), usage, quality, product class and product users.

In some instances, the line between positioning, brand image and USP may be blurred and it is not always clear which approach has been pursued. However, as long as a Big Idea that works emerges, this should not present too many difficulties.

Exhibit 8.10

Inherent drama (Burnett)

Leo Burnett was the founder of one of America's leading advertising agencies, one that would later become an international force. Belch and Belch (1998) describe his inherent drama approach as a belief that 'advertising should be based on a foundation of consumer benefits with an emphasis on the dramatic element in expressing these benefits.' The drama should therefore show that the advertiser understands why the consumer should purchase the product or use the service. In the 1980s Nescafé Gold Blend used this approach in order to show what the coffee might be able to do for the consumer. They launched their highly successful 'Couple' campaign in 1987 and since then there have been three couples involved in advertising mini-soap-operas. Each advertisement leaves the viewer wondering what will happen next and the coffee is at the heart of the tension. According to Robinson (2000), the campaign pushed sales of Gold Blend up by 70 per cent and transformed it from being a minor player into the second biggest coffee brand in the UK.

Advertising appeals

The Big Idea is the foundation upon which advertising can be built. Therefore, when the Big Idea has been found, the advertising agency can set about turning it into advertising that will be seen, heard and/or read. Firstly, the advertising appeal must be decided on and, secondly the creative execution style must be developed.

The advertising appeal 'refers to the approach used to attract the attention of consumers and/or influence their feelings toward the product, service or cause' (Belch and Belch, 1998). According to Armstrong and Kotler (2003), advertising appeals should possess three characteristics:

- They should be **meaningful**, emphasising benefits that make the product more desirable or interesting.
- They must be **believable**.
- They should be **distinctive** so as to help the target audience differentiate the advertiser's offer from those of its competitors.

There are two main types of advertising appeals that are used in order to attract the attention of the target audience. These are rational appeals and emotional appeals. Therefore, the advertiser must know what motivates their target audience. In some instances, the advertising agency may recommend a combination of the two types of appeals so as to have an impact on the head and the heart.

Rational appeals

Rational appeals *focus on the functional needs and expectations of the target audience. Use information and logical discussion to persuade the target audience.*

Rational appeals focus on the functional needs and expectations of the target audience for the product or service being advertised. Rational appeals use information and logical discussion to succeed in the power of persuasion. Depending on the circumstances, consumers tend to be motivated by rational motives such as safety, comfort, hunger, pain relief, health and economics. People also use rational criteria when evaluating products and services. Examples of these might include performance, quality, technological capability, efficiency, durability and reliability.

Weilbacher (cited in Belch and Belch, 1998) further identified a number of advertising appeals which can be classified as rational appeals:

- **feature appeal**. In this case the advertisement focuses on the dominant traits of the product or service.
- **competitive advantage appeal**. Ryanair and the telecommunications company, Sprint, identify their main competitors and show how their own services are more price competitive.
- **favourable price appeal**. Electrical retailers, Power City and DID Electrical, focus on low prices.
- **news appeal**. Eircom might use this type of appeal to tell their target audience about the introduction of lower prices. When the mobile service providers, O2, Meteor and Vodafone, improve their coverage, they might highlight this fact through advertising

with news appeal. In saturated markets, such as the FMCG sector, manufacturers launch new, improved versions of their products and focus on these innovations when advertising. Advertising might also be used to celebrate an organisation's anniversary. This message tells the target audience that the advertiser has been around for a long time and will continue to be around for a long time to come.

- **product/service popularity appeals**. Advertising is used to tell the target audience how many customers a company has and, as a result, advertisers instil confidence in potential customers. Bank of Scotland (Ireland) highlight their popularity by referring to their status as the third largest business bank in Ireland.

Exhibit 8.11

Emotional appeals

While rational appeals focus on benefits and features, **emotional appeals** focus on the target audience's social or psychological need for the product or indeed their need to avoid the product, service or action. Emotional appeals exploit human feelings in a number of areas including belonging, status, rejection, acceptance and embarrassment. For example, some car companies aim to make an impression on their target audience by appealing to the person's need to convey their status in society by the car they drive. Esat Digifone (now O2) ran a television advertising campaign in the 1990s. This featured a handsome man in a night-club who is attracted to a good-looking woman. When she leaves, she slips him her phone number and he cannot believe his luck. He goes outside and calls her immediately but his grating voice and thick accent brings about a change of mind in the

Emotional appeals *focus on the target audience's social or psychological needs.*

woman. In conclusion, Esat Digifone suggests that, in these circumstances, a text message would have been more effective. The advertisement touches on rejection and the human need for acceptance.

Psychological needs are driven by feelings or states such as love, affection, happiness, nostalgia, self-esteem, fear and sorrow. For example, Bord na Móna evoke feelings of nostalgia in their television advertisements for peat briquettes. The cosy images of happy families, pets, friends and lovers snuggling up beside a roaring fire to the sound of the Marino Waltz conjure up happy memories for the target audience. At the other extreme, road safety advertisements have become more graphic in their approach in order to connect with psychologically driven feelings.

Creative execution style

The creative execution style 'refers to the way a particular appeal is turned into an advertising message presented to the consumer' (Belch and Belch, 1998). The following are the most widely used creative execution styles and are summarised in Table 8.3.

Table 8.3 Creative execution styles

- Slice of life
- Dramatisation
- Humour
- Factual
- Demonstration
- Technical expertise
- Scientific evidence
- Comparison
- Endorsement or testimonial
- Personality symbol
- Animation
- Fantasy
- Controversy

Slice of life

This shows the product or service being used in a typical setting. Very often, it is intended that the people used in the advertisements come across as 'real' people in real-life situations. The cleaning product Flash takes this approach.

Dramatisation

The product or service is presented as the 'star' of the advertisement. Brands like Impulse, Cadbury's Milk Tray, and Nescafé Gold Blend use this style of advertising and depict their products as essential catalysts to the occurrence of particular situations.

Humour

Humour is widely used in advertising. The main thrust of the humour should not be mocking or cause offence to a particular segment of the population. Where an advertisement is being used as part of a global or transnational campaign, research should be conducted so as to ensure that the humour is understood and appreciated by all.

Factual representation

Information concerning a product or service's features and benefits are presented in a factual way. Dell Computers adopt this style in their press advertisements and list their products' features. This style is often suited to high-involvement purchases that are risky for the purchaser. This is because the buyer needs to have a lot of information before feeling confident enough to make a purchase.

Demonstration

Some products are complex and difficult to explain verbally or textually. In these situations, television might be an appropriate medium to use because the advertiser can demonstrate the product being used. This style is seen on television shopping channels and is widely used to advertise DIY and exercise equipment.

Technical expertise

This style highlights the advertiser's technical expertise when it comes to making a product or delivering a service. One of the best-known examples of this approach is Del Monte's 'The man from Del Monte says yes' campaign. It is intended to draw attention to the care taken by Del Monte when sourcing its ingredients. Bulmers also use this approach in their 'Nothing added but time' and 'All in its own good time' campaigns. These approaches endorse their cider-making capabilities.

Scientific evidence

This style builds a product or service's credibility by presenting scientific evidence to back up claims made by the advertiser. Visual supports such as charts and graphs are often used in print and television advertising. Cosmetics companies such as L'Oréal use this approach in order to counter the growing cynicism towards beauty products. Many moisturising creams claim to reduce wrinkles and, while the use of beautiful 'older' models may only deepen cynicism, scientific research endorsing the claims may be more plausible (see Exhibit 8.13).

Comparison

This style makes comparisons between the advertiser's product or service and that of a competitor. Laws on comparative advertising in Ireland and the UK have slackened considerably but any claims must be true and backed up where necessary. For a long time, advertisers used this approach without actually mentioning the name of the competitor. For example, this was an approach favoured by advertisers of washing powders. More recently, airlines and telecommunications companies have used the comparative style.

Endorsement or testimonial

The main focus of this style is to have a product or service endorsed by a celebrity, an expert or a 'real' person. It is important that the source chosen is credible and does not behave in a way that is likely to undermine the advertisement. Celebrities are widely used to endorse products, for example, Flora proactiv and Jack Charlton, Shredded Wheat and Ian Botham, L'Oreal and Andie MacDowell. An increasingly celebrity-obsessed culture means that advertisers must be careful when working with celebrities. For example, Pepsi paid Britney Spears millions of dollars to appear in their advertising. This back-fired when she was photographed drinking Pepsi's main competitor Coca-Cola.

Exhibit 8.13

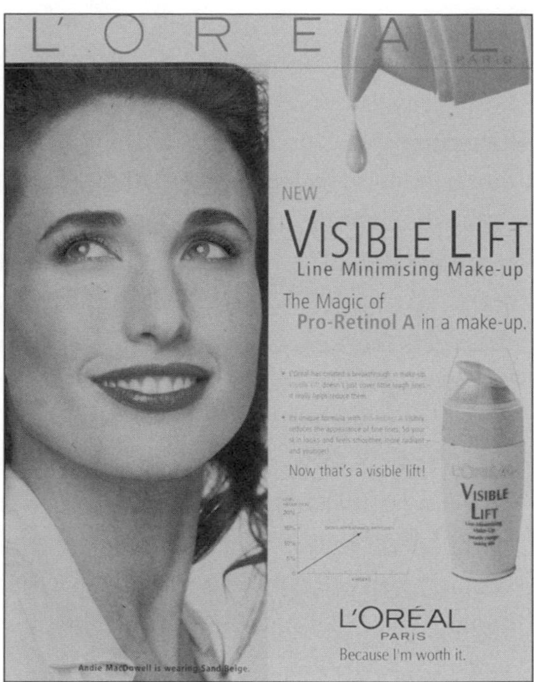

Testimonials from 'real' people can be very effective. Flora proactiv uses well-known people in its advertising but it also features ordinary people. They tell their own story of their experience with the product in a way that people can relate to. The slimming product, Slimfast, features satisfied customers who show photographs of what they looked like before and after using Slimfast.

Personality symbol

In this style, a personality symbol is created to represent the brand and bring its values alive. For example Old Mr Brennan and Brennan's Bread, Tony the Tiger and Kellogg's Frosties, Captain Birdseye and the Birdseye range of products and Lyons Tea's Minstrels. Personality symbols are not always animated but may be real people and animals. For example, Statoil use an actor to play the part of Norwegian manager, Del Monte have developed their 'Man from Del Monte' personality and Andrex and Dulux both use dogs to symbolise their brands. In 1999, Unilever, who own the Birdseye range, decided to get rid of the original Captain Birdseye and replace him with a younger version. However, they reversed their decision when sales plummeted by 20 per cent. Even though market research had strongly indicated that consumers were tired of the old Captain Birdseye, they did not embrace the change (*Irish Independent*, 21 October 2002).

Animation

Animation is very popular in advertising campaigns aimed at children, although it is used in adult-oriented advertising as well. It varies in terms of sophistication from the animation of straightforward, two-dimensional drawings to the more sophisticated, computer-generated, three-dimensional approach. Examples of the former approach include Hovis Bread, Cadbury's Caramel and some direct response insurance companies like First Call Direct. The high-tech approach was adopted by Lucozade when they launched their Lara Croft campaign. According to Chris Cawley, Chief Executive of the advertising agency, Cawley Nea, 'cartoons give an image longevity. You don't have to worry about them falling from grace or becoming old so they can attract a following that spans generations' (*Irish Independent*, 21 October 2002).

Fantasy

Brand advertisers use emotional appeals and the fantasy style is often found in advertisements concerning perfumes, cars, luxury brands, chocolate and alcoholic drinks. Well-known examples include Opium, Cadbury's Flake, Smirnoff Ice and Carlsberg.

Controversy

Some advertisers adopt a controversial style to make an impact and court publicity. While this style may result in the banning of an advertisement, this might not deter the advertiser because a ban often results in widespread media coverage and public debate. Consider the two examples (below) which demonstrate how advertising bans resulted in publicity for Levi and Carlsberg.

Levi ad rubs standards body up the wrong way

A poster advertising Levi jeans and carrying the words 'Rub yourself' was likely to cause grave and widespread offence, the Advertising Standards Authority has ruled. Its ruling followed a number of complaints that the poses adopted by models in the poster were provocative and sexual and deeply offensive and embarrassing to women. The offending poster showed a young man standing with his back to a wall and embracing a young woman who is standing in front of him with her back turned towards him. Such images, said complainants, should not have been displayed at bus shelters where young children waiting for buses would be exposed to such images. In their response, Levi said the posters complied with standards of taste and decency in

Ireland and they did not feel it contained anything likely to cause grave or widespread offence. The textured backgrounds were designed to work with the poses to show that the textured effect of the product had been achieved by rubbing up against various surfaces. But upholding the complaints, the ASAI said it concluded the posters, and in particular the words 'Rub yourself' were likely to cause grave and widespread offence and contravened the advertising code.

In another ruling the authority upheld a complaint about the 'builder's bum' Carlsberg TV commercial, but it did not consider the advertisement was likely to cause grave or widespread offence or offend against the rules on sex stereotyping. The commercial shows three young men going together on holiday who are depicted drinking Carlsberg on arrival in their holiday apartment. A shot of workers on an adjacent building site showed the construction workers were young women with one of the women builders 'showing cleavage of the upper part of her bottom.' A woman who complained about the commercial said she found it offensive and was upset by the way it trivialised and objectified women. She felt it degraded women and also contained a message that was 'only for the boys'. Carlsberg replied that over a 12-month period this was the first complaint about the advertisement and they did not believe it had caused grave or widespread offence. They also did not accept it had degraded women or was in very bad taste. While it upheld the complaint, the authority said it did not consider the commercial was likely to cause grave or widespread offence. However, it was concerned about the attractiveness of the commercial for young people and that in an advertisement for alcoholic drinks featuring young people, three separate occasions of drinking were shown. This created an attractive depiction of holidaying based on drinking alcohol that was likely to be of particular appeal to male minors. It did not consider that this presentation complied with the requirements of the code of advertising standards.

Source: *Irish Independent*, 23 October 2002

The use of the controversial style can backfire, as Benetton, the Italian-based global clothing company discovered to their expense in 2000. In a push to gain a foothold in the lucrative US market they signed a multi-million-dollar deal with the US retail giant Sears. They were not there long when they launched their 'Death Row' poster campaign that featured real inmates from Death Row. This offended and angered the victims' relatives who lobbied the retailer until Benetton were expelled from all of Sears outlets. The story was covered on television and in newspapers. Unlike other controversies 'enjoyed' by Benetton, the Death Row campaign did not have a happy ending for the company and resulted in millions of dollars worth of lost sales.

All of these styles can be used on their own or in combination with others. For example, a common approach is to combine slice of life with humour.

Implementation

When the advertising appeals and creative execution styles have been agreed, words, images and sounds are developed and finalised. Obviously, images are not required for radio advertising and some advertisers do not use words in visual media such as print and television. For example, with the exception of the Benetton brand mark and the words 'United colours of Benetton', Benetton use only imagery to get their message across.

Copy
The written or spoken element of an advertisement.

Visual
The graphic aspects of an advertisement. Includes photography, illustrations, diagrams and logos.

Audio
The aural or sound component of advertising.

The proper terminology for words and images is copy and visual respectively. **Copy** refers to the written or spoken element of an advertisement. The **visual** refers to the graphic aspects of an advertisement and includes photographs, illustrations, diagrams and company logos. **Audio** refers to the aural or sound component of advertising. The copy component of the advertisement is the responsibility of the copywriter while the art director is responsible for the visual component (refer to Chapter 4 for more on this).

Copy

Advertising copy consists of a headline, sub-headline, body copy and signature.

Headlines

The headline is the attention-grabbing, most dominant written or spoken part of an advertisement. This one sentence or phrase targets the communication at a particular audience and encourages them to stay with the remaining messages contained in the advertisement. Ogilvy (1983) stated that 'on the average, five times as many people read the headlines as read the body copy. It follows that unless your headline sells your product, you have wasted 90 per cent of your money.' He also contended that 'the headlines that work best are those which promise the reader a benefit – like whiter wash, more miles per gallon, freedom from pimples, fewer cavities.'

The following types of headlines are just some of the approaches most commonly used by copywriters (*IPA Handbook*, 1997):

- **direct**. The main message of the advertisement or the main product benefit is identified. One of HMV's Christmas 2002 advertisements took this approach – 'Get money-off vouchers worth £100 when you buy any of these chart titles.'
- **indirect**. Reference to the product, service or organisation is made in such a way that it will arouse the curiosity of the target audience.
- **discursive**. A quotation from someone in a conversational situation is used to stir up feelings of empathy or interest among the target audience. The explorer Henry Matthews was used in the headline of an American Express print advertisement –

'when I was 5, it was holidays with my parents. At 11, holidays with the school. At 21, holidays with the lads. At 35 holidays with my kids. Now I'm going somewhere on my own' (*Observer Sport Monthly*, December 2002).

Accord Marriage Care use the same approach in their radio advertisements when a man admits that what he thought was a good marriage ran into difficulties.

- **news**. Words and phrases like 'announcing', 'introducing', 'new' aim to create excitement and interest in the advertiser's message.
- **question**. A question can be used to arouse and keep the target audience's interest until the question is answered or a solution is offered. In a press advertisement, Bank of Scotland (Ireland) asked 'How much could you save by remortgaging your home over the phone?' (*The Irish Times*, 15 February 2003). The remainder of the advertisement provided answers to the question.
- **selective**. The headline is used to reach out to specific market segments by asking people to self-select. Headlines such as 'Tense, nervous headache?', 'Hayfever sufferers' only appeal to people suffering from these ailments.
- **command**. The target audience is told exactly what is expected of them. Retailers often use this technique in order to instil a sense of urgency in the target audience and to impress upon them the importance of calling in to their nearest retail outlet.
- **provocative**. Some headlines purposely set out to evoke an emotional response. Provocative headlines are used in charity advertising in order to motivate the target audience to take action.
- **testimonial**. A person with expertise or positive experience of the product or service lends their name to its promotion in the headline.
- **endorsement**. The product or service is endorsed by a celebrity or loyal user.

Exhibit 8.14

The people of Ethiopia need help . . .

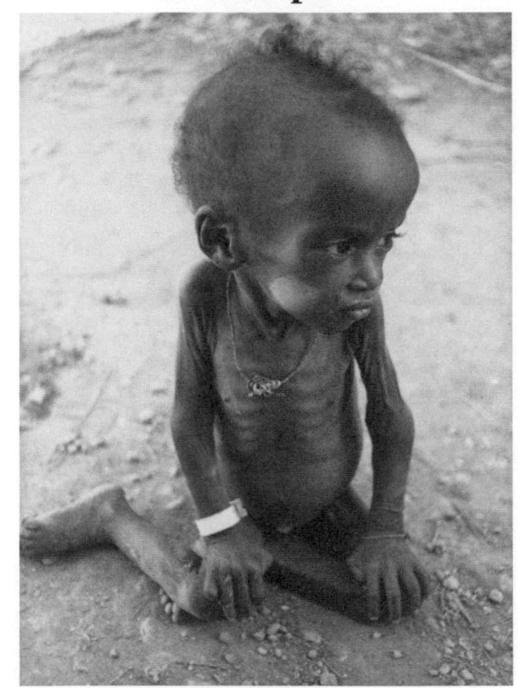

. . . and they can't wait for ever.

GOAL, PO Box 19,
Dun Laoghaire, Co. Dublin.
Telephone: 01-2809779

- **curious**. This approach aims to draw the target audience into the advertisement through the use of an intriguing headline that merits further investigation. Sure deodorant for men used the following headline in order to arouse curiosity – 'Medicals involving rubber gloves; pregnancy tests; *Guns & Ammo* readers'. It concludes with the tagline, 'For whatever makes you sweat' and a picture of a can of Sure for men.

The sub-headline

Not all advertisements use sub-headlines but, when they are used, their purpose is to provide a link between the headline and the body copy. In October 2002, Jurys ran a press advertisement with the headline 'Home is where the heart is.' This was intended to arouse curiosity and on further reading, the sub-headline 'from €49 per room' made the message clearer. In this case, the use of a low price in the sub-headline would ensure that the reader finished reading the ad. A number of sub-headlines might be used in an advertisement in order to draw the target audience's attention to particular sub-messages.

Body copy

Body copy consists of the main verbal or written part of the advertisement. It expands on the promises or messages contained in the headlines and sub-headlines. It might identify and empathise with target audience needs and then go on to offer a solution. The main objective is to motivate the target audience to do something.

Body copy should not use jargon that the target audience will not understand. While it is intended to motivate the target audience, it should never over-promise or communicate false information. The advertiser should also remember that noise levels surrounding advertising are high and the target audience is likely to encounter distractions. Therefore the body copy should make its point as quickly as possible.

Signature

Most forms of advertising close with a signature that identifies clearly who is behind the advertising. Therefore, it usually contains the name of the advertiser and, in many cases, it includes contact details. Increasingly, the signature contains a **tagline** that encapsulates key information about the organisation such as its core competence, main proposition, vision, promise, values or strengths. Some examples of well-known taglines are as follows:

Tagline
Encapsulates key information about the organisation in just one phrase.

- 'Ryanair – the low fares airline'
- 'Western Union Money Transfer – the fastest way to send money worldwide'
- 'Miele – anything else is a compromise'
- 'The art of performance – Jaguar'.

The visual component of advertising

The visual component of advertising is concerned with the appearance of an advertisement. It consists of the images being used, and the way in which any printed information is presented. Obviously, the techniques used to depict the visual components vary depending on the types of media being used.

In the case of print advertising the art director must decide what style they will use:

- If an image is being used, will it be executed in photographic, hand-drawn illustrative, or computer-generated form?
- Will the final image be in black and white or colour, or a combination of the two?
- How will the information be presented? For example, scientific information, research findings, and comparisons might be represented in chart or graph format.
- What typeface, also known as a font, will the headlines, sub-headlines and body copy appear in? **Typefaces** are sets of types or characters in a particular design. Examples include Times New Roman, Courier and Arial. Many organisations adopt the same typeface for all printed communications and some go so far as to design their own (see Chapter 3).

Typeface *Set of types or characters in a particular design.*

What size typeface will be used? Headlines are usually printed in the largest font in the advertisement, sub-headlines are smaller, and the body copy is smaller again. With regard to text and font size, it is important that the target audience can read it without strain. Mandatory inclusions, such as those seen in financial services advertisements, tend to be in a very small font size (i.e. the 'small print').

In television and cinema advertising, important visual aspects include the setting, the filming style, and the appearance of the actors and product (Some of these are dealt with in Chapter 2 under Semiotics, page 31).

Audio

Audio is the spoken words, music and sounds that are used in broadcast advertising. Some advertisements might include all of these, while others may involve only one of these. Therefore, the creators of advertising must consider the following:

If words are being used, what tone of voice should be used to say them? In Ireland, some of RTE's leading actors and presenters are used by advertisers because of their delivery style. The actor, Alan Stanford, is used in many organisations' radio advertisements. The drawback is that if an actor is heard in too many advertisements, listeners or viewers might be confused as to what is being advertised.

- Should the message be delivered in the form of a catchy jingle? Good jingles are very memorable and can deliver a message very effectively.
- Music is often used to stir emotions and evoke certain feelings. Does the music already exist or does it have to be composed especially for the advertisement? If it already

exists, should the original version be used? If so, permission has to be sought and fees must be paid. This might prove expensive, so an alternative to this might be to record a different version. Those who permit their music to be used may reap significant financial rewards over and above the fee received from the advertiser. For example, Vodafone's use of the Dandy Warhols' single in their broadcast advertising helped catapult the song to number one in the singles charts.

Davies (2003) argues that many advertisers have turned their backs on the copy element of advertising in their quest for memorable visual elements. He states:

> 'It's easy to see how business has been seduced by the perceived power of image. We're apparently living in a high-octane visual culture, where media-savvy consumers expertly decode and store the thousands of sponsored images machine-gunned at them every day. But the bullets are in danger of losing their penetrative power. There's a suspicion that the iconography of commerce has played itself out and is now caught in an endless repeat cycle, as over-familiar graphic ideas, styles and tics are regurgitated at decreasing intervals ...
>
> 'Highly sophisticated manipulators of visual language, marketers and designers all too often get waylaid in the finer details of image making, overlooking the most potent communication tool of all – words. Engaging, relevant content, and a consistent, recognisable, tone of voice should be essential ingredients in all corporate communications. If writers are involved in the key early stages of a project as creative partners, they can help to shape and develop the strategic thinking behind the design process, creating a compelling synergy between words and images.'

In practice, advertisers should pay attention to both the visual and copy components of advertising and work to ensure that their messages are being communicated in the most effective manner.

Evaluating advertising

Advertisers and account handlers in advertising agencies must be able to evaluate the work of creative teams in an objective manner. All too often, good work is rejected because of the personal likes and dislikes of a key decision-maker. Just because the decision-maker does not like the colour pink or the appearance of one of the actors in the advertisement, does not mean that it will not work. To guard against this, and to remove subjectivity from the process, those put in charge of evaluating advertising would be well advised to do so with the aid of a framework. Before we look at such a framework in detail, it is worth stressing that the following questions must always be asked and considered when evaluating advertising:

- Who is the advertisement aimed at?
- Will it appeal to the target audience?
- Will it help achieve the advertising objectives?

The following framework (summarised in Table 8.4) was first devised by Unilever but is used by many advertisers and top advertising agencies around the world. It evaluates advertising against ten criteria.

Table 8.4 Ten principles for evaluating advertising

1. It has impact.
2. It concentrates on one Big Idea.
3. It is simple and clear.
4. It involves the target consumer.
5. Its promise discriminates the brand from its competitors.
6. It is credible and feels genuine.
7. It integrates the brand name with the central idea.
8. It establishes and/or develops a relationship with the consumer.
9. It must build the brand personality.
10. The idea must be campaignable.

Source: McConnells Advertising Agency (2000)

1. Create impact

In order to communicate with the target audience, an advertisement must first grab its attention. This is easier said than done – consumers are exposed to anywhere between 500 and 3,000 advertising messages every day. The National Safety Council made an impression on its target audiences in a series of advertisements about road safety. Their 'Shame' advertisement is featured in the case study at the end of this chapter. McCann Erickson in Belfast created the campaign and they and their client were awarded a Gold Award at the 2002 Advertising Effectiveness Awards for this advertisement. They also won the Grand Prix and Gold for their seat-belt usage advertisement.

2. Concentrate on one Big Idea

The brand's benefit should be conveyed to the consumer by one Big Idea. This can be a visual and/or aural expression that is exclusively linked to the brand.

During the dot.com surge in the late 1990s, there was a surge in advertising in order to make people aware of the new companies and their websites. One such company was the financial services provider, breathe.com. Their TV advertising centred on imagery and sounds suggesting breathing activity and it served to build brand awareness. The execution of the idea proved arresting and unexpected. Creatively, it was a breath of fresh air!

3. Make it simple and clear

If advertising contains too many thoughts and ideas, the target audience will be confused and worse still, will lose attention. The execution should be simple and the expression should be unambiguous. Most importantly, the target audience should understand what is expected of them.

Ronseal, the paint manufacturers, are exponents of the simple and clear school of advertising. Their TV advertisements usually feature a DIY expert demonstrating one of the products and saying the now famous tagline, 'It does exactly what it says on the tin.'

One Direct, An Post's financial services operation, sells its services direct to the public over the phone. Their advertising always features their telephone number and leaves the viewer, listener or reader in no doubt as to what they should do – pick up the telephone and call One Direct.

However, simplicity and clarity does not necessarily mean that everything needs to be spelled out to the target audience, as shown in the Specsavers advertisment in Exhibit 8.15. Advertisers should remember that real communication is two-way and that the consumer should participate.

Exhibit 8.15 Specsavers advertisement

4. Involve the target consumer

Effective advertising should have immediate dramatic impact, which arouses the interest of the target audience and holds that interest. It should also elicit a favourable emotional response by appealing to the consumer's self interest, relating to a known need or problem and promising satisfaction or a solution to that need or problem.

Deodorant products present a challenge to advertising agencies. For most people deodorant is considered a necessary, low-involvement purchase. However, in 2002, Sure tapped into the emotional aspects of personal hygiene. The Big Idea in the TV advertisement was the chance meeting between a 20-something woman and her ex-boyfriend, who is accompanied by his new, attractive girlfriend. The woman panics when she is confronted by the man with whom she was once very intimate but, despite all of this she need not worry, because she is wearing Sure deodorant. The strength of the advertisement is the way in which it succeeds in involving the target audience.

5. Differentiate the brand from its competitors with its promise

An advertisement must communicate a benefit to the target audience. This benefit should help distinguish the brand from competing brands. In today's competitive environment, this is a very difficult task. Many organisations recognise that, while they find it difficult to differentiate their product from those of their competitors, they can create differences through brand advertising. Therefore, the brand must communicate difference and this is achieved by highlighting important brand values (for further information about values, look back at Chapter 3).

Petrol is a highly homogeneous product and most consumers depend on triggers such as branding, price and location to differentiate the various suppliers. The suppliers recognise this fact which is reinforced in the advertising of Shell and Statoil. Shell's advertising focuses on the environment and Statoil's advertising focuses on price and forecourt retailing.

6. Make it credible and genuine

Advertisers must not mislead the target audience. Therefore, any statements and demonstrations must be true so that the target audience will accept them. While humour is commonplace in advertising, the fundamental brand benefit must always seem obtainable.

In 2001, Lever Brothers enlisted the services of Gillian Quinn, wife of ex-Irish footballer, Niall Quinn, to star in their TV and radio advertisements for the washing detergent, Surf. Due to the nature of her husband's job, she genuinely appears to have a challenging washing load.

In contrast, the late 1990s saw the likes of Procter & Gamble and Lever Brothers losing faith in their hair shampoo advertisements. Research told them that the models appeared to have impossibly shiny hair and this seemed unrealistic and unachievable for most consumers.

7. Integrate the brand name with the central idea

The Big Idea should be inextricably linked to the brand name and must only be remembered in association with the brand.

Budweiser's 'Wassup!' campaign was a huge success in the 1990s and the brand name became inextricably linked to the slang expression.

For several decades, Andrex have featured Labrador puppies in their advertisements. When consumers see a puppy of that breed, they automatically associate it with the Andrex brand.

8. Establish and/or develop a relationship with the consumer

Relationships are built on mutual understanding. The situations shown, the people depicted, the language and tone of voice used, all demonstrate the advertiser's understanding of, and sympathy with, the consumer's lifestyle and aspirations.

In 2001, AIB Bank launched their 'Your life, Anything is possible, Be with AIB' campaign. The series of advertisements focused on current and potential customers rather than on the bank. It also communicated that AIB is aware of what's going on in people's lives against the backdrop of a changed Ireland, an Ireland that has given many people new opportunities, wealth and possibilities (Moriarty, 2002).

The advertising should also induce a strong positive feeling towards the brand and, therefore, establish a preference for and confidence in the brand.

When the Irish food manufacturer, Green Isle, launched its Goodfellas range of pizzas in the 1990s, it used advertising very successfully to build the new brand. Ireland is not renowned for its pizzas but the Italian community in New York is. The Goodfellas advertisements centred on an Italian-American family making and eating fine pizza. By disguising its Irish origins and building strong brand values, consumers felt confident buying the brand, and Goodfellas quickly became a success story in food retail outlets.

9. Build brand personality

Each advertisement affects the consumer's perception of the brand. If any one advertisement conflicts with that perception, it will cause, at best, a neutral feeling, or, at worst, a negative feeling. Therefore, it is vital to ensure consistency since each advertisement helps to build or reinforce the desired brand personality.

The soft drink manufacturer, Tango, used advertising to good effect when they set about infusing the brand with personality. The zany 'You've been Tango'd' campaign changed the fortunes of the brand. While keeping the same packaging, pricing structure and distribution strategy, a radical change in their advertising yielded an impressive improvement in their sales.

10. Make it campaignable

A truly good central idea will be used in a number of advertisements, or even a series of campaigns. The Big Idea should be capable of development.

For many years, the Irish advertising agency, McConnells, has created advertising for the National Lottery. Their 'It could be you' series of advertisements has evolved into the 'It could be them/him/her' series.

Andrex and their Labrador puppies have retained their ability to capture the attention of the target audience.

Lager brands such as Carlsberg and Heineken are known for their Big Ideas which are developed and used in several advertisements.

Measuring advertising effectiveness

Marketing research can be conducted before, during and after an advertising campaign. At the very least, advertisers should carry out research after a campaign to see if the advertising objectives have been achieved.

Research prior to the launch of a campaign

When a significant amount of money is invested in an advertising campaign, it may be prudent to carry out research prior to its launch. Such research may be done at the creative stage in order to find out which creative idea is the best. A number of ideas might be presented to a focus group. According to Rogan (2003), focus groups 'usually consist of eight to ten people, together with a moderator, who meet for a group discussion about a particular subject'. In this case, the subject involves advertising, and the people chosen should be representative of the overall target audience. While the findings of focus group research can be insightful, care should be taken not to read too much into the results. Any research conducted at the creative stage is challenging for the members of the focus group. They are often invited to comment on **concepts**, i.e. rough ideas that do not yet exist in final form. While an idea for radio or print advertising is quite easy and relatively cheap to simulate, the same cannot be said of television or cinema advertising. Focus groups might be asked to base their judgements on storyboards. **Storyboards** are a one-dimensional technique used by advertising agencies to tell the story of an advertisement through the use of photographic, illustrative or computer-generated images. Many people find it difficult to imagine what these might look like as moving images. As a result, this might cause the focus group to reject a perfectly good idea.

Concepts
Rough ideas that do not yet exist in final form. Used to trigger discussion in focus groups.

Storyboards
One-dimensional technique used to tell the story of an ad through the use of photographic, illustrative or computer-generated images.

Test marketing
Transmission of an advertisement to a restricted audience.

Some advertisers use **test marketing** before fully implementing an advertising campaign. This involves producing an advertisement and transmitting it to a restricted audience. When using radio, newspapers and outdoor, this is a viable option. As explained in Chapter 7, there is a strong local radio and newspaper network in Ireland. This allows advertisers to expose target audiences to the advertisement in selective geographic areas only. Similarly, outdoor advertising sites can be booked on a selective basis. This activity is followed up with marketing research to ascertain whether or not it has achieved the advertising objectives. External environmental events and company-specific factors must be taken into account when analysing the results.

Research during an advertising campaign

Burnett and Moriarty (1998) identify three main types of research that can be carried out during an advertising campaign. These are coincidental surveys, attitude tests and tracking studies.

Coincidental surveys

This approach entails making random telephone calls to members of the target audience. It is most often done for advertising campaigns being transmitted on broadcast media. Each person is asked to divulge what stations or programmes they are watching or listening to. Their levels of spontaneous and assisted awareness, as well as their understanding of the advertisement, are researched. This type of research can prove very useful because it highlights problems at an early stage and prompts advertisers to switch to alternative channels or other media vehicles, or to make changes to the actual advertisement. In the case of radio advertising, the voice-over and the message can be changed quite easily. When interpreting the results of this type of research, it is important to measure awareness and understanding levels of the advertisement itself as opposed to relying on audience figures for particular channels and media vehicles. Remember, effective reach is a far more important figure than reach alone (see Chapter 7).

Attitude tests

The purpose of this type of research is to measure the strength of people's attitudes, either positive or negative, towards things like the advertisement itself, and the product, service, brand and/or organisation in question. There are a number of ways of doing this.

Rating scales

Rating scales are where respondents are invited to indicate their attitudes, feelings and views on a pre-determined scale.

The **Likert scale** is a widely used rating scale and offers a range of choices from, for example, 'strongly agree' right through to 'strongly disagree'.

This ad conveys a healthy image for Brand X (please circle one):

Strongly agree	Agree	Neither agree or disagree	Disagree	Strongly disagree

The **semantic differential** presents 'bipolar adjectives on a scale, and respondents are asked to indicate on the scale the point that reflects their view.' (Rogan, 2003) For example, a sample of an advertiser's target audience might be asked to indicate on the following scale their views about Brand X following an advertising campaign.

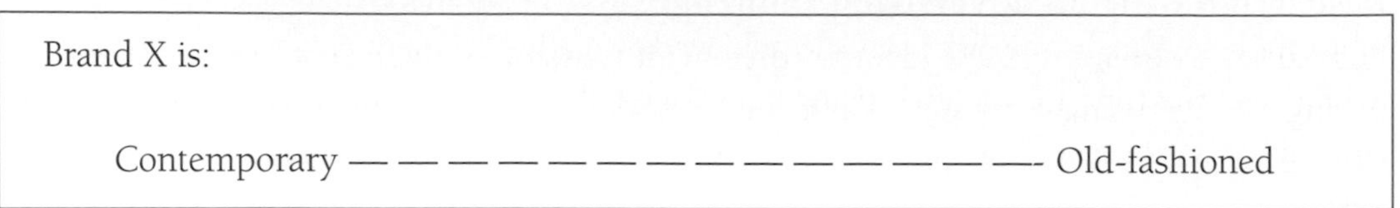
Brand X is:

Contemporary ——————————————————- Old-fashioned

Answers given can then be analysed and used to judge the effectiveness or otherwise of Brand X's advertising campaign.

The use of rating scales involves a highly structured approach to marketing research and does not afford the respondent much flexibility.

Open-ended questioning techniques/focus groups

Focus groups can be held to allow the respondent greater freedom of expression. This allows the advertiser to use open-ended questioning techniques to get inside the minds of its target audience. However, focus groups are time-consuming and expensive.

Tracking studies

Tracking studies are used to follow up the purchase activity or behavioural change in a specific consumer or group of consumers over a period of time. As illustrated in the 'Shame' case study (page 230), tracking studies were used to compare the target audience's behaviour before, during and after the campaign.

Research after a campaign

While it may be advisable to carry out research before and during an advertising campaign, it is essential to do it after a campaign. This facilitates learning and improvement and assists future decision-making. It also informs the advertiser whether or not the advertising was effective and represented a sound financial investment.

Recall tests are used to test the target audience's memory. **Spontaneous recall** is tested to see how many people can remember the advertisement without having to be prompted, whereas **prompted recall** provides clues to help people remember the advertisement in question. Obviously, high levels of spontaneous recall are better than prompted recall, but research must be conducted to find out whether respondents have favourable feelings towards the advertisement.

As illustrated in the 'Shame' case study, attitude change research was conducted to find out whether the advertising resulted in attitude changes. For this to be meaningful, attitudes must be measured prior to the commencement of the campaign.

Summary

Advertising is used by organisations for diverse purposes, from sales-oriented reasons to brand-building reasons. The creative brief is a written document that guides the creative team in the creation of effective advertising. Creative strategy details exactly how the objectives set out in the brief will be achieved. Creative strategy consists of the Big Idea which sets the tone for an advertising campaign. There are two main types of advertising appeals – emotional and rational – and they must be meaningful, believable and distinctive. The creative execution style is the way in which the big idea and the advertising appeals are presented to the target audience. When making an advertisement, great care and attention is given to the words, sounds, appearance and style. When evaluating advertising, it should be done objectively and ten criteria have been identified that can be used for this purpose. Marketing research should be conducted before during and after advertising campaigns to help measure effectiveness and to assist in a continuous learning process.

Useful websites

www.iapi.ie Institute of Advertising Practitioners in Ireland

Review questions

1. Explain in detail the reasons why organisations use advertising.
2. Using examples to illustrate your answer, identify five types of advertising.
3. Discuss why creativity is so important in advertising and state whether or not you think that great creativity leads to great advertising.
4. Describe a process that might help nurture advertising creativity.
5. Critically assess the various approaches used when coming up with the Big Idea.
6. Compare and contrast rational and emotional advertising appeals.
7. Using examples to illustrate your answer, describe the various creative execution styles typically used in advertising.
8. Discuss the role of marketing research in advertising.

Exercises

1. You are a brand manager for a new range of sportswear for football, running, tennis and general keep-fit enthusiasts in the 18–44 age group. It is being launched in Ireland in 12 months' time and is already successful in the United Kingdom, France and Germany. You know that you will be launching it with an advertising campaign and must now write a comprehensive creative brief for your Irish advertising agency.

2. Select a press advertisement, a television advertisement and, a radio advertisement and using Table 8.4 (page 222), evaluate whether or not you think they are good advertisements. In all cases, give reasons for your answer. What would you have done differently, if anything?

References

Armstrong, Gary and Kotler, Philip, *Marketing: An Introduction*, 6th edition (Pearson Education, Inc., 2003).

Belch, George E. and Belch, Michael A., *Advertising and Promotion: An Integrated Marketing Communications Perspective*, 4th edition (The McGraw-Hill Companies, Inc., 1998).

Brierley, Sean, *The Advertising Handbook* (Routledge, 1995).

Burnett, John and Moriarty, Sandra, *Introduction to Marketing Communications: An Integrated Approach*, (Prentice Hall Inc., 1998).

Davies, Jim, 'Optical delusions' (*Financial Times – Creative Business*, 10 February 2003).

Institute of Public Administration, *Marketing Communications* (Institute of Public Administration, 1997).

Moriarty, Brenda, 'Developing a Service Brand', Marketing Institute Seminar on Customer Care: The Ultimate Competitive Advantage (November, 2002).

Ogilvy, David, *Ogilvy on Advertising* (Prion Books Ltd, 1983).

Reeves, R., *Reality in Advertising* (New York: Alfred A. Knopf, 1961).

Ries, A. and Trout, J. *Positioning, The Battle for Your Mind* (McGraw-Hill, New York, 1981).

Robinson, Mark, *Channel 4/Sunday Times: 100 Greatest TV Ads* (Harper Collins, 2000).

Rogan, Donal, *Marketing: An Introduction for Irish Students*, 2nd edition (Gill & Macmillan, 2003).

The Oxford English Reference Dictionary, 2nd edition (Oxford University Press, 1996).

Wells, William, Burnett, John and Moriarty, Sandra, *Advertising: Principles and Practice*, 4th edition (Prentice Hall International Inc., 1998).

Young, J. W., *James Webb Young's Technique for Producing Ideas* (Lincoln, IL: NTC Publications, 1975).

Case study

'Shame' anti-drink-driving – an example of effective advertising

Road fatalities in Ireland are higher than the nearest European neighbour, Great Britain. Driver-alcohol is a major cause of road deaths. It is the second biggest killer on the roads after excessive speed.

Marketing background

Extensive five-year analysis of cross-border road statistics identified male car drivers as being over-represented in those responsible for alcohol-related fatalities. Male car drivers aged 17–24 were the most over-represented making them the primary target audience, followed by 25–34-year-old males.

Before the launch of 'Shame', attitudes towards drink-driving were measured revealing that less than a third of drivers agreed they could not drink any alcohol without their driving being affected. Among the primary target audience less than a fifth of drivers believed in a zero alcohol level when driving. Over a third of drivers and almost half of 17–24-year-old males agreed it was acceptable to drive after having two drinks.

The campaign needed to change attitudes to reduce the number of people being killed or seriously injured due to driver alcohol as every unit of alcohol has an impairing effect on driving. Independent qualitative research conducted in February 2000 explored why certain males persist in driving after drinking and what the most powerful deterrents might be. This research identified the need to dramatise the conscience of the driver and the 'Shame' of being responsible for a child's death resulting from an accident where only a small amount of alcohol was drunk.

Marketing strategy

The marketing strategy was to move drink-driving from a position of social stigma to one of personal 'Shame' – designed to work in tandem with the established 'brand' of 'Never ever drink and drive.' The end sequence line 'Never ever drink and drive – could you live with the shame?' was designed to evoke not just the shame of killing a child with all its consequences, but also the sequence of shame which is implicitly consequential to drinking and driving – arrest, imprisonment, loss of job, loss of licence, loss of dignity and personal humiliation.

Advertising objectives

1. To position drink-driving as shameful.
2. To improve attitudes among target male drivers by decreasing the acceptability of driving after consuming alcohol and increasing the number of safe drivers who believe they cannot consume any alcohol without affecting their driving.
3. To save lives.

Execution – creative strategy

The television advertisement 'Shame' opens on an innocent little boy playing in his garden. He kicks a football and scores into his football net and runs around like a professional punching the air. The ad then dissolves to an ordinary decent bloke

(ODB) in a suit, (23, attractive, carefree) as he throws his sports bag into his car. It then switches to the ODB at football training with his mates as he scores a goal and replicates exactly the triumphant action of the little boy. The ad then cuts to ODB having a pint after training. He is seen driving home, relaxed. He loses concentration, his car clips the kerb resulting in the car rolling over dramatically before crashing down over a hedge into a garden falling on the little boy who is crushed to death. The ad ends on the tragic scene and ODB standing shocked, stunned and shamed amid the tragedy. Voice-over and end titles reveal 'Never ever drink and drive – could you live with the shame?'

'Shame' as a concept and emotion spans every aspect of drink-driving. The end sequence line is delivered over the tragedy on-screen as a challenging, probing question but not in a didactic preachy tone of voice, which research indicated would alienate the target audience. Personal relevance is a vital component of the creative strategy. This is designed to be every man's story and every man's nightmare. 'Shall I tell you about my life?' – the opening lines from 'Man of the World' by Fleetwood Mac, musically drives home personal relevance, with ironic potency. The creative involves the audience in both the world of the victim and the world of the perpetrator, showing how these two worlds collide instantly because of the impairing effect of alcohol on driving.

Results

In January 2001, 'Shame' was the third highest spontaneously recalled advertisement in the Irish Marketing Journal Adwatch Top Ten after Guinness and Budweiser. At the same time, two months after the launch, 86 per cent of all drivers who drink and 85 per cent of the target audience of 17–24-year-old male drivers recalled seeing 'Shame' when prompted.

Attitude change

55 per cent (January 2001) of 17–24-year-old male drivers who drink agreed they could not drink any alcohol without their driving being affected, a 36 per cent improvement on baseline. Prior to the launch of the campaign 71 per cent of 17–24-year-old male drivers who drink felt they could drink one or more units of alcohol without affecting their driving. By January 2001, this had fallen to 45 per cent. Among 17–24-year-old male drivers who drink there was a 36 per cent decrease in the acceptability of driving after one drink (from 71 per cent in August 2000 to 35 per cent in January 2001). There was a 20 per cent decrease in the acceptability of driving after two drinks, from 45 per cent in August 2000 to 25 per cent in January 2001.

Prior to the launch of 'Shame', drink-driving was considered to be 'extremely shameful' by 69 per cent of 17–24-year-old male drivers, when compared to other shameful behaviour such as sexual abuse and drug-dealing. In the two months following the launch, the shamefulness of drink driving had increased with 78 per cent of the target audience believing it to be 'extremely shameful'.

Impact

When asked to what extent the campaign made them think about the dangers of driving after one or more drinks, a huge 80 per cent of drivers who drink felt the campaign made them think 'a lot' about the dangers and a further 16 per cent claimed it made them think 'a little' about the dangers. The campaign has impacted on 96 per cent of drivers who drink and 94 per cent of 17–24-year-old male drivers who drink by making them think about the dangers of driving after one or more units of alcohol.

Behaviour change

In the 12 months following the launch of 'Shame', there were 14 fewer deaths on the roads in the Republic of Ireland compared to the preceding 14 months. Robust figures for a period of five years are needed for real change to be measured.

Lifestyle change

The Irish Times on 13 September 2002 reported that the managing director of Heineken Ireland (Ireland's second largest brewer) said, 'a 20 per cent jump in off-licence sales of both Heineken and Coors Light in the half-year to June 30th resulted from a marketing drive by the company as well as "lifestyle changes" among drinkers. Growing awareness over the drink-driving issue meant many Irish drinkers now preferred to drink at home more often than before.'

Conclusions

The anti-drink-driving campaign, 'Shame', improved attitudes and contributed towards reduced road deaths. The campaign achieved 86 per cent awareness, a 36 per cent decline in the acceptability of driving after one drink, and an increased perception that drink driving is 'extremely shameful' among the target audience.

Source: The National Safety Council and The Institute of Advertising Practitioners in Ireland, *Advertising Effectiveness Cases 2002* (www.iapi.ie 2002)

9

PUBLIC RELATIONS

The aims and objectives of this chapter are:

- to explore the many facets of public relations, and in particular:
  - to define public relations and differentiate between marketing public relations and corporate public relations
  - to understand the reasons why organisations use public relations
  - to build media relations and write a press release
  - to differentiate between the many tools available to organisations when implementing public relations programmes
  - to understand the crucial aspects of crisis management
  - to prescribe methods of measuring the effectiveness of public relations.

Introduction

The term 'public relations' (PR) is recognised and widely used by many people. However, it is often misused and misunderstood. It is frequently confused with terms like press release, press relations and publicity, all of which will be explained in detail later in the chapter. Practitioners have seen their profession ridiculed in the media and parodied in popular comedy programmes, like the BBC's very successful *Absolutely Fabulous*. Consequently, a career in public relations is wrongly perceived as the perfect job for people who enjoy parties and meeting A-list celebrities. Another charge made against the profession is its unscrupulous manipulation of the media in order to secure the publication or broadcast of overly favourable stories about client companies.

The reality of PR and those who work in the industry is very different. This chapter demonstrates its worth as a sophisticated communications tool, which is used for a variety of reasons. PR professionals work long hours and are required to have excellent writing skills, superb organisational skills and highly tuned interpersonal skills which can be used in a number of very different situations.

According to Alan Dixon of Keating and Associates (2003), the PR industry in Ireland consists of approximately 140 companies. Only six employ between ten and 20 people and five of these are owned by international networks. Of the remaining companies in the industry, approximately 40 employ more than one person and less than ten, while the remaining are one-person outfits.

The true meaning of PR

Many definitions have been proposed for **public relations**. As highlighted by Harrison (2000), it means, quite simply 'relations with the public'. One of the most frequently used definitions is the one developed by the Institute of Public Relations in the UK (1999). It states that 'public relations is about reputation – the result of what you do, what you say and what others say about you. Public relations practice is the discipline, which looks after reputation – with the aim of earning understanding and support, and influencing opinion and behaviour. It is the planned and sustained effort to establish and maintain goodwill and mutual understanding between an organisation and its publics.' This definition captures the complexities and challenges posed by PR:

***Public relations (PR)** concerns a firm's relations with the public.*

- Its success is highly dependent on the actions and behaviour of all employees. Roger Haywood (1991) endorses this view and sees public relations as 'the projection of the personality of the organisation'. The personality of the organisation emanates from the employees and in many situations, the employees are the brand.
- Customers' word of mouth can sustain or undermine a firm's reputation. PR activity attempts to encourage customers to speak positively about the organisation.
- It is not an *ad hoc* activity but one that requires full-time attention and considered planning. Therefore it is a strategic tool.

Its target audience is wide and varied and may require several different approaches.

Product PR and corporate PR – what are they and how are they different?

It is important to go beyond the more traditional definitions of PR which tend to emphasise its importance at a corporate level. In practice it is also used in product and individual promotions. This is because the concept of IMC has become more important to firms. For example, when Sony launched Playstation 2 in November 2001, publicity was generated when various media ran news stories about the new product and this contributed to rapid product sales.

Product PR, also known as **marketing PR**, is defined by Harris (1993) as 'the process of planning, executing and evaluating programmes that encourage purchase and consumer satisfaction through credible communications of information and impressions that identify companies and their products with the needs, wants, concerns and interests of consumers'.

***Product PR** aims to encourage purchase and consumer satisfaction through credible communication of information and impressions.*

This endorses Cutlip *et al.*'s (1985) view that marketing PR is 'not only concerned with organisational success and failure but also with specific publics: customers, consumers and clients with whom exchange transactions take place'.

Corporate PR *seeks to identify, establish and maintain mutually beneficial relationships between an organisation and its publics.*

This definition contrasts sharply with their view of **corporate PR** which they define as 'a function of management seeking to identify, establish and maintain mutually beneficial relationships between an organisation and the various publics on whom its success and failure depend'. Pickton and Broderick's (2001) definition focuses on the broad nature of corporate PR. They see it as 'those parts of public relations not directly concerned with a marketing or brand focus but taking a broader corporate or whole business perspective'.

It should be stressed that even though marketing PR and corporate PR take different perspectives, one can influence the other's publics. Ryanair announced its massive expansion plans to the business community after the attacks on 11 September 2001 – this type of corporate PR can indirectly affect marketing activity as consumer confidence in the company grows and more people choose to fly with them.

Smith (1998) suggests that product PR is the responsibility of the marketing manager, while corporate PR tends to be the responsibility of the corporate communications director. The main differences between product and corporate PR are summarised in Table 9.1.

Table 9.1 Main differences between product and corporate PR

Product PR
- Actively encourages sales
- Focus on company products and brands
- Audience most likely to consist of customers, potential customers, distributors
- Responsibility of marketing manager

Corporate PR
- Not directly involved in brand promotion
- Broad business perspective
- Very varied audience
- Responsibility of corporate communications director

Publics

In the Institute of Public Relations' definition, the term 'publics' is used but not explained.

Publics in a PR context *Various target audiences that PR activity is aimed at.*

Kotler and Armstrong (2003) view a public as 'any group that has an actual or potential impact on a company's ability to achieve its objectives. An organisation's **publics in a PR context** can be described as the various target audiences that an organisation's communications activity is aimed at. Typically, an organisation might have to communicate with some or all of the publics in Figure 9.1.

Figure 9.1 Publics

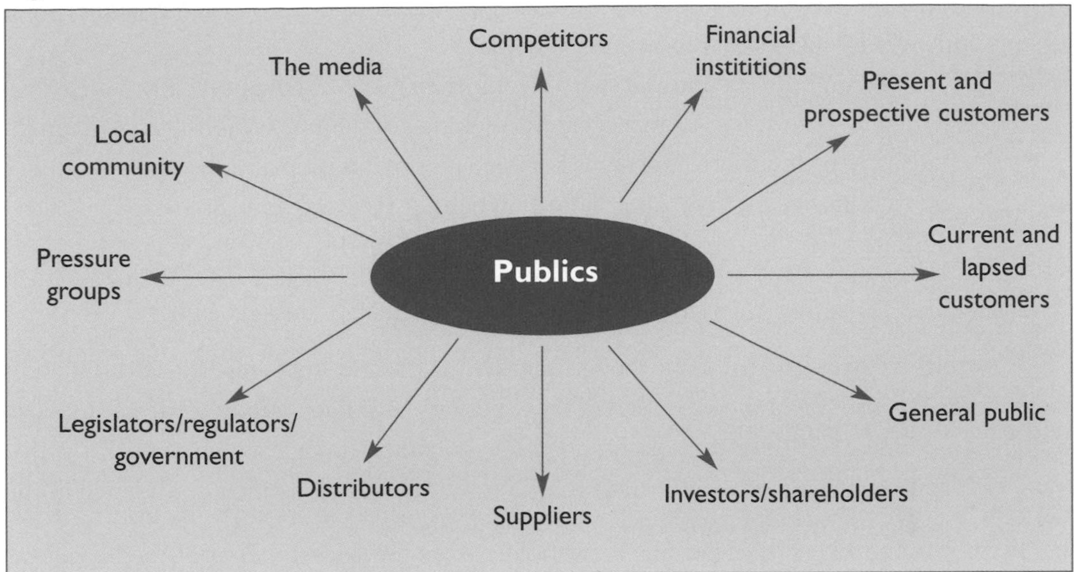

The importance attributed to each of an organisation's publics may vary, depending on the situation. For example, when a publicly quoted company publishes financial results, financial institutions, investors and shareholders, including staff, are usually the most important publics. When the same business launches a new product, employees, distributors, prospective and current customers, and competitors are the most important publics. Both examples highlight the fact that employees should be seen as a key audience for most PR activity. Unfortunately, many companies do not acknowledge this, which means that often employees are last to hear the news.

The role of PR

Kitchen and Papasolomou (1997) state that 'its real role extends to establishing understanding between an organisation and those publics that have either a potential or actual interest in it.' PR contributes positively to the achievement of non-marketing objectives, such as building and sustaining positive employee relations. The main aspects of the role of PR follows in detail – Table 9.2 provides a brief summary.

Table 9.2 The role of public relations

- Central in building an organisation's positive image
- Helps draw attention to new products and makes advertising campaigns more effective
- Counters bad publicity
- Motivates employees and attracts suitable employees

PR is central in building an organisation's positive image

A positive image is important for the growth and development of many organisations because it can help:

- persuade consumers to buy more of its products
- attract employees
- attract shareholders
- maintain good relations with local communities and local authorities.

PR is used to build an organisation's positive image. For example, the Body Shop has tended to use PR rather than advertising to communicate its mission and beliefs to its various publics. This approach is perhaps more credible for a firm that espouses environmental values because its communications appear as news as opposed to planned and paid-for advertising slots.

According to Harris (1993), PR can be used to position companies as leaders and experts in their field. For example, many of the economists working with leading Irish banks and stockbrokers have become household names. Broadcast and print media call on the likes of Dan McLaughlin to comment on significant economic events. This in turn raises the profile of their employers.

PR can draw attention to new products

PR can help draw attention to new products and make advertising campaigns more effective. When a business launches a new product, advertising may be central to the communications strategy. However, an advertising campaign can have more impact and achieve greater recognition if it is accompanied by extensive PR activity, such as radio interviews and newspaper articles.

PR can counter bad publicity

PR can help counter bad publicity. When the UK retail giant Tesco acquired the Irish retail group Quinnsworth, customers and suppliers were concerned that the supermarket chain would source most of its products in the UK. Through a combination of advertising and PR, Tesco reassured concerned parties that where possible, products would be sourced in Ireland.

PR can influence employee motivation and recruitment

Employee motivation and recruitment can be positively influenced by PR. Superquinn uses PR to instil a sense of pride in employees. Employees frequently hear, read or see news items relating to Superquinn's excellent customer service, which motivates them to live up to their reputation. Consequently, when it comes to recruitment, a positive image helps to attract those people most likely to be able to live up to such an image.

Building and maintaining relations with the media

Strong media relations are a vital ingredient in successful PR. Time spent building contacts with influential people working in broadcast and print media is a necessary investment. Without these, an organisation's news and stories will not be published and senior management will not be given media access. At the same time, the media depend on PR agencies and their clients for newsworthy items, so it is important that mutually beneficial relationships are nurtured.

Many businesses employ the services of a PR agency in order to exploit their network of long-established relationships with key contacts across the media.

Press releases

The **press release** is an essential tool used by PR agencies and their clients when dealing with the media. It is a typed document that presents details of the proposed news item. Photographic material regularly accompanies these documents. The inclusion of photographs tends to be more important when sending material to regional newspapers.

Press release *Typed document sent to the media containing details of a proposed news item.*

The problem is that journalists and editors receive so many press releases every day. Consequently, many agencies and their clients often prefer to arrange briefing meetings where they can talk to their media contacts about particular news items. Information given at such meetings can then be reinforced by the distribution of press releases.

How to build and maintain strong media relations

The following guidelines should be followed when working with the media if strong, productive relationships are to exist (see Table 9.3 on page 241 for a summary).

1. Provide real and accurate news

Always give your media contact real and accurate news so as to instil trust. Someone may think something is newsworthy, but each item should be critically assessed from the media's point of view. Will it appeal to their readers? Will it attract the attention of their listeners or viewers?

2. Carefully construct the press release

Careful attention must be given to the construction of press releases. Journalists and editors are very busy people and do not have time to read releases in their entirety. Adhering to the following guidelines makes their jobs a little easier and may increase the likelihood of press releases being published:

- Ensure that the most important information is at the beginning of the press release.
- Use wide margins where recipients can write notes.

- Use 1.5 line spacing.
- Highlight key messages by using bullet points.
- Choose an exciting font to attract interest but ensure that it is legible.
- Keep the press release no longer than two pages.
- Always include a contact name, phone number and e-mail address so that the recipient can follow up on the information in the release.

3. Distribute the press releases in each contact's preferred form

It is important to discover how the press contact likes to receive information – fax, e-mail, hard copy. Increasingly, their preference is for e-mail, but it is important to find out in advance whether or not they can accept attachments. If not, they should not be sent.

4. Personalise press releases for each media contact

Individual press releases should be written for each contact. A blanket or standard press release requires less work, but it lacks direct appeal for specific media vehicles. When sending a press release to a number of media contacts, the language, style, and content should be targeted for the target audience of each media vehicle. This might mean following the editorial style of each vehicle. For example, *The Irish Times* and *The Irish Star* convey their news in very different ways and the language used in press releases should reflect this. Some agencies and their clients offer exclusive stories to a particular media contact, on the basis that excellent coverage in one media vehicle is better than limited coverage in many. This tactic also helps establish strong media relations with both parties benefiting.

5. Respect the deadlines of media contacts

It is essential to know and understand the deadlines that drive media contacts. They do not want to receive telephone calls at stressful times. Also, if they have agreed to use a news item, they must have everything they need in plenty of time for their deadline. For example, the deadline for most Sunday newspapers is Friday evening.

6. Check the photographic style guidelines for each publication

When photographs are being used in the news item, it is necessary to find out in advance who is responsible for the photography. Some publications like to use their own photographers so as to ensure that the style of photography suits their newspaper or magazine. Others accept client-generated photographs. In this case, the client or its PR agency must clarify in advance whether or not there are any specifications, which must be adhered to, such as black-and-white or colour photography.

7. Understand the media contacts and the areas that interest them

Clients and their PR agencies must get to know their media contacts and understand the areas that interest them. If a contact has a particular interest in a subject, cause or issue, this should be known. A news item can be written from a particular angle that will grab their interest and increase the likelihood of the article being published. Gaining such information is usually done by engaging in social activities with the contact, such as lunch or dinner.

8. Complement the media contact's own resources

PR agencies and their clients should complement the media contact's own resources by providing access to information and key personnel when they need it, thus making their job easier.

Table 9.3 Building and maintaining strong media relations

- Distribute real and accurate news
- Invest time in the careful construction of the press release:
  - Place important information at the beginning
  - Use wide margins
  - Use 1.5 line spacing
  - Highlight key messages with bullet points
  - Keep to two pages or less
  - Include contact details in case of need for follow-up
- Distribute press releases in each media contact's preferred form
- Personalise press releases for each media contact
- Respect deadlines
- Check whether guidelines for photographic material exist
- Understand media contacts and the areas that interest them
- Complement media contact's own resources

The PR tool kit

One of the most widely used PR tools is the press release, as we have just seen. There are also many other methods available to companies when engaging in PR activity and these are identified and explained in this section. Deciding which one to use depends on an organisation's objectives, target audience, available budget and resources.

Publicity

Publicity is the 'non-personal communication about an organisation or its products that is transmitted through a mass medium in the form of news but is not paid for by the organisation' (Skinner, 1990). There are many reasons why organisations might decide to use publicity (Table 9.4):

Publicity
Non-personal, unpaid-for communication that is transmitted through a mass medium in the form of news.

Table 9.4 Reasons for using publicity

• To increase awareness of an existing product or brand • To launch a new product • To create, revitalise or change a company's corporate image • To circumvent legislation

- **to increase awareness**. Publicity can help increase awareness of an existing product or brand. Celebrities are often employed to generate publicity in such situations. In January 2002, it was announced that Catherine Zeta Jones would be the new face of Estée Lauder, replacing Liz Hurley. This news was covered in the media and drew attention to the Estée Lauder brand.
- **to launch a new product**. In an increasingly crowded advertising environment, publicity can be used to help launch a new product, and draw attention to advertising activity. In Ireland, many FMCG manufacturers draw attention to new products by funding quizzes on radio programmes like 2FM's *Big Breakfast* and the *Ian Dempsey Breakfast Show*.
- **to create, revitalise or change corporate image**. When organisations create, revitalise or change their corporate image, they often attempt to attract media attention. In its continuing efforts to change its fortunes, Marks & Spencer signed a clothing contract with David Beckham in February 2002. The intention is that news of this will give Marks & Spencer clothes more appeal with a younger, more fashion-conscious target audience.
- **to circumvent legislation**. Some organisations use publicity to circumvent legislation. This prevents them from using key elements of the marketing communications mix. As the communications options available to tobacco companies diminish, many are turning to publicity. However, this has come under increased scrutiny from EU legislators, and it is likely that the tobacco industry will not be able to use publicity in future.

Publicity is generated in a number of ways including press releases, press conferences, the staging of events, speeches, conferences, attendance at trade shows, and sponsorship. Sometimes publicity is unplanned, but it is much more advantageous to enjoy the fruits of carefully planned publicity and integrate it with other elements of the marketing communications mix.

Costs of publicity

Despite the fact that publicity is not directly paid for by the organisation, there are a number of associated costs which must be taken into account. These costs are financial and human:

- preparation time required to research and write press releases
- the hire of photographers and associated costs, such as the development and processing of film
- organisation of press conferences
- if the publicity is directly related to a particular event, the considerable costs involved in organising the event itself
- entertaining media contacts
- fees charged where an outside PR agency is employed
- administration costs, such as printing, couriers, faxes, phone etc.

Therefore, in order to assess the true cost of publicity, all of the associated costs must be taken into account.

The differences between publicity and advertising

There are a number of differences between publicity and advertising and these must be evaluated when deciding which one to use or indeed, whether they should be used together.

Publicity enjoys high levels of credibility

Often, publicity is perceived by the target audience as an independent evaluation of a company's product or an objective evaluation of a situation, which may have arisen in a business. Its presentation in the form of news builds credibility. However, the level of credibility enjoyed is usually directly related to the status of the media vehicle.

Meanwhile, advertising messages are considered biased, and determined and written by the company itself, thus seeming to give little consideration to target audiences' needs for balanced, objective information.

Publicity is seen as informative

Publicity is seen as informative, whereas many people consider advertising to be persuasive and manipulative.

Advertisers have full control over the format and content of their advertisements

One of the most appealing characteristics of advertising is that advertisers have full control over the format and content of their advertisements. This means that the media cannot alter them.

In contrast, companies cannot control publicity items and editors frequently alter or totally rewrite press releases. Even if publicity is achieved, it may not send out the desired message. Many restaurants rely on publicity since advertising is too expensive. However, this puts them at the mercy of food critics who write articles highlighting the good and the bad points of their experiences. Such articles create publicity for the restaurants in question but if it is negative the consequences can be far-reaching.

Advertisers can pay to guarantee transmission or print time and placements

When advertisers buy advertising time and space, they can decide when and where their advertisement will be broadcast or printed. With publicity, timing and positioning cannot be guaranteed. Even if assurances are given that a news item will appear on the front page of a newspaper, the occurrence of unpredictable, significant news events can displace previously planned items.

Publicity items are not usually repeated

Since publicity items are not usually repeated, it is very important that the desired message is communicated in that one presentation. In contrast, a firm can pay to have an advertisement repeated as often as it chooses.

Publicity time is usually free of charge

In many circumstances, publicity items are not paid for while advertising time can be very expensive. However, as illustrated earlier, this does not mean that publicity is without cost.

Speeches, interviews and presentations

Speeches, interviews and presentations are a very credible way for organisations to communicate their views to key publics. The reputation of the venue or occasion where speeches and presentations are delivered determines the likely levels of publicity that can be generated. The calibre of the people giving speeches can also attract publicity. For example, when Sir Anthony O'Reilly delivers a speech, the media watch with interest and may broadcast or print related stories before and after the event. Such activity is often accompanied by photo-calls.

When an employee from an organisation is planning to engage in an interview with one of its key publics, such as the media, shareholders, or employees, preparation is the key to success. In advance of the interview, an outside agent should put the interviewee through a rigorous 'mock' interview that tests their knowledge of the key facts and figures. Also, it is invaluable to put them through a questions-and-answers session so that they are fully prepared for any eventuality.

When media journalists want an interview, they might telephone and request a telephone interview there and then. Employees and senior managers should not engage in impromptu interviews because they do not give interviewees time to prepare. They should be rescheduled for a time that suits both parties. By refusing to give an interview under any circumstances, media relations might be damaged. When interviews are recorded for subsequent transmission on television or radio they are usually edited. Therefore, it is important that the interviewee keeps this in mind and ensures that the key messages are communicated at the beginning of the interview.

Corporate advertising

Corporate advertising aims to promote the organisation, as opposed to directly selling a particular product or brand. There are five main categories:

Corporate advertising *promotes the organisation rather than a specific product or service.*

Patronage advertisements

Patronage advertisements aim to convince people to buy from a particular company, without focusing on a specific product or service. Such advertisements are regularly used by large organisations offering a wide range of products or services.

Patronage ads *aim to convince people to buy from a particular company.*

Exhibit 9.1 shows how the insurance company, Allianz, uses patronage advertisements to build goodwill towards their organisation without highlighting individual services. This particular advertisement was published on 30 September 2002, the day after Europe won golf's prestigious Ryder Cup. It illustrates how Allianz integrate their sponsorship activity with their advertising.

Exhibit 9.1

Public information advertising

Public information advertising *When organisations need to deliver information to a large number of people.*

Public information advertising is used when organisations need to deliver information to a large number of people. When members of SIPTU in Aer Lingus went on strike in March 2001, Aer Lingus ran advertisements to inform ticket holders of cancelled flights.

Also in March 2001, the Department of the Marine and Natural Resources placed many advertisements advising the public on best practices in order to reduce the likelihood of foot-and-mouth disease breaking out in the Republic of Ireland.

Exhibit 9.3

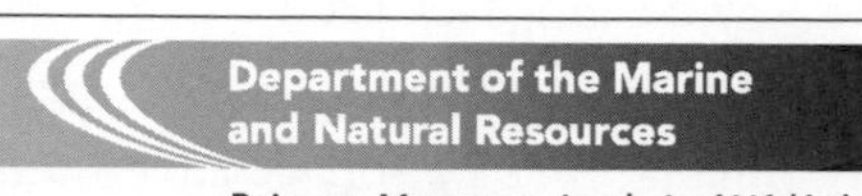

Roinn na Mara agus Acmhainní Nádúrtha

Guidelines in relation to Angling and Foot and Mouth Disease Controls

The following guidelines are based on the recommendations of the Expert Group in relation to FMD controls and have been prepared by the Department of the Marine and Natural Resources in consultation with the Department of Agriculture, Food and Rural Development, the Department of Tourism, Sport and Recreation and the Central and Regional Fisheries Boards. The guidelines are applicable to all persons involved in the angling sector including domestic and visiting anglers, fisheries boards, private fishery owners and tourism angling promoters.

The content and application of the guidelines will be kept under constant review particularly in the light of further recommendations of the Expert Group which is now faced with the reality that the FMD virus is present in Ireland.

Prohibitions

- Anglers should, until further notice, refrain from fishing where this involves entry onto land to which animals of susceptible species may have had access since 1 February 2001. Susceptible species are cattle, sheep, pigs, goats and deer.
- Eel fishing should not take place until further notice.
- All angling competitions should be postponed for the present due to the likelihood of attracting persons who are in the highest risk groups for the spread of the FMD virus.
- Fishing activity should not take place within any area declared by the Department of Agriculture, Food and Rural Development to be a restricted zone.

Where angling is permitted

Prior to undertaking fishing activities, the operators of angling facilities, including sea angling, should consult with their local regional fisheries board in relation to fishing access points and fishing protocols. Angling clubs and individual anglers should consult with their local regional fisheries board in relation to specific areas of intended fishing activity prior to commencing fishing. The Fisheries Boards will assist in designating suitable fishing areas where practicable.

Baits

Anglers who wish to use baits consisting of organic material e.g. maggots, larvae, worms, etc., should only use such baits where they can be sure that all the material has been sourced in the State and not from a restricted zone. Imported organic baits should not be used.

Tourist anglers

Anglers from the UK and other countries where FMD infection has been confirmed should be discouraged from travelling to Ireland especially those who may have had any contact with susceptible species.

Fisheries owners and managers

Fisheries owners and managers should ensure that access to their fisheries is confined to anglers who comply with these guidelines and any guidelines issued by the Department of Agriculture, Food and Rural Development.

Fisheries Boards

Fisheries Boards may resume stocking and transfer of fish where necessary subject to non-entry onto agricultural land and the use of disinfectant in accordance with Department of Agriculture, Food and Rural Development guidelines. Fisheries Board staff should continue to avoid unnecessary entry onto agricultural land. Where entry onto agricultural land is necessary they shall comply with the guidelines issued by the Department of Agriculture, Food and Rural Development.

Disinfection procedures

Operators of angling facilities should comply with the Department of Agriculture, Food and Rural Development guidelines regarding appropriate disease control notices and disinfection facilities. In addition, those in the highest risk groups (i.e. those involved in the agriculture and agribusiness sectors) along with people from restricted zones must follow the specific guidelines for these groups issued by the Department of Agriculture, Food and Rural Development.

These guidelines are subject to ongoing review and/or change.

For further information contact:

Press & Information Office: Tel:(+353-1) 6199507. Fax: (+353-1) 6766161. E-mail: Press_Office@marine.gov.ie

Latest information available on the WEB at: www.irlgov.ie/marine/pressrelease

Public information advertising is also used when a company needs to recall a product that has some sort of defect.

Public position advertising *Used to clarify a company's stance on an issue or problem.*

Public position advertising clarifies a company's stance on a certain issue or problem. In 1998, Tesco ran an advertisement that clearly stated its policy with regard to the use of Irish beef suppliers.

In 2000, Iarnrod Eireann launched a campaign to address growing concern about the lack of investment in the rail infrastructure. In the campaign, they acknowledged that they had a long way to go but that an investment programme was underway which would address many of the problems.

Exhibit 9.5

Exhibit 9.6

Public perception advertising

Public perception advertising is used to project a particular company image. Many organisations try to project a 'green' image and this is clearly illustrated in Exhibit 9.6.

Public perception advertising
Used to project a particular company image.

Public service or advocacy advertisements

Public service or advocacy advertisements are where organisations align themselves to particular social causes. Many organisations seized the opportunity to become involved in the Special Olympics World Games, which were staged in Ireland in 2003. Exhibit 9.7 illustrates how An Post used their association with the Special Olympics World Games.

Public service or advocacy ads
Organisations align themselves to particular social causes.

Exhibit 9.7

Lobbying

Legislative forces are very significant in shaping an organisation's environment. They are part of the macro environment and as such, they are outside the direct control of most organisations. However, rather than waiting for legislation to be passed and implemented, many organisations and industry representative bodies engage in lobbying which Pickton and Broderick (2001) describe as 'approaches to influence such bodies as the government and other persuasive groups to favour the interest of the lobbyist'.

As petrol and diesel prices increase, the Automobile Association (AA) and haulage industry representatives have been lobbying the Government to reduce duties on fuel. Meanwhile, environmental lobbyists are seeking higher taxes and duties on fuel, in order to encourage greater use of public transport.

Since the 1990s, progressively restrictive legislation regarding smoking in public places has been introduced by successive governments. Lobbyists working on behalf of the tobacco and publican industries have been lobbying in an effort to soften the legislation. However, anti-smoking pressure groups have been lobbying for even greater restrictions on the tobacco industry.

Lobbying is not only used to influence government representatives. Consider the following issue that did not involve the Government. Thousands of sports fans in Ireland resorted to lobbying when the cable television service provider, NTL dropped the Eurosport channel from its cable package in 2002. Websites were set up so that irate fans could register their dissatisfaction and media vehicles were used as platforms from which these fans could voice their opinion.

Paul Allen, Managing Director of Paul Allen & Associates, dismisses the legitimacy of what he calls 'three main myths about the lobbying process' (*Marketing*, March 2002):

- **Public representatives are important influencers in the legislative process**. Politicians vote on the party line almost every time, which means that they carry very little influence on their own.

- **Politicians are the focus of lobbying activities**. Senior and middle-ranking civil servants in government departments are usually more useful to lobbyists than politicians. Allen argues that effective lobbyists build relationships with the civil servants responsible for drafting policy and laws. He points out that once an issue goes to the Dail, it is too late to exert any influence.

- **Money buys influence**. The days of the 'brown envelope' are well and truly gone, due to the immense media exposure given to the practice.

Allen advocates that effective lobbyists use discretion and avoid publicity in many cases. They engage in behind-the-scenes activity and employ the appropriate tactics for each particular situation as opposed to the same tactics every time.

Voluntary donations

Many organisations make voluntary donations to local communities, charities and sports clubs. Such donations differ from sponsorship (which is dealt with in Chapter 11) because they are given without putting any obligation on the beneficiary. However, to capitalise on these donations, companies often attempt to generate some publicity.

Company newsletters and magazines

In large organisations where employees are based in different locations, newsletters are a good way of communicating relevant news and information. Traditionally, they were printed documents but, increasingly, companies are using intranets to publish newsletters. Intranets are an in-company version of the Internet that enable staff to communicate electronically with each other.

Newsletters are also used to communicate with other publics such as customers, shareholders and distributors. Many newsletters aimed at consumer markets print lifestyle-oriented articles on health, diet and holidays. It is intended that this approach will be seen as less 'hard sell' because many of the articles indirectly promote company products and services rather than using direct selling techniques. Competitions are also a common staple in such newsletters. The banks and utilities avail of regular communications through bills and statements to send out their newsletters. Tesco incorporates vouchers into its quarterly magazine.

Site visits

Offering key publics the opportunity to visit company sites is a very powerful way of communicating. Many multinational corporations locating in Ireland recognise the need to promote good relations with local communities. One way of doing this is to open their doors to site visits, so that people will gain a greater insight into the company's operations.

Well-known Irish companies such as Waterford Crystal, Jerpoint Glass and Louis Mulcahy (pottery) use visits as a way of promoting their products to national and international tourists. They allow visitors to witness the products being made and this often motivates the visitors to purchase something before leaving.

Product placement

As organisations worry about a growing level of cynicism towards advertising, they are seeking more subtle ways of promoting their products. Many are turning to product placement. The objective is to ensure that an organisation's product is seen or mentioned on broadcast media or in print media. Examples can be seen all around us. Carrie Bradshaw, the main character in the TV comedy, *Sex and the City*, uses her Apple laptop in every episode. Celebrities are often photographed wearing leading clothing brands. Each year, the Oscar ceremony is used by leading fashion houses to promote their latest designs.

Actors enthusiastically agree to wear these outfits. Publicity for both the designer and the actor can be considerable. Liz Hurley's career took off when she was seen wearing what is famously referred to as 'that dress', designed by Versace.

Tobacco companies are looking closely at this area because legislation has severely curtailed their ability to promote their products. Cigarettes and cigars are smoked by leading actors in mainstream movies and TV series in a drive to make smoking cool again and to circumvent stringent marketing communications legislation.

Competitions

Competitions are usually categorised as a sales promotions tool. However, they are also part of the PR tool kit. In Ireland, radio is frequently used for this purpose. Radio offers organisations the opportunity to be part of a successful programme, without having to advertise. Since deregulation, the number of radio stations has increased considerably and audiences are well segmented. The *Ian Dempsey Breakfast Show* on Today FM is a mix of music, comedy sketches and competitions. Companies pay thousands of euros to have their products featured as the prize in the competition. These companies also provide attractive prizes such as holidays, cash or cars in order to have their name and product mentioned. In return, they are guaranteed a large, relevant audience and they become part of that audience's entertainment. When the prizes are unusual or very valuable, the company is often able to generate additional publicity in the media.

Crisis management

'A crisis is a dramatic change, usually for the worse, which may arise as a result of an accident, through someone's negligence or because of criminal behaviour, such as product tampering or sabotage. Crises, disasters, scandals and emergencies are the very essence of hard news and always receive extensive coverage in the media' (Harrison, 2000). Therefore a crisis presents major challenges for the organisation in question. The way it deals with the crisis may prove vital for recovery and survival. According to Fill (2002), crises are emerging with greater frequency due to the proliferation in the number and influence of consumer groups, the advent of instantaneous communications, the pace of the advancement of technology, which contributes to errors, and extreme climatic changes, which are leading to an increase in natural disasters.

Dramatic change is difficult to predict but this should not prevent companies from planning for even the most unlikely eventuality. Even though some crises are outside an organisation's control, many are not and can be planned for. According to Tracey Stafford, Drury Communications (2002), companies must put in place a crisis management plan that can be implemented should the need arise. To do this, management must identify possible, often unlikely, scenarios that could occur and then plan accordingly. Figure 9.2 identifies the main principles of crisis PR. As well as scenario-building during the preparation stage, companies should rehearse the plan in order to test it.

A crisis is very interesting to journalists. This means that they usually want information before the full extent of the crisis is known. It is important that they are given some information so that they do not begin to talk to unauthorised sources. It is widely acknowledged that, in February 2002, AIB handled the early stages of a major crisis very well. Michael Buckley, Chief Executive, was available to the media when the news of a $691 million (€789 million) fraud at their US subsidiary hit the headlines. One dealer, John Rusnak, achieved fame overnight and remained at the centre of the crisis. In the days that

Figure 9.2 Crisis management

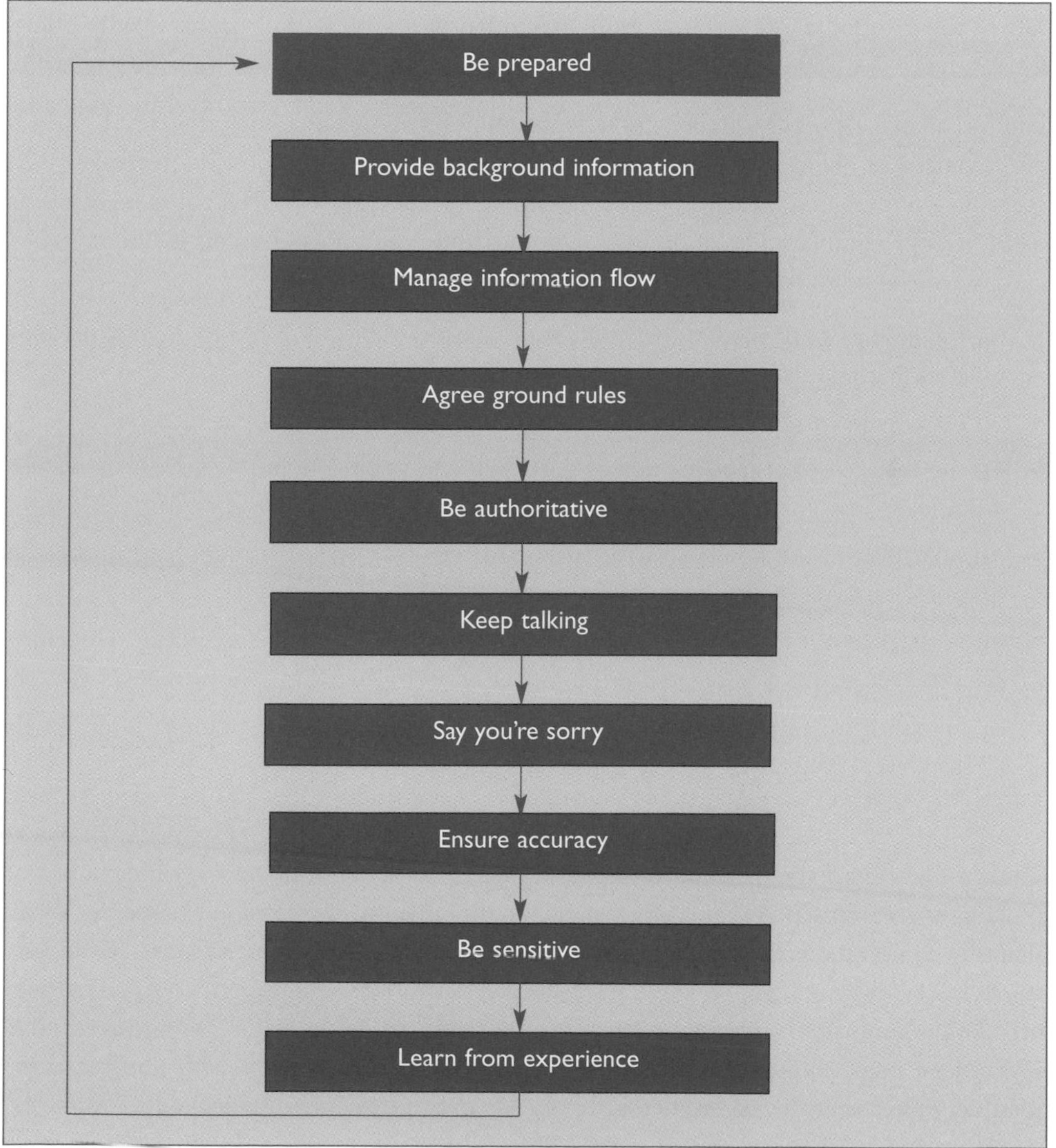

Source: Harris (2000)

followed the initial shock, senior executives and board members continued to talk to the media. A few weeks after the news had broken, *The Irish Times* (23 February 2002) carried a headline 'AIB undertakes charm offensive to assuage nervous investors.' This 'charm offensive' required the bank to keep talking to the media and another key public, their major shareholders. While they continued to answer questions about the crisis, they also tried to counter the bad news with positive news about their financial performance in Ireland.

Once the initial intensity of a crisis has calmed down, organisations must resolve any problems that still remain and learn from the whole experience. This may involve investigations, and these can sometimes result in court cases and possible imprisonment.

Measuring the effectiveness of PR

Like so many elements of the marketing communications mix, the true level of PR's effectiveness is difficult to measure. Traditionally, practitioners have primarily used quantitative measures, which involves measuring media exposure. The company itself or its PR agency compiles a book of press clippings and monitors all broadcast coverage and carries out the following evaluation:

- in the case of print media, the number of column inches devoted to a company and related matters
- in the case of broadcast media, the number of times the company is mentioned
- in the case of visual media, such as television and print, the number of times images associated with the organisation appeared
- the position of the news – was it front-page news or was it buried deep inside the publication? Was it headline news?
- the existence of positive and/or negative reportage
- the extent of articles
- the quality of the media vehicle in which the news appeared and whether or not it was capable of reaching the desired public or publics
- the costs that would have been incurred if the company had bought the space.

The problem with the quantitative approach is that it only addresses quantity and not quality. Just because an organisation is given widespread media coverage, does not mean that the target audience has been affected or that the campaign objectives have been achieved. Leading practitioners in the UK are addressing this issue and advocate the use of qualitative evaluation techniques that can be used in conjunction with quantitative techniques. According to Cowlett (2000), qualitative techniques not only monitor how many people are receiving PR messages, but they also assess the quality of the messages, and people's attitudes. Favourability ratings and opinion research are at the heart of this evaluation. The downside for companies is that this type of research is costly, but the question should not be whether they can afford to do it, but whether they can afford not to do it.

Summary

PR is a very complex element of the marketing communications mix. It is used to communicate with diverse audiences. These audiences may be internal and external. A key success factor in PR is media relations and the way in which an organisation relates to key media figures. The press release is used by organisations to get their point across to journalists. The PR tool kit is very diverse and includes publicity, speeches, interviews and presentations, corporate advertising, lobbying, voluntary donations, company newsletters and magazines, site visits, product placements and competitions.

While publicity is often viewed as free, there are many financial and human resource costs associated with it.

Crises occur more regularly in today's turbulent business environment and PR is an increasingly important tool when dealing with crises.

Like many elements of the marketing communications mix, the effectiveness of PR is difficult to measure, but industry professionals are developing ways of addressing this difficulty.

Useful organisations

Public Relations Institute of Ireland (PRII) www.prii.ie
Public Relations Consultants Association (PRCA)

Review questions

1. Compare and contrast the terms 'corporate PR' and 'marketing PR'.
2. Explain the role of PR and use examples to illustrate your answer.
3. Prescribe how good media relations might be nurtured by an organisation or its PR agency.
4. Identify and explain the key PR tools available to organisations.
5. Set out the key principles of crisis management.
6. Critically assess the methods used to measure the effectiveness of a PR campaign.

Exercises

1. Select an organisation of your choice with a particular piece of news. Identify three media vehicles which you think should cover their story and write three press releases for three media contacts.

2. There have been a number of high-profile crises in recent years. Select one and critically assess how the company dealt with the crisis. Do you think they dealt with it well? If not, how would you have handled it if you had been their advisor?

References

Armstrong, Gary and Kotler, Philip, *Marketing – An Introduction* (Pearson Education, 2003).

Blythe, J., *Marketing Communications* (Financial Times/Prentice Hall, 2000).

Cowlett, Mary, 'How to measure the effectiveness of PR' (*Marketing*, pp. 37–38, 14 December 2000).

Cutlip, S., Center, A. H. and Broom, G. J., *Effective Public Relations* (Englewood Cliffs, NJ: Prentice Hall, 1985).

Fill, Chris, *Marketing Communications: Contexts, Strategies and Applications*, 3rd edition (Pearson Education Limited, 2002).

Harris, T., *The Marketer's Guide to PR: How Today's Companies Are Using the New Public Relations to Gain a Competitive Edge* (Wiley, 1993).

Harrison, Shirley, *Public Relations: An Introduction*, 2nd edition (Thomson Learning, 2000).

Haywood, R., *All about Public Relations*, 2nd edition (McGraw-Hill, 1991).

Institute of Public Relations Handbook (Institute of Public Relations, 1999).

Kitchen, P. J. and Papasolomov, I., 'Marketing public relations: conceptual legitimacy or window dressing?' (*Marketing Intelligence and Planning*, Vol. 15, No. 2, pp. 71–84, 1997).

Pickton, D. and Broderick, A., *Integrated Marketing Communications* (Financial Times/ Prentice Hall, 2001).

Skinner, Steven J., *Marketing* (Houghton Mifflin, 1990).

Case study

Supermac's public affairs campaign against fraudulent/exaggerated claims

BACKGROUND

Public liability insurance costs have rocketed for Supermac's restaurants in the past few years as the result of fraudulent claimants targeting fast-food restaurants to make a quick buck. Individual Supermac's restaurants have experienced increases in premiums of 300 per cent against costs in 2001, despite having very low levels of claims against them.

Supermac's found the toilets in many of their branches to be the most regularly used location for such set-up incidents to be orchestrated. In an attempt to combat a trend that seemed to be reaching epidemic proportions, Supermac's installed a hidden camera above the wash hand basins in a Galway branch (it should be stressed that neither the urinals nor cubicles were visible from the camera, and personal privacy was not invaded). Signs were placed alerting customers to the presence of cameras in the restaurant.

The camera caught an incident where three young men entered the toilets, splashed water on the floor, practised a few skids and then one ultimately feigned a fall. A claim was subsequently filed against Supermac's in Galway by this young man, with the claimant pursuing a maximum award of €38,000 in the Circuit Court for the alleged neck and head injuries caused by the fall. The claimant discovered that Supermac's had this footage and withdrew his case, but only hours before it was due to be heard in court (the solicitors still received their fees, also a common occurrence when cases are settled on the steps of the court). Incensed, Supermac's had hoped to pursue the false claimant, but were advised by the Gardai that this was only possible if the claimant had perjured himself in court.

Supermac's are not alone with the problem of fraudulent/exaggerating claimants and escalating insurance costs. Irish business is being burdened increasingly by the propensity of certain individuals to make money from personal injury claims. Small and medium-sized businesses seem to be suffering the brunt of these costs, with ISME reporting at least one member, a manufacturing business employing over 100, which was considering closing its doors due to untenable insurance costs. It is very difficult to quantify exactly how much these claims, both real and bogus, cost the economy every year. In 2001 the Irish Business and Employers' Association (IBEC) companies reported that, on average, personal injury claims cost each firm €48,797. In 2000, the cost of personal injuries to the Irish public and private bodies was over €1.5 billion, and IBEC anticipates this figure will have increased by 40 per cent in 2001 and will increase a further 50 per cent in 2002. Legal costs account for between 40–44 per cent of these figures, and it is a widely held belief that certain elements of the legal profession, known as ambulance chasers, drive up the cost of claims, both in the percentage of awards they can claim and the fees they charge.

Insurance companies often do not defend cases vigorously enough. This can be accounted for by lack of investigative resources, but a settlement is sometimes seen as a cheaper option than the legal route. The perceived 'loss' situation, where the loser must cover both parties' legal costs, is seen as too risky and it is believed to be easier and less costly to settle for a lesser sum outside the legal system.

Supermac's currently have 111 public liability claims outstanding against their 46 restaurants and this level of claims would not be seen as unusual in the restaurant sector. In Supermac's experience, a significant proportion of these (up to 50 per cent) are believed to be exaggerated, with a further 25 per cent estimated to be fraudulent. Upon checking with Insurance Link, the database service of the insurance industry, Supermac's was able to tell that 40 per cent of these claimants had made at least one prior personal injury claim, if not multiple claims, in the last five years. It must be stressed that Supermac's absolutely and categorically recognise the right of genuine victims to pursue compensation if they have been injured or disabled in an incident outside of their control. However, the trend of feigned personal injuries and ensuing claims, especially in the quick-service restaurant area, has been alarming.

THE BRIEF

Supermac's were angry at the inequity of the system and that they were unable to pursue a criminal, through the courts or via the Gardai, despite the criminal's attempt to defraud the company for a substantial sum of money (plus the potential legal costs involved). It was important to stem the flow of scam artists making bogus claims against Supermac's restaurants. Supermac's needed to be positioned as an establishment that fought back and were intolerant of this type of trickery and fraud. It had to be understood by these criminals that they would no longer be allowed to behave in this manner unchecked. On a national level, the government had to be made aware that this issue will ultimately cost jobs, and claims are bleeding Irish business dry as opposed to this being a 'victimless' crime.

Key challenges:

- to prevent the perpetration of fraudulent claims in Supermac's restaurants.
- to bring fraudulent and exaggerated personal injury claims to the attention of the judiciary, the government and the Gardai as the criminal activity it is, and seek their immediate and concerted action on this
- to change the public's perception of these crimes – that this is not a victimless crime, but instead is hugely costly to business and the economy.

Objectives:

- to prevent Supermac's restaurants being targeted by personal injury fraudsters on the make
- to re-open the Galway case, and have the perpetrators pursued as criminals while also making an example of them in the press
- to encourage the Fraud Squad to consider false personal injury claims as fraud, whether perjured in court or not, and pursue them as a criminal act
- to place this as an important employment issue on the political agenda – jobs will be lost if the cost of insurance continues to rise
- to provide a platform for employer and business groups to unite and argue their case.

Strategy

After devising a media strategy to raise awareness of the blatant nature of these frauds against Irish business, it was decided that Supermac's would need third-party endorsement to show this is a wide-ranging problem and not unique to the fast-food industry. Meetings were scheduled with IBEC, the Irish Small and Medium Enterprises (ISME), the Chambers of Commerce Ireland (CCI), the Small Firms' Association (SFA) and the Vintners' Federation of Ireland (VFI). Supermac's received the endorsement and support of each organisation, and a commitment to support the media strategy. Other groups and businesses including CIE, Dublin Corporation, the new claims section of the NIMA and the Irish Insurance Federation (IIF) were all also briefed and supported the press conference with their attendance.

Charles Flanagan TD (Fine Gael) and Pat Rabbitte TD (Labour) were briefed in their capacity as members of the Joint Oireachtas Committee on Enterprise and Small Business. The rest of the Committee was subsequently briefed on the campaign and a presentation invited. Noel Treacy TD (Fianna Fail), Minister of State at the Department of Education and Science and at the Department of Enterprise, Trade and Employment (with responsibility for Science and Technology), was also informed of the campaign, and offered his support.

Supt. Willie Magee, head of the Fraud Squad, also met with Supermac's to discuss the pursuit of fraudulent claimants, and immediately arranged for the Galway case to be re-opened and the claimant to be re-questioned. Supermac's wanted to present the video footage of the set-up accident to the media, and scheduled a press conference to do this. Along with the footage of the false claimant and his two accomplices feigning the accident, a further video was shown. The second video was of a drunken reveller attempting to slide down the banister of a Supermac's restaurant staircase, falling between the two flights and landing 15 feet below. He was then seen getting up and walking away. Two days later he came into the store threatening to claim for a broken leg which he claimed he received during a fall on the restaurant's stairs. He did not pursue the claim once he learned of the video footage which clearly documented his own recklessness in attempting to slide down the banister in such a drunken state.

Attendance at the press conference was very high. It included RTE radio and television news, Primetime (RTE, TV3 news, *The Irish Times*, the *Irish Independent*, the *Irish Examiner*, the *Star*, the *Mirror*, Irishhealth.com, *Health and Safety Times*, FM104, 98FM and LiteFM.

Results

News and editorial coverage of the press conference was phenomenal, and spanned over six days, both before and after the press conference. More importantly, it fostered debate on the subject for weeks afterwards. TV3 followed up the story three weeks later and *The Irish Times* worked on a follow-up. The story dominated the national news on the day of the conference: RTE Radio News at 1, RTE1 SixOne News, RTE1 Nine O'Clock News, Network 2 News2, 11pm, TV3 News at 5.30 p.m., 6.30 p.m. and 11 p.m. RTE's Primetime did a 24-minute feature on the topic and held a debate between a member on the medical profession and a director of the Law Society. Coverage was also in the *Evening Herald*, the *Sun*, *Business and Finance*, the *Sunday Business Post* and the *Sunday Tribune*. There was also huge regional interest including interviews with Pat McDonagh for Cork 96FM, FM103/County Sound, WLR FM, the *Limerick Leader* and *Kerry's Eye*. The *Irish Mirror* also followed the investigation further by checking the court records of the day and tracking down the claimant and interviewing him. He claimed to be 'very sorry' and blamed his folly on his youth at the time (he was 16 then, and is now 21).

Supermac's called for people who perpetrate fraudulent and exaggerated claims for personal injury to be pursued as criminals. Supermac's own case in Galway was immediately re-opened and the false claimant re-questioned.

Six solicitors representing clients involved in claims against Supermac's checked with legal counsel for Supermac's to see if video evidence was available of their client's alleged incident.

It is too early to quantify a reduction in fraudulent claims against Supermac's restaurants, but it seems the perception of Supermac's restaurants as somewhere to make a quick buck with a fraudulent claim has changed dramatically. The *Mirror*'s 'outing' of the perpetrator added to the feeling of humiliation that a criminal could suffer if found out.

Pat McDonagh, Chief Executive of Supermac's, has been approached by numerous other businesses in a similar situation, keen to campaign further on the issue. These businesses have included other fast-food chains, a supermarket chain, a department store chain, and a petrol station chain to name a few. An alliance has formed to continue lobbying on the issue, and Supermac's are no longer campaigning on their own.

The resultant publicity from the case raised the profile of the issue in the media and on the political agenda. Discussion on the topic reached many of the local and regional newspapers and radio talkshows. Questions were raised about the legal costs involved in each case and the irresponsibility of insurance companies settling claims too easily.

The political parties have enthusiastically adopted this issue in their party policy. Every political party has included something on this topic in their election manifesto.

The business groups involved, IBEC, ISME, the SFA and the VFI all agreed to make this a central plank of their work coming up to the 2002 election. The

Supermac's campaign breathed new life into a topic which had grown tiered for them.

The Personal Injury Assessment Board, after languishing for close to four years, is now firmly back on the political agenda and demands have been made for its establishment immediately and for the inclusion of public liability claims in its remit. Minister Treacy's office promised that the Board would be operational before the election.

BUDGET

The campaign cost less than €10,000.

This case study, by Supermac's Family Restaurants and Fleishman-Hillard Saunders, was entered in the PRII Awards, 2001/2 and was published on www.prii.ie.

10

SPONSORSHIP

The aims and objectives of this chapter are:

- to examine key aspects of sponsorship, and in particular:
    - to explain what is meant by sponsorship
    - to give reasons for its growth
    - to set objectives that can be achieved through sponsorship
    - to identify different forms of sponsorship
    - to appreciate the possible risks associated with sponsorship activity
    - to select the most appropriate sponsorship activity in order to achieve a given set of objectives
    - to prescribe ways of measuring the effectiveness of sponsorship activity
    - to appreciate sponsorship's fit with other tools in the marketing communications mix.

Introduction

'Commercial sponsorship is an investment, in cash or in kind, in an activity, in return for access to the exploitable commercial potential associated with that activity' (Meenaghan, 1991). The thrust of this definition is endorsed by the Incorporated Society of British Advertisers (ISBA, 1993). It defines sponsorship as the 'payment of a fee by a company in return for the right to a public association with an activity, item or person, where the purpose is the achievement of a commercial objective'. Some key points emerge from these two definitions. Since sponsorship involves, in many instances, the investment of significant sums of money, a return on this investment is expected. Therefore, before committing to sponsorship activity, an organisation must identify clearly and in quantifiable terms, exactly what it wants to achieve. The other point made about sponsorship is that there are many options available to organisations interested in investing in the activity. These will be examined later in the chapter. Sponsorship is attractive to organisations committed to IMC. This chapter shows how it has the potential to fit with an organisation's advertising, public relations, sales promotions, personal selling and direct marketing activities.

Industry overview

In 2003, Amárach Consulting published a report about the outlook for sponsorship in Ireland. Their findings revealed that the sector is very buoyant. In 2002 investment in sponsorship worldwide was €27.26 billion. North American organisations accounted for almost 40 per cent of this total, investing €10.78 in sponsorship in 2002, while European companies allocated €7.93 billion. It is interesting to note that, despite a downturn in the world economy, expenditure on sponsorship is projected to increase in 2003 (as shown later in the chapter, this may be at the expense of other elements of the marketing communications mix, in particular advertising). The level of spend on sponsorship in Ireland in 2002 was just under €60 million and this is projected to increase by 5 per cent in 2003. Amárach point out that buoyant spend in Ireland in 2002 was due, in part, to the World Cup and new activities such as Nissan's sponsorship of the Irish Open Golf event, the Bank of Ireland's renewal of its GAA football sponsorship, and BUPA Ireland's sponsorship of Ireland's first ever outdoor ice rink at Smithfield Plaza.

Table 10.1 Overview of sponsorship expenditure worldwide

	2002 (€)	2003 (€, projected)	Increase (%)
Ireland	59.85 million	63 million	5
European companies	7.93 billion	8.27 billion	4.2
North American companies	10.78 billion	11.75 billion	8.9
Worldwide	27.26 billion	29.27 billion	7.4

Source: Amárach Consulting, 2003

Amárach conducted qualitative research among 12 Irish sponsorship decision-makers to find out what they considered examples of best practice in 2002. The top sponsorships mentioned in order of frequency are shown in Table 10.2. It is interesting to note that five of the sponsorships identified were alcohol brand sponsors.

With figures of the magnitude shown in Table 10.1, it is easy to understand why there has been a move away from *ad hoc*, unplanned sponsorship towards a more considered strategic approach. It is not so long ago that a large proportion of senior executives made sponsorship expenditure decisions on the basis of personal interests and requests from friends. This approach is unsustainable in an environment that demands that all expenditure can be justified on economic grounds. Sponsorship programmes should only be undertaken if it is going to benefit the company investing in the activity, as well as the recipient of the investment.

Table 10.2 Top sponsorships mentioned by decision-makers

Rank	Sponsorship of 2002
1	Guinness and GAA All-Ireland Hurling Championships
2	Heineken European Rugby Cup
3	Bank of Ireland and GAA All-Ireland Football Championships
Others	Carlsberg and FAI Irish Team
	Guinness and Cork Jazz Festival
	AmEx World Golf Championships in Kilkenny
	Murphy's Irish Open
	Vodafone and Radio Traffic Reports

Source: Amárach Consulting, 2003

Reasons behind sponsorship's growing popularity

Research on the growing levels of sponsorship expenditure highlighted above has shown that these levels are set to increase. There are a number of reasons for this. These are summarised in Table 10.3.

Table 10.3 Reasons for growing interest in sponsorship

- Increasing levels of clutter in the advertising environment
- Rising cost of production and media for advertisers
- Huge range of sponsorship options to choose from
- Widespread media coverage of many activities
- Globalisation and the need to reach out to target audiences across the world
- Legislative restrictions in some industries
- Technological developments which make it easy for target audiences to avoid advertising
- Continued fragmentation of consumer markets
- Ability of sponsorship to appeal to a range of audiences

Clutter

The level of clutter in advertising is on the rise, and this makes it increasingly difficult for advertisements to be noticed. This has prompted advertisers to seek alternative ways of getting noticed. Sponsorship often delivers a captive audience to the sponsor. For example, if someone attends a golf tournament, the sponsor has many opportunities to deliver its messages.

Rising production and media costs in advertising

The production and media costs associated with advertising are increasing at a time when advertisers are looking for better value for their money. Sponsorship enables companies to target their messages more effectively, thereby reducing wasteful expenditure.

Range of sponsorship options

The number and types of sponsorship opportunities are increasing all the time. The prevalence of sporting, arts and leisure activities is well known, but other developments have presented new opportunities. Even during the prosperity of the Celtic Tiger era, and especially since its demise, the Irish Government is shifting responsibility onto private industry to assist in the provision of public services such as better roads, schools, third-level institutions, hospitals, etc. Some institutions have found that assistance in the form of sponsorship is a viable option for all concerned. For example, the education sector often turns to industry for assistance when implementing ambitious development plans. University College Dublin (UCD) has obtained funding from the likes of Lochlann Quinn and Dr Michael Smurfitt in order to establish undergraduate and post-graduate centres of excellence for education in business. The sponsors and the university both win – the sponsors' brands gain integrity and kudos from being associated with a university of world renown, and UCD can offer programmes that may not have gone ahead without the proper funding.

Media coverage

Allied with the growth in sponsorship opportunities has been the increased media coverage they have been given. The advent of digital television has been accompanied by the coverage of less mainstream sports and leisure activities. Dedicated sports channels such as Eurosport and Sky Sports not only bring the more popular sports like soccer and tennis into consumers' sitting rooms, they also guarantee the coverage of minority sports like cycling, table tennis, and sidecar racing. Arts and history channels strongly appeal to audiences with a deep interest in the arts, culture and history. Lifestyle channels ensure that DIY, cooking and gardening enthusiasts are provided with a wealth of programmes.

Globalisation

Globalisation presents many challenges for organisations wanting to communicate across cultural boundaries. The translation of messages contained in advertising often presents difficulties and has led many global organisations to allocate significant portions of their budgets to sponsorship. The 'swoosh' of the Nike logo requires no translation when it adorns the signage at major international sports events. These events, and the symbols associated with them, are then beamed into the homes of millions of consumers around the world.

Legislation

Two of Ireland's oldest and most established industries, tobacco and alcohol, have witnessed a severe curtailment in the options available to them when it comes to promoting their products and communicating with their target audiences. This is a result of stringent legislative restrictions that have been implemented at both national and EU level. The tobacco industry has suffered most. Until recently, sponsorship was used by the tobacco industry as a way of circumventing legislation outlawing the advertising of their products, but even that option is being closed off. Pressure groups are calling on the Irish Government to introduce similar legislation aimed at the drinks industry in order to curb the growing incidence of alcohol abuse (see Chapter 5 for an in-depth examination of the tobacco industry's legislative environment).

Technology

Technology has motivated companies to seek ways of overcoming their target audience's ability to avoid their messages. According to Meenaghan (1998), 'the consumer market, while undoubtedly more literate and sophisticated, is also highly fragmented and increasingly empowered by technology to control its consumption of a proliferation of media options.' Remote controls, video recorders and TiVo all make it easier for people to avoid television advertising. For some advertisers, this has called into question the long-term viability of the medium.

Fragmentation of consumer markets

Sponsorship is ideally placed to deal with the difficulties presented by fragmenting consumer markets. Target audiences voluntarily segment themselves by the very nature of the types of events they attend, the activities they participate in, the places they go and the interests they pursue.

Broad appeal

Sponsorship is used to reach a diverse target audience including staff, customers, government, distributors and suppliers.

Advantages and disadvantages of sponsorship

There are a number of advantages associated with sponsorship (summarised in Table 10.4).

Advantages

Access to specific audiences

As already mentioned, sponsorship is utilised by many organisations because of its ability to give them access to specific audiences. Therefore, it might prove more cost-effective than traditional mass advertising campaigns because there is often less wastage. For example, if an organisation wants to reach consumers with an interest in GAA sports, press advertising enables them to communicate with their target audience but they might also end up transmitting their message to people who have no interest in the GAA. If the same company sponsors a GAA-related event or team, the message is more likely to only reach the desired target audience.

Table 10.4 The advantages and disadvantages of sponsorship

Advantages

- Provides access to specific audiences
- Integrates well with other elements of the marketing communications mix
- Helps improve or maintain relations with key audiences

Disadvantages

- Impossible to prevent some potentially damaging external occurrences
- May suffer as a result of adverse publicity associated with a sponsored team, person or an actual event
- Potential to alienate opposition fans
- Incidence of distractions

Good integration with other elements of the marketing communications mix

Sponsorship can be executed in such a way that it integrates well with other elements of the marketing communications mix. Public relations activity is often linked with sponsorship, and works hard to ensure that maximum news coverage is enjoyed. This is referred to as **media leverage**, whereby maximum usage is made of an event. Photographic and video material might be used in company brochures and direct mail elements; footage and images for advertising might be generated at sponsored events. Sales promotion activities such as tastings and coupon distribution are commonplace at many sponsored events. Some sponsors use events to gather names and contact details for their databases.

Media leverage *When maximum usage is made of a sponsored event.*

Relations with key audiences can be improved or maintained

Sponsorship is used to improve or maintain relations with key audiences. When organisations sponsor events, they usually receive a quota of tickets as part of their contract. This allows them to invite potential and existing customers and employees, agents, partners, distributors, media representatives and suppliers. In the business-to-business sector, successful relationship-building is vital. The relaxed environment of a sporting contest or a music concert provides a setting more conducive to the formation of strong relationships than the formal environs of a boardroom.

However, there are a number of disadvantages associated with sponsorship. Any organisation intending to engage in sponsorship should be aware of them.

Disadvantages

Unforeseen circumstances

Unlike advertising, the final outcomes of sponsorship cannot always be controlled. An organisation might invest a lot of time and effort planning a sponsorship programme, only to see an outside variable change the desired outcome. Outside variables include industrial disputes, adverse weather conditions, terrorism, war, political uncertainty, scandals, disease epidemics and health scares. In 2001, two environmental shocks rendered a lot of sponsorship planning and preparation void. At the beginning of 2001 there was an outbreak of foot-and-mouth disease centred in the United Kingdom. In an effort to prevent its spread, many outdoor events around Ireland were postponed, including the St Patrick's Day Parade and the remaining matches in the Six Nations Rugby Championship. The fallout from the 11 September attacks in the United States in 2001 led to the cancellation of high-profile events, including golf's Ryder Cup which was due to be held in Ireland. In all cases, the sponsors involved were powerless to change the situation, even though they had already invested considerable resources in planning for the events and publicising their involvement in them. The threat of serious acute respiratory syndrome (SARS) threatened the 2003 Special Olympics World Summer Games.

Adverse publicity associated with team, person or event

The behaviour of the sponsored person or team may reflect badly on the company. When Ireland qualified for the 2002 World Cup Finals, many companies clamoured to be associated with the team. When news of difficulties between the manager, Mick McCarthy, and his captain, Roy Keane, hit the headlines, there were fears that the Irish team would collapse. For many of the sponsors, such a prospect would have negated months of planning and investment. However, the controversy meant that the team enjoyed even greater media coverage. This meant that sponsors' logos were visible more often than had originally been anticipated. Whenever any member of the team was interviewed on television or photographed, they were wearing clothes that carried the Eircom logo, the main sponsor of the team.

At the 1996 Olympic Games, Irish swimmer, Michelle de Bruin, won four medals. These wins signalled a significant improvement in the swimmer's form and, as is usually the case in such circumstances, questions were raised as to the reasons for these improvements. A controversial doping test two years later fuelled the public's doubts. Even though de Bruin remains a multiple Olympic medal holder, a major achievement for any Irish athlete, she is considered a high-risk person for organisations to associate with for sponsorship purposes.

The performance of a sponsored team or person may reflect badly on the sponsor. For example, tennis player Anna Kournikova's inability to win a tier-one tennis tournament is beginning to concern her many sponsors.

Sometimes adverse publicity is associated with an event as a result of spectator's behaviour. This is a problem that has dogged English football and, at one stage, many sponsors threatened to withdraw their support if the Football Association did not address the issue of adverse behaviour and hooliganism.

The extract below demonstrates how sponsors sometimes take measures to diffuse the likelihood of negative publicity:

Jones bows to pressure from her sponsors

Marion Jones ended her association with the disgraced former coach of Ben Johnson, Charlie Francis, under pressure from her Sponsor Nike. Jones's decision to cut her ties with Francis came after Nike, her biggest sponsor, warned she was in danger of ruining a multimillion-dollar advertising campaign based on her for the 2004 Olympics if she continued to attract so much negative publicity.

Source: *The Irish Times*, 7 February 2003

Alienation of opposition fans

Associations with particular teams or sports stars may alienate the sponsor from supporters of the opposition. Fans of teams in the English Premiership football league are passionate in their dislike of opposition teams. This dislike can, in some cases, extend to anything associated with these teams, including sponsors.

Distraction levels

While sponsorship is considered a good way of circumventing clutter, sponsors often have to compete with a number of powerful distractions. In the case of event sponsorship, the event itself might prevent spectators from even noticing a sponsor's presence. Sponsored events are often ambushed by competitors and this is dealt with later in this chapter (page 275). Broadcast sponsorship (the sponsorship of television and radio programmes) is very popular, but the distractions identified in Chapter 6 must be considered.

Sponsorship objectives

Properly executed, sponsorship is capable of meeting a wide range of objectives aimed at diverse audiences including current and potential customers, employees, suppliers, channel members and the media. Before engaging in any sponsorship activity, specific objectives must be set so that the results can be measured (see Table 10.5 for a summary).

- **to generate organisation awareness**. Sponsorship might be used to generate general awareness of an organisation. For example, when the mobile communications service provider Esat Digifone changed its name to O^2 in 2002, they implemented an integrated marketing communications campaign that involved advertising, direct marketing, sponsorship and public relations. They sponsored a new event called 'Party in the Park'.

Table 10.5 Sponsorship objectives

• To generate general awareness of a company • To build awareness of specific products and services • To launch new products and services • To forge links between a brand and particular market segments • To change perceptions held by target audiences towards an organisation, brand or product • To build relationships with key customers, channel members and the media • To attract new employees and channel members • To encourage potential customers to try new products • To add to company databases

- **to build awareness of specific products or services**. Heineken enjoy a high profile as a result of their sponsorship of rugby's European Cup. It is referred to as the 'Heineken Cup'.

- **to help launch a new product or service**. Sponsored events provide a venue where samples of a new product can be distributed to the target audience in a relaxed environment.

- **to forge links between a brand and a particular market segment**. Guinness is synonymous with the Cork Jazz Festival and the enthusiasts attending every year identify strongly with the brand. Sports sponsorship is heavily utilised by companies looking to achieve this objective.

- **to change target audience perceptions**. Sponsorship is used to reinforce advertising messages aimed at changing perceptions held by target audiences towards an organisation, brand or product. In an effort to shake off a jaded image, sports brand Dunlop signed sponsorship deals with top tennis players James Blake and Thomas Johansson (*Sunday Times*, 5 January 2003).

- **to build relationships with key audiences**. Sponsorship is used to build relationships with key customers, channel members and the media. When an organisation sponsors an event, it is entitled to a quota of tickets. These are used for the purposes of corporate hospitality. Sponsors should endeavour to invite influential journalists and photographers to attend events with a view to securing positive media coverage. Many sponsors employ the services of a public relations consultant to assist them with this task.

- **to attract new employees and channel members**. Sponsorship raises an organisation's profile and is often used to attract new employees and channel members. When organisations are seen to sponsor major events, this helps make them more attractive to potential recruits and partners.

- **to build company databases**. Sponsorship helps many organisations add names to their databases. Sponsored events often provide organisations with the opportunity to gather the names and personal details of potential customers, channel members and employees.

Types of sponsorship

There are three main types of sponsorship: broadcast, event and cause-related sponsorship.

Broadcast sponsorship

Broadcast sponsorship entails the sponsorship of parts of, or entire, television or radio programmes. It is one of the fastest-growing types of sponsorship and is predicted to continue to enjoy popularity among sponsors. This is due, in part, to a relaxation of the laws governing this approach and also to the proliferation of television and radio channels across Europe.

Broadcast sponsorship *Sponsorship of parts of or entire television or radio programmes.*

According to research conducted by Amárach Consulting in 2002, four of the top ten most frequently mentioned sponsorships in Ireland were broadcast sponsorships. Females seem to be very aware of broadcast sponsorships, in particular, 15–24-year-old females. Research into prompted awareness revealed that in October 2001, 73 per cent of Irish adults aged 15–74 were aware of Eircom's sponsorship of RTE's weather forecast and 72 per cent were aware of Cadbury's sponsorship of *Coronation Street* on UTV (see Table 10.6).

Broadcast sponsorship is capable of achieving many of the same objectives as advertising but it is seen as an effective way of cutting through the increasing levels of clutter present in advertising slots. While it is usual for television viewers to change channels when advertisements are broadcast, they are less likely to avoid broadcast

Table 10.6 Prompted awareness of broadcast sponsorships

Rank	Sponsorship	Percentage of all Irish adults aged 15–74 October 2001	Number of all Irish adults aged 15–74 October 2001
1	Eircom & *Weather Forecast* – RTE	73	2.06 million
2	Eircell & *Who Wants to be a Millionaire* – RTE1	73	2.06 million
3	Cadburys & *Coronation Street* – ITV	72	2.04 million
4	Hibernian & *Crimeline* – RTE1	54	1.54 million
5	11850 & *Fair City* – RTE1	53	1. 5 million
6	Aero & *Midweek Movies* – RTE1	52	1.47 million
7	Baileys & *Friends* – Network 2	44	1.23 million
8	Daz & *Emmerdale* – ITV	38	1.06 million
9	Eircom & *Weather Forecast* – TV3	35	1 million
10	Renault & *Late Late Show* – RTE1	34	954,000

Source: Amárach Consulting, 2002

sponsorship messages. In many cases, they are seen as part of the credits to a programme and audiences may even look forward to them. When Eircell (now known as Vodafone) sponsored RTE's *Who Wants to be a Millionaire* quiz show, they used short, amusing vignettes at the beginning and end of advertisement breaks, and at the end of each show. When this is executed well, viewers look forward to the sponsor's message and it becomes part of the programme.

Sponsors find broadcast sponsorship appealing because their brands become inextricably linked to the programme. Therefore, by sponsoring a very popular programme, the audience's goodwill is transferred to the sponsor's brand. Television networks around the world spend large amounts of money in order to secure the rights to popular programmes like *Friends* and *ER* because they can use them to attract sponsors. In Amárach Consulting's 2002 research, one in four Irish adults claimed that their attitude towards the sponsor was 'a lot more positive' as a result of their favourite sponsorship, while 37 per cent felt 'a little more positive' towards the sponsor. The research also revealed that the number one driver of the sponsorship's appeal was a 'preference for the programme'. Respondents who disliked a sponsorship felt that the sponsor did not suit the programme, and 43 per cent of the respondents aged 15–74 stated that they preferred organisations to use broadcast sponsorship than to engage in advertising during the same television programme.

Radio sponsorship is used in Ireland and Amárach's research revealed that Kellogg's sponsorship of the *Ian Dempsey Breakfast Show* on Today FM enjoyed the highest awareness in October 2001. One in five adults were aware of the sponsorship without being prompted, while prompted awareness was four in ten Irish adults (see Table 10.7).

Table 10.7 Prompted awareness of radio programme sponsorship

Rank	Sponsorship	Percentage of all Irish adults aged 15–74 October 2001	Number of all Irish adults aged 15–74 October 2001
1	*Ian Dempsey Breakfast Show* & Kellogg's – Today FM	39	1.09 million
2	*Premiership Live* & Carlsberg – Today FM	21	585,000
3	2FM *Sports Results* & Texaco – 2FM	19	524,000
4	*Most Wanted with Dusty Rhodes* & Eircell Ready To GO	18	513,000

Source: Amárach Consulting, 2002

As a result of the research, Amárach Consulting arrived at some very positive conclusions for broadcast sponsorship (see Table 10.8).

Table 10.8 Summary of research findings into broadcast sponsorship in Ireland

- It is a powerful tool for keeping brands 'front-of-mind', particularly when the target audience consists of young people and females
- Broadcast sponsorship of sports coverage can be a highly cost-effective option to sponsorship in sporting fields
- In Ireland, RTE broadcast sponsorship achieves significantly better results than other channels
- Sponsor fit is a core influencer in a broadcast sponsorship's success
- Broadcast sponsorship makes consumers feel more positively towards sponsors
- Consumers are more positive towards broadcast sponsorship than advertising
- The broadcast sponsorship market potential is strong, with room for expansion of TV and radio sponsorship on RTE

Broadcast sponsorship includes product placement. It is used in the film and entertainment industry. Companies negotiate with production companies to have their products featured in films or television programmes in exchange for a fee and this, in turn, contributes to the production costs of the film or programme. The sponsor gains the goodwill of specific market segments by associating with popular films and television programmes.

Initially, broadcast sponsorship was very popular with sponsors because it was significantly cheaper than advertising. However, as it grows in popularity, sponsors are bidding up the costs of being associated with popular programmes. This increase can be reconciled by the fact that audiences are more likely to see or hear the message than an advertisement.

Event or activity sponsorship

A cursory glance at the promotional material associated with many events and activities reveals the extent of sponsorship in these areas. While it is more lucrative for sponsors to be involved in high-profile events or activities, i.e. those capable of attracting media coverage, local events also attract sponsorship. The appeal of event and activity sponsorship lies in its ability to reach specific audiences, both those that attend the event and those that watch it on television.

Sport

Sports events and the athletes involved in the events attract significant levels of sponsorship. In 2002, more than €22 billion was invested in sports sponsorship world wide (*Irish Independent*, 2002). Nike is heavily involved in sports sponsorship. For example, in order to reach golfers, Nike sponsors the highest-profile golfer in the world, Tiger Woods. In tennis, it sponsors André Agassi. These sportsmen are global brands in their own right and, by associating with them, Nike reinforces its own status as a global company.

Sponsorship of specific athletes involved in high-profile events is an effective way of attracting the attention of consumers. The tennis player, Anna Kournikova, is perhaps less well known for her tennis prowess than for her beauty. Even when she is practising, large numbers of adoring fans turn out to see her. Her mass appeal explains why she netted more than Stg£7 million in 2001 through lucrative sponsorship deals in a year when she was rarely able to play tennis because of a foot injury (*Irish Independent*, 2002). Martin (1996) points out that sponsorship of high-profile athletes also helps the sponsor to achieve the following :

- to strengthen brand name recall
- to reinforce product image
- to give the message credibility
- to increase the product's appeal
- to improve advertisement recall
- to improve the likelihood of product purchase.

Sports and the arts are two areas capable of attracting high levels of sponsorship. Broadcast giants like Sky have made the globalisation of specific sporting events possible. The English Premiership football league attracts significant sponsorship and its growing popularity around the world means that sponsors can cross cultural borders. For example, Manchester United's fortunes are followed across Europe and the club boasts a significant fan base in Asia.

Within particular sports, there exists a wide range of sponsorship opportunities. Staying on the football theme, it is now commonplace to secure sponsorship for team clothing, clubs, players, man of the match, stadiums, equipment (even the ball) and the pitch. Depending on the depth of the sponsor's involvement, they can purchase the rights to have their name included as part of the competition's name. For example, the Football Association of Ireland secured a sponsorship deal with Eircom in 1999. Ireland's national league is officially referred to as the Eircom League. This means that the company enjoys extensive coverage across the various media.

The arts

The arts covers a wide range of disciplines – popular, classical, jazz and blues music, visual arts such as painting, photography and sculpture, and performing arts, such as dance, theatre and film. This is very appealing to sponsors because they can target very specific market segments. Radio stations often sponsor pop concerts because they know that the people attending these events make up a significant proportion of their desired target market. They also gain considerable kudos from being associated with particular pop groups. The Bank of Ireland has enjoyed a long relationship with the Proms, a series of classical concerts, and Guinness's relationship with the Cork Jazz festival is well known and well established. This is not always the case. Very often, there arrives a time when companies do not renew sponsorship contracts. There are a number of reasons for this. They may not have the required budget to continue the sponsorship. The association may no longer fit with their marketing strategy. Legislation may prevent them from continuing the sponsorship, as is the case for tobacco companies. For example, Gallahers sponsored Ireland's prestigious, world-class snooker tournament for many years but, with the introduction of new legislation, this was outlawed. The tournament organisers believed that it would be difficult to find a replacement sponsor because the tournament held such strong associations with the tobacco industry. However, the Department of Health saw this as an opportunity and stepped in as the main sponsor because they saw it as a way of reaching smokers and of delivering an anti-smoking message. Another tobacco company, PJ Carroll, used to sponsor the Irish Open golf tournament. It was a successful partnership and the tournament was called the Carrolls Open. When they stopped sponsoring the event, Murphy's Stout became the main sponsor. This is a challenging situation for the new sponsor and must be supported by advertising in order to eradicate past associations and to create new ones.

Event-related sponsorship and relationship-building

Event-related sponsorship is ideally suited to relationship-building. Sponsors usually use their quota of tickets for corporate hospitality. They invite important and potential customers, opinion leaders and channel partners to attend the event. However, this often causes resentment within the organisation because most employees are not involved in this activity. Unless it is presented to employees as a value-adding activity that will result in a more prosperous business, staff will perceive it as yet another perk for executives who are already well paid.

Uncontrollable aspects of event-related sponsorship

A difficulty with event or activity sponsorship is the adverse publicity that may arise. Unlike advertising, there are many variables in sponsorship that cannot be controlled. In 1998, the Tour de France came to Ireland. This was also the year when numerous drugs scandals were unearthed, most notably in the Festina-sponsored team. Team doctors and managers were imprisoned. Being associated with the sport became a high-risk activity. This risk is not unique to cycling and it is generally accepted that the use of performance-enhancing drugs is endemic in most sports. Associations with pop stars can also be risky because widespread use of recreational drugs.

Cause-related sponsorship

There is a significant difference between **cause-related sponsorship** and charitable donations. Charitable donations entail a company making a donation to a particular cause or non-profit organisation without necessarily

Cause-related sponsorship
Done with a view to having a positive impact on the sponsor's corporate or brand image. Beneficial to both parties.

benefiting from it in commercial terms. Therefore, the main beneficiary of charitable donations is the recipient. It may be appropriate or possible for the donor to generate goodwill among target audiences by generating publicity, thereby creating positive associations.

Cause-related sponsorship is done with a view to having a positive impact on an organisation's corporate or brand image. Therefore, it is intended that it will be beneficial to both parties. Different forms of cause-related sponsorship can be implemented. Tesco's 'Computers for schools' campaign is a good example of cause-related sponsorship. They undertook to donate computers to schools in exchange for coupons that shoppers were entitled to when they shopped in Tesco. Schools benefited from the scheme and Tesco benefited because it encouraged teachers and pupils' parents to shop regularly in their shops.

Transaction-based programmes *The sponsor makes a donation to a worthy cause every time a customer buys one of their products or uses their service.*

Some companies run **transaction-based programmes**. This is when the sponsor undertakes to make a donation to a worthy cause every time a customer buys one of their products or uses their service. Major credit card companies often use this type of sponsorship to attract and retain new customers. Every time a customer uses their credit card, the sponsor makes a donation to a pre-determined worthy cause. One such example of transaction-based sponsorship is shown below:

All credit to UCD and AIB

In 2002, University College Dublin and AIB launched a credit card exclusively aimed at UCD graduates and staff. It is called the UCD AIB Affinity Credit Card and UCD stresses the fact that it benefits the credit card holder and UCD. The key selling proposition of the card is the fact that by signing up for and using the card, deserving causes will benefit:

AIB has committed to donate €12.70 to a fund of the new cardholder's choice when their new card is issued.

AIB will make a donation to UCD every time the cardholder uses their card.

AIB donates a percentage of the cardholder's annual spend to a fund of their choice.

As well as offering the philanthropic benefits outlined above, the credit card offers the user other benefits including competitive interest rates, no annual fee, discounts at designated outlets and regular updates on events in UCD. This example of transaction-based sponsorship illustrates how all parties stand to gain from such an initiative – in this case it is the cardholder, UCD, AIB and charitable causes.

Source: University College Dublin mail shot, 24 May 2002

In the case study at the close of this chapter, the most ambitious example of cause-related sponsorship ever seen in Ireland is explored.

Ambush marketing

Before embarking on a sponsorship programme, sponsors draw up a contract between themselves and the event or activity owners. This sets out clearly what rights the sponsor can expect to enjoy in exchange for their investment. It also states clearly what exactly the sponsor is sponsoring:

- the event title, e.g. the Eircom League
- the series title, e.g. the Sanex Tour in tennis
- a category, e.g. Pepsi might buy the category rights at an event. No other soft drinks company can call themselves the official soft drinks sponsor at that event
- an award, e.g. man of the match
- the scoreboard, e.g. Rado's sponsorship of scoreboards used in tennis tournaments
- promotional material, including brochures, sales promotions and advertising.

However, contracts offer little protection against **ambush marketing**. Meenaghan (1996) states that 'the practice whereby another company, often a competitor, intrudes upon public attention surrounding the event, thereby deflecting attention to themselves and away from the sponsor, is now known in the sponsorship business as ambush marketing.'

Ambush marketing
A company intrudes on public attention surrounding an event and deflects attention to themselves and away from the sponsor.

Problems often arise when the rights to broadcast sponsorship are not related to the event sponsorship. This presents ample ambush marketing opportunities to competitors. As can be seen in the extract below, such a situation allowed Qantas to position itself as apparent Olympic sponsor in 2000 through its high-profile media presence, and this overshadowed its competitor, Ansett, the official sponsors at the Olympics.

Going for gold

The Olympic Games is a very attractive proposition for many sponsors. High-profile global corporations spend millions being official sponsors to the Games. At the 2000 Olympics in Sydney, Australian and international companies invested $2.6 billion in sponsorship. However, many well-known corporations managed to raise their profiles even further by engaging in ambush marketing.

At the 1996 Atlanta Games Reebok were official sponsors. However, through clever ambush marketing stunts, Nike achieved 51 per cent consumer awareness as a result of the Games. One coup in particular brought Nike a lot of attention. They sponsored Michael Jordan's golden shoes, as they carried him to Olympic gold.

> At the 2000 Sydney Games, Australia's airline, Ansett sponsored the Games. However, their competitor Qantas were perceived as official sponsors because they ran television advertisements at peak viewing time.
>
> Source: O'Clery, Conor, 'Money talks loudest at Sydney sports fest', (*The Irish Times*, 29 September 2000)

Meenaghan (1996) identifies a range of ambush strategies which are now commonplace:

- Sponsor media coverage of an event.
- Sponsor a sub-category within an event and exploit this aggressively.
- Make a sponsorship-related contribution to the Players' Pool. The Players' Pool represents a pool of funds contributed by sponsors to a team. It is then divided between team members.
- Plan advertising that coincides with the sponsored event.
- Develop imaginative ambush strategies – such strategies have the added bonus of attracting significant news coverage (as in the example of Nike's stunt at the 1996 Atlanta Olympics described above).

The term 'ambush marketing' suggests that the perpetrator is engaging in an illegal activity. This is not the case, but it does undermine the effectiveness of sponsorship. While interest in sponsorship has never been stronger, the costs of participating in it are increasing all the time. Therefore, sponsors, in their quest for greater efficiencies and accountability, want to ensure that they are getting value for money. Some practitioners worry that ambush marketing will end up ambushing sponsorship because many sponsors are questioning the wisdom of investing in an event or activity if it does not afford them the highest profile.

Sponsorship selection

Sponsorship used to be an *ad hoc* activity, frequently determined by senior executives' hobbies, interests, preferences and friends. This method of selection is unacceptable in a cost-conscious environment and, more importantly, can damage corporate or brand image. Sponsorship is now a multi-million-euro business in Ireland and more often, it is approached with the respect it deserves. The type of sponsorship chosen is usually influenced by a number of factors:

- sponsorship objectives
- available budget
- in-house views on and experience of sponsorship
- the advice and recommendations of external agencies
- the availability of appropriate events, activities, causes and television and radio programmes.

Since many organisations in Ireland are part of multinational corporations, sponsorship decisions are often made by head office. For example, when Vodafone purchased Eircell, many of the events previously sponsored by Eircell were not continued by Vodafone. Figure 10.1 summarises the steps involved in selecting sponsorship activity, described in detail below.

1. **Refer to corporate and marketing objectives**. Decision-makers must refer to their organisation's corporate and marketing objectives. What is the organisation trying to achieve? This helps ensure sponsorship does not conflict with other marketing activities.
2. **Relate sponsorship to marketing communications objectives and strategy**. Decision-makers must be fully aware of their organisation's marketing communications objectives and strategy. Sponsorship works best when it is integrated with other elements in the promotions mix. This may involve setting up multi-disciplinary teams comprising colleagues and representatives from outside agencies. This ensures that a consistent message is sent to target audiences.
3. **Establish sponsorship objectives**. Sponsorship objectives inform everybody about what exactly the organisation hopes to achieve through sponsorship.
4. **Agree sponsorship strategy**. The sponsorship strategy identifies the type of sponsorship activity that will enable the organisation to meet its sponsorship objectives. The main options are broadcast, event or cause-related sponsorship.

Figure 10.1 Selecting sponsorship activity

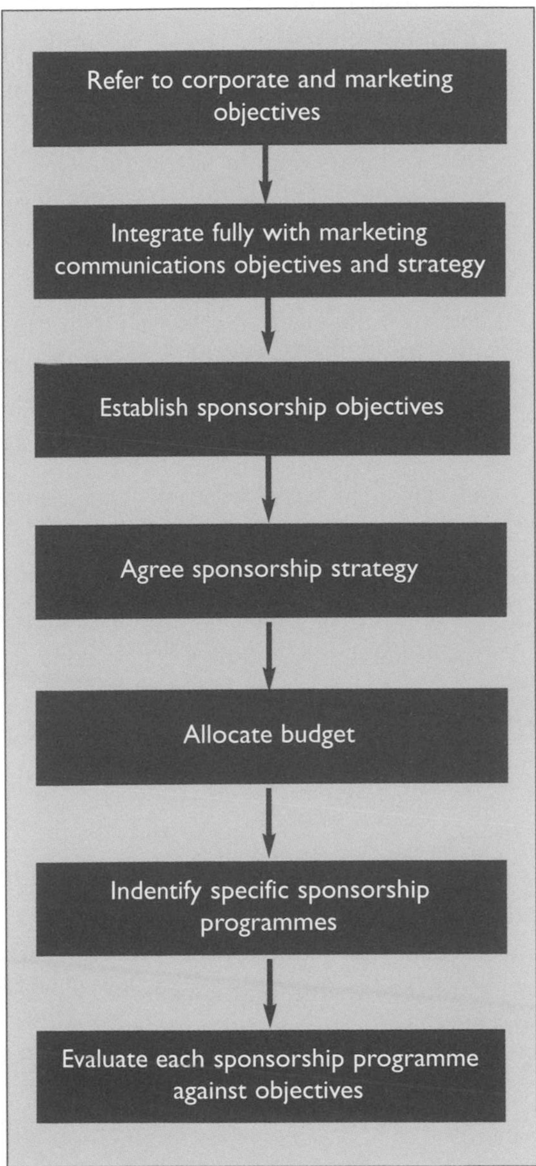

Source: Meenaghan (1995)

5. **Allocate budget**. In reality, many organisations set their sponsorship budget before agreeing on the objectives and strategy. Then they engage in sponsorship they can afford. Best practice states that objectives and the most appropriate activity should precede budget-setting.

   Budgeting for sponsorship programmes should be comprehensive. Some sponsors only include the cost of actually sponsoring the event, person, activity, broadcast or cause. They omit the preparation costs involved. For example, preparation for Bank of Ireland's sponsorship of the 2003 Special Olympics World Games commenced in 2000 (*The Irish Times*, 2002). In the lead-up to the actual event, they invested significant amounts of time and money in publicising the bank's involvement in order to achieve maximum leverage from the investment.

   Preparation is not the only expense. A general rule of thumb in the industry states that sponsors should spend the same on advertising as on the actual sponsorship programme. This helps ensure maximum recall. While the advertising costs can ultimately be allocated to a separate budget, organisations should ensure in advance that they are able to spend the desired amount on advertising. If not, they should question the wisdom of investing in the sponsorship programme in question.
6. **Identify and evaluate specific sponsorship programmes**. Once sponsorship alternatives have been identified, they must be evaluated against the sponsorship objectives. The following evaluation criteria are used:

   - Does the sponsorship programme compliment corporate or brand values?
   - Does it facilitate the fulfilment of the sponsorship objectives?
   - Does it reach the required target audience?
   - Is it likely to be sabotaged by ambush marketing?
   - What are the terms of the contract, i.e. category exclusivity, sole sponsorship rights, tickets for hospitality etc.?
   - If it is an event, is there any likelihood that it will not take place?
   - If it is a person, is there any likelihood that they will behave inappropriately or sustain injury?
   - How much does it cost?

   These criteria can be likened to traffic lights. When answering the questions, the organisation should not proceed with the sponsorship programme if they are confronted with too many amber and red lights.

Evaluating sponsorship effectiveness

Organisations want greater accountability when it comes to spending money on marketing communications. The effectiveness of some elements of the marketing communications mix is easier to measure than others, for example, direct marketing. Sponsorship effectiveness is measured using quantitative and qualitative techniques.

Quantitative techniques

Quantitative techniques usually involve measuring levels of event and media exposure. The level of **event exposure** is based on the number of people who attended the event. This works on the assumption that, by being there, they were exposed to the sponsor's message. In order to estimate this, the event organiser must provide accurate attendance figures to the sponsor. At the negotiation stage of the sponsorship contract, the sponsor must be satisfied that the organiser has the appropriate procedures and resources in place to measure attendance accurately. In many cases, technology plays a central role in this.

Event exposure
Using the number of people who attended an event to estimate the level of exposure to sponsorship.

Another quantitative measure is the level of **media exposure** enjoyed by the event. The sponsor can then quite literally count the number of times their name was mentioned and their logo appeared on television, on the Internet, and in newspapers and magazines. Based on listenership, viewership and readership figures, the sponsor can estimate the number of people who have been exposed to their messages.

Media exposure
Using the number of times the sponsor's name was mentioned in various media. Utilising listenership, viewership and readership figures to estimate the number of people who have been exposed messages.

Both techniques provide a measure of reach and frequency, i.e. how many people did the sponsor reach and how often. However, quantitative techniques do not take into account whether or not the sponsor's presence registered with the target audience. Viewers are usually engrossed in the event and may not even notice the sponsor. Therefore, qualitative research techniques should be used in conjunction with quantitative techniques so as to provide the sponsor with a more critical analysis.

Another quantitative technique tests recall to find out whether or not the sponsor's activity has been noticed. Questionnaires are used to ask respondents a series of unprompted questions. For example, the respondent might be asked if they know who sponsors a particular event. If they are able to answer the question without prompting, this means that the sponsorship has made some sort of impact. If they do not know, the next series of questions prompt the respondent. For example, the person might be asked if they know which bank sponsors a particular event. If they still do not know, the questionnaire provides a list of banks, which includes the right answer. Incorrect answers might provide useful information. If a significant number of respondents give the same incorrect answer, it might mean that some form of ambush marketing is taking place.

When carrying out marketing research, questions should be included to assess whether or not the activity has achieved the sponsorship objectives and to determine the impact of the sponsorship on the sponsor's image. That someone is aware of the sponsorship activity does not mean that it is effective.

Another quantitative technique is to investigate the impact of sponsorship on sales. However, this is not easy to measure because external environmental factors and other elements of the marketing mix and the marketing communications mix contribute to sales levels.

Qualitative techniques

Some sponsors conduct more in-depth research and use qualitative techniques to probe the opinions of target audiences more fully. While structured questionnaires provide a lot of valuable data, the results may highlight issues that require further investigation. Individuals are invited to participate in focus groups or one-on-one interviews. These techniques afford sponsors the opportunity to get inside the heads of their target audiences and to find out more about their attitudes towards the organisation's sponsorship activity. Interviewees might be asked for suggestions regarding appropriate sponsorship activity.

Summary

Sponsorship is an investment of cash or benefit-in-kind in an activity, in return for the sponsor's right to commercially exploit their involvement. Research shows that sponsorship spend in Ireland and around the world remains strong and is set to continue growing. This is largely at the expense of advertising, which experiences high levels of noise. There are three main sponsorship activities and they are event sponsorship, broadcast sponsorship and cause-related sponsorship. Research carried out by Amárach Consulting reveals that broadcast sponsorship is particularly effective in Ireland. One of the greatest causes of concern for sponsors is the growing incidence of ambush marketing.

Since sponsorship is an investment, organisations should ensure that it meets a number of criteria before committing to it. The sponsorship activity should help an organisation meet its overall corporate objectives. In order to assess whether or not the sponsorship activity has achieved its objectives, the sponsor should conduct quantitative and qualitative research.

Review questions

1. Identify reasons why sponsorship is such a popular element of the marketing communications mix.
2. Critically assess the advantages and disadvantages of sponsorship.
3. Describe the type of objectives that can be achieved through sponsorship.
4. Identify and describe the main types of sponsorship. Use examples to illustrate your answer.
5. What is ambush marketing?
6. Prescribe a framework for selecting sponsorship.
7. Critically assess the use of quantitative techniques for evaluating sponsorship effectiveness.

Exercise

Select three organisations that currently engage in sponsorship activity. Carry out research to find out what they are doing (if anything) to leverage this sponsorship.

References

Amárach Consulting, *Broadcast Sponsorship Success: Research to Inform the Industry for 2002 and Beyond* (Amárach Consulting on behalf of RTE, March 2002).

Amárach Consulting, *Sponsorship in Ireland: Outlook 2003* (Amárach Consulting, February 2003).

Incorporated Society of British Advertisers, *Sponsorship: What you should Expect from the Parties Involved* (ISBA Publications, 1993).

Martin, James H. and Boler, Mary Jo, 'Is the athlete's sport important when picking an athlete to endorse a nonsport product?' (*Journal of Consumer Marketing*, Vol. 13, No. 6, 1996).

Meenaghan, Tony, 'The role of sponsorship in the marketing communications mix' (*International Journal of Advertising*, 10(1), 35–47, 1991).

Meenaghan, Tony, 'Managing sponsorship effectively', in Meenaghan, Tony and O'Sullivan, Paul (eds), *Marketing Communications in Ireland* (Oak Tree Press, 1995).

Meenaghan, Tony, 'Ambush marketing: a threat to corporate sponsorship' (*Sloan Management Review*, 38(1), 103–13, 1996).

Meenaghan, Tony, 'Current developments and future directions in commercial sponsorship' (*International Journal of Advertising*, 17(1), 3–28, 1998).

Purnell, Sonia, 'Battle of the super babes' (*Irish Independent*, 24 June 2002).

Case study

2003 Special Olympics World Summer Games

INTRODUCTION

The 2003 Special Olympics World Summer Games was the largest sporting event to ever occur on the island of Ireland. It is intended that the Games will leave a lasting positive legacy in Ireland, raising awareness of learning disabilities through an educational programme targeted at schools and third-level institutions. The Premier Sponsor and the Games Partners contributed over €11.5 million to the Games. Given the sums involved, sponsorship of the Games was an investment decision. This view is encapsulated by Lisa Browne of Bank of Ireland (the Premier Sponsor), who observes, 'we view sponsorship as a business decision. It is an investment and as such we expect a return on our investment. The way we measure it is in terms of our marketing and business objectives.' In the eyes of the sponsors, the key attribute that sponsorship of the 2003 Special Olympics World Summer Games bestows upon them is association with a highly visible good cause. As Gary Finnerty of An Post put it, one of the key benefits of being a Games Partner is 'association with a good cause and generally to be perceived as a good corporate citizen.' Lisa Browne of Bank of Ireland observed, 'it has been wonderful in terms of generating good PR for the bank.'

The commercial sponsorship of the 2003 Special Olympics World Summer Games was a pyramid structure. At the top was the Premier Sponsor, Bank of Ireland, which at the outset provided €3 million and provided a further €1 million to promote the Games. On January 2002 the euro became Ireland's official currency. Bank of Ireland saw this as an opportunity for its customers to support the 2003 Special Olympics World Summer Games directly. The bank arranged collection points in all of its branches where customers could donate their old Irish and European currency. These collections raised in excess of €1 million.

The next layer of sponsorship consisted of Games Partners. These were six leading Irish companies, which committed themselves to provide €1.27 million each in either cash or in kind. The third layer of sponsorship consisted of suppliers who provided services including public relations, photography, design and production facilities. These companies provided 'either payment in kind or cash of €317,435'. The Premier Sponsor and all of the Games Partners each had a designated sporting venue during the World Games in June 2003 and also acted as lead sponsor for specific programmes prior to the games. For example, Bank of Ireland's designated sporting venue during the Games was Morton Stadium and was the sponsor of the Host Towns programme.

Branding

Branding was an essential part of the 2003 Special Olympics World Summer Games dynamic as it increased awareness about the event. Sponsors believed that the key to gaining a return on their investment was that the 2003 Special Olympics World Summer Games Limited maintained tight control over the application of the brand. The sponsorship manager, Rory Smyth, first vetted all applications of the brand by the individual sponsors for approval. This helped ensure that the image of the brand was not tarnished by inappropriate application. The sponsors also expected the organisers to rigorously protect the brand from use by organisations other than official sponsors. The regulations regarding the branding of the sponsor company was very strict and was laid out in the sponsorship contract. For each company's designated campaign and venue their brand was prominently placed with the brands of all the other Games Partners in view, though with a smaller logo.

The Premier Sponsor

Bank of Ireland, as Premier Sponsor, spent €4 million on its sponsorship. At the outset, the bank initiated contact indicating it would be interested in participating in the sponsorship programme. Bank of Ireland regards all its sponsorship as investments that are measured against both its marketing and business objectives. According to its Sponsorship Manager, what attracted it to the 2003 Special Olympics World Summer Games was that it offered so much more as a method of energising and motivating employees. The company's strategy was to make sure that 'Bank of Ireland's contribution results in a better experience for everybody that is involved' (Lisa Browne, 2002). Within its sponsorship they had three marketing objectives. Firstly, to strengthen awareness of the bank's Premier Sponsorship. Secondly, to motivate target audiences to take required action, and thirdly to ensure all communications demonstrate empathy with the 2003 Special Olympics World Summer Games.

Bank of Ireland was the sponsor of the Host Town Programme, which welcomed and accommodated the athletes and coaches for the four days before the World Games in June 2003. Every Host Town application form had to have the signature of the local bank manager and a staff member on its Host Town Committee thus sponsorship of this programme enabled the branches at a local level to take ownership of the sponsorship.

Bank of Ireland supported its sponsorship of the event with both a regionally and nationally based public relations campaign. The bank utilised the brand of the 2003 Special Olympics World Summer Games on both internal and external communication, including ATM slips. It also utilised its branch network to inform the public of other initiatives in which the 2003 Special Olympics World Summer Games were involved. It provided two days' additional leave for every two days of holidays taken by an employee to participate as a volunteer.

The Games Partners

There were six Games Partners and they were Aer Lingus, An Post, Eircom, O'Brien's Irish Sandwich Bars, RTE and Toyota. Eircom's and O'Brien's roles are examined below.

Eircom

Eircom's sponsorship was a continuation of a standing sponsorship arrangement going back 17 years. The initial sponsorship took the form of cash donations and the sponsoring of the national Special Olympics programme called Special Olympics Ireland. Eircom was also the main sponsor of the National Games in 2002. 2003 Special Olympics World Summer Games formally approached Eircom and made a presentation to the company, although many informal contacts would have been built up over the years. The sponsorship was one in which the staff also got interested and excited. The ultimate decision to become a partner was undertaken by the then chairman of the organisation Mr Ray McSharry and the Board of Directors of the company. The contracts Eircom had with 2003 Special Olympics World Summer Games and Special Olympics Ireland were separate. Eircom believes its long association with the Special Olympics movement brought a great understanding to the World Games, which was unique among the other sponsors.

Eircom was the telecommunications provider for the Games as, according to Carol McMahon of Eircom, 'that is our skills, our knowledge, and we are giving that to them.' Eircom's donation was part benefit-in-kind and included the cost of line rental and calls and other hard-cash costs. Eircom Consult, the company's consultancy company, provided a comprehensive advice plan to 2003 Special Olympics World Summer Games Limited. Eircom chose the Law Enforcement Torch Run as its designated sponsorship programme because it had experience of the event in its sponsorship of Special Olympics Ireland. It saw benefits in Law Enforcement Torch Run in that it had a high visibility throughout Ireland. Its designated venue during the Games was University College Dublin where the football and basketball tournaments were played. This was a natural fit because of their sponsorship of the national football league and the international football team. In 2003, its telephone directories went to every home in the country, which featured Special Olympics athletes. The 2003 Special Olympics World Summer Games branding was used on all billing and Eircom television commercials.

Eircom's definition of successful Games included consumer brand awareness and also the utilisation of the sponsorship within Eircom. According to Carol McMahon of Eircom, 'it is a very good vehicle for internal communications among staff.' This was especially important for the company, as it had undergone two changes in its corporate governance structures in recent years. Eircom's brand values are described as 'professional, progressive and friendly' so the World Games were seen as a perfect fit.

O'Brien's Irish Sandwich Bar

O'Brien's was somewhat different from the other Games Partners in that its contribution of €1.27 million came in the form of direct contributions from its own funds, benefit-in-kind contributions and voluntary financial contributions from fund-raising activities organised by O'Brien's. It should be noted that O'Brien's is a small organisation, when compared to the other Games Partners and thus, at a practical level, would not have had the financial resources to fund the €1.27 million contribution independently. What O'Brien's lacked in direct financial resources, it more than made up for as a passionate advocate for the Games in both the communities in which its sandwich bars operate and its wider network of commercial suppliers.

When Brody Sweeney, CEO of O'Brien's, heard about the 2003 Special Olympics World Summer Games he contacted the organisation and said he wanted to be part of it. 'He just felt it was right and he wanted to do it.' He wanted to get involved from the point of view of raising awareness about learning disabilities and secondly because it was good for the company to be associated with such an event. O'Brien's sponsored the Volunteer Programme and had the RDS as its designated venue. O'Brien's had the same commitment of €1.27 million as the rest of the Games Partners but much of this was in kind. It provided 20,000 sandwiches a day for the ten days of the Games. What made it unique in comparison to the other Games Partners was that the remainder was made up of money that the organisation generated from fund-raising. Its contract with the 2003 Special Olympics World Summer Games required the company to meet monthly fund-raising targets.

To provide this benefit-in-kind and to complete the logistical challenge involved, O'Brien's were assisted by many of its ordinary customers and suppliers. According to Maurice Knightly, Operations Director, the suppliers came on board enthusiastically, more so than the franchise partners. He supposed it was because they were trying to promote their brand and boost sales also. In addition to the company's network of partners, other companies which were not normally suppliers of O'Brien's were contacted to assist in the operation. One of these was Freshways, a wholesale sandwich maker, which had the state-of-the-art equipment enabling them to churn out thousands of sandwiches. O'Brien's acting alone would have been unable to achieve this as the company is comprised of small retail outlets, that are mainly controlled by franchise partners, and a support office.

On the labels of the lunches, as occurred at the National Games which O'Brien's used as a test run, the sandwich packages had O'Brien's 2003 Special Olympics World Summer Games label stating also Freshways' support. Maxwell House, which is not the company's coffee supplier, supplied the coffee for the National Games. According to Knightly, 'they saw it as an opportunity to get their brand out to more people.' O'Brien's believe that it was easier to ask for assistance from others as they were aware that the 2003 Special Olympics World Summer Games were a once-off event and that it would not be coming back year after year.

O'Brien's contract with 2003 Special Olympics World Summer Games required it to raise specific amounts of money each month. O'Brien's fund-raising included a concert which raised €27,500. The artists, including Sinead O'Connor, gave their time for free. The administration costs for the event only came to €1,000.

O'Brien's saw several commercial benefits from their sponsorship of the Games.

Relative to the other Games Partners this is a small, but rapidly expanding company. The Volunteer Programme received national exposure through TV, newsprint and mail shot advertisements. On every campaign O'Brien's was acknowledged as the sponsor of this programme. The logic for selecting this programme was reinforced by O'Brien's Special Olympics Co-ordinator, Alyne Healy when she noted, 'we thought we would probably get the biggest coverage on that end of it [the Volunteer Programme].' All the 30,000 volunteers wore a t-shirt with O'Brien's logo on it. This raised the profile of the brand. Association with a non-profit organisation further strengthened the O'Brien's brand. Again as Alyne Healy observed, 'I think everyone sees the benefit of being involved with a non-profit organisation in terms of sponsorship and brand awareness and goodwill.' For O'Brien's, the definition of a successful sponsorship in this case was greater exposure of their brand and products and that it carried out its commitment to deliver €1.27 million through fund-raising and benefit-in-kind to the Games. It wanted to be seen to be a company that has the capacity to deliver on its promises.

This excerpt is reproduced with kind permission from a case written by Peter McNamara, Garrett Murray and Carolin Grampp, UCD Business School, and with the help of Paul Brown, 2003 Special Olympics World Summer Games Limited, *2003 Special Olympics World Summer Games: Managing a Stakeholder Network*, (University College Dublin, 2003).

11

SALES PROMOTION

The aims and objectives of this chapter are:

- to explore sales promotion as a whole
- to examine its role as part of the marketing communications mix, and in particular:
  - to define sales promotion
  - to examine the reasons why sales promotion has become such a popular element of the marketing communications mix
  - to explain the objectives of sales promotion
  - to differentiate between the sales promotion activities aimed at consumers, the trade and sales forces
  - to describe and critically assess the types of sales promotion tools available
  - to explore the downside of sales promotion activity
  - to prescribe a framework that assists in the implementation of effective sales promotion programmes
  - to assess sales promotion's fit with the other elements of the marketing communications mix.

Introduction

Sales promotion is a marketing communications tool that offers incentives to consumers, the trade, business buyers and sales representatives. Its primary objective is to secure sales. Properly used, it is an important component of the marketing communications mix and can motivate buyers who have not responded to other promotional techniques. However, as this chapter explains, sales promotion is frequently abused and over-used by marketers. As a result, it has a tarnished image when compared to advertising, public relations and sponsorship. This image is justified in many cases because the culprits consistently implement sales promotions programmes for short-term gain, while ignoring the longer-term implications of their actions.

This chapter dispels the myth that sales promotion should only be used as a tactical tool and will examine the strategic role it can play in a properly planned integrated marketing communications programme.

What is sales promotion?

There is general consensus among the authors of marketing communications literature as to the meaning of sales promotion. It uses incentives in order to achieve specific action-oriented objectives (see Shimp, 1997; Burnett and Moriarty; 1998; Semenik, 2002). While some people perceive sales promotion as an aggressive activity that bases its appeal primarily on price attractiveness, sales promotion offers additional value to the target audience. Therefore, the onus is on the marketer to find out what constitutes value for each market segment and to base subsequent sales promotion activity on this information. All too often, promotions focus on giving the customer more product at a lower price when in fact they would have been prepared to pay the full price while welcoming other value-adding initiatives. Perhaps this is best illustrated in the following quotation: 'The incentive is additional to the basic benefits provided by the brand and temporarily changes its perceived price or value' (Shimp, 1997).

When marketers engage in sales promotion, there is usually an expectation that the activity will enjoy an immediate, positive response. The incentives are designed in such a way that they will motivate the target audience to take action.

Table 11.1 provides a summary of these views of the characteristics of sales promotion. Sales promotion is used both for tactical and strategic purposes. Tactical reasons for using sales promotion might include the need to respond to a competitor's actions or the need to boost sales which are lagging behind sales targets. Pickton and Broderick (2001) refer to this application of the tool as a quick fix, deployed in order to respond to certain situations that require immediate attention. Therefore, such activity is not sustainable or advisable in the long run.

Table 11.2 Key characteristics of sales promotion

- Incentive-based activity
- Seeks action-oriented responses
- Expects immediate responses
- Should offer additional value over and above the regular offer

There are strategic reasons for using sales promotion. By their very nature, strategic sales promotions are 'planned as part of a larger pre-planned campaign and sustained marketing communications effort, integrated with a range of sales promotions and other marketing communications activities' (Pickton and Broderick, 2001). An example of a strategic sales promotion is Superquinn's Superclub loyalty scheme which adds value for customers and strengthens their loyalty. It is integrated with direct marketing activity and used as a focal point in some of Superquinn's advertising with a view to increasing store traffic.

Reasons for the growth in sales promotion

Sales promotion is enjoying sustained growth levels in Ireland. This mirrors trends in other EU countries and the US. In 2001 work by sales promotion agencies in Ireland on behalf of their clients was estimated to be worth €45–€50 million and growth projections for 2002 were 10 per cent (*Marketing Magazine*, April 2002). A rapidly changing and sometimes volatile marketing environment has contributed to this growth.

See Table 11.2 for a summary of the reasons for growth in sales promotion, the details of which follow here.

Table 11.2 Reasons for the growth in sales promotion

- Growing retailer power as a result of loyalty schemes, electronic data interface (EDI), centralised purchasing and own brands
- Declining brand loyalty among consumers
- Consumer sensitivity to sales promotion
- Short-term sales focus in many organisations, reinforced by the brand management organisation structure
- A tight labour market during the 'Celtic Tiger' phase of the Irish economy.

Retailer power

Since the 1990s, the Irish food retail sector has undergone significant consolidation. Domination by a few companies – Dunnes, Tesco Ireland, and to a lesser extent Superquinn, Supervalu and newcomers Aldi and Lidl – has seen the balance of power shifting away from product manufacturers and brand owners into the hands of retailers. Their domination has been aided by a number of factors.

Loyalty schemes

Tesco Ireland, Dunnes and Superquinn operate club cards that provide them with immense amounts of customer information that is held on databases. Consequently, they know far more about their customers than the manufacturers know about them. This is worrying for manufacturers because retailers' customers are manufacturers' end customers. If knowledge is power, then the retailers' customer databases have strongly tipped the balance of power into the hands of the retailers.

Electronic data interface (EDI)

EDI gives the retailer instant access to information about sales and stock levels. If a product is not selling, retailers have the information they need to call upon the manufacturer to help them move the product. This help usually takes the form of a sales promotion and, if this does not work, the retailer can delist the product (i.e. stop stocking it) and give the valuable shelf space to more popular lines.

Centralised purchasing

The main food retailers employ purchasing professionals to purchase stock directly from the manufacturer or main distributor on behalf of an entire retail network. Prior to its introduction, individual managers purchased stock for their own branches from wholesalers. This meant that, in many cases, the wholesalers and the manufacturers held the balance of power. With the advent of central purchasing, retailers buy direct from the manufacturers and can exert much greater pressure on them in order to avail of the keenest prices. They are also in a much better position to negotiate for marketing support (these are usually sales promotions and are examined in detail later in this chapter, page 293). The power that emanates from a centralised purchasing regime is set to accelerate, with what Perkins (2001) refers to as a 'frenzy of corporate activity' in the European retail sector which has seen a number of mergers, acquisitions, and alliances between major retailers.

Own brands

The spectacular rise in popularity in the UK of supermarket retailers' ranges of own brands is well documented. However, for various reasons, the Irish consumer was slower to make the switch. For example, when Tesco acquired Quinnsworth in 1997, own-brand products accounted for around 6 per cent of sales, while in the UK, own-brand products accounted for 50 per cent of Tesco's sales (Vignali, 2001). Since then there has been a significant improvement in own-brand quality and Irish consumers are at last showing signs of switching their allegiances away from manufacturers' brands towards retailers' own brands.

Declining brand loyalty

Retailers are committed to the development and promotion of quality, cost-competitive own brands. This trend is not confined to the food retail sector. Retailers such as Boots, Woodies, B&Q and fashion retailers all enjoy considerable success in this area. Allied to this, and as a result of increased competition in Ireland, there has been a proliferation of manufacturers' brands in recent years. This means that consumers are faced with greater choice. Meanwhile, there is a perception among consumers that competing brands are similar in quality. Therefore, they are willing to try a range of brands in their quest for a mix of quality and value for money.

Consumer sensitivity to sales promotions

If consumers can choose from a much greater range of products of similar quality, sales promotion activity often helps simplify the choice. Attractive incentive-based promotions play a major role in precipitating impulse purchases at the point of sale.

Short-term focus

Sales promotion activity is widely used in the FMCG sector. Organisations in this sector generally utilise a brand management structure. This gives responsibility to individual managers for the success of a brand or a portfolio of brands. Challenging monthly sales targets are set for each brand. As a result, brand managers often resort to sales promotion activity in order to achieve immediate results that will impact positively on sales. While a strong advertising campaign can influence sales, the results usually take much longer to materialise than those resulting from sales promotion activity. Also, an advertising campaign takes much longer to devise and produce, whereas many sales promotions can be implemented in a short time period.

In a system that rewards and promotes brand managers on the basis of their ability to reach their sales targets, it is easy to understand why sales promotion is a popular choice. However, there are risks to this approach for the long-term health of a brand (see page 306).

Greater drive for accountability

There is much greater pressure on those responsible for marketing communications to demonstrate high returns on expenditure. This helps to explain why sales promotion and direct marketing are experiencing growing popularity. In both cases, it is possible to measure response levels and attribute sales to specific campaigns. For example, if a company distributes money-off coupons, the number of coupons redeemed is counted. Therefore, brand managers can provide quantitative information to senior management very soon after a sales promotion campaign has been implemented. Conversely, an advertising campaign is more likely to take longer to have an impact on sales, and direct effects are not always straightforward to quantify.

A tight labour market

Sales promotions are used to retain staff. Until the mid-1990s, staff retention in Ireland was not a major problem because unemployment rates of 17 per cent meant that there was little job mobility and employees remained with companies on a long-term basis. This changed in the wake of the economic boom and, when unemployment plummeted to levels as low as 4 per cent, workers became more mobile and could move from job to job. In an effort to retain staff, employers used a number of methods to retain staff, including better pay, bonuses, share options and sales promotions. Sales promotions were used to incentivise and reward staff activity (see page 294 for more on this).

Role of sales promotion

Sales promotion is aimed at three main groups:

- consumers
- trade
- employees.

As well as enabling organisations to achieve the objectives explained below, an overriding objective of all sales promotion activity is that it supports and enhances all other marketing communications activity.

The role of consumer-oriented sales promotion

As illustrated in Figure 11.1, consumer-oriented sales promotion is targeted at the end consumer. Its main purposes are:

Figure 11.1 The role of consumer-oriented sales promotion

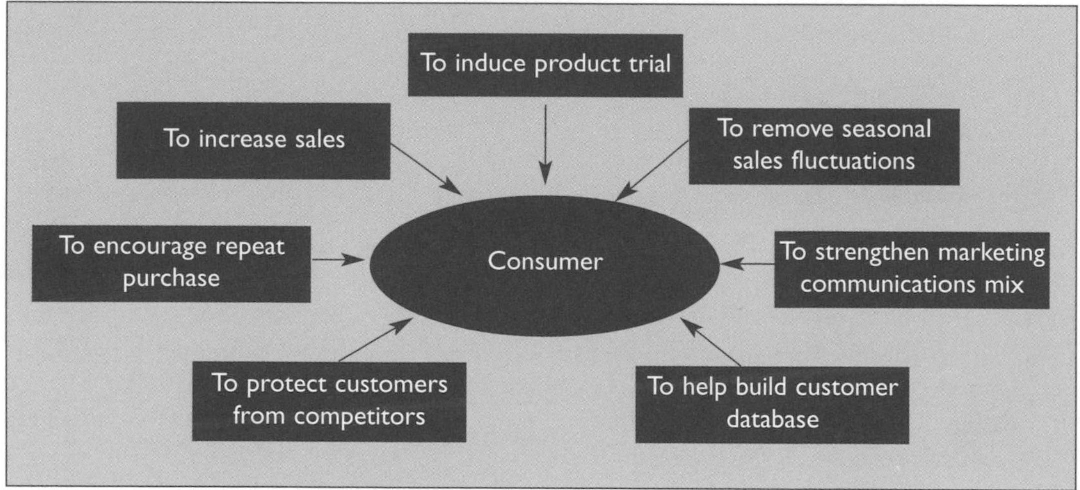

- **to induce trial of a new or existing product**. When organisations launch a new product or introduce an existing product to a new market segment, sales promotion is used to motivate consumers to try the product.
- **to increase sales of an existing product**. In order to increase sales among existing customers, companies might suggest additional uses for the product. For example, Kraft offer recipe sheets with their Philadelphia cheese range in order to highlight the many uses of the product.
- **to encourage repeat purchase among existing customers**. Techniques such as on-pack money-off coupons, free or subsidised gifts, and rewards based on purchase levels, are used to encourage consumers to purchase products more regularly.
- **to remove customers from the purchase cycle**. Some sales promotion techniques, such as 'buy one, get one free' serve to load customers with large quantities of a product. This takes them out of the purchase cycle for a longer period of time and may shelter them from competitor advances.
- **to smooth out seasonal fluctuations**. Some products are associated with certain times

of the year and many customers do not buy them at any other time. For example, cranberry sauce is associated with Christmas, but sales promotion can be used to encourage consumers to use the product on other occasions such as Sunday lunch or as an accompaniment for salads.

- **to strengthen other elements of the marketing communications mix**. Many organisations use sales promotion in conjunction with advertising, public relations and direct marketing. This might help an advertisement, mail shot or press release break through the clutter and make an impression on the target audience.
- **to encourage consumers to provide personal information**. Sales promotion is used by organisations to build and add to their databases. For example, Ireland's leading mortgage provider, PermanentTSB ran a competition in conjunction with *The Irish Times* in 2003. The prize was €10,000 towards the winner's mortgage or an equivalent cash amount. All entrants had to provide their name, address and phone number.

The role of trade-oriented sales promotion

As we saw earlier, retailers in many sectors have seized the initiative when it comes to dealing with manufacturers. This has led to an increase in the use of sales promotion aimed at retailers or 'the trade' as they are referred to. This activity is seen as another way of building retailer loyalty. There are many reasons why manufacturers engage in trade-oriented sales promotion (see Figure 11.2 for a summary):

- **to secure shelf space for new products**. Shelf space in retail outlets is valuable and retailers can only afford to stock products that will sell. Therefore, they prefer to display familiar products with a proven track record. The use of incentives may help persuade retailers to stock a new product.
- **to encourage retailers to stock larger quantities**. When retailers have large quantities of a product in stock, they are likely to put greater effort into selling the product. It is in the manufacturer's interest to encourage retailers to hold larger quantities of their products in stock. This approach may serve to discourage the retailer from stocking rival products, and also diminishes the likelihood of the retailer running out of stock. When outlets run out of stock, it increases the possibility of customers switching to competitor brands.
- **to secure increased and/or better shelf space**. The position occupied by a product in the retail environment contributes significantly to its success or failure. Manufacturers use sales promotion to persuade retailers to give them prime in-store locations for their products. While well-known brands are able to leverage their names, less well-known manufacturers are forced to offer more than a good product in order to stake their claim to a good location in the retail environment.
- **to gain permission to display point-of-purchase materials**. Many manufacturers like to install items such as posters, free-standing display units and leaflets promoting their products in retailers' premises. However, they represent the loss of valuable selling

space. Manufacturers and product distributors may have to offer retailers incentives in exchange for permission to put up point-of-purchase displays.

- **to smooth out seasonal sales fluctuations**. Retailers do not want to stock too many products. With the benefits that EDI brings (see page 289), they are even more reluctant to hold unnecessary surplus stock. Some manufacturers are affected by seasonal variances in demand for their products, but, with the co-operation of the retailer and the support of marketing communications, they can sometimes sell such products off-season (see above, page 293).
- **to gain advantage over competitors**. Trade sales promotion is used to position a manufacturer more favourably. By offering incentives such as advertising support, training and discounts on bulk purchases, manufacturers might be able to gain advantage over competitors. Of course, many incentives can be copied easily by competitors.
- **to motivate retailers' salespeople to recommend certain products**. Manufacturers might run competitions for the best retail sales representative. Being 'the best' depends on sales volume. While this type of promotion may prove highly rewarding for the salesperson, the customer may lose out. Without knowing it, they may be advised to buy an inappropriate product. This may not become apparent for some time, but if they need to buy a replacement product at some stage, they are unlikely to return to the retailer where they first bought the product.

Figure 11.2 The role of trade-oriented sales promotion

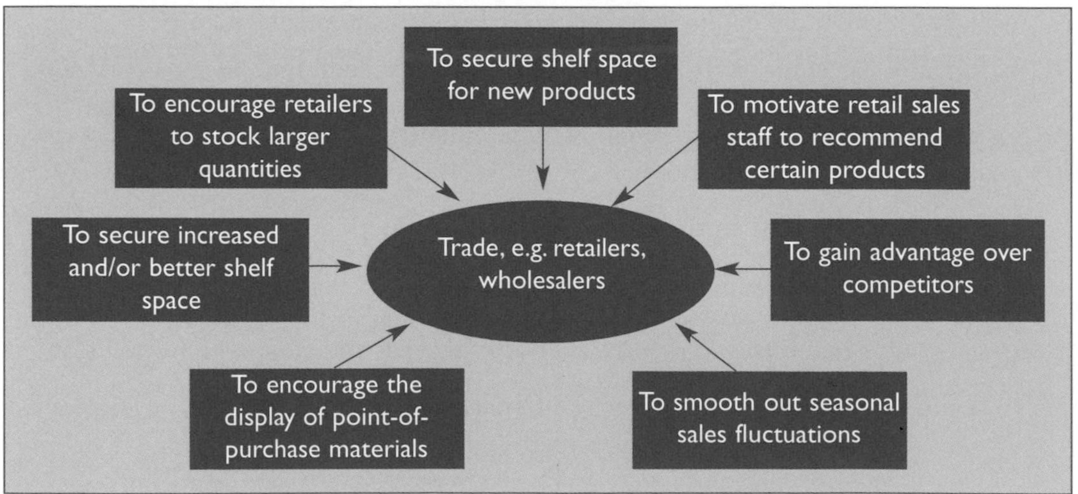

The role of employee-oriented sales promotion

An important target audience for sales promotion is employees. The incentives and supports can have a very positive impact on an organisation's sales performance. In addition, some companies use sales promotion techniques in order to cultivate loyalty among staff. In times of economic boom, sales promotion contributes to staff retention, thus enabling companies to remain competitive.

Figure 11.3 illustrates the main purposes of employee-oriented sales promotion:

Figure 11.3 Role of employee-oriented sales promotion

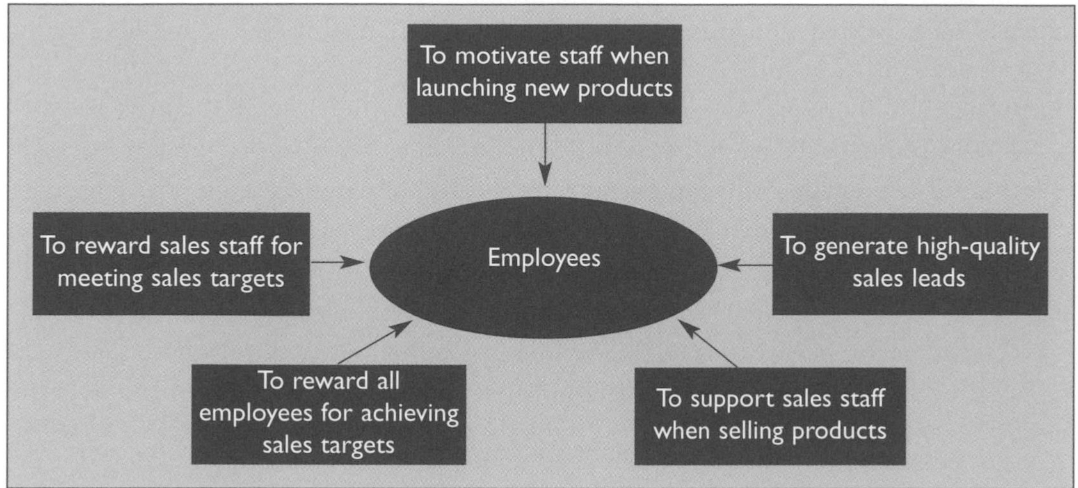

- **to motivate staff when launching new products**. It is often easier for sales staff to meet their targets by selling existing products. Therefore, they may need specific incentives to motivate them to sell new products. Sales promotion techniques are used for this.
- **to reward sales staff for meeting sales targets**. Sales promotion techniques can be used by organisations to motivate and reward sales representatives.
- **to reward all staff in an organisation for sales achieved**. Many organisations recognise that it is not only the front-line employees who contribute to sales figures. Sales promotion is used to reward all staff, thus recognising their contributions to commercial success.
- **to support sales staff in their efforts to sell products**. Just as retailers need visual aids to enhance products, sales staff also require support material in order to sell products.
- **to generate sales leads**. Many organisations use sales promotions to reward staff for generating sales leads. Some organisations grade the sales leads on the basis of their quality. Quality is evaluated by tracking the total number of leads which are converted into sales, the monetary value of the sales, and the potential life-time value of the new customer.

Consumer-oriented sales promotion tools

Consumer sales promotions are, as the name suggests, aimed at the end consumer. As retailer power grows, manufacturers need to counter this by ensuring that consumers want their products. In using sales promotions, the manufacturers are trying to make their products more desirable so consumers will pull their products through the distribution channel. This approach is based on the premise that if the sales promotion tools used are appealing enough, the consumer will demand that the retailer sell the product. The following sales promotion tools are used by organisations to help them achieve consumer-oriented objectives.

Sampling

Sampling *When free or discounted samples of a product are made available to the target audience.*

Sampling is a technique whereby free or discounted samples of a product are made available to the target audience. It is very effective because the consumer experiences the product first-hand and, if a favourable impression is made, the desire to purchase may be strong. However, sampling is relatively expensive and tends to be more effective for FMCGs because the products are relatively inexpensive in the first place. Sampling works best for products whose effects can be judged immediately. Otherwise, there may not be sufficient product contained in the sample for it to have the desired effect. Samples reach consumers in a number of ways.

Door drops

In Ireland this is a common distribution method and it is not unusual for a number of non-competing companies to collaborate and share delivery costs. However, it can be wasteful because samples are delivered to all houses in a neighbourhood, regardless of whether or not a member of the target audience resides there. Feminine hygiene product manufacturers use door drops to deliver free samples but these are wasted in all-male households.

Direct mail

To reduce wastage of the type indicated above, some companies use direct mail to distribute their samples. This means that they are not necessarily sent to everyone living in a particular area. Instead, the samples are sent to those consumers most likely to use the product. While postage costs mean that this method is quite expensive, it is less wasteful. Lyons Tea used this approach in a seasonal mail shot coming up to St Patrick's day. It contained a teabag that could either be used by the recipient or forwarded to an overseas friend of the recipient (See Exhibit 11.1).

On-pack sampling

A sample of a product is attached to another non-competitive, often complementary product, for example, Roma pasta and Dolmio pasta sauces, and Cadbury's drinking chocolate and confectionery items, often provide vehicles for one another. The difficulty with this approach is that the main product assumes an unusual shape and can present difficulties for retailers when stacking their shelves. Even more crucially, the packs may

Exhibit 11.1

Someone you know missing the taste of home?

This St. Patrick's Day, send a friend or loved one a little reminder of home. Wherever they are in the world, cheer them up with a comforting cup of LYONS tea sent all the way from Ireland.

Enclosed you'll find a self-sealing envelope containing 3 LYONS Original Blend teabags, ready to be addressed, stamped and posted. There's also space to write a personal message.

So even though you can't be there, let them know you're thinking of them.

Enjoy a cup of LYONS tea yourself - enclosed you'll find a coupon for 50c off your next purchase of LYONS Original Blend 80's teabags.

Because there's life, there's LYONS

take up more space than usual and this is unpopular with retailers because they do not receive additional revenue with each sale.

Magazine sampling

The main advantage of magazines is that they enable the marketer to reach specific target audiences. Samples are regularly attached to teenage magazines, and the cosmetics industry avails of the wide range of women's magazines to introduce readers to their products. Some samples are contained within magazines. For example, cosmetics companies use gatefolds (see page 161) to carry perfume samples. This makes a much greater impact than attempting to describe a smell.

Retailers often experience problems when samples are attached to the covers of magazines, because people steal the samples and in the process, damage the covers. This has led a rise in the number of magazines complete with samples being sent to retailers in clear plastic packaging. However, this involves considerable costs and environmental consequences. An alternative is for the retailer to keep the sample behind the counter and give it to the customer when they buy the magazine. This means additional work for the retailer.

Consumers must be cautious of some samples that accompany magazines. In Ireland, many publications originate in the UK. Personal computer magazines from the UK often carry free CD-ROMs. When Internet usage became more popular in people's homes, many UK Internet service providers (ISPs) gave away CD-ROMs with magazines which, when installed, connected the user to the Internet. They were aimed at the UK market and did not carry warnings to alert non-UK residents to the fact that while all log-on charges were at local rates, these rates were only applicable to UK residents. Irish users who installed the disks, and accessed the Internet through ISPs in the UK only discovered this, sometimes shocking, fact when they received their phone bills, which were much higher than usual. Why was this? It was because they had been surfing the net via the UK so call charges were based on the cost of a call from Ireland to the UK.

In-store sampling

Retailers allow a certain amount of in-store sampling to take place in their stores. This involves a representative from the product manufacturer's company setting up a stand in a retail outlet and distributing free samples for customers to taste or use. This method is very effective because it takes place at the point of purchase, thus making it possible to motivate impulse purchases. In order to reinforce positive reactions and to encourage purchase, customers are usually given a money-off coupon for the product in question. While this method of sampling is very effective, retailers only permit a limited amount of tastings at any one time. Therefore, negotiations must take place between the producer and the retailer early in the year in order to gain permission and to agree schedules. Retailers might request a producer to run tastings in particular outlets to accelerate the sales of flagging products.

Sponsored events

Sponsors use events to distribute samples of their products, which results in targeted distribution (see Chapter 10).

__Coupons__ entitle the holder to money off specific products.

Coupons

Coupons are a widely used sales promotion tool and they entitle the holder to money off specific products. While retailers' co-operation is essential, coupons do not interfere with their shelf space. They also mean that the retailer does not have to reduce the retail price. Therefore, the manufacturer bears the full cost of the promotion. Consequently, coupons are quite popular with retailers.

Coupons are effective when used in conjunction with in-store tastings (see above). They might encourage consumers to try new products because they feel that by not paying the full price and this reduces any risk. Coupons are also used to attract consumers who may not otherwise be prepared to pay the full price. However, such support should not continue in the long run, so an organisation should investigate whether or not these consumers are ever likely to be prepared to pay the full price.

There are a number of disadvantages associated with coupons:

- Many companies use coupons to attract new customers to purchase established products. However, the coupons are often distributed in a non-targeted manner. This means that loyal consumers, who would have paid the full price anyway, avail of the discount.

  Technology can go some way towards rectifying this problem. Since the advent of loyalty card schemes, retailers have the potential to target coupons at specific customers. They can analyse the purchasing habits of cardholders and use this information to persuade manufacturers to provide the retailer with coupons in order to increase sales of certain products or to reward loyal customers for buying particular brands. In addition, retailers can send out coupons for own-brand products in an effort to persuade customers to switch from a manufacturer's brand. For example, a retailer can see that a customer is buying Kerrygold butter on a regular basis. In order to persuade that person to switch to Tesco's own brand, they can send out a mail shot containing coupons for their own-brand butter. They know that the customer buys butter, so the challenge is to persuade them to switch their brand allegiance.

Manufacturers work with the likes of the Internet company, pigsback.com, to target their coupons at the right people. When a consumer registers with pigsback.com, they are asked to supply information about themselves. This enables pigsback.com to build individual customer profiles. Manufacturers and service providers specify the type of consumers they want to target and devise special offers in order to appeal to them. Pigsback.com then match these specifications with their database and communicate a tailored range of special offers to those who are most likely to respond. For example, when registering, someone may have stated that they drink wine. When a wine distributor goes to pigsback.com with a special offer, this person will probably be informed and invited to avail of the offer.

They also give consumers the opportunity to select coupons for FMCGs that most appeal to them. Regular e-mails invite the addressee to view coupons for a range of branded goods and to click on those that they would like to use. Having done this, the addressee can print off their own personalised set of coupons and use them with the retailer before the expiry date. The main advantages of this are:

1. The manufacturer does not waste money printing coupons that will never be used. Instead, the user incurs the printing costs. The coupons only end up with those who really want them.
2. Not only can the manufacturer track the number of coupons that have been redeemed, but, due to the fact that the coupons are personalised, manufacturers also know exactly who has responded. That person's name becomes part of the manufacturer's database. This is very important due to growing retailer power.

- Coupon redemption rates tend to be low. **Redemption rates** refer to the number of consumers who use the coupon. A few factors contribute to low redemption rates. Coupon users need to be organised and resolute in their intention to redeem the coupon. Many people are disorganised and forget to bring coupons with them when they go shopping.

Redemption rates
The number of consumers who actually use coupons.

Also, in Ireland, there used to be a certain amount of stigma associated with using coupons, and as a result, consumers did not want to be seen presenting them at the checkout.

Mis-redemption of coupons in retail outlets incurs costs. Many companies who distribute coupons have a wide range of products and different versions of each. For example, Donegal Catch might distribute money-off coupons for their Chunky Cod Fillets range but a customer may present the coupon when purchasing haddock. Whether or not it is accepted depends on the vigilance and care taken by the checkout assistant. In such cases, the coupon is usually accepted and the manufacturer pays for the mistake.

Unlike sampling, consumer response to coupons is rarely immediate. This contributes to low redemption rates because, even though the consumer intent is there, they may initially forget to bring the coupon with them when they go shopping. To introduce a sense of urgency, manufacturers often include usage deadlines, for example 'Valid until ...', with a date indicating the deadline by which the coupon must be redeemed.

Coupons are distributed to consumers through a number of channels:

- **Direct mail** and **email** are used frequently.
- **Printed media** – newspaper and magazine advertisements – include coupons and the reader cuts them out.

Bounce-back coupons *Included on product packaging and entitle the product user to money off their next purchase.*

- Some manufacturers print coupons on product **packaging**. These are redeemable against the customer's next purchase, and are known as **bounce-back coupons**.
- When **in-store** sampling is conducted, those who try the product are usually given a money-off coupon to reinforce their purchase intent. Manufacturers often use this technique in retail outlets and pubs. Also, point-of-purchase displays are used to carry product-specific literature that might also incorporate coupons.
- **Outdoor distribution** can be used, for example, to distribute coupons to commuters. This often results in wastage because it is a relatively untargeted method of distribution.
- As we saw in Chapter 10, **sponsored events** are often used to distribute coupons. Compared to some of the other distribution methods, this is generally well targeted.

Cash refunds

Consumers are sometimes offered cash refunds when they buy the product in question. To receive the refund, the customer must take the initiative and send proof of purchase to the manufacturer. The cash is then posted out to the consumer or credited to their bank or credit card account. Retailers are not required to do anything in this instance. The manufacturer can develop a direct relationship with respondents and add them to their database. Unless the refund is very attractive, response rates tend to be low because the consumer actually has to do something to get the refund.

Bonus packs

Bonus quantities of a product are given to consumers in a number of ways:

- Larger packaging contains more product at no additional cost, for example, 50 per cent. The manufacturer incurs additional one-off packaging costs. However, these packs require additional retail shelf space and do not generate additional profit for the retailer.
- Extra units of the existing product size are offered at no additional cost, for example, Boots regularly offers three items for the price of two.

Bonus packs *Bonus quantities of a product given to consumers in the form of larger packaging or additional packs.*

The main purpose of using bonus packs is to remove consumers from the purchasing cycle for long periods, thus keeping them away from competitors' products and promotions.

Bonus-pack promotions are easier to implement and manage than other consumer sales promotions. However, it is difficult to track exactly which consumers availed of the offers. They tend to appeal primarily to price-sensitive consumers who are not loyal to any particular brand. Therefore, the manufacturer may not enjoy long-term benefits from this method.

Premiums

Premiums are gifts or discounted items that are offered with a product. They are intended to act as an additional incentive to the consumer to buy a particular product and, in many cases, they add value to the core product. They either come free with a product or as self-liquidating premiums. **Self-liquidating premiums** are where the consumer meets some or all of the cost of the premium. They may also have to pay for delivery costs. Consumers have to do more to avail of self-liquidating premiums. This means that redemption rates are often much lower than on-pack premiums.

Premiums *Gifts or discounted items.*

Self-liquidating premiums *Where the consumer pays some or all of the cost of the premium.*

Premiums are distributed in a number of ways:

- free and attached to or in the core product's packaging, for example, Kellogg's breakfast cereals
- free and located near the core product
- available on request from the distribution outlet on presentation of proof-of-purchase of the core product
- available direct from the manufacturer. The consumer may have to collect a number of coupons and send them back to the manufacturer. Depending on the promotion, the consumer may have to pay for the premium and cover any postage and packaging costs. Unlike point-of-purchase distribution of premiums, this method allows the manufacturer to increase its database and build a direct relationship with the consumer.

There are a number of drawbacks associated with premiums:

- The quality and image of the premium can have a negative impact on the core product. If a brand strives to promote a quality image, provision of a cheap, low-quality premium might damage the brand.

- Premiums are expensive. In promotions where the consumer has to send off for the premium, administrative costs to the company are high. These costs entail stock control, packing and distribution. It can also be difficult to accurately predict the response level. Over-estimation results in the purchase of a surplus number of premiums, while under-estimation can lead to delivery delays. This can have detrimental effects on customer loyalty and perceptions of service quality.
- On-pack premiums present difficulties for retailers. Unless the premium is actually contained within the existing packaging, on-pack premiums can be irregular in size and add significantly to the area usually occupied by the core product. It involves surrendering more shelf space for no extra profit. In countering this argument, manufacturers contend that such promotions lead to an increase in the number of units of a product being sold. Nevertheless, the retailer may refuse to stock such promotions or decide to locate them in a less favourable location.

Competitions, free draws and lotteries

Competitions are regularly mailed to customers in magazines. They usually pose questions, the answers to which can be found within the publication. This method is used by the likes of Tesco, Eircom, AIB Bank and the VHI. The questions are deliberately easy so as to maximise response levels and, where appropriate, product purchase.

Competitions that require respondents to devise slogans about the product are very popular in Ireland. For years, Lyons Tea has used this approach and the prizes are usually significant, for example, cars, or mortgage payments covered for ten years.

Free prize draws usually require the participant to do nothing but submit their name, contact information and sometimes some additional details.

The prizes on offer should reflect the core values of the brand and should not undermine them in any way. There is also a danger that the competition itself can detract from the brand. It is not clear whether or not this form of sales promotion builds brand loyalty because some consumers merely buy the product in order to participate in the competition and they never intend purchasing the product again. Manufacturers view competitions and lotteries as a way of building customer databases so that they can build more direct contact with consumers.

Loyalty schemes

Technology has enabled many companies to develop loyalty schemes. Customers are given smart cards that record purchase information. The cardholder is awarded points that are then translated into money-off vouchers or they can be used to 'purchase' products. Retailers use these schemes to reward their customers and to persuade them to buy certain products. For example, Superquinn works with suppliers and offers cardholders bonus points if they purchase certain products.

Trade-oriented sales promotion tools

Manufacturers have at their disposal many sales promotion tools that can be used when dealing with their distributors. More and more retailers are by-passing wholesalers and purchase directly from the manufacturers. The more buying power enjoyed by the retailer, the greater the need for the manufacturer to implement generous sales promotion programmes aimed at these powerful customers. This helps ensure that the manufacturer is granted all-important shelf space for their products.

Trade allowances

The primary objective of offering trade allowances is to increase the likelihood that distributors will stock a particular product or range of products. Essentially, allowances are given in the form of product, cash, discounts, special payment terms and special delivery agreements.

Product or merchandise allowances

When distributors order merchandise, the manufacturer gives them additional stock free of charge. In exchange for this, the distributor might give the product a prime location or may actively promote its sale. Once the distributors have sold the products they paid for, additional sales represent a very high profit. Ideally, manufacturers would prefer the cost savings to be passed on to the end consumer.

Discounts

Some manufacturers offer discounts based on orders received. These are shown on the final invoices. The objective is to encourage distributors to purchase large quantities.

Special payment terms

Manufacturers negotiate payment terms that meet the needs of their distributors. This may entail offering extended payment periods.

Slotting fees/allowances

In many countries, larger, more powerful retailers charge manufacturers fees in exchange for shelf space for new products. This particular practice has been the subject of much scrutiny in Ireland and other EU countries. It is seen by some as unfair practice but retailers argue that they need financial compensation to cover the cost of stocking new products with no proven track record. They also maintain that the cost of rearranging merchandise to make way for new products is an expensive task and that they should be paid for doing it.

Point-of-purchase displays

Many manufacturers provide their distributors with point-of-purchase material. This consists of promotional material that is used in the retail environment to attract the attention of consumers. It includes free-standing displays, stickers, demonstration equipment, posters, packaging, carrier bags and display cabinets. Depending on the power and revenue-generating ability of the distributor, and the expense of the materials involved, the manufacturer provides these items free of charge or at a reduced rate. Point-of-purchase materials are influential in the retail environment and often stimulate impulse purchases. Some manufacturers assist with the installation of these items. In the Irish mobile phone market, retail outlets expect to receive point-of-purchase support from the phone manufacturers and the service providers.

Brochures, leaflets, catalogues

These provide information for the trade and their customers. Detailed versions of company literature are usually provided for sales personnel, while abridged versions may be supplied for consumers.

Sales training

Sales training is provided for the trade in instances where they are required to sell complex or speciality products like computers, electrical products and DIY equipment. These programmes are supported with sales and technical manuals. The better the sales representative understands a particular make, the more likely they are to promote it. Premium brand manufacturers, like cosmetic companies, believe that sales representatives must embody the brand's values. These brand values are imparted on training programmes.

Contests and incentives

These are used to motivate retail sales staff and are similar to those used for the manufacturer's own staff. Typically, they reward sales staff on the basis of sales volume and the value of that volume. However, these programmes can be a cause of concern to managers in retail outlets. Sales staff may promote a particular product in order to benefit from an incentive scheme. Consequently, customers may be persuaded to buy products that do not exactly meet their needs. This may lead to dissatisfaction with the retailer and the manufacturer, causing them to switch to competitors the next time they need to purchase a related product.

Co-operative advertising

Co-operative advertising is where manufacturers support channel members' advertising activity. In return, the distributor highlights the manufacturer's products in the advertisements and draws attention to the products in the retail environment.

Employee-oriented sales promotion tools

Many of the tools already outlined under consumer- and trade-oriented tools are used to motivate and retain staff. The most commonly used tools are premiums, competitions and incentives, loyalty schemes, support literature and training. For example, Superquinn extends its Superclub points to staff and point allocation is based on sales. Staff-oriented sales promotions are dealt with in Chapter 13, which examines personal selling.

Table 11.3 provides a summary of sales promotion tools.

Table 11.3 Sales promotion tools

Consumer-oriented	Trade-oriented	Staff-oriented
• Sampling	• Trade allowances	• Premiums
• Coupons	• Product allowances	• Competitions
• Cash refunds	• Discounts	• Loyalty schemes
• Bonus packs	• Slotting fees	• Training
• Premiums	• Special payment terms	• Support literature
• On-pack	• Point-of-purchase displays	
• Self-liquidating	• Brochures, leaflets, catalogues	
• Competitions, free draws, lotteries	• Sales training programmes	
• Loyalty schemes	• Contests and incentives	
	• Co-operative advertising	

Sales promotions and the marketing communications mix

The most successful sales promotions are those that integrate fully with other elements of the marketing communications mix. Technology has the ability to make many sales promotions campaigns more effective. It also blurs the line between sales promotion and direct marketing. For example, should the loyalty programmes being run by Ireland's leading retailers be categorised as sales promotions or as direct marketing? The reality is that they combine both disciplines. Similarly, how do you categorise the Internet initiatives like pigsback.com. They appear to focus on sales promotions, but use technology to help ensure that each participant gets the most out of the scheme. Sales promotion is frequently used by advertisers to grab their audiences' attention. Power City's big advertising idea is built around sales promotions. Their messages focus on price reductions and limited time periods in which to avail of such offers. During the World Cup of 2002, the radio station 98FM advertised the fact that they were hosting a party in Annabelle's night club during the Ireland/Germany match. To make their offer more attractive, they promised all attendees a complementary bottle of Miller beer on arrival.

Companies involved in sponsorship activity employ sales promotion techniques at events. For example, food and drinks companies might offer free product tastings and distribute money-off coupons to the attendees.

The downside of sales promotion

Some or all of the sales promotion tools described in this chapter regularly overwhelm consumers and the trade. While the results of these campaigns are relatively easy to measure in the short term, there are long-term consequences that must not be ignored.

While sales promotions are usually successful at accelerating purchase decisions in the short term, it often transpires that consumers are merely 'on loan' from competitors. As soon as the price returns to a non-discounted level, consumers might migrate to other brands.

Brand equity *The financial value that a firm puts on a brand.*

The most worrying aspect of consumer sales promotions is their long-term effect on brand equity. **Brand equity** is the financial value that a firm puts on its brand. The value is determined by many factors, including consumers' perceptions of the brand. The frequency and types of sales promotion used influences these perceptions. Many sales promotions fail to communicate the brand's core values and attributes. Instead they focus on price. If a brand is regularly subjected to sales promotions, it might be devalued in the consumer's mind. Consumers may begin to believe that there is something wrong with the brand or they may not be prepared to pay the full price for the product or service.

Of course, some firms such as Ryanair and Lidl successfully differentiate themselves on the basis of highly competitive prices. This enables them to build brand equity as a result. However, unless price differentiation is a long-term and sustainable strategy, over reliance on sales promotions is not advisable.

Checklist for creating sales promotions that work

1. Testing

It is advisable to test a sales promotion with a representative sample of the entire target audience before executing the entire campaign. This will indicate the likely level of response to the offer. Testing is particularly important when premiums are involved because it will help the organisation estimate the likely quantity required in order to fulfil the offer.

2. The sales promotion must be easily understood

The more complex the promotion, the lower the response rates are likely to be. Complexity can also place pressure on customer service staff as consumers inundate customer helplines with queries. Also, the resulting confusion and the way it is handled may have a negative impact on the brand.

3. The sales promotion should be distinctive

It is difficult to be original in today's crowded market. Most techniques have been tried and tested. However, before embarking on a campaign, organisations should be aware of what competitors are doing and ensure that the proposed promotion is different.

4. Operational aspects must be planned

Many sales promotions represent the commencement of a dialogue between the consumer and the organisation. This must be planned so that each response is dealt with efficiently. For example, when consumers send off for premiums, they expect to receive them within a short period of time (unless otherwise stated). They expect them to be in stock and in good condition when they arrive. Fulfilling such expectations requires planning and has human resource implications. Many organisations recognise that they do not have the necessary resources in-house, and employ the services of an outside organisation.

5. The brand must not be compromised

The offer should be in keeping with the brand's core values. If a company spends money on advertising campaigns that draw attention to certain core values, it is vital that sales promotions do not communicate conflicting values. For example, if premiums are offered, their quality should reflect the brand's quality. If a premium falls apart, the recipient attributes its poor workmanship to the company who offered it to them and not to the manufacturer of the premium.

Summary

Sales promotion is an acceleration tool that is used to motivate consumers, trade and employees into making purchases. It has enjoyed growing popularity in Ireland and other European countries for a number of reasons. Irish and European food retailers hold immense power over their suppliers and own information about their suppliers' purchasing patterns as a result of loyalty schemes. Retailers are consolidating and using their strength and experience to engage in central purchasing. Another weapon in their armoury is high-quality own brands. In many product sectors, consumers have less brand loyalty and are more sensitive to value-driven sales promotions. Manufacturers want to use results-oriented marketing communications tools and sales promotion meets this requirement.

Sales promotion motivates consumers and trade to try new products and stock up on existing ones. It can also encourage them to buy products on a regular basis. Producers of seasonal products use sales promotion to smooth out sales fluctuations. Sales promotion may help secure vantage points for products in retail outlets. There is a wide range of sales promotion tools to choose from, including sampling, coupons and premiums for consumers.

Sales promotion integrates well with other elements of the marketing communications mix and draws attention to the message. However, organisations should use sales promotion sparingly. Even though it can deliver impressive results in the short term, it may inflict long-term damage on brand equity.

Useful websites

www.spii.ie Sales Promotion Institute of Ireland
www.pigsback.com pigsback.com

Review questions

1. Discuss reasons why sales promotion has grown in popularity in Ireland.
2. Examine in detail the role of sales promotion. Use examples that you are familiar with to illustrate your answer.
3. Critically assess the various consumer-oriented and trade-oriented sales promotion tools.
4. Discuss the advantages and disadvantages of sales promotion.

Exercise

Visit a supermarket and look for three consumer-oriented sales promotions. Categorise them using Table 11.3 on page 305 as a guide. Critically assess the following:

- Do the sales promotions occupy a good space in the supermarket?
- Do you think they cause problems for the retailer?
- Do you think they support the brands or do they undermine them?

To the best of your knowledge, are the various promotions supported by any other marketing communications activity, for example, advertising, public relations, direct mail?

References

Burnett, John and Moriarty, Sandra, *Introduction to Marketing Communications: An Integrated Approach* (Prentice Hall, 1998).

Perkins, Ben, 'The European retail grocery market overview' (*British Food Journal*, Vol. 103, No. 10, pp. 744–8, 2001).

Pickton, David and Broderick, Amanda, *Integrated Marketing Communications* (Financial Times/Prentice Hall, 2001).

Semenik, Richard J., *Promotion and Integrated Marketing Communications* (South-Western, 2002).

Shimp, T. A., *Advertising, Promotion and Supplemental Aspects of Integrated Marketing Communications*, 4th edition (Dryden Press, 1997).

Vignali, Claudio, 'Tesco's adaptation to the Irish market' (*British Food Journal*, Vol. 103, No. 2, pp. 146–63, 2001).

12

DIRECT MARKETING

The aims and objectives of this chapter are:

- to examine direct marketing and its role in integrated marketing communications, and in particular:
  - to define 'direct marketing'
  - to explain the reasons for its growth in Ireland
  - to help you understand the types of objectives that direct marketing can fulfil
  - to demonstrate the value and importance of a good database and the challenges inherent in its compilation and maintenance
  - to help you critically assess the various direct marketing media
  - to assess direct marketing's relationship with other elements of the marketing communications mix
  - to evaluate the role of technology in direct marketing.

Introduction

Direct marketing carries with it many negative connotations for marketing practitioners and the target audiences that they are trying to reach. Mention 'direct marketing' to a group of people and at least one person will think or say 'junk mail'. While some direct marketing communications deserve this derogatory label, so-called 'junk mail' does offer firms an effective way of communicating directly with existing and potential customers in a highly personalised manner.

Another misconception about direct marketing is that it is the same as direct mail. This ignores the range of direct marketing media available to organisations and fails to celebrate the strategic value of the discipline.

Direct marketing is well placed to play a central role in a business environment that places increasing emphasis on relationship marketing. It is well placed to take advantage of technological advances that have been made and continue to be made (see Chapter 14).

Finally, direct marketing has the potential to assist organisations in their quest to fully integrate all elements of the marketing communications mix. Perhaps it is these aspects that may help elevate direct marketing from its lowly position in the marketing communications mix to its rightful place alongside the other elements.

What is direct marketing?

Direct marketing
An interactive way of marketing that uses one or more media to effect a measurable response and/or transaction at any location.

Direct marketing is one of the elements in the marketing communications mix. As well as fulfilling an important marketing communications function, it is used to support firms in the distribution of their products and services to existing and potential customers. Both aspects are highlighted in the American Direct Marketing Association's (ADMA) definition, which states that 'direct marketing is an interactive system of marketing which uses one or more advertising media to effect a measurable response and/or transaction at any location' (cited in McDonald, 1998). The definition raises three important direct marketing characteristics – it is interactive, its results are measurable and it has location flexibility.

Interactivity

Unlike some of the other elements in the marketing communications mix, direct marketing is interactive. It enables firms to communicate with individuals in a personalised manner. The more information a firm holds about an individual, the more tailored the communications can be. The interactive nature of direct marketing means that the firm and the targeted individual can engage in two-way communication. Direct marketing campaigns actively encourage individuals to respond by e-mail, telephone or mail. These responses give firms valuable information about respondents. In turn, this information is used to refine and improve subsequent communications.

Measurable responses

The performance of a direct marketing programme campaign can be measured. Firms can count the number of responses they receive. This enables them to calculate the overall effectiveness of a campaign. To do this they must record:

- the number of people contacted and the investment required
- the number of responses received and the handling costs incurred in dealing with these responses
- the number of respondents who fulfilled the organisation's objectives, for example, purchased a product, agreed to meet a sales person.

Many firms recognise the role direct marketing plays in customer relationship management. It fits well with the shift from transaction-based marketing (i.e. one-off sales) to relationship marketing (i.e. long-term, mutually beneficial relationships between the firm and the customer). Firms must track respondents' long-term activity to estimate the true cost of the initial and subsequent direct marketing activity. For example, many people respond to direct mail campaigns because they offer attractive incentives. Once respondents have received the incentives, they may sever all links with the firm. While initial analyses suggest that the campaigns were successful, further examination would reveal that the campaigns were costly and ineffective.

Location

Direct marketing activity can be conducted without building expensive retail outlets and without the assistance of agents and distributors. This is an attractive option for many firms because it enables them to enjoy direct relationships with their customers. It may also save them money that can instead be invested in technology such as the Internet and telecommunications. In Ireland, the banking and insurance sectors are investing heavily in the provision of direct marketing networks, for example, call centres. This move means that AIB Bank and the Bank of Ireland have been able to close some of their physical retail outlets.

Test-ability

There is a further aspect of direct marketing that is not mentioned in the ADMA's definition and that is its facility for testing. All elements of the marketing communications mix require significant investment and it is often difficult to predict in advance which programmes will succeed. Even the most highly skilled practitioners in the industry experience failure. However, the costs of failure can be prohibitive, particularly in television advertising. A certain amount of marketing research can be carried out in advance of an advertising campaign to find out whether the target audience likes it. However, because this research is not conducted under 'real' conditions, it may prove unreliable.

Direct marketing testing involves the manipulation of independent variables, such as price or creative treatment, and going live to small samples of the target audience with different versions of a campaign. Response levels are used to evaluate which approach works best before exposing the entire target audience to the campaign. Therefore, testing minimises the likelihood of implementing a campaign that does not work.

Testing is examined in more detail later in this chapter.

The growth of direct marketing

Since the 1980s, Europe and the United States have experienced significant levels of growth in the use of direct marketing. It is difficult to measure the actual size of the direct marketing industry in Ireland because its activity is difficult to track fully. It incorporates call centres, inserts with customer bills and statements, mail shots, e-mail and direct response advertising. Despite this, it is widely acknowledged that it is a significant industry and a number of factors have contributed to this trend (summarised in Table 12.1):

Table 12.1 Reasons for the growth in direct marketing

- Growing consumer cynicism towards traditional media
- Fragmentation of traditional media and consumer audiences
- Call for greater accountability of marketing communications expenditure
- Improvements in database technology
- Advent and widespread availability of desktop publishing
- The liberalisation of the telecommunications sector
- Growth in credit card usage
- Growing retailer strength
- Cash-rich, time-poor consumers

- **growing cynicism towards traditional media**. Consumers have demonstrated growing dissatisfaction and cynicism with the more traditional methods of communication, such as advertising.
- **fragmentation of media and audiences**. As we saw in Chapter 7, traditional media, such as television and radio, have fragmented. Similarly, consumer audiences have fragmented and differences between segments is more pronounced. These changes have prompted many advertisers to question the merits of investing large sums of money in advertising, when direct marketing techniques allow them to communicate with target audiences as individuals.
- **call for greater accountability**. Marketing departments are under pressure to account for their expenditure on marketing communications. As explained in Chapter 8, it is often difficult to measure the effectiveness of advertising, whereas marketing communications elements that seek responses from target audiences, such as direct marketing and sales promotion, are more accountable.
- **improvements in database technology**. Continuing improvements in technology enable large and small firms to build and maintain comprehensive customer databases (see below). There has been a dramatic decline in the costs associated with the collection, maintenance and usage of customer information. This gives firms the capability to tailor their marketing communications and target specific messages at individuals.
- **desktop publishing**. The advent of desktop publishing allows firms to produce their own promotional material in-house at a relatively low cost.
- **liberalisation of the telecommunications sector**. The liberalisation of the telecommunications sector across Europe, allied with technological advancements in telecommunications hardware and software, has precipitated a growth in the number

of call centres and in-house telemarketing facilities. These receive calls from current and potential customers (in-bound calls), and enable firms to make telephone calls to current and potential customers (out-bound calls). Liberalisation has also led to very high levels of mobile phone ownership. This allows firms to contact target audiences through non-voice methods, such as SMS (short message service) and MMS (media message service).

- **credit card usage**. Until the 1990s boom, Irish consumers did not use credit cards to the same extent as their European counterparts. They have subsequently caught up and this gives consumers greater flexibility when buying products and services because they can pay for them over the phone and on the Internet.
- **growing retailer power**. The growing strength of retailers across Europe and the United States has motivated manufacturers to establish direct relationships with the end user of their products.
- **cash-rich, time-poor consumers**. Many consumers are cash-rich and time-poor. Consequently, they attach great importance to time and, in many instances, they do not want to eat into their leisure time visiting retail outlets and business premises. Many welcome the opportunity to gain direct access to products and services from home or work. Mail, phone and the Internet facilitate this.

Like their international counterparts, many marketing practitioners in Ireland acknowledge the trends outlined above. Some have worked in countries where the merits of direct marketing are well regarded. They subsequently returned to Ireland, bringing their positive experiences and expertise with them. In response, many advertising agencies established direct marketing subsidiaries and a number of specialist agencies also emerged. According to the Irish Direct Marketing Association's (IDMA) 2003 directory, there are 15 agencies listed under the categories 'direct marketing agency' and 'direct marketing consultant'. Of these, three are subsidiaries of advertising agencies. Elsewhere in the directory, five additional advertising agencies draw attention to their expertise in direct marketing.

The IDMA was founded in 1988 in recognition of the growing interest and commitment to direct marketing in Ireland. It is the official representative body for the Irish direct marketing industry. An important part of its remit is to set standards for its members and help eradicate the industry's negative image. It has an educational role, as some members voiced concern at the lack of formal training in the area of direct marketing. As a result, the Diploma in Direct Marketing was launched and has attracted a student cohort from both client and agency organisations.

In the 1990s, the Irish Government's industrial policy contributed to the growth in direct marketing activity. The Industrial Authority of Ireland (IDA) was charged with establishing Ireland as a location for call centres. Global players, such as Citibank and Dell, were persuaded to locate their call centres in Ireland. This enticed third-level graduates, many with language skills, to pursue careers in these centres. As a result, Ireland has a pool of skilled employees capable of working in telemarketing.

Direct marketing objectives

Firms use direct marketing to achieve a range of objectives (summarised in Table 12.2):

Table 12.2 Direct marketing objectives

- To generate sales leads
- To build and enhance a database
- To generate sales
- To create cross-selling opportunities
- To persuade customers to upgrade
- To attract lapsed customers

- **to generate leads**. Many organisations use direct marketing to support the sales function. In particular, out-bound telemarketing is often used to secure appointments that are subsequently followed up with visits from sales representatives.
- **to build a database**. Databases are at the heart of direct marketing. However, unidentified potential customers may exist and a direct marketing campaign can be used to find these people and to encourage them to make contact. Direct response advertising is used to motivate responses from interested people.

Exhibit 12.1

How much could you save by remortgaging your home over the phone?

3.0% APR variable

Well, when you add up the difference a lower interest rate could make to your repayments, the saving could run into thousands. And that's not the only advantage of remortgaging over the phone. You also get the flexibility of longer opening hours and great customer service to make the whole process entirely hassle-free. Better still, this whole package has been put together by one of the most reliable and well-established names in the business – Bank of Scotland.

The facts speak for themselves

For starters, the rate is a staggeringly low 3.0% APR. And that's not a special offer that only lasts for a few months.

Bank of Scotland's Price Promise' guarantees that its standard variable rate will never be more than 1.5% above the published European Base Rate*. Just think how much you could save over the lifetime of your mortgage simply by switching to a better rate. It could add up to thousands of pounds over the years. Compare the example below with your existing mortgage payments.

If you were paying a €100,000 repayment mortgage over 20 years, the rate would be 3.0% APR with a monthly repayment of just €554.60 (based on a loan to value of 70%).

What's more, for customers looking for a lower loan to the value of up to 60%‡, Bank of Scotland now offer a Tracker Mortgage, which tracks the European Base Rate* for the **life** of your mortgage, not just a set period. So if you've been thinking about remortgaging, this offer from such a credible lender is well worth considering.

Raise extra money when you remortgage

Another bonus of remortgaging with Bank of Scotland is that you can raise additional funds. In fact, you could get up to €75,000 from the equity in your property by simply switching your existing mortgage to Bank of Scotland. You can also add any extra legal expenses to your overall loan amount too.

So, what do I do next?

Simply call Bank of Scotland and you can remortgage your home over the phone, so think of the time you could save. The opening hours are longer, 8am to 8pm, seven days a week, giving you more flexibility.

When you phone, you're guaranteed to get a friendly person answering your call. And just as importantly, you can be sure that you're also talking to a mortgage expert who's qualified to answer all your questions. They'll do their best to explain everything as clearly as possible, without using any jargon.

How long does it take?

When you're looking to remortgage, you're bound to want a quick decision. No one likes to be kept waiting while mortgage lenders make their minds up. That's why Bank of Scotland provides quotations and provisional approval in a matter of minutes. As you'd expect, they'll also do everything they can to make the whole process as fast and trouble-free as possible.

What next?

If you've got more questions or you just want to get started, it's free to call Bank of Scotland's friendly advisers now on **1800 556 577**.

We promise you won't find an easier way to remortgage your house.

Call FREE on 1800 556 577†

quoting response code IRMTG550. Lines are open: 8am – 8pm, 7 days a week.

BANK OF SCOTLAND

- **to build and strengthen customer loyalty**. Many direct marketing media provide privacy when the firm and their customers communicate, for example, mail and telephone. This enables firms to reward customers on an individual basis. Irish supermarkets have the potential to offer totally unique rewards to each of their loyalty card holders, based on the types of products they purchase, the frequency of their visits, and the monetary value of their purchases. This approach overcomes the tendency of many firms to offer incentives and rewards to new customers, while ignoring loyal customers.

  In the business-to-business sector, firms use direct marketing to keep their customers informed about new products. Increasingly, this information is conveyed by e-mail in the form of e-newsletters (see Chapter 14).
- **to generate sales**. Firms use direct marketing to generate sales. In business-to-business markets, and consumer markets, telemarketing, e-mail, direct mail, and direct response advertisements are used to specifically invite target audiences to purchase something. Sales promotion techniques motivate the target audience to take action, for example, free gifts and price reductions.
- **to create cross-selling opportunities**. Cross-selling is when a firm sells products and services, from one or more parts of its business, to customers already buying products from another part of the business. For example, firms in the financial services sector utilise customer databases to cross-sell. As their customers grow older, and encounter different circumstances, many previously irrelevant financial products become important. Banks have access to very detailed customer information and use this to identify products that they are likely to need.
- **to persuade customers to upgrade**. Upgrading occurs when customers buy a more sophisticated or comprehensive version of a particular product or service. For example, the Automobile Association (AA) has a range of options available to customers seeking cover for vehicle recovery. Through direct marketing techniques, they attempt to persuade customers who purchase the most basic cover to upgrade to one of their more comprehensive options.
- **to attract lapsed customers**. For various reasons, customers may cease to remain customers. When this occurs, they are categorised as lapsed customers. Not all firms can identify these people, but when they can, direct marketing is used to try and attract them back as customers. This technique often succeeds because the target audience is already familiar with the firm that communicates with them. Therefore, they are more likely to take notice of the message.

  For example, the current affairs magazine, *The Economist*, uses direct mail in conjunction with out-bound telemarketing to persuade past subscribers to renew their subscriptions. They use monetary discounts and free gifts to strengthen the appeal of their proposition.

The database – the engine that drives successful direct marketing

At the heart of all successful direct marketing campaigns is an excellent database. A database is a structured set of data held in a computer. In direct marketing, databases serve a number of purposes:

- the storage and comparison of marketing information
- the ranking of customers in terms of loyalty
- the targeting of direct mail, e-mail, and telemarketing campaigns
- the support of sales force activities
- the enhancement of customer service.

Improvements in database technology have contributed to direct marketing's ascendancy because it is relatively straightforward, through the use of sophisticated software, to build strong customer relationships with regular communications. Various software packages exist, but they should, at the very least, enable the firm to carry out a number of key tasks:

- testing (see below)
- tracking of individuals, i.e. every encounter that a person has with the firm should be observed and recorded
- the implementation of effective loyalty programmes (see below)
- the comparison of each record on the database – this is possible because the information relating to each individual is held in database fields. This allows firms to compare the profiles of individuals and examine each individual's activity. The number of fields per contact varies from industry to industry and from firm to firm. Typical fields relating to individuals in consumer markets are shown in Figure 12.1.

Organisations should achieve consistency when setting up database fields. This means that each entry should follow the same format. This simplifies the data input (also referred to as datacapture) task and facilitates like-with-like comparisons.

Building a database

Information held on a database is gathered from a number of sources. At the very least, all firms should strive to record up-to-date and relevant information about their customers.

Prospects *Those who have the potential to become customers.*

Another important group of individuals is **prospects**. These are not customers but have the potential to become customers. Drayton Bird (1993) has this to say about prospects: 'I believe the object of business is to locate a prospect, make that prospect a customer and then turn that customer into a friend.' Firms should categorise them as:

- **cold prospects**. These people are unlikely to become customers. They may have been customers in the past and severed contact with the firm for a variety of reasons, for example, irreconcilable differences, change of address, no further need for the product or service. Some cold prospects have never been customers and have had no previous contact with the firm. They might be satisfied with the firm's main competitors.

Figure 12.1 Database fields for a consumer

Title	First name
Surname	
Street name and number	
Town	
County	
Home telephone number	Mobile phone number
E-mail address	
Date of birth	Marital status
Occupation	Number of children
Date of last transaction	Hobbies and interests
Value of last transaction	

- **warm prospects**. These people may have voluntarily contacted the firm or may have been customers in the past. Where no previous relationship with the firm exists, their profile suggests that they would like to become customers.
- **hot prospects**. This group demonstrates tremendous goodwill towards the firm and would like to become customers. Certain barriers may prevent them from becoming customers, for example, a firm's location or opening hours, but once these are removed, the likelihood of them becoming customers improves. Hot prospects also include existing customers. They present cross-selling and upgrading opportunities. Dissatisfied customers of key competitors should be included in this category.

The above categories enable firms to engage in cost-effective campaigns. It is much better to target hot and warm prospects first. However, some firms concentrate resources on cold prospects. This does not make economic sense because response rates are bound to be low.

Prospects are identified in a number of ways:

- Some people may have demonstrated to a firm, through their actions, that they are interested in becoming customers, for example, they voluntarily contacted the company, they responded to an advertisement.
- Their profile is similar to that of existing customers, for example, they have the same interests, occupation, are from the same age group.
- They used to be customers.

Information on customers and prospects is obtained from internal and external sources. Most firms have access to information that already exists. Internal sources of information include the following:

- order forms
- invoices
- guarantee and warranty forms
- delivery details
- general enquiries
- loyalty card schemes
- records generated by sales representatives
- repair and maintenance records.

Many firms realise that internal information sources do not fully meet their needs. They can turn to external sources to enhance their databases:

- **questionnaires** that gather additional information from customers and prospects
- **sales promotions** that require participants to send back personal information. These are used to acquire customer data and identify new prospects. For example, in an effort to identify prospects, FMCG manufacturers offer money-off coupons that can only be obtained when respondents submit personal information about themselves.
- **direct response advertising** that invites target audiences to make contact with the firm through the provision of response devises, such as coupons, telephone numbers and/or e-mail addresses.
- **lists of contacts** who match the profile of existing customers, which can be obtained from list brokers. These are available to rent or buy. If the latter option is chosen, the list becomes their property of the buyer and no other firm can avail of the same list. When buying or renting lists, firms should only deal with reputable companies that guarantee the supply of accurate, up-to-date lists that exclude individuals who do not wish to receive direct marketing communications. Leading specialists in the compilation and supply of lists in Ireland include Precision Marketing Information (PMI) (for consumer lists) and Kompass (business-to-business lists). PMI compiles its lists from the electoral register and annual surveys of 100,000 consumers. Kompass holds information on 115,000 Irish companies and 180,000 contact names (*IDMA Directory*, 2003).

Database maintenance

A database can be likened to a living, growing creature. It must be nurtured and cared for if it is to perform at its optimum. Databases conform to the old adage 'garbage in, garbage out' and can only change if they are instructed to do so.

Information about the individuals on a database changes regularly. When someone takes the trouble to inform a firm of these changes, the relevant fields on the database must be amended. Changes typically involve contact details, marital status and occupation. If a firm continues to use the old data, it creates a very bad impression and results in customer dissatisfaction.

Individuals do not always bother to communicate changes in their personal details. Therefore, firms undertake regular database checks by contacting individuals, and verifying that the information held about them is correct. This is often done by out-bound telephone calls or by post. While the former method is more costly, it is more effective.

Another source of annoyance to individuals is the occurrence of duplicate contacts. This may arise because a person appears twice on the database. The computer reads the information and 'sees' two individuals because some of the fields contain different data. Irish postal addresses cause many of these problems. Outside the metropolitan areas, many people do not live on roads or streets with names and numbers. Successful delivery of post often depends on the knowledge of postal workers because residents might have at least two versions of their address. Databases read these versions as separate records and unless a process of deduplication is carried out, individuals run the risk of receiving the same communication more than once. **Deduplication** is a process that removes duplicate records from a database. It involves human interaction with the database. When internal human resources are scarce, firms employ external specialists to go through the records on their databases to identify and delete duplicate data, i.e. to ensure that an individual only appears once on the database. The process presents the opportunity to eliminate any inaccuracies, such as spelling mistakes.

Deduplication *The removal of duplicate records from a database.*

Another vital function of database maintenance, is the removal of individuals who no longer wish to be included. Under the Data Protection Act, an individual has the right to be removed from a firm's database. They are entitled to pursue legal action if they continue to receive unsolicited approaches from the company involved. Therefore, registering such requests and taking action is a vital part of database maintenance.

Another aspect of maintenance is security and firms should have clear policies in relation to this:

- Company databases can be made accessible to all staff. However, only a few designated employees should be able to make changes to the information.
- Back-up versions of the database should be held, preferably in a different location so that in the event of an act of destruction, the valuable asset survives.

- The threat of computer viruses is a constant one, so firms should invest in software to protect their databases from viruses.

Table 12.3 provides a summary of the key elements of database maintenance.

Table 12.3 Seven vital elements of database maintenance

1. Always amend records when requested to do so by an individual.
2. Check and verify the accuracy of information on a regular basis.
3. Deduplicate records and eliminate inaccuracies regularly.
4. Action any requests for removal from the database.
5. Have clear policies on staff access to the database.
6. Always keep a back-up copy of the database.
7. Install virus protection software.

Direct marketing and testing

As stated earlier, one of the strengths of direct marketing is that it allows firms to test the effectiveness of certain variables before exposing the entire target audience to a campaign. This enables the direct marketer to fine-tune a campaign in order to achieve the best possible results. There are a number of variables that can be tested. The main ones are:

- **the target audience**. Whether a firm uses its own database, or buys or rents a list from an outside source, it is advisable to test whether or not the target audience is receptive to the proposed campaign. A sample of the list is exposed to the campaign and if their response is favourable, the campaign might be executed in full to the remaining people in the target audience.
- **the offer**. This is the element of the campaign that encourages the target audience to respond (O'Malley *et al.*, 1999). According to Stone *et al.* (1995), various aspects of the offer can be tested and these include:
  - price
  - incentives
  - benefits
  - exclusivity
  - ways of using the product
  - competitive comparison
  - newsworthiness
  - image
  - celebrity endorsement.
- **the timing of the campaign**. The success of a telemarketing campaign is particularly sensitive to timing. Contacting a person at the wrong time causes irritation and makes

a positive response less likely. Timing also takes into account the frequency with which the direct marketer should contact an individual. Firms dependent on subscribers usually make contact with the customer well in advance of the subscription expiry date. If at first they do not succeed in securing a renewal, more communications follow.

- **the creative aspects of the campaign**. Examples of creativity in direct marketing include style of photography and imagery, language, headlines, materials used (e.g. paper stock), formats (e.g. size of envelopes), and tone of voice (e.g. friendly or formal). Even though firms are well advised to test the creative aspects of a campaign, it is important that they do not do anything that will undermine the integrity of the brand. In order to prevent this, many companies have strict guidelines in place (see Chapter 3).

When variables have been tested, the results are analysed. The approach that yielded the best responses is usually executed to the entire target audience. The Internet is ideal for carrying out testing and the firm can make necessary changes very quickly in order to increase response rates.

Direct marketing media

Direct marketing media fall into two main categories – those that are personally addressed and those that are unaddressable. The former category is possible because of the availability of a list which is either generated from a firm's own database or acquired from an outside source. Unaddressable media are used when individual names and contact details are not known. Direct marketing media are the various vehicles that enable firms to transmit direct marketing programmes.

Addressable direct marketing media

There are three main types of addressable direct marketing media: direct mail; telephone; and the Internet. The Internet's role as a direct marketing medium is dealt with in Chapter 14. Here, we concentrate on the more traditional direct marketing media, direct mail and telephone.

Direct mail

Direct mail is any form of marketing communication that is delivered through the letterbox. A typical direct mail pack, also known as a **mail shot**, consists of an outer envelope, a personalised letter (in most cases), a leaflet or brochure, a reply device (possibly incorporating an application form) and a prepaid reply envelope. Some mail shots contain additional inserts but if the pack exceeds a certain weight, it is liable for higher postage rates, and this has budget implications.

Direct mail
Any form of marketing communication that is delivered through the letterbox.

Mail shot
Actual item that is sent through the post.

Direct mail usually carries the name and address of the target but sometimes this information is not available. In such circumstances, firms can avail of a service from An Post that delivers unaddressed mail shots to certain areas. These households are considered likely to accommodate the types of individuals being sought.

Banks and credit card companies, the ESB, Bord Gais, Eircom, O2 and Vodafone use customer statements as vehicles for direct mail. These are known as **statement stuffers**. They are cost-effective because they make use of a piece of correspondence that is sent out on a regular basis. Most customers open this piece of mail because it involves financial issues.

Statement stuffers
Pieces of direct marketing material sent to customers with their regular statements.

Direct mail is the vehicle most commonly associated with direct marketing. It is ideally suited to the following tasks:

- reinforcing customer loyalty, for example, Tesco Ireland send quarterly mail shots to Clubcard holders, containing a magazine and vouchers
- generating sales
- cross-selling and upgrading customers
- reactivating lapsed customers
- communicating important information to customers, for example, notification of mergers and acquisitions. When TSB Bank and Irish Permanent merged, they notified their customers by post. Also, new product launches.

Properly used, direct mail should never be categorised as junk mail because it enables companies to tailor their communications and products or services to suit the needs of each segment or individual. This capability means that mail shots should be relevant and interesting, thus minimising waste.

Direct mail facilitates a certain amount of creativity and the creative team can enjoy freedom when designing a range of approaches and formats, for example, envelope size and shape. In reality, cost restricts creativity, and strict budgets should be set before creative work commences.

Unlike a television or radio advertisement, direct mail has the potential to enjoy a longer shelf life. It might remain in the house or work environment for a long time and enjoy the attention of multiple readers.

Research has found that direct mail is difficult to ignore because it is usually addressed to a person. If the recipient of a mail shot already has a relationship with the firm, they are more likely to take notice of the mail shot.

From a firm's perspective, direct mail offers privacy. When a firm transmits a television advertisement, its competitors can see what it is doing. Direct mail offers firms the opportunity to launch new products or set special price levels without competitors' or other customers' knowledge.

Direct mail is ideally suited to testing. Typical aspects that are tested include the following:

Mailing lists

If a firm intends renting or purchasing a mailing list, it can send a mail shot to a sample of the list to evaluate whether or not it is suitable, before committing to use the entire list.

Envelope design

A firm might test whether or not the inclusion of a headline on the envelope improves response rates. Sometimes, headlines stop people opening the mail shot because they suspect that it is 'junk mail'. On the other hand, if the headline arouses interest and is relevant to the individual, it might motivate them to open the envelope.

Contents of the cover letter

Many direct mail letters conclude with a 'PS' that draws attention to an important message. Some firms test whether or not to use a 'PS', while others test the content of the 'PS'. The wording of headlines within a cover letter might be tested to find out which one is most effective.

The use of incentives

Direct mail allows firms to test whether or not incentives improve response rates. Different types of incentives can also be tested.

Numbers of items enclosed

Some practitioners believe that the more items in a mail shot, the more opportunities the firm has to get its message across. However, there is a perception among many consumers that direct mail has an adverse effect on the environment, and that the more items a mail shot contains, the more damaging it is. Firms should strike a balance, and enclose the appropriate number of items to achieve their objectives.

Reply devices

Research shows that the provision of a reply device that is free to the respondent increases response rates. The firm might test whether or not a free phone number is more appropriate than the inclusion of a postage-paid reply envelope. Testing might reveal that some segments prefer to use the telephone while others prefer to use the post. Many firms allow people to respond by e-mail, but it is worth noting that the respondent bears the cost.

The success or failure of a direct mail campaign is easily measured. The number of mail shots sent and the number of responses received is recorded. Most importantly, the volume of business directly attributable to the mail shot is calculated. Therefore, if the mail shot generates a high response, it is even more important that firms analyse the amount of business generated by the activity.

Despite its popularity with direct marketing practitioners, direct mail still attracts a certain amount of bad press and seems unable to throw off the 'junk mail' tag. This is because many firms persist in using poor-quality lists and are not sufficiently selective when deciding who should receive direct mail. They also fail to make each piece of communication relevant to the recipient. As a result, response rates tend to be very low (less than 1 per cent in many cases) and this results in firms being less than enthusiastic about direct mail.

Even when direct mail is personally addressed to someone, it is not guaranteed to reach the right person. Someone else in the household, or office in the case of business-to-business mail shots, might screen the mail and decide what is important and what isn't.

While Irish households receive relatively small amounts of direct mail each year compared to their counterparts in the UK and the US, there is a perception that too much mail is arriving in our letterboxes. However, Nua (March, 2002) reported the findings of a survey that was conducted by GartnerG2 in the US. The survey found that US businesses are turning to e-mail instead of traditional direct mailings. It also found that direct mail appears to have reached its peak in the US and that the amount of direct mail sent to US households was set to decline by 15 per cent in 2002. While the volume of direct mail generated in Ireland lags significantly behind the US, these findings may point to a trend that could dilute Irish firms' interest in direct mail and see them focusing more on electronic delivery of direct marketing communications.

The onus is on Irish companies to be more selective and relevant when using direct mail. When this happens, consumers and buyers will be happy to receive direct mail and response rates will improve.

Table 12.4 summarises the advantages and disadvantages of direct mail.

Table 12.4 The advantages and disadvantages of direct mail

Advantages

- Enables firms to send tailored, relevant communications
- Facilitates a certain amount of creative freedom
- Has a longer shelf life than traditional advertising media
- Allows the sender to avoid the scrutiny of the competition and other customers
- Facilitates extensive testing
- Results can be measured

Disadvantages

- Still dogged by the 'junk mail' image
- Not always guaranteed to reach the intended target
- Tendency to deliver very low response rates.

Telemarketing

Telemarketing is the use of the telephone for direct marketing purposes. It is usually described as in-bound or out-bound. **In-bound telemarketing** occurs when an individual telephones a firm either in response to an invitation to call, or unprompted. **Out-bound telemarketing** occurs when a firm contacts customers and/or prospects in order to sell, gather information and/or impart information. Telemarketing is ideally placed to play a significant role in integrated marketing communications programmes. Increasingly, the 1800 number is in advertising, sponsorship and public relations campaigns. This allows respondents to telephone the firm free of charge.

Telemarketing *The use of telephone for direct marketing purposes.*

In-bound telemarketing *Where an individual telephones a firm, either by invitation or unprompted.*

Out-bound telemarketing *Where a firm contacts customers and prospects to sell, gather or impart information.*

Telemarketing is used to carry out many of the tasks done by direct mail, such as selling to existing customers, identifying prospects, reactivating lapsed customers and disseminating information. Many firms use telemarketing to provide better customer service and enhance customer relationships, for example, technical support.

Depending on the quality of the list, out-bound telemarketing is targeted and the message can be personalised to suit each individual contact. This improves cost-effectiveness. Also, unlike direct mail, the organisation can be sure of reaching the intended target. If someone is not available, the caller can try again.

Telemarketing involves human interaction. This means that if one approach is not leading to the desired responses, an alternative approach can be introduced easily. This is not so easy with direct mail because significant printing costs might be incurred and a relatively long delay might ensue.

Advance research informs telemarketers as to the best time to contact the target audience. If this information is utilised, it makes the target audience more receptive to the advances of an organisation, whereas an ill-timed telephone call makes a bad impression.

If someone has a query about a piece of direct mail, they may forget to follow it up. With telemarketing, queries from the target audience can be answered immediately.

Changes in consumer lifestyles and a greater prevalence of shift work mean that around-the-clock access to a company is very important. Involvement in telemarketing facilitates this need.

Like direct mail, telemarketing is well suited to testing. Lists, scripts, the proposition, incentives, and timing can all be tested on sample audiences and the results can be learned quickly.

While telemarketing is popular with many firms, there are some disadvantages associated with its use. Poorly trained call-centre staff reflect badly on a firm's image. Many firms outsource telemarketing to specialist agencies. When screening these agencies, stringent selection criteria must be put in place so as to ensure that all customer and prospect experiences are positive.

Research shows that out-bound telemarketing is more successful when the target has an existing relationship with the firm. Unsolicited telephone calls from unfamiliar firms do not enhance telemarketing's image. Furthermore, if the call centre contacts the prospect at an inappropriate time, irrevocable damage can be done.

Table 12.5 summarises the advantages and disadvantages of telemarketing.

Table 12.5 The advantages and disadvantages of telemarketing

Advantages
• Facilitates highly targeted, direct communication
• Human interaction allows approach modification as and when necessary
• Contact can be made at a time when the target is most receptive
• Delivers an immediate two-way response
• Highly suited to testing
• Most effective when a relationship between the target and the organisation already exists
• The calibre of the call-centre staff can adversely affect brand image
Disadvantages
• The calibre of the call-centre staff can adversely affect brand image

Unaddressable direct marketing media

Unaddressable direct marketing media *Direct marketing media that do not use the target audience's personal details.*

Direct marketing is usually more effective when it is personally addressed to the target audience. However, many firms only have limited databases and do not know the names and contact details of their target audience. Sometimes **unaddressable direct marketing media** are used to make contact with the target audience. These are media that do not use the target audience's personal details. There are a number of unaddressable direct marketing media available to firms.

Direct response advertising

Direct response advertising *Advertising that sets out to persuade the target audience to make contact with the advertiser.*

Direct response advertising is used to persuade the target audience to make contact with the advertiser. Radio, television, newspapers and magazines are often used for this purpose. 1800 telephone numbers and website addresses are heavily advertised to make it easy for the target audience to contact the advertiser. Respondents' activity must be tracked, so as to facilitate an evaluation of the effectiveness of these advertisements. When a customer or prospect telephones a call centre, they should be asked how they heard about the company and the telephone number. This is particularly important if the firm is running a series of advertisements across a range of media. Recording this information allows them to evaluate the effectiveness of particular media vehicles and it informs future decisions. The biggest challenge for direct response television advertising is to motivate viewers to stop viewing in order to respond to the advertisement.

The differences between traditional and direct response television media planning are illustrated in Table 12.6.

Table 12.6 The differences between traditional and direct response advertising

	Brand media	DRTV
Objectives	• To gain high coverage and frequency within a target audience	• To generate consistent levels of in-bound calls to live operated call centre
	• To achieve high brand awareness figures in research	• To generate the maximum numbers of enquiries possible, at the lowest possible cost per head
Strategy	• High-rating peak-time spots, generally heavily weighted. Short bursts of activity, with a high volume of spots in order to reach as many people within the target market • Dominate the TV medium in order to concentrate the consumer's mind on the product or service being advertised	• A combination of peak and off-peak but more towards the off-peak • Ongoing regular TV presence in order to generate a regular stream of enquiries • Emphasis placed on cost-effective delivery of leads, not awareness, coverage and frequency, or audience delivery.

Source: Browne (1997)

Many newspaper and magazine advertisements carry free phone numbers, website addresses and response coupons. If the same advertisement is placed in a range of printed media vehicles, a tracking code is included on coupons so that the firm knows which vehicle or vehicles attracted the highest number of responses.

Newspapers present advantages and disadvantages to direct marketers:

- They facilitate fast testing because the lead-time between booking and placing an advertisement is quite short. Provided the design of the advertisement is quite simple, necessary changes can be implemented at a relatively low cost.
- They enjoy a relatively short life. If the reader does not respond immediately, subsequent response is unlikely and the direct marketer must move on to the next option.
- The advertisement must compete with many others, and the articles for the reader's attention.

Magazines also present advantages and disadvantages:

- The reproduction quality in a magazine is far superior to a newspaper. This is important for firms wanting to present a quality image.
- Most magazines have a much longer life than newspapers. This means the likely response period is much longer.
- While they are a good medium for testing, long lead-times for placing advertisements and long production periods mean that findings take longer to compile.

Direct response radio advertising is popular with many firms. In Ireland, radio is very popular and is well segmented. Radio production costs are relatively low and this means that the medium is well suited to testing because it is relatively easy to alter messages. As a general rule of thumb, responses tend to be fast but they need to be because the messages are short-lived. The advertisements must compete with those of other companies and with the content of the radio schedules. To succeed, the advertisements must be very catchy and memorable so that listeners can recall contact details. This explains why the use of catchy jingles is very prevalent. They also require frequent repetition.

Direct response advertising requires a very different creative approach to mainstream advertising. Since the primary objective is to elicit a response, the advertisement must be designed accordingly. Some advertisers have found, to their cost, that just because an advertising agency has an excellent track record in creating advertising that works, it does not necessarily have the expertise to create direct response advertising that works.

Inserts in printed materials

Some firms place loose promotional literature, known as inserts, in printed media. For example, Dell regularly places detailed sales leaflets in a range of daily and Sunday newspapers and other publications. Their primary objective is to sell computers and to encourage prospects to telephone them with enquiries. Other publications are also available to carry inserts, for example, the Eircom telephone directory.

Inserts give firms much greater control over quality and content. They have greater freedom to determine the size and format of the insert, although they are usually quite costly to produce. They allow the advertiser to convey more information than is possible in a conventional press advertisement. However, an over-abundance of them in any one publication causes annoyance and leads to complaints about clutter. There are also concerns about the environmental impact of inserts.

Door drops

Door drops are a popular way of reaching the target audience directly. However, they are far less effective than personalised mail shots and because of the blanket approach, they can be quite wasteful as they reach individuals who are not part of the target audience. In many urban areas, householders are inundated with door drops. This is perceived as clutter and lacks impact.

Direct marketing and the other elements of the marketing communications mix

Direct marketing is regularly used in conjunction with other elements of the marketing communications mix.

Advertising

As discussed above, direct response advertising implicitly sets out to evoke a response from the target audience. However, even mainstream advertising often incorporates response mechanisms. While the primary objective might be to generate awareness or change target audience attitudes, a secondary objective might be to encourage people to contact the advertiser.

Sponsorship

As with advertising, the primary objective of sponsorship activity is not usually to generate responses. However, sponsored events are used to gather the personal details of target audiences. Signage at sponsored events, and clothing worn by people working at an event, might carry the sponsor's website address or free phone number.

Public relations

In many firms, there is a strong link between customer care and technical support, and the public relations function. People who handle customer queries on the telephone are the firm's 'voice'. Their professionalism or incompetence makes a lasting impression on the caller.

Increasingly, the Internet is used to distribute e-newsletters and maintain ongoing contact with individuals. Queries traditionally handled by the public relations department are often dealt with by visits to the firm's website.

Sales promotion

Sales promotion and direct marketing are ideal bedfellows. In many cases the line between the two elements is blurred. Is a supermarket's loyalty scheme direct marketing or a sales promotion? Are coupons and competitions, sales promotion or direct marketing? The reality is that sales promotions are more cost-effective and targeted when used in conjunction with direct marketing techniques. Also, direct marketing campaigns that use relevant and targeted sales promotion techniques create impact. For example, cosmetics company, Clinique, in conjunction with their approved retailers, mail customers to inform them of in-store promotions. They make an impression on the target audience because they use Clinique products.

Proper utilisation of databases enables firms to track the long-term effects of sales promotions and to evaluate which ones are cost-effective.

Personal selling

Personal selling is the most expensive element in the marketing communications mix. Many firms use direct marketing to make sales representatives more efficient. Instead of a salesperson sitting at their desk all day making telephone calls to make appointments with prospects and customers, direct mail and out-bound telemarketing is used. This frees up a salesperson to spend more time with prospects and customers and to build stronger relationships.

Future developments in direct marketing

While Chapter 14 deals specifically with the Internet and its relevance for direct marketing, There are some other developments worthy of note:

SMS and MMS

SMS stands for 'short message service' and MMS stands for 'media message service'. Firms use SMS to send text messages to target audiences with mobile phones. MMS is a newer facility that enables firms to send images to people's mobile phone.

Opt-in
Where the data subject has to give permission before direct marketers can contact them by e-mail, fax, automatic calling machine and SMS/MMS.

Both SMS and MMS are '**opt-in**'. This means that firms must have an individual's permission before sending messages to their mobile phone. Nonetheless, SMS is considered a good way of reaching younger audiences because they communicate through text messages every day. According to a report published by Amárach Consulting, a third of 15–24-year-old mobile phone users are sending over 20 text messages per week (see Table 12.7).

Table 12.7 Use of SMS

Age category	Mobile users using text messaging (%)
15–19	85
20–24	74
25–34	57
35–49	40
50–64	40
65+	27
Total	**57**

Source: *Consumer TrendWatch Technology Quarter* 2, (Amárach Consulting, 2003)

Advertisers tap into the power of txt

R U xpriencd? You betcha. It's a love affair that has not gone unnoticed by marketers. What makes texting so attractive to advertisers is that it is as up close and personal as marketing gets. 'Only 20% of people have access to the web at any one time but 80% of the population has a mobile phone,' says Declan Clancy of Data Conversion Systems. 'As such, it really is the letterbox in your pocket.'

Working with Bloom, the advertising agency, recently Clancy devised a promotional campaign for Lifestyle Sports. In it, competition questions were positioned at points of sale in 67 Lifestyle Sports stores as well as via radio and press. Answers were sent by text to a special phone number. Correct entrants immediately received a return text offering them prizes ranging from discount vouchers to free sports kit. To redeem these, they had to present the text to store staff. By varying the questions over different media, the company could see which advertising channel had been most effective. This is knowledge that will help eliminate waste in future campaigns, says Clancy.

During the five-week promotion more than 86,000 entries were received. Central to its success was Lifestyle's decision not to use a premium tariff text rate, says Fiona Boyle, marketing manager. Although it would have seen the company recoup some of its investment, it opted instead to make the competition as accessible as possible, she says. The use of short messaging service (SMS) technology – including validation systems and return texts to winning entrants – added €30,000 to the campaign's costs. For this it accumulated a database of 30,000 unique customer phone numbers which, due to the analysis software used, are identifiable by their interest in sport. All entrants were asked if they would like to receive further text messages from the company. 'Ultimately, the real success of the campaign will depend on what we do with the database,' says Boyle.

'Whenever, Wherever', the hit single by Shakira, the Colombian pop singer, provides further proof of the power of text. To support the single's Irish launch last year, Sony Music and Puca, an SMS marketing company, teamed up to run a text messaging competition on RTE's Aertel in the week before the release. Viewers were invited to text the word 'Shakira' to a special phone number. Those who did were rewarded with CDs, vouchers, posters and T-shirts. There were 6,000 entries and, of those, 67% opted to receive future SMS news from Sony Music about Shakira. The single entered the charts at No 1. Says Eleanor McCarthy, Sony Music Ireland marketing director: 'Although the budget for the SMS element of the campaign represented only a small proportion, we feel it really kick-started the campaign. Shakira was virtually unheard of outside the US and Latin America in 2002 and Sony Music had the task of creating awareness of her as an artist in a market already crowded with young female singers. We wanted to create a buzz about her in the youth audience, and SMS was a logical route as it is their communication media of choice.'

Puca has also devised SMS campaigns for brands such as Coca-Cola and Cadbury. Sarah Shortman, general manager, says: 'SMS represents permission marketing at its best. It is highly targeted and accountable and, because it is database-driven, you can see exactly how many people responded. What's more, response rates to SMS marketing can be as high as 11%.' By contrast traditional mail shots typically generate a response rate of 3–4%.

Source: *The Sunday Times*, 8 June 2003

Interactive television

The advent of digital television facilitates greater targeting because of the growth in special interest channels. Digital television also presents opportunities for interactive direct response advertising. Subscribers to Sky Digital can connect to the network through a modem and this enables them to interact with advertisers. This facility has the potential to make television advertising accountable and will enable advertisers to calculate the effectiveness of their advertisements.

Data protection

Data protection is the 'protection of personal privacy ... against the threat of computer power ... by regulating computer use ... by giving people new rights and is now also extended to manual files' (Joe Meade, Data Protection Commissioner, IDMA 2003 Seminar, 29 April 2003).

The Data Protection Acts (1988 and 2003) contain eight key principles

1. Data is fairly obtained.
2. Data is collected for a specific purpose.
3. Data is processed in a manner compatible to why it was collected.
4. Data is relevant and not excessive.
5. Data is kept safe and secure.
6. Data is kept accurate and up to date.
7. Data is not kept for an excessive period of time.
8. The holder of the data must comply with access requests of the data subject.

In April 2003, the 1988 Data Protection Act was amended. It stipulates that before direct marketers can use e-mail, fax, automatic calling machines and SMS/MMS for direct marketing purposes, the data subject must opt-in. This simply means that the direct marketer must receive permission before they can use these media to contact people. Opt-in is also referred to as permission-based marketing and is set to become the norm for other addressable direct marketing media.

The case study at the close of this chapter demonstrates the seriousness with which this issue is being treated.

Summary

Direct marketing is an interactive marketing system that uses various media to effect a measurable response at the target audience's preferred location. One of its great assets is its facility to test various aspects of a campaign in real circumstances with a small representative sample of the target audience before transmitting it to the entire audience.

Direct marketing in Ireland has experienced growth for a number of reasons, including the fragmentation of traditional media and consumer markets, significant technological developments, deregulation in the telecommunications sector, growing retailer power, and marketing managers' desire for greater accountability in marketing communications.

Direct marketing is used to achieve a range of objectives and these are driven by the need to encourage responses from target audiences. The database plays a pivotal role in direct marketing and its quality often determines the success or otherwise of a campaign. Therefore, attention must be given to maintaining, developing and protecting the database.

There are various direct marketing media and these are divided into two categories, addressable and unaddressable. Addressable incorporates any medium that enables the firm to personally address the target audience when they make contact. Unaddressable media are used when the names and contact details of some or all of the target audience are unknown.

A review of the other elements of the marketing communications mix shows that direct marketing techniques are often used to make them more effective. Perhaps the key to the link between the elements is information and the carrier of that information, the database.

Significant developments in direct marketing fall into two main categories: technology, and data protection.

Useful websites

www.comreg.ie	Commission for Communications Regulation
www.dataprivacy.ie	The Office of the Data Protection Officer
www.dma.ie	Direct Marketing Associates
www.idma.ie	Irish Direct Marketing Association

Review questions

1. Critically assess the main characteristics of direct marketing.
2. Discuss reasons behind the growth in direct marketing in Ireland.

3. What objectives does direct marketing achieve? Illustrate your answer with examples.
4. Critically assess the role of the database in direct marketing.
5. Prescribe best practice for maintaining and protecting databases.
6. What is meant by testing? Explain how it works.
7. Critically assess the various addressable and unaddressable direct marketing media.
8. Evaluate the role of direct marketing in relation to other elements of the marketing communications mix.

Exercise

Select a piece of direct mail and identify elements that you think could be tested. Critically assess the mail shot. Do you think it was tailored for the individual involved? What does it do well? What could it do better?

References

Bird, Drayton, *Commonsense Direct Marketing*, 3rd edition (Kogan Page, 1993).

Browne, Julian, 'Direct response television, masterclass', (*Go Direct* November/December, 1997).

McDonald, William J., *Direct Marketing: An Integrated Approach* (McGraw-Hill, 1998).

Nua (March, 2002, www.nua.ie).

O'Malley, Lisa, Patterson, Maurice and Evans, Martin, *Exploring Direct Marketing* (International Thomson Business Press, 1999).

Stone, M., Davies, D. and Bond, A., *Direct Hit: Direct Marketing with a Winning Edge* (Pitman, 1995).

Case study

MBNA Bank, and the Office of the Data Protection Officer

INTRODUCTION

A number of individuals contacted The Office of the Data Protection Officer to complain about the receipt of direct marketing contacts from MBNA Bank, a financial institution specialising in credit cards. Some individuals were unhappy about receiving unsolicited telephone calls at their homes, while one individual – who had received a number of unwanted mailings and telephone calls over a period of several months – had gone to some lengths to remove his details from MBNA's direct marketing databases, but apparently without success. In investigating this series of complaints, two distinct but related issues arose for consideration:

- MBNA's response to individuals' requests to opt out of direct marketing
- Eircom's practice of adding telephone directory details onto other large databases – the practice of 'teleappending'.

MBNA'S RESPONSE

As regards the difficulties and concerns of individuals about direct marketing, the Officer raised the issue with MBNA and found the bank to be co-operative and helpful. The bank stressed its desire to comply fully with data protection law, and the Officer had no reason to doubt the bank's *bona fides* in this regard. At a meeting with MBNA representatives, the bank explained that personal information was obtained from two principal sources:

- application forms (which included an 'opt-out' tick box, for those who did not wish to receive direct marketing
- a direct marketing agency called PMI, which maintains an extensive database (derived in large part from the electoral register) to facilitate the direct marketing of Irish residents.

The bank was fully aware of individuals' legal right to be removed from direct marketing databases, and had detailed procedures in place to ensure that this right was honoured. The bank acknowledged that these procedures had clearly failed for the complainant in this case.

The Office insisted that fuller details be provided as to why the procedure had failed so badly in the case of the complainant in question. Having investigated the matter, MBNA concluded that the problem had arisen due to deficiencies in communications with its direct marketing associate, PMI. MBNA said that more stringent checking procedures had been put in place, and that direct marketing staff had been re-educated with a view to addressing these deficiencies.

Section 2(7) of the Data Protection Act, 1988 provides that, on request, a person's name must be removed from a direct marketing list. In the circumstances of this case, the Officer concluded that the Bank was, in this instance, in breach of its data protection obligations. He also found it appropriate, in the interests of fairness, to place the Bank's failure in this instance in proper context. He noted that the bank issues of the order of 2,000,000 direct mailings every year, and process about 40,000 'do not contact' requests. The evidence would appear to indicate that they succeed in complying with the great majority of such requests, and he had no basis for doubting their stated commitment to complying with data protection law. He also noted that the bank had taken concrete steps to prevent a recurrence of this matter.

'TELEAPPENDING'

As regards the separate issue of telephoning people at home, MBNA explained that the phone numbers had been made available for direct marketing purposes via Eircom. The Officer therefore decided it would be appropriate to raise this matter with that organisation, which was the data controller in respect of the telephone directory database. In his discussions with Eircom, he established that the phone company offered a commercial service to clients which involved Eircom automatically appending telephone numbers in bulk onto other databases of names and addresses – such as direct marketing databases derived from the electoral register. This process was referred to as 'teleappending'. The Officer suggested to Eircom that the disclosure of telephone directory data in this context was not a disclosure which was compatible with the purpose for which subscriber data was held by Eircom, in the absence of the clear consent of subscribers, and that the disclosure was therefore contrary to section 2(1)cii of the Data Protection Act, 1988. In essence, the Officer took the view that the purpose for which Eircom held the data was the provision of a traditional 'look-up' directory service. This service was quite distinct from the population of third-party databases, which would effectively allow direct marketers to generate 'reverse-searchable' directories. In his view, such a potentially far-reaching application of personal data would need to be subject to additional clear consent from subscribers.

Following discussions, Eircom indicated its acceptance of the Officer's position on this matter, and that the practice of teleappending would be discontinued until the consent issues could be resolved. The Officer did, however, accept that limited forms of teleappending – for example, to update databases automatically, where an extra digit had been added to existing telephone numbers – were not incompatible with data protection law.

This case illustrates the sensitivities attaching to telephone directory information, and confirms the Officer's view that the data protection and privacy rights of telephone subscribers cannot be taken for granted. He is satisfied that Eircom appreciates this point of principle, and this is borne out by its positive response to his concerns in this case.

Source: www.dataprivacy.ie (The Office of the Data Protection Officer, May 2001)

13

PERSONAL SELLING

The aims and objectives of this chapter are:

- to examine key aspects of personal selling and its role in the marketing communications mix, and in particular:
  - to explain what is meant by personal selling
  - to describe its key characteristics
  - to demonstrate personal selling's role in the marketing mix
  - to explain when to use personal selling
  - to help you appreciate personal selling's fit with the other tools of the marketing communications mix
  - to classify salespeople according to the type of sales activity they undertake
  - to provide a framework for designing sales force strategy and structure.

What is personal selling?

Personal selling is the term used to describe sales activity that is carried out directly between the buyer and the seller through personal media. The 'carrier' of the organisation's message is the **sales representative** or salesperson. The collective term for a firm's sales representatives is **sales force**. Unlike other channels for marketing communications, the message is very adaptable and capable of being targeted in order to appeal directly to the needs and reactions of an individual or group of buyers. Therefore, personal selling is the most interpersonal and interactive element of the marketing communications mix, and the salesperson serves as a vital contact point between a firm and its customers. Indeed, for many customers, the salesperson is the company and becomes the living embodiment of its values.

Personal selling *Face-to-face interaction with one or more prospective customers for the purpose of making a sale and building long-term mutually benefit.*

Sales representative *The person who carries the firm's message direct to the target audience.*

Sales force *The collective term for a firm's sales representatives.*

Traditionally, personal selling concentrated primarily on single, one-off transactions, without necessarily seeking repeat purchases from the same customers. This was at a time when competitors tended to be scarce and potential customers were plentiful. However, as markets became more competitive, many firms found it necessary for long-term survival to adopt the concept of relationship marketing. According to Gronroos (1994), relationship marketing sets out to 'identify and establish, maintain and enhance and, when necessary, terminate relationships with customers and other stakeholders, at a profit so that the objectives of all parties involved are met; and this is done by mutual exchange and fulfilment of promises'.

Similarly, Armstrong and Kotler (2003) embrace the concept of **relationship marketing** in their contention that selling activity should aim to 'build long-term, value producing relationships' while seeking out ways of solving customers' problems.

This concept has had a major impact on the sales function in many firms and has led to greater emphasis on relational selling or relational exchange. Vitale and Giglierano (2002) define relational exchange as 'customer–supplier relationships where the interaction recognises the long-term benefit of the combination. Interdependence is an accepted, even fostered, element of the relationship.' This represents a major shift from transactional selling which focuses on each individual sale without taking long-term prospects into account.

Table 13.1 summarises the key characteristics of personal selling.

Table 13.1 Key characteristics of personal selling

- Direct sales activity carried out between the seller and the buyer
- Interpersonal and interactive
- The sales representative is the embodiment of the selling organisation's brand values
- Evolving from transaction-oriented towards building relationships and solving the buyer's problems

Personal selling and the marketing mix

As illustrated in Figure 13.1, the management of all components of the marketing mix should emanate from the organisation's overall marketing strategy. In turn, the marketing strategy should take into account the company's mission and corporate objectives.

The marketing communications strategy is part of the overall marketing strategy and involves decisions about the role of each element in the marketing communications mix. The sales and marketing functions must work closely together to put in place a fully co-ordinated marketing communications plan. In reality, rivalry and conflict may exist between the two functions. Organisational factors tend to be the primary source of these problems:

- The sales force may not be involved in formulating the organisation's overall marketing strategy. This means that they feel no sense of ownership towards the resulting strategy. Consequently, they may put in place a sales strategy that sets out to fulfil a completely different set of objectives.
- Some organisations may be driven by the sales function. In such cases, it may be

acceptable for them to develop a sales strategy before a marketing plan exists. This merely serves to reinforce the gulf and lack of synergy between sales and marketing.

Figure 13.1 Personal selling and the marketing mix

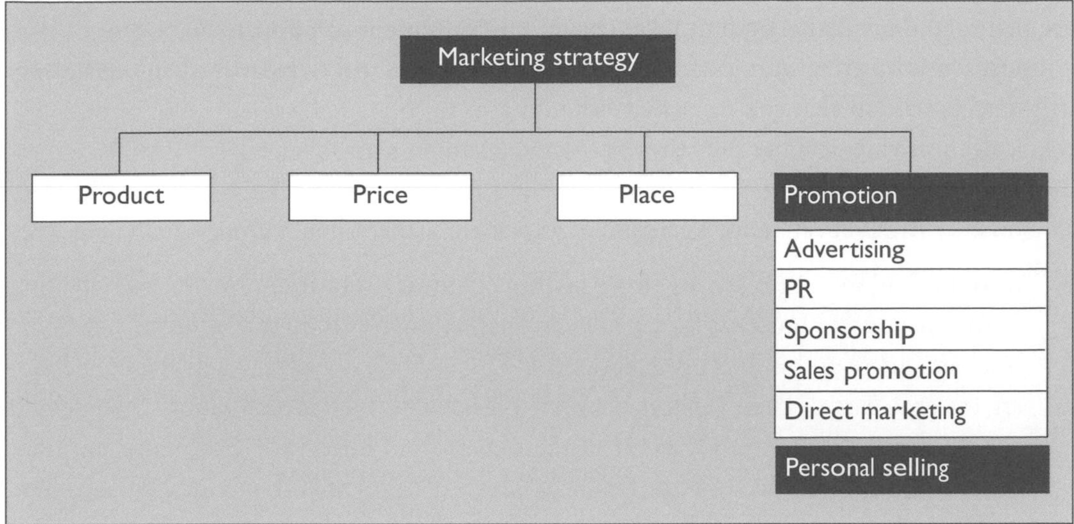

Personal selling and the marketing communications mix

This section takes a closer look at the role of personal selling and its relationship with the other elements of the marketing communications mix.

When to use personal selling

The decision to use particular elements of the marketing communications mix depends on a number of factors. Similarly, there are a number of factors that are taken into account when deciding whether or not to use personal selling (see Table 13.2 for a summary).

Table 13.2 Evaluating when a company should use personal selling

- Nature of the information
- Size, nature and importance of the target audience
- Marketing objectives
- Cost and effectiveness of personal selling in relation to the other elements of the promotions mix
- Channel strategy
- Customer requirements for a sales representative

The nature of the information

If the information is complex, face-to-face, personal communication may be more effective. This gives the sales representative an opportunity to answer questions and address individual concerns.

The size and nature of the target audience

When a firm attempts to communicate with a small and easily identifiable target audience, it may be more effective to meet directly with the relevant people. This approach is prevalent in the business-to-business sector, where personal selling is the more widely used element of the marketing communications mix. It is even more appropriate when the firm's proposition is of great importance to the target audience and when particular customers are very significant to the selling organisation.

The marketing objectives

Personal selling is effective for firms looking to achieve the following:

- **to build and maintain strong, long-lasting customer relationships**. Firms operating in the business-to-business sector use personal selling techniques to achieve this. Some firms are adept at this and bring about a situation where their sales representatives are an integral part of their customers' own businesses. In these situations, the selling organisation is considered a factor in their customers' successes. Such customers are likely to become strong advocates of the selling organisation and may generate business leads. More importantly, such close-knit relationships may keep competitors away.
- **to encourage action from the target audience**. Advertising is effective at building awareness and direct marketing important in building leads. However, in certain situations, personal selling may be the most appropriate way of persuading the target audience to take action. While this may not prove possible or practical in situations where the target audience is large, it is a viable option in the business-to-business sector. By identifying and listening to each member of the buying centre or decision-making unit (DMU), the sales representative evaluates what it would take to persuade each individual or company to take action. Different things are important to different audiences so the sales representative may need to negotiate on the basis of the following:
    - price
    - payment terms
    - delivery times
    - after-sales service
    - training.

Cost of personal selling in relation to the other elements of the marketing mix

There is a tendency for many firms, in particular, small to medium-sized enterprises, to consider certain elements of the promotions mix as being beyond their means. Advertising is often not considered because of this perception, whereas direct mail is widely used by smaller firms. However, the initial cost per contact of direct mail is more expensive than advertising. The reality is that it may be possible to offset the costs of direct mail against the day-to-day running expenses of a business, for example, postage and stationery costs. It is not as easy for these same businesses to 'hide' advertising costs. Some firms do not take into account the full cost of having a sales representative out on the road. Salary and commission are not the only costs associated with a sales representative. Other costs which might be taken into account include:

- the provision of a company car – usually firms lease or buy cars. However, some sales representatives use their own cars and receive a monthly car allowance instead
- motor insurance and motor tax, petrol or diesel, and servicing costs
- mobile phone charges
- supply of a laptop computer – while not all sales representatives have a laptop computer, they are used more often. They enable the user to:
  - make sales presentations
  - gain ready access to customer data
  - keep in touch with their organisation through the Internet
  - input and update important information
- the entertainment of current and potential customers
- daily subsistence – when sales representatives are out on the road all day, they are entitled to an allowance for meals
- accommodation – it is not unusual for sales representatives to travel long distances. This may necessitate overnight stays that must be reimbursed.

When these expenses are added to salary and commission, the cost of keeping just one sales representative on the road may easily exceed €80,000. Therefore, when managers devise the marketing communications strategy, and consider ways of implementing it, they must consider the costs of using each element of the promotions mix. In addition, they need to consider whether or not the elements under consideration will be capable of achieving marketing and marketing communications objectives.

Channel strategy

Since the 1990s, there has been a significant change in many firms' approach to channel strategy and management. There is greater emphasis on streamlining networks and reducing the number of layers between the manufacturer or service provider and the end customer. At the same time, many retailers, service providers, fast-food restaurants, and pubs with multiple outlets have introduced central purchasing and purchase directly from the manufacturer. These changes have reduced the number of contact points in buying organisations.

Customer requirements for a sales representative
The move away from transactions towards relationships motivates buyers and sellers to take a long-term view when doing business together. In many cases, the buyer requires or even demands the services of a sales representative.

The relationship between personal selling and the other elements of the marketing communications mix

A recurring theme throughout this book is the importance of achieving integration between all elements of the marketing communications mix. Earlier in this chapter, we saw how difficult it could be to integrate personal selling with other marketing activities. However, personal selling can be supported by and enhance some or all of the other elements in the marketing communications mix.

Advertising

According to Jobber and Lancaster (1997), advertising is used to make the sales representative's job easier by conveying information to the target audience in advance of any contact they might have with a sales representative. If this is done properly, it lays foundations and the sales representative can build on the prospective customer's knowledge.

Advertising is used to encourage potential customers to make contact with the company. Coupons that invite the target audience to contact the advertiser can be included in direct response press and magazine advertisements. A large number of firms incorporate free phone numbers, e-mail addresses and website details in their broadcast and print advertising so that potential customers will make themselves known to the advertiser. Respondents to this form of advertising may prove an important source of leads for the sales team.

Sales promotion

Sales promotion is used to make products more attractive to a firm's channel members. Salespeople use sales promotions to persuade channel members to stock their products. These usually come in the form of incentives such as free products, competitions, point-of-purchase material, co-operative advertising and training.

Sales promotions are used in advertising to generate added interest in a product. An attractive promotion may motivate prospective customers to make contact with the firm. These leads are given to sales representatives, who use the lure of the sales promotion to close the sale. Therefore, according to Burnett and Moriarty (1998), sales promotions can be an effective way of adding value to the personal selling effort.

Public relations

The sales representative is an important public relations tool. For many customers, the sales representative is the living embodiment of the firm's values. In the customer's eyes, they are the firm. Of course, depending on the calibre of the salesperson, this may prove positive or negative. An excellent sales representative is an invaluable asset from a public relations perspective, while an incompetent sales representative does untold damage to a firm's long-term reputation and credibility.

Sales representatives should also be involved in formal public relations activity. They might accompany current and prospective customers on plant tours. Since many Irish firms are part of multinational corporations, it is not unusual for current and potential customers in Ireland to be brought on plant tours to subsidiaries in other countries. This presents relationship-forming opportunities because the two parties get to spend a significant amount of time together.

Some firms encourage sales representative to become involved in community-based activities. They might also be encouraged to give talks at events organised by professional bodies like the Marketing Institute and the Institution of Engineers in Ireland (IEI). Such events present networking opportunities and the potential to meet prospective customers, while reinforcing and reassuring existing customers of their expertise.

Many firms take stands at selected trade shows and sales representatives work at these stands. It is envisaged that this activity will contribute to sales, either directly or indirectly since trade shows are important for building a firm's profile.

Sponsorship

A carefully devised sponsorship strategy provides sales representatives with a powerful selling aid. Sponsorship of sports and the arts is very popular with sponsors. The guarantee of a quota of tickets to each sponsored event is just one of the benefits for the sponsor. These tickets are used to entertain potential customers and to reward valuable customers. The enjoyable nature of these events gives sales representatives the opportunity to forge strong relationships. However, an increasing number of private and public organisations have introduced codes of conduct that preclude staff from accepting invitations to such events, in case it could be construed as bribery.

Direct marketing

The use of direct response advertising as a personal selling support tool was described earlier. There are other direct marketing tools that are used to support the sales effort. In the business-to-business sector, direct mail is sent to target audiences containing information about new products. All mail shots should incorporate a reply device so that the recipient contacts the sender. These responses provide sales leads for the sales force.

A growing number of firms use telemarketing to reduce the workload of sales representatives. In-bound and out-bound telemarketers are used to handle queries, process straightforward sales and set up appointments for visits from salespeople. This reduces the sales representative's workload and allows them to spend more time with important existing and potential customers.

The Internet is a very important direct marketing tool and is used to support sales representatives. Obviously, its role depends on the sophistication of the website and the level of investment in its design and maintenance.

Managing the sales force

When a firm's marketing objectives and strategy are established, the sales manager crafts a sales strategy to accomplish specific sales objectives. Sales management is used to ensure that these objectives are achieved. Churchill *et al.* (1990) proposed a framework for analysing sales management and this is reproduced in Figure 13.2.

Types of selling situations

Before examining the sales management function, we should take a look at types of selling situations (see Table 13.3). Salespeople are classified according to the type of sales activity they undertake. There are three categories but it is important to note that a combination of all three is often used by firms.

Table 13.3 Types of sales activity

- Order takers
- Order creators/missionary salespeople
- Order getters
  - New business salespeople
  - Organisational salespeople
  - Consumer salespeople
  - Technical support salespeople
  - Merchandisers

Order takers

There are inside and outside order takers in many firms. Inside order takers do not go out to visit customers. Instead, the customer contacts them, either by telephone, e-mail, in writing or in person. Therefore, order taking is a largely reactive, transaction-oriented activity. Examples include retail salespeople and telemarketing personnel.

In contrast, outside order takers respond to customer requests but do so by visiting the customer's premises. Like inside order takers, they do not adopt a proactive stance. Increasingly, outside order takers are being replaced by telemarketers. They fulfil many of the same tasks in a more cost-effective way.

Figure 13.2 Overview of sales management

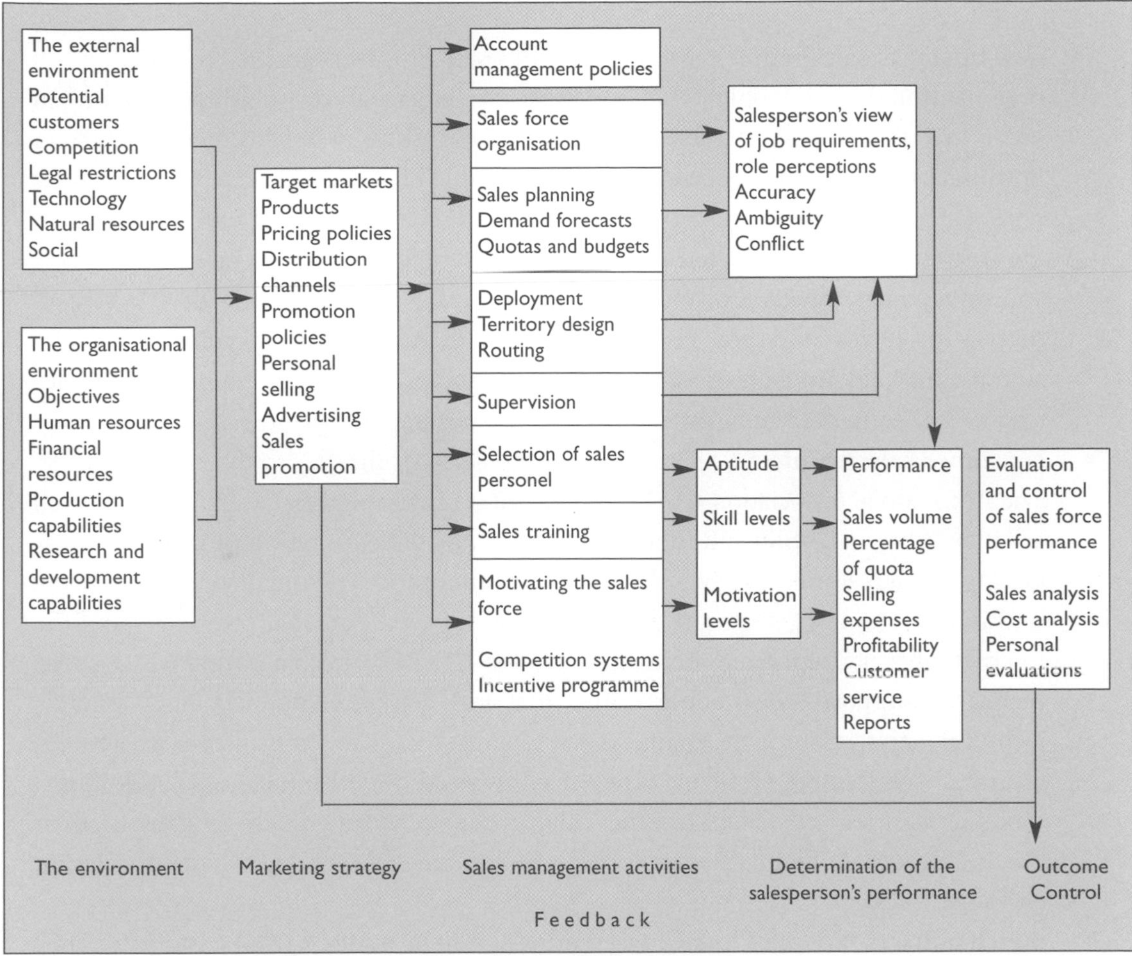

Source: Churchill *et al.* (1990)

Order creators/missionary salespeople

Order creators', or missionary salespeople's, objective is not to make a direct sale, but to persuade customers to specify or recommend the sales representative's product or service in appropriate situations. This is common in a number of sectors in the Irish economy. For example, lighting and building materials sales organisations engage in missionary selling to architects and consultants so that they will specify the use of their products in building projects. Book publishers specialising in educational texts target key individuals in the Department of Education and Science, teachers and lecturers so that they will specify their books on syllabuses. It is hoped that a large number of students will, in turn, purchase the recommended texts.

Order getters

Unlike order creators, order getters' objective is to persuade customers to place orders directly with themselves. Jobber and Lancaster (1997) divide this activity into five main categories:

- **new-business salespeople**'s task is to identify new prospects and sell to them
- **organisational salespeople**'s main objective is to engage in relationship marketing in order to cultivate and maintain long-term relationships with customers. In larger organisations, this may necessitate team selling. Team selling occurs when sales representatives from a number of departments, all selling different products, approach the customer as a co-ordinated unit. The objective is to cross-sell a range of products and satisfy many needs. For example, Siemens provide customers with solutions to diverse problems and are involved in many areas, including communications, automation, and software design. It often advantageous for multidisciplinary sales teams to be formed to fulfil a customer's needs successfully.
- **consumer salespeople** sell their products and services directly to the end consumer. The Automobile Association (AA) positions sales representatives at retail outlets such as Liffey Valley in Dublin and they sell subscriptions direct to new customers. Double-glazing, conservatories and encyclopaedias are other products sold direct to consumers in this way. However, since the advent of high-powered personal computers and the Internet, encyclopaedias are increasingly sold in CD-ROM format or online.
- **technical support salespeople**. Firms that sell complex products must provide technical support through engineers or technicians. They must solve customers' technical queries and problems. They may also see opportunities to sell additional products to these customers or they may recommend upgraded versions of their existing products. Technical support salespeople are often the recipients of relevant customer feedback.
- **merchandisers** provide a link between firms and their trade or retail customers. They advise channel members on point-of-purchase (POP) displays so that products are shown off to their best advantage. Firms often create their own POP materials and supply them to channel members at a discounted price or free of charge. They assemble the displays and make it easy for retailers to use them. Mobile phone service providers, such as Vodafone and O2, take merchandising very seriously and give their retailers a lot of support in this area.

Sales management activities

Figure 13.2 (page 347) presented an overview of the sales management function. Key sales management activities are explained below.

Sales force organisation

This is the way in which salespeople and their tasks are structured. Sales force organisation is largely dependent on the nature of the product being sold, the number of prospects and customers, and their location, and the firm's resources. Some firms give salespeople responsibility for specific geographical areas, while others give them responsibility for specific industry sectors, for example, pharmaceuticals, dairy, and textiles.

Some individual prospects or customers may be so important to a selling organisation that they merit the full-time dedication of a salesperson or even an entire team. This is known as key account management. For example, some customers, or clients, as they are more usually known, are so important to their advertising agencies, that an entire team comprising account handlers and creatives are committed to servicing their business 100 per cent of their time. The ESB is one of Ireland's main buyers of power equipment, and as a result, suppliers in this area allocate the time of one or more sales representatives to building long-term relationships with them.

Finally, some organisations sell a range of products, and give salespeople specific responsibility for selling just one or a related range of products.

Determining the size of the sales force

A firm's resources help determine the size of the sales force. However, the sales objectives should be the driving force behind the size of the sales force. These enable the sales manager to calculate how many salespeople are required to ensure that sales objectives are achieved.

Lone selling or team selling

Increased interest in relationship marketing has given rise to a greater preponderance of team selling. This is applicable in selling organisations that have a wide range of products and services. Products from many different business units may be very relevant to the customer. Team selling enables the sales force to identify cross-selling opportunities and, from the customer's perspective, it is a more efficient way of solving problems.

Inside or outside selling

Some firms use a combination of inside and outside selling. Some customer needs are easily served by a telephone call, while others require in-depth meetings and the dedication of an outside salesperson. Improvements in telecommunications technology have persuaded some organisations to replace outside salespeople with inside telesales staff. While it is a more efficient approach in many instances, firms must ensure that they do not lose touch with their customers. This problem may arise because the interpersonal aspect of personal selling is superseded by an efficient, production-line approach. One way of ensuring that this does not happen is to use a combination of the two in a complementary way.

The recruitment, selection and training of salespeople

According to Doyle (2002), various studies agree that successful salespeople are likely to have the following traits:

- high levels of motivation
- empathy – good salespeople are able to listen to customers and relate to them. This enables them to build long-lasting customer relationships
- self-confidence – salespeople must believe in themselves so current and prospective customers will believe in them too.

Planning for any element of the marketing communications mix depends on what an organisation is trying to achieve. The recruitment of salespeople is no different and, while the above traits provide useful recruitment guidelines, the organisation must understand the characteristics of their target market and consider the nature of the product or service being sold. These factors, together with the sales objectives, determine the profile of the person best suited to a particular selling role.

The personal selling element of the marketing communications mix cannot be controlled and made uniform in the same way as advertising. People deliver the message, and no two people are the same. Training helps ensure that salespeople behave within certain parameters.

Training should be ongoing but a newly recruited salesperson should be informed and trained in the following areas:

- **company background**. Salespeople familiarise themselves with the origins of the company. Some prospective customers feel more comfortable dealing with organisations if they know something about the founders, length of time in existence, geographical locations, number of employees, and areas of expertise.
- **company values**. These provide the salesperson with a behavioural 'roadmap'. For example, if an organisation's values are to be progressive, efficient and innovative, salespeople should be taught what these words mean in the sales context. What does 'progressive' mean to the salesperson? What does 'efficient' mean? What does 'innovative' mean? Acceptance and enactment of company values increase the likelihood of salespeople behaving in a more uniform way.
- **product**. Salespeople should know everything about the products they are selling.
- **target audience**. Salespeople must know as much as possible about the target audience. This enables them to tailor their messages and appeal to different needs.
- **competitors**. When current and prospective customers engage in the purchasing process, they often compare and contrast the merits of a number of competing firms. They usually meet with salespeople from these firms. Salespeople should know as much as possible about their competitors so that they can differentiate their own company's offering. This is often achieved by highlighting the shortcomings of competitors.
- **administrative tasks**. Salespeople are usually required to carry out administrative

specific call plans that must be adhered to over a specific time period. As well as directing salespeople, the sales manager must motivate them.

At the start of the financial year, it is usual to hold an annual sales conference. In large, dispersed organisations, this presents an excellent opportunity for the entire sales force to meet and exchange ideas and views. It is also used to present the sales plan and the marketing communications schedule for the year.

In addition to the annual sales conference, monthly sales meetings are often scheduled. Selling is a lonely profession and these meetings help re-energise the sales force. Sales managers might use these occasions to congratulate good performers and encourage those who have experienced a difficult month. These formal sales meetings are used to disseminate relevant information, for example, a comparison of sales performance against sales targets, new product information, previously unanticipated marketing communications activity and competitor information.

The sales force must be motivated to do their best. The sales manager shapes expectations and instils a belief that effort and performance are rewarded. We have just seen that, while money is a significant element of any compensation plan, it is not and should not be the only incentive used to encourage sales representatives to achieve their targets. For example, recognition and promotion are powerful motivators.

Evaluation

This must be carried out in order to ascertain the success or otherwise of the sales plan. It helps the sales manager identify the sales force's training needs. From the salesperson's perspective remuneration can depend on it. Evaluation therefore analyses the performance of the sales force. De Burca and Lambkin (1993) contend that performance evaluation has several elements and they are:

- **aggregate performance**, i.e. the performance of the entire sales force when measured against the organisation's sales targets
- **individual performance**, i.e. the performance of each salesperson
- **objective output**, i.e. measurable aspects of performance, such as the profitability of the selling function
- **subjective measures**, i.e. customer service provision. This necessitates the acquisition of feedback from customers.

Salespeople themselves are required to provide information in order to assist with the evaluation process. They are required to submit regular expense claims, call plans and sales reports, from which the sales manager evaluates efficiency and effectiveness.

The personal selling process

The personal selling process outlined in Figure 13.3 on page 352, is a representation of the nature of the tasks carried out by salespeople. While it concentrates on the activity involved in securing a transaction, much of the salesperson's time should be dedicated to building relationships with existing customers.

Figure 13.3 Personal selling process

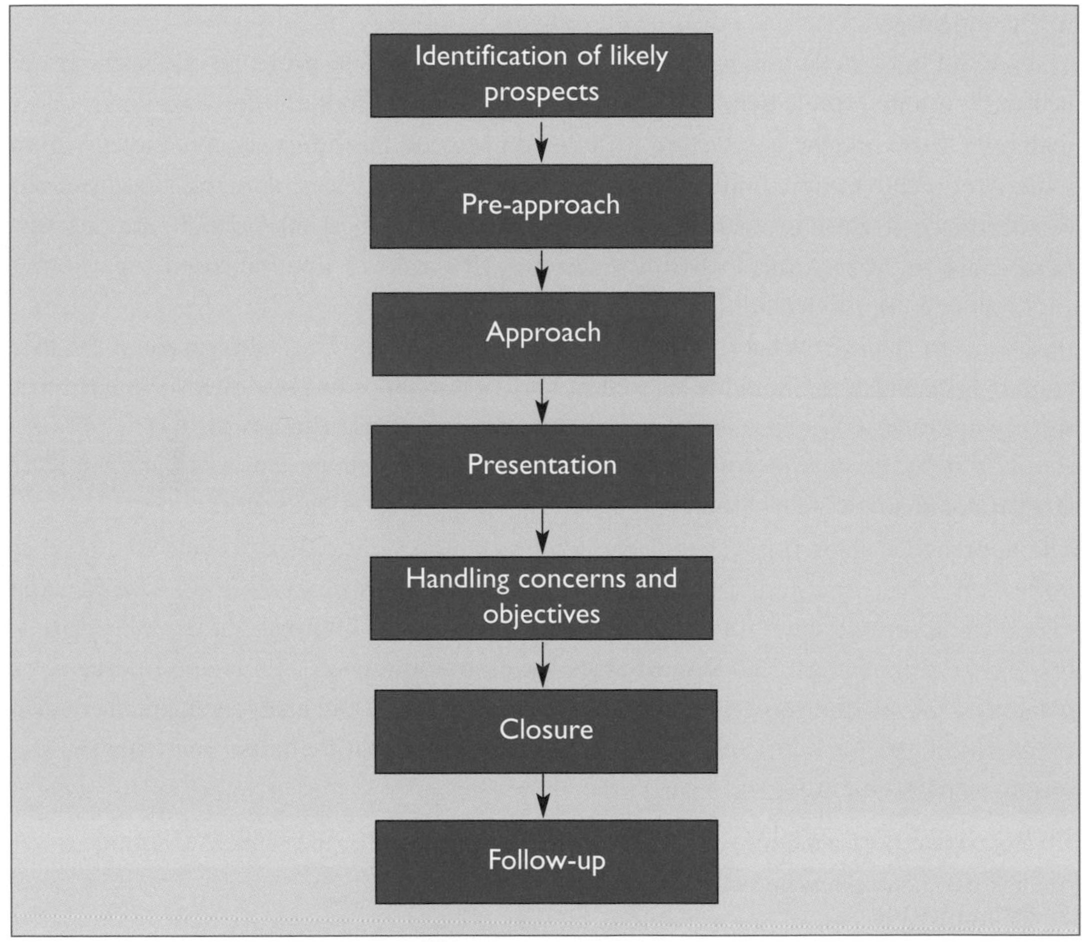

1. Identification of likely prospects

The identification of likely prospects involves research. Sales representatives usually do this. Some firms involve other staff, for example, marketing executives. Sales representatives should make it their business to know what is happening in their market. By scanning the information contained in newspapers, specialist magazines, tender documentation and the Internet, they discover what activities prospective customers are involved in. This enables them to identify activities that require the purchase of certain products and services. Also, salespeople speak to current customers, suppliers and network partners with a view to obtaining leads. Word of mouth and recommendations from existing customers are effective ways of identifying potential customers. Increasingly, salespeople are supported in this task by other elements of the marketing communications mix, such as direct marketing (see above). At this stage of the process, each prospect must be evaluated in terms of its long-term revenue-generating potential. Time spent doing this means that the salesperson's energies are not diverted away from targeting prospects with potential.

2. Pre-approach

The second stage of the process is referred to as pre-approach. When the salesperson has isolated a number of likely prospects, they immerse themselves in the prospect's business with a view to knowing more about it than the prospect does. This has more relevance in today's competitive environment than ever before because successful selling is really about partnership with the customer. If the salesperson can bring new information or a different perspective to the prospect at their first meeting, this makes a strong impression.

At the pre-approach stage, the salesperson sets objectives for the first contact. What do they want to achieve? What information do they want to find out? The nature of the first contact is considered. Should it be by letter or telephone, or in person? Investing time in the pre-approach stage increases the likelihood of success at the approach stage.

3. Approach

The approach stage is the first time the salesperson and the prospect come into contact with each other. Therefore the impression left by the salesperson is a key factor in the continuance or otherwise of the relationship. If the contact is by telephone or in person, the salesperson must use the opportunity to listen to the prospect and determine what they want. The salesperson must also use this opportunity to tell the prospect about their own organisation, paying particular attention to aspects that will interest the listener. The salesperson should work to ensure that they arrange a follow-up meeting to make a presentation that is specific to the prospect's needs.

4. Presentation

If the approach stage succeeds, the salesperson engages in the presentation stage of the process. This can take place in a number of venues, although the selling organisation may want to invite the prospect to a meeting in their premises. This allows the prospect to find out more about the organisation. In some situations, it might be important for the prospective customer to observe the manufacturing process or for the salesperson to demonstrate a particular product. The salesperson might also make a presentation that demonstrates they were listening to the prospect at the approach stage and they have thought about ways in which they can be of assistance. Some firms have corporate videos that are shown to the prospect at this stage. However, due to technological advancements, it is now possible for salespeople to compile prospect-specific multimedia presentations that focus on specific concerns and opportunities.

5. Handling of any concerns and objections

Potential customers rarely listen to presentations without commenting or asking questions. Therefore the handling of any concerns and objections is very important. Salespeople should be empathetic and should listen carefully to what the prospect is saying. An ability to interpret the prospect's body language may be required because people do not always say exactly what they are thinking. If the salesperson does not succeed in finding out what the prospect is thinking, all further contact may be terminated. When known, concerns and objections can usually be resolved and the salesperson's ability to do this might enable the selling process to proceed.

6. Closure

At the closure stage of the salesperson seeks to secure an order from the prospect. It entails finalising the terms and conditions of the order, such as product specifications, training requirements, after-sales service, delivery deadlines, warranty, and, of course, price. Price is an aspect which can cause embarrassment but unless this is clarified with the prospect, closure is not possible. Therefore, the salesperson must have the necessary negotiation skills. Depending on the relative power of the prospect, and their perceived importance to the selling organisation, they might attempt to exert considerable downward pressure on the price. It is important for the salesperson to remember that a sale at any price is not always a good thing. At this stage of the selling process, the salesperson might deploy some sales promotion techniques in order to make the offer more attractive.

7. Follow-up

The follow-up stage of the selling process is essential if the selling organisation intends building long-term relationships with new customers. Depending on the nature of the product or service involved, this stage might entail the sales representative personally delivering the product or visiting the customer to see it in use very soon after closure. It may simply involve a telephone call to ensure that the new customer is happy with their purchase.

Follow-up does not end there. The salesperson should create opportunities to maintain regular contact with the customer. Further sales opportunities may emerge during these interactions. Also, they allow the salesperson to observe competitor activity and anticipate likely threats. Direct marketing techniques are used from this stage on and might take the form of loyalty schemes and regular personal communications delivered by mail or e-mail.

Despite the growing realisation among organisations that they should engage in relationship marketing, the personal selling process remains oriented towards a transaction-led approach. While many aspects of this process remain valid, some firms need to do more to encourage team selling, advocate the long-term merit of working in partnership with customers, and invest time in post-sales activity.

Many firms use the Internet to support the personal selling function. This is examined in Chapter 14.

Personal selling in context

In highly competitive markets, professional salespeople are a crucial differentiator. They use their expertise and problem-solving skills to form long-lasting relationships with customers. In this final section, we will have a brief look at the pros and cons of personal selling:

- **flexibility**. When compared with advertising, public relations and sponsorship, personal selling facilitates greater flexibility. Verbal and non-verbal signals from customers indicate their levels of enthusiasm for the selling message. Consequently, sales representatives can evaluate each situation and tailor their messages to maximise effectiveness. This helps build relationships.
- **one-on-one communication**. Advertising, and to a lesser extent sponsorship and public relations, communicates with mass audiences, while personal selling facilitates one-on-one communication. This characteristic also plays a key role in the delivery of customer service.
- **less wastage**. Assuming that the sales force targets the right people, personal selling is far more targeted, and incurs less wastage than advertising.
- **high cost per contact**. The cost per contact of personal selling is high and tends to be much greater than other elements of the marketing communications mix. There are many costs associated with the maintenance of the sales function. Some firms use telesales and the Internet to reduce personal selling costs. Both of these support the sales force and allow them to spend more time on value-adding activities, such as maintaining relationships and spending time with key customers.
- **difficult to control**. While the interpersonal nature of personal selling is very positive, there is a downside. It is difficult to control because individuals carry out personal selling and each person is different. Extensive training and support help minimise variations and help ensure that sales representatives are more likely to behave and communicate in the desired way. In contrast, advertising is completely within the firm's control.
- **recruitment, selection and supervision**. Economic boom and recession present different challenges in terms of recruitment, selection and supervision. An economic boom, like that experienced in Ireland in the 1990s, makes it difficult to find suitable candidates for vacant positions. Once a candidate has been found and trained, the problems do not stop there. Retention is one of the biggest problems as successful sales representatives accept more lucrative offers from competitor firms. If the incumbent organisation wants to pursue relationship marketing, constantly changing personnel

makes this difficult to achieve. During an economic downturn, motivation is a problem. Prospects and customers have less money. This makes the selling process very difficult. If sales representatives rely on commission-based earnings, morale can become very low.

Summary

Personal selling describes the sales activity that is carried out directly between the buyer and the seller through personal media. Therefore it is the most adaptable element of the marketing communications mix and allows the salesperson to adapt the message to suit each individual.

Using cost per contact as a measure, personal selling is the most expensive element of the marketing communications mix. Therefore, each firm should carefully evaluate when it is most appropriate to use personal selling. This evaluation takes into account the nature of the information being conveyed, the size and nature of the target audience, the marketing objectives, the cost of personal selling in relation to other elements of the marketing mix, and the channel strategy.

With proper planning, personal selling works well with the other elements of the marketing communications mix. Advertising and direct marketing are used to generate sales leads, and sales promotion is used by salespeople at the closure stage of the selling process. A firm's sales force is a public relations tool, and salespeople become the face of the firm.

Salespeople are classified according to the type of sales activity they undertake – order takers, missionary salespeople, and order getters. Sales management helps ensure that the sales force achieves the sales objectives. Salespeople are compensated for their efforts in a number of ways and the most widely used method in Ireland is basic salary plus commission and bonus.

The personal selling process is broken down into seven inter-related steps. The salesperson must demonstrate good listening skills, problem-solving ability, interpersonal skills and negotiation skills to implement the process successfully.

Personal selling is a very powerful marketing communications tool in that it is flexible, it facilitates one-on-one communication, and it results in less wastage than say, advertising. However, the cost per contact is high, a salesperson's behaviour is difficult to control, and the recruitment, selection and supervision of sales representatives present many challenges.

Useful website

www.salesinstitute.ie Sales Institute of Ireland

Review questions

1. What is personal selling? In your answer, critically assess the difference between transaction selling and relational selling.
2. Describe and discuss the factors that determine the role of personal selling in each individual firm.
3. Discuss the relationship between personal selling and the other elements of the marketing communications mix.
4. Identify the different types of sales activity and explain each one.
5. Discuss in detail the role of sales management.
6. Critically assess the various compensation plans used in Irish firms.
7. Describe in detail the personal selling process.

Exercise

Interview a sales manager in a firm of your choice. Ask them to describe in detail the selling process they use in order to secure new customers. Compare their answers with Figure 13.3 on page 354 and critically assess whether or not you think their process is effective. Give reasons for your answer. What recommendations, if any, would you suggest to improve their process?

References

Armstrong, Gary and Kotler, Philip, *Marketing: An Introduction*, 6th edition (Pearson Education Inc., 2003).

Burnett, John and Moriarty, Sandra, *Introduction to Marketing Communication: An Integrated Approach* (Prentice-Hall, 1998).

Churchill, G. A. Jr, Ford, N. M. and Walker, O. C. Jr, *Sales Force Management: Planning, Implementation and Control*, 3rd edition (Irwin, Homewood, 1990).

De Burca, Sean and Lambkin, Mary, 'Sales force management in Ireland' (*Irish Marketing Review*, Vol. 6, 1993).

Doyle, Peter, *Marketing Management and Strategy*, third edition (Pearson Education Limited, 2002).

Gronroos, C., *From Marketing Mix to Relationship Marketing: Towards a Paradigm Shift in Marketing*, (Management Decisions, 1994).

Jobber, David and Lancaster, Geoff, *Selling and Sales Management*, 4th edition (Pitman Publishing, 1997).

Vitale, Robert P. and Giglierano, Joseph J. *Business-to-Business Marketing: Analysis and Practice in a Dynamic Environment* (South-Western/Thomson Learning, 2002).

14

ONLINE MARKETING COMMUNICATIONS

The aims and objectives of this chapter are:

- to define some key terms associated with the Internet
- to identify the characteristics of the Internet as a marketing communications medium
- to explain the benefits of using the Internet for marketing communications
- to describe the key success factors in web design
- to examine how each element of the marketing communications mix can be implemented on the Internet.

Introduction

Chapter 6 examined the more traditional media associated with marketing communications. However, since the 1990s, new media options have become available to organisations engaging in marketing communications. In the past, business customers were the primary users of these new technologies. This meant that they were not considered appropriate media for the transmission of messages to consumer markets. Since the mid-1990s an ever-increasing number of consumers have been able to access the so-called 'new media' outside the workplace through computers, digital television and mobile phones. AC Nielsen (2001) found that, in just 12 months from March 2000 to March 2001, the active Internet audience in Ireland grew by 75 per cent to 572,000 and the total Internet audience grew 69 per cent to almost 1.2 million. Their research, from the marketer's point of view, highlighted other interesting data too:

- 16 per cent of the Irish Internet audience is in the 12–17 age group.
- 82 per cent more females visited websites in March 2001 than at the same time the previous year.
- There was a 105 per cent increase in the 65–99 age group; an 81 per cent increase in the 55–64 age group; and a 66 per cent increase in the 50–54 age group.

According to the research company Amárach, (20 August 2002), by the end of June 2002,

38 per cent of all Irish adults were using the Internet. This is the equivalent of 1,065,000 adult users and represented a 5 per cent increase on the figures recorded in 2001.

While the rate of growth in Internet usage is slowing down, statistics like these cannot be ignored by Irish marketers.

Key terms

Much of the terminology associated with the Internet has made its way into everyday language. However, many terms are not fully understood and can cause confusion. For instance, what is the difference between the Internet and the World Wide Web? While there is a difference between them, the Internet and World Wide Web are used interchangeably to convey the same meaning. According to Armstrong and Kotler (2003), the **Internet** is a 'vast public web of computer networks that connects users of all types all around the world to each other and to an amazingly large "information repository". The Internet makes up one big "information highway" that can dispatch bits at incredible speeds from one location to another.' The **World Wide Web** is the multimedia version of the Internet that was introduced in 1993 and when people talk about the Internet, they should, strictly speaking, talk about the World Wide Web (Pickton and Broderick, 2001). The introduction of the World Wide Web means that the Internet's role as a strategic business tool is more effective. For the purposes of this chapter, the term 'Internet' will be used.

The Internet *A public web of computer networks that connects users around the world.*

The World Wide Web *The multimedia version of the Internet.*

E-business *The use of IT for buying, selling, servicing customers and working with business partners.*

E-commerce *Buying and selling supported by electronic means.*

E-marketing *Communication, promotion and sale of products and services over the Internet.*

Uniform Resource Locator (URL) *Used to locate specific websites.*

Internet protocols *control and direct the passing of data across the network.*

Other terms that require definition are e-business, e-commerce and e-marketing. **E-business** 'embraces all aspects of the use of information technology in business. It includes not only buying and selling, but also servicing customers and collaborating with business partners' (Rowley, 2001). **E-commerce** refers to the 'buying and selling processes supported by electronic means, primarily the Internet', while **e-marketing** is 'the 'e-selling' side of e-commerce – company efforts to communicate about, promote, and sell products and services over the Internet' (Armstrong and Kotler, 2003). The primary focus of this chapter is on e-marketing, with particular emphasis on the role of marketing communications.

While the term 'website address' is often used when referring to the location of a website, the correct term is the **Uniform Resource Locator (URL)**. It enables the user to locate a specific website. For example, Kellogg's URL is http://www.kelloggs.ie/. The user does not have to key in the **Internet protocol** (e.g. http://) and in many cases, the company's name alone is sufficient. Internet protocols 'control and direct the passing of data across the network' (Ellsworth and Ellsworth, 1997).

Characteristics of the Internet as a marketing communications medium

Before someone actually visits an organisation's website, the Internet can be described as operating in a pull environment. This means that the information on the website cannot really be pushed at the person until they actually visit the website (Figure 14.1). In recognition of this, many organisations use traditional marketing communications activity in order to pull visitors into their sites. This can be likened to advertising done by FMCG manufacturers to create consumer preferences and ensure that their products are actively demanded from the retailers.

Figure 14.1 Push and pull environment

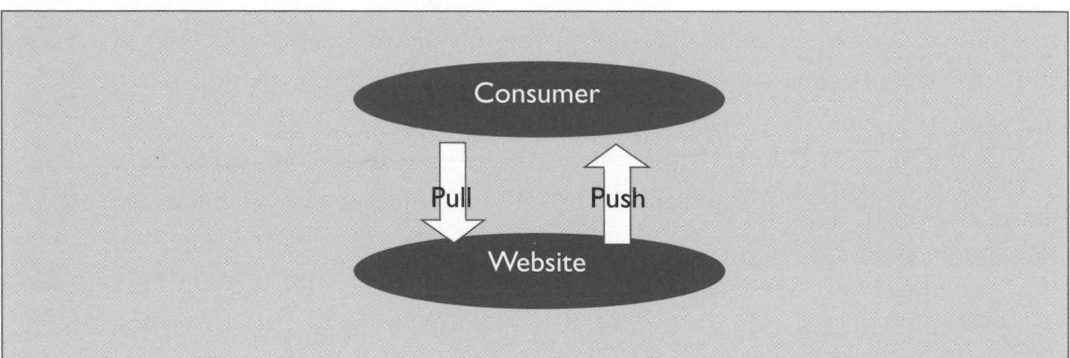

In the 1990s, a boom in conventional advertising occurred as new and existing organisations set about informing audiences of their arrival on the Internet. Many of these advertisers were part of the dot.com vanguard and their demise coincided with a downturn in the global economy. This caused a downturn in the fortunes of the global advertising industry. Target audiences were made aware of various websites as a result of extensive broadcast and print advertising. Many organisations also used publicity to draw attention to their websites. These techniques are still used, although Internet-based techniques are also used to attract visitors. These will be examined later in the chapter.

When someone actually enters a website, the owner can create a push-type marketing environment by using a range of techniques, including online sales promotions, direct marketing and advertising.

The characteristics of the Internet can be considered under four main areas. They are communication style, social presence, control of communication content and control of communication contact (Peters, 1998; O'Malley *et al.* 1999).

Communication style

This refers to the temporal (or time) dimension of communications. Marketing communications methods are either synchronous or asynchronous. **Synchronous**

communication style means 'there is little or no time lag between the giving, receiving and responding aspects of communication between parties.' **Asynchronous communication** 'would include a time lag' (Peters, 1998). As illustrated in Figure 14.2, personal selling exhibits a highly synchronous communication style because the giving, receiving and responding aspects of communication are simultaneous. This is due to the face-to-face nature of personal selling. It contrasts sharply with direct mail, which is strongly asynchronous because there is always a time lag between the giving and receiving of information. Furthermore, the time lag between the receipt of information and response can be quite significant. Like personal selling, telemarketing is highly synchronous. The Internet or electronic commerce displays synchronous characteristics and fares well in comparison to direct mail. As technology improves and facilitates even faster information exchanges, Internet time lags will diminish.

Synchronous communication *Little or no time lag between the giving, receiving and responding aspects of communication between parties.*

Asynchronous communication *Includes a time lag.*

Social presence

Social presence is the feeling that communication exchanges are 'sociable, warm, personal, sensitive and active' (Peters, 1998). It is strongly influenced by the channel attributes. As illustrated in Figure 14.2, personal selling exhibits an extremely high level of social presence. Communication is face-to-face. This means that non-verbal cues can be observed, interpreted and acted upon. While the ability to observe body language is the most valuable type of non-verbal communication, telemarketers use tone of voice to gauge the mood of the target. Electronic commerce exhibits a medium social presence but the provision of chat rooms and instantaneous e-mails creates a greater sense of social presence. Once again, direct mail, one of the key direct marketing media, fares relatively badly in terms of social presence. It is more akin to TV advertising.

Social presence *The feeling that communication exchanges are sociable, warm, personal, sensitive and active.*

Figure 14.2 Level of social presence in personal and non-personal communications methods

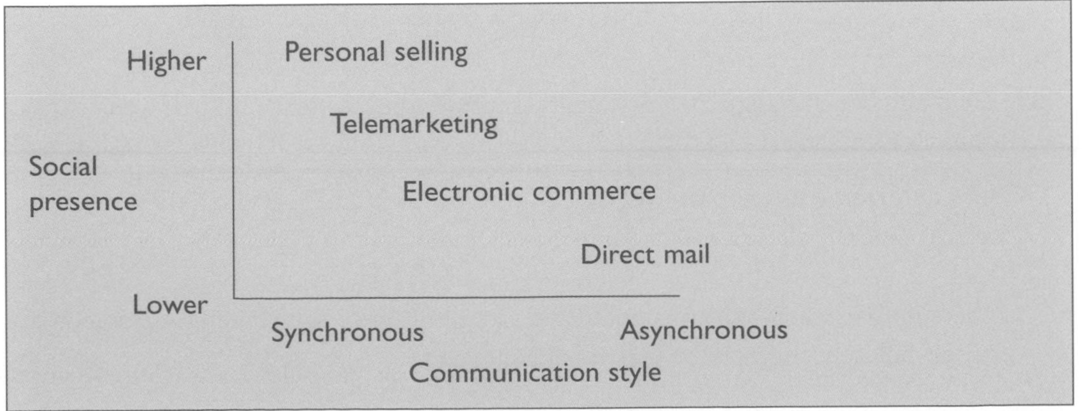

Source: Peters (1998)

Consumer control of contact

Consumers are more likely to engage in computer-based marketing activity if they have control over when contact is made. This is a significant advantage of the Internet because it gives consumers control over timing. In such circumstances, they are more likely to respond positively to the communication.

Consumer control of content

Interactive *When users are able to control the content, or presentation, of the message.*

With regard to the Internet, 'content can be customised by either users or by senders. Where users are able to control the content, or presentation, of the message it is said to be **interactive**' (Peters, 1998). In this environment, consumers can supply content to chosen websites by e-mailing the company or companies involved or by sending messages to electronic bulletin boards. For example, amazon.com encourages customers to review CDs, DVDs and books that they have purchased and to rate them. This information is available on the website for other customers and serves as electronic word of mouth. As shown in Figure 14.3, electronic commerce offers consumers greater control over content than personal selling, which tends to be controlled by the sales representative. While telemarketing appears to fare well in terms of consumer control of content, this is far more likely during in-bound telemarketing (when the consumer initiates the call) as opposed to out-bound telemarketing (when the organisation initiates the call).

Figure 14.3 Consumer control of content and contact in different marketing communications

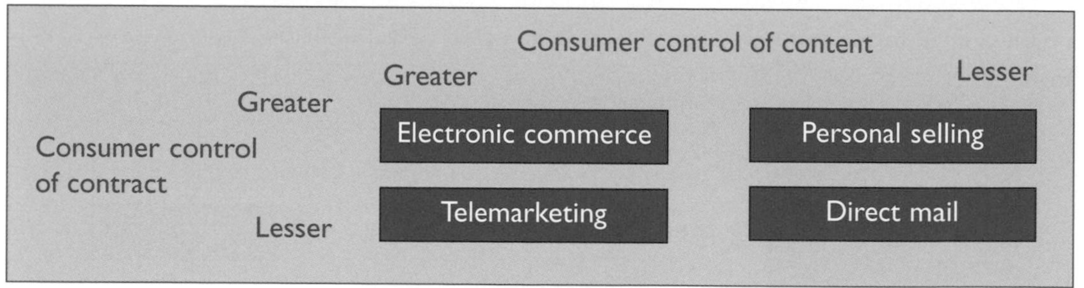

Source: Peters (1998)

The benefits

There are many benefits associated with marketing communications on the Internet (these are summarised in Table 14.1):

- **Users determine usage patterns**, that is, when, where and how often they access the Internet, since it allows users round-the-clock access throughout the year (Rowley, 2001).
- It offers **global reach**, which is undifferentiated but, once someone has made contact over the Internet, they can be individually targeted.

Table 14.1 The benefits of marketing communications on the Internet

• Users can determine usage patterns
• Global reach
• Powerful tool in building long-term customer relationships
• Interactive
• Enables consumers to take a proactive approach with suppliers
• Can be used to support channel strategy

- It is **a powerful tool for building long-term customer relationships**. Once a person has visited a website and registered their details, an organisation can keep in regular contact via e-mail. For example, pigsback.com regularly contacts its customers by e-mail with tailored sales promotion offers directly related to the contact's tastes and interests.
- It is **interactive**, unlike television, cinema, radio, press and outdoor media. As already explained, interactivity implies that all parties can influence and are involved in the communication process. Therefore it is not a passive medium. Figure 14.4 shows how consumers can communicate with each other and how customers often enter other websites from their initial entry point.
- It **enables consumers to be proactive**. The Internet turns marketing communications on its head. Traditionally, the organisation initiated marketing communications activity.

Figure 14.4 Interactivity, the difference between traditional media and the Internet

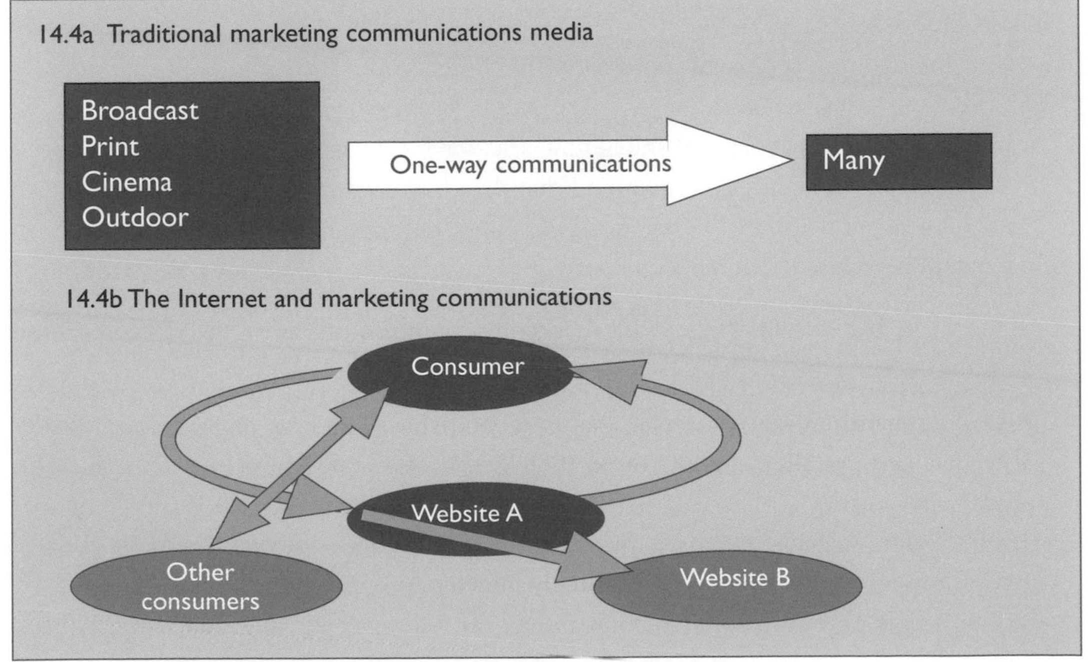

The Internet enables the customer to be more proactive when searching for suppliers and in many cases it has shifted the initial emphasis from 'organisation-to-potential-customer contact' to 'potential-customer-to-organisation contact'.

- It **supports channel strategy** by building customer goodwill and complementing the organisation's other sales channels, as opposed to selling its products directly. For example, the global drinks giant Diageo uses its website to enhance its extensive portfolio of brands. While it is not used to sell its brands directly to consumers, it is used to enhance brand image and to generate strong demand in the relevant outlets.

  Increasingly, however, the Internet is being used as a selling tool and is capable of carrying out online transactions with visitors to the website. By cutting out agents, they can save money. Examples include Ryanair.com and, more recently, Aer Lingus and aerlingus.com:

Aer Lingus website strategy pays dividends

Many of the world's biggest airlines have finally managed to trade their way out of the calamitous post 9/11 slump, but Aer Lingus has literally clicked its way out of trouble, via its aerlingus.com website. The firm has not spent a single cent advertising or marketing any other element of its operation since December 2001. It has ploughed all its marketing and advertising resources instead into aerlingus.com.

The Irish Times has learned that during one week recently the airline sold 45 per cent of all its tickets via the site – which has become a sort of electronic shopfront. Aer Lingus executives admit the strategy involves taking the odd leaf out of Ryanair's book, but so be it.

In a strange way Aer Lingus has become aerlingus.com. The hackneyed shamrock symbol, long associated with the 'old' Aer Lingus, has not been used in marketing the airline in at least a year. The airline is now a national carrier with a small 'n'.

Marketing the site has even included that dreaded word of all traditional carriers, 'cheap', in relation to fares. 'That was certainly a culture shock to some people in here,' said a company source this week. Although the firm continues to operate a telesales service and to sell tickets through the travel trade, the firm is not shy in stating that it wants aerlingus.com to sell more than 80 per cent of tickets online.

Ryanair.com has already exceeded that level. It is also offering more – car-parking at selected British airports, for example – on its site right now than Aer Lingus. But aerlingus.com and Ryanair.com are unlikely to call the battle off for some time. In future, value-added services will be the name of the game. If the websites are the new shopfronts, Ryanair has already packed its windows with an array of wares. You can buy a mortgage, home insurance and life insurance and personal loans from its site. Aerlingus.com is not that all-encompassing yet. But it may find that once you emphasise the online route, you have to go all the way. Already the airline is selling insurance via aerlingus.com. The company's chief executive, Mr Willie Walsh, regards aerlingus.com as a major factor behind the turnaround in the airline's fortunes. 'It has helped us reduce our distribution costs which has translated into the widespread availability of cheap seats. Our guarantee is that you will always find the cheapest Aer Lingus fares on our website. That promise has been the key to the success of marketing the Internet as a sales channel,' he says. Three years ago about 9 per cent of the airline's revenue per ticket was going on commission, this is now down to 1 per cent. The cost of selling its product (airline tickets) has fallen from €163 million in 2001 to an anticipated €79 million this year. This is good news for Aer Lingus and its shareholder, the Government, but bad news for the travel trade and possibly for Ryanair, at least on routes such as the Dublin–Stansted service which are booked mainly via the website.

Mr Walsh says whatever eventually happens in the cyberspace battle between the airlines, Aer Lingus's decision to put so much emphasis on the site has been the right one. But having stolen some of Ryanair's clothes, Aer Lingus must broaden its Web offering. Already some US airlines offer all-in holidays via the web, others offer specialist packages. The sites of Ryanair and Aer Lingus, may represent new ways of marketing, new forms of selling, but they are currently judged only on fares. But how will they do if they become all-embracing travel portals, offering everything from fishing gear to pleasure crafts by just clicking your mouse?

Source: *The Irish Times*, 9 January 2003

Key success factors in web design

According to Kompass Ireland (2000) first-time visitors to a website account for 73.38 per cent of its visitors. Only 16.2 per cent return for two or four visits. Therefore, organisations should take a number of factors into account when designing websites in order to impress first-time visitors to their websites and increase the likelihood of frequent visits.

Table 14.2 Key success factors in web design

- Layout and ease of use
- The provision of interesting and extensive content
- Regular content updates
- Interactivity
- Relevant, helpful links to other websites
- Secure transaction facilities

Layout and ease of use

When consumers first started using the Internet, many complained that websites were difficult to use or navigate. They made information retrieval difficult. This meant that the user was less likely to return. While it is acceptable that a website consists of numerous screens that equate to the paper version of pages, they should be indexed. This means that the user can return to them easily during their visit. Many websites use icons in order to assist navigation.

Graphics, photographs, moving images and video material tend to occupy large areas of space on a website. Unless the user has a very powerful computer and has an ISDN phone line, they can take a long time to load. In Ireland, Internet access costs are high. This means that slow-loading images cause annoyance because many of the Internet service providers (e.g. Eircom, Esat Bt) charge private users on the basis of time spent online. Therefore, access costs should be taken into consideration when designing a website.

The provision of interesting and extensive content

If website content is very interesting to visitors and impossible to explore in just one visit, they are more likely to return. Of course, it is also important that a website is capable of fulfilling visitors' information requirements. However, this does not mean that they should be heavily text-based. Many user-friendly websites convey information through a combination of text and images. Care should be taken to ensure that the external audience is kept in mind when compiling information. Therefore the site should be free of jargon, which is usually only understood by internal audiences.

Regular content updates

Websites should be updated regularly in order to reflect relevant developments and changes. Many organisations draw attention to new products and special offers on the home page of their websites. These techniques can be used to draw visitors further into the website.

Interactivity

The term 'interactive' was explained earlier (page 363). An interactive website gives visitors greater control over the content and enables them to communicate with the organisation itself. As illustrated in Figure 14.4, many websites encourage visitors to communicate with each other through chat rooms or to post their views on a notice board.

Links

When consumers use the Internet to gather information, a website's links can be important. Links enable visitors to go directly from one website to another. The quality and relevance of a website's links contribute to its success and the regard in which it is held.

Transaction-based orientation

Some products and services are ideally suited for sale over the Internet and so it may be important that a website can facilitate transactions. There are many security issues associated with online credit card transactions. Unscrupulous individuals have been able to break into less secure sites and gain access to customers' credit card details. This makes consumers reluctant to make online purchases unless they can be persuaded that organisations have invested in the necessary software to minimise any associated risk.

The marketing communications mix and the Internet

This section examines elements of the traditional marketing communications mix and their compatibility with the Internet.

Advertising

In Ireland, interest in advertising on the Internet can be attributed to the increase in the number of people using the Internet. However, it should be remembered that not everybody has access to the Internet. Those who do have access often encounter irritating problems caused by the telecommunications infrastructure. Most users who access the Internet at home do not have high-speed ISDN lines. This means that access tends to be slow and this contributes to high access costs.

The Internet's interactive and highly targeted nature is very attractive to advertisers. Online advertising enables advertisers to change their messages frequently. According to Kompass Ireland (2000), the Internet allows the advertiser to 'quantify in real time what's working or not, and respond just as fast'. Changes can be made to offline advertisements but they take longer to implement and usually incur significant costs. Another major advantage of online advertising is that response levels can be measured accurately (see below).

A number of online advertising formats are available.

Banner advertisements

These can be static or animated and usually contain a company name, a message and an enticement to click (*The Economist*, 9 October 1999). If someone clicks on a banner advertisement, the user is transported to the advertiser's website. This is referred to as a **clickthrough**. Banner advertising costs are based on cost per thousand (CPM) impressions and clickthrough rates:

Clickthrough
When someone clicks on a banner advertisement they are transported directly to the advertiser's website.

- **CPM impressions** occur 'when a visitor to a website views a page where an ad is displayed, whether the ad is seen or not' (Kompass Ireland, 2000) The CPM impressions method provides an accurate visitor count to potential advertisers. However, it does not inform them as to the effectiveness of placing an advertisement on a particular website. It can be compared to television advertising – just because an advertisement is broadcast during a particular programme, it is not necessarily noticed by the target audience.

- A **clickthrough rate** is 'the number of times your banner advert is clicked on by a visitor' (Kompass Ireland, 2000). For obvious reasons, advertisers prefer costs to be calculated using this method. If someone clicks on a banner advertisement, it means that it has been seen and acted upon. Clickthrough rates tend to be low and in 2001 Amárach Consulting published findings that suggested 65 per cent of Internet users never clicked on a banner advertisement and that those who did, could not remember what ad they had clicked on (*The Irish Times*, 30 July 2001).

  According to Hofacker and Murphy (1998) clickthrough rates can be improved by changing certain aspects of banner advertisements:

  - the inclusion of animation, thereby introducing movement to the website
  - cryptic messages in order to arouse curiosity
  - posing questions to get visitors more involved in the website
  - 'call to action' phrases so as to elicit a response and initiate a relationship.

  They also stress the importance of placing banner advertisements on websites that contain content aimed at the desired target audience.

  Hofacker and Murphy state that clickthrough rates can be used to test web banner copy and analyse actual behaviour. This compares favourably with research into traditional advertising because it concentrates more on attitudes. Due to the irrational nature of people, attitudes and intentions do not always equate to actual behaviour.

Pop-ups

These are 'extra little windows that proliferate across your screen when you visit certain sites' (*Financial Times*, 18 October 2002). Many people consider them intrusive and, to eliminate them, the user must click on them. While they do provide a steady income stream for Internet companies, the following extract shows that their value is being questioned:

Pop-ups popping off

David Gand, executive vice-president of product marketing at AOL, announced that in the new version, 'We cleaned up the user experience – there are fewer pop-ups,' it was an unusual admission. Even more grown-up was Ted Leonsis, AOL's vice-chairman: 'If it's bothering the customers, you shouldn't do it.'

AOL's advertising and e-commerce revenues in 2001 amounted to $2.7 billion. Jon Miller, chief executive, summed up the change of heart: 'The most important thing we offer advertisers is the chance to be part of a service that consumers love, and we've determined that pop-ups aren't the best way to do that.' However, the company will continue to use pop-ups for its own alerts and to advertise AOL Time Warner special offers.

AOL's main rivals, MSN and Yahoo refuse to forswear pop-ups entirely. 'We have very few pop-ups and cap their frequency,' says Michelle Rutter, head of pan-European sales and trade marketing at MSN, adding that MSN has several new formats in the pipeline.

Lindsay Biggart, marketing director for Yahoo UK and Ireland, says that: 'Our consumer research illustrates pop-ups have a detrimental brand effect, for both us and the advertiser.

Mark Cullen, client services director, ARC Interactive, a digital marketing agency, says: 'My view is that pop-ups were always the home of lazy creative and lazy media planning strategies. Sure, it's easy to grab half a second's-worth of attention by throwing something at the eyeballs of a consumer but most agencies have moved on and are now creating immersive communications, where the user feels that time looking at and interacting has been worthwhile – stepping into and taking part in the ad, for example.'

For Internet advertisers, the trouble has been finding a course between print advertising, which is static but does not disrupt the reading of the article, and TV advertising, which disrupts the flow of the broadcast but excuses itself by being entertaining. The print model used to consist mainly of banners, but new formats allow ads to be placed prominently in the centre of the page, allowing the text to flow around them.

Source: *Financial Times*, 22 October 2002

Webmercials

Some firms adapt a television commercial especially for use on the web and they usually run for five to seven seconds. Interesting examples of webmercials can be seen at www.kmgi.com (www.medialive.ie).

E-mail advertising via newsletters

Many organisations produce an online newsletter, referred to as an e-newsletter or e-zine that is sent by e-mail to a list of contacts. Some allow other appropriate organisations to take out advertisements in their e-newsletters (Kompass Ireland, 2000). We will re-visit this under Public Relations and Direct Marketing (see pages 372 and 374).

Microsites

These are limited areas on the web managed and paid for by an external company (Armstrong and Kotler, 2003). For example, a mortgage provider might create a microsite on an estate agent's website in order to provide free advice about mortgages. The site can go on to promote specific services from that particular mortgage provider.

Affiliate programmes

This is when one organisation promotes its products and services on specialist websites. These sites are likely to be visited by the desired target audience. The host website owner is rewarded on a commission basis. That is, they receive commission on any sales resulting from the website presence. For example, amazon.com have formed a number of affiliate programmes that allow them to provide direct access to their website from non-competitive websites.

Intermercials

These appear between content on a website. However, they are very unpopular with users and are seen as clutter.

According to Elkin (2002), a survey of 5,000 Internet users has revealed that online consumers who feel an affinity for a website's content are much more likely to notice and be affected by that particular website's advertisements. It found that a user's affinity for a website is influenced by:

- word of mouth
- satisfaction with the content
- 'Favourite' status within an interest category, for example, news, sport, hobbies. 'Favourite' status is when an Internet user saves a website address and adds it to a file called 'Favourites'. This gives the user quick and easy access to chosen websites.

The survey found that 75 per cent of high-affinity users felt that ads interfered less with their experience of accessing content, compared to 31 per cent of low-affinity users. The findings of the survey mirror similar findings in relation to traditional media. That is, if the target audience likes a particular media vehicle, they may be more sensitive and receptive to accompanying advertising.

The extract below illustrates how well-known FMCG companies have used online advertising, in conjunction with traditional advertising to considerable effect in the United States.

Kimberly-Clark, Colgate report online ad success

Kimberly-Clark Corporation and Colgate-Palmolive both report that adding online components to the mix for two test advertising campaigns substantially increased brand awareness for their products.

The latest studies involved campaigns for Kimberly-Clark's Kleenex SoftPack (tissues) and Colgate-Palmolive's Colgate Total Toothpaste brands involving magazine, TV and Internet advertising. The studies suggest that online spending should be about 10 to 15 per cent of the overall media mix in low-involvement categories such as packaged goods and that the best interactive marketing is an emotion-packed complement to offline media, defined here as TV and magazines. The research also suggests that rejiggering online and offline media levels may offer a better return on investment.

Shifting even 5 per cent of the media budget can open a competitive edge, said Rex Briggs, principal of the research consultancy Marketing Evolution. 'If a traditional marketer does optimise its media mix and a competitor doesn't, they'll get between 5 and 15 per cent better results without spending a dollar more,' he said.

STUDY GOALS

In launching its Kleenex SoftPack line extension, Kimberly-Clark wanted to know how online media within the mix could build brand awareness and drive trial. 'We were actually impacting and reaching light TV viewers and non-TV viewers,' said Brad Santeler, associate director of interactive services for Kimberly-Clark. TV ads only reach about 42 per cent of Kleenex's target audience. The brand was spending 75 per cent of its budget on TV, 23 per cent on print and just 2 per cent online. By boosting its online spending, Kimberly hoped to supplement the light reach of TV and complement magazine advertising. The combination of print and online advertising helped raise brand awareness among its target audience for SoftPack from 34.7 per cent to 42.7 per cent; brand image from 35 per cent to 41.8 per cent; purchase intent from 24.2 per cent to 34 per cent; and bundled trial intent from 43.9 per cent to 55.7 per cent, according to the company.

18–49-YEAR-OLDS

Colgate's findings revealed that online was the most cost-efficient means of reaching 18–49-year-olds for Colgate Total toothpaste. Colgate wanted to increase purchase preference among occasional and non-Total users, but it was only putting 7 per cent of its budget toward online, while 78 per cent went to TV and 15 per cent was earmarked for magazines. The findings showed that TV ought to have been 75 per cent of the mix, magazines 14 per cent and online 11 per cent. TV, while effective, doesn't hit about 40 per cent of the target audience – light TV watchers or non-TV watchers. Upping online media allocation for the campaign helped Colgate gain incremental reach it wouldn't have otherwise had, according to the company.

> 'What's significant for Colgate is they were able to generate purchase preference more cost-efficiently with online media ... on a dollar-for-dollar basis, compared to the other media used,' Mr Briggs said. 'If it costs you $1 per new person you make want to buy your products with online advertising, a $1.23 for TV, and $1.84 for magazines, it's something you have to look at.'
>
> Source: Elkin (2003)

Public relations

According to Ashcroft and Hoey (2001), the web can be used to raise an organisation's profile. This can be achieved in a number of ways:

- the promotion of new initiatives
- a change or improvement of image
- improving or enhancing customer service.

Depending on how they are done, these methods can improve or weaken an organisation's reputation. In Chapter 9, public relations activities were explained. It is quite possible to carry out many of these activities on the Internet.

New product launches and dissemination of important information

Information about new products and other company information can be posted on a website. Good design helps ensure that a visitor is drawn to the information each time that they visit the website. It is important that this information is updated regularly in order to keep visitors interested and keen to return.

New product and general company information can also be distributed directly via the online equivalent of a newsletter, the e-newsletter. These are sent to various stakeholders such as staff, shareholders, distributors, the media and current and prospective customers via e-mail. They usually incorporate links giving the recipient direct access onto the sender's website.

Launch and distribution of annual reports

The print and distribution (i.e. postage) costs associated with paper-based annual reports are very high. The Internet enables organisations to publish their reports on their websites, thus passing many of the costs onto the audience. Anyone accessing an annual report in this way incurs Internet access costs and if they decide to print it out, this cost is borne by them and not the originator. While the paper annual report still exists, the Internet lessens the need to produce and distribute as many copies.

Distribution of press releases

Many journalists prefer to receive press releases by e-mail. In addition, many organisations make their press releases available to their website visitors. This means that even if they are not published in printed media or broadcast on TV or radio, they can still reach the target audience via the Internet.

Reproduction or broadcast of presentations

Presentations and speeches by key personnel are important PR vehicles. An organisation's website is ideally suited to carrying the script or overhead aids. In some cases, video footage of the occasion is put on the website so visitors with the appropriate computer software can see and hear the presentation or speech being delivered.

Point of contact

An important function of an organisation's public relations is to act as a point of contact with its various stakeholders. A well-designed, informative website can fulfil this role and reduce the number of telephone calls received by the person responsible for public relations. To further reduce the number of telephone contacts, online access to the organisation via e-mail can be encouraged.

Internal communications

An organisation's intranet is a site that offers employees information and the ability to communicate with each other. It is usually only accessible to an internal audience and, while many intranets can be visited outside the office, security codes are usually required. While the intranet is a vital channel in many organisations for communication with and between employees, care should be taken to ensure that it does not become the sole means of communication. Electronic communications are often open to misinterpretation, so regular face-to-face interaction should be maintained.

Sponsorship

While banner advertising (see page 367) is the most prominent form of organisational presence on most websites, there would appear to be potential for content sponsorship. An organisation or an organisation's brand gains exposure on a host website (or websites) by sponsoring special content. An advantage is that online sponsorship presents the possibility of exposure to a highly targeted audience.

The Irish website www.skool.ie is an online information service for second-level students. It provides information on a range of topics including exams, health and finance. AIB Bank is one of the main sponsors and, while they do not provide specific information about their own services, their logo appears on the site.

Sales promotion

Sales promotion techniques are widely used on websites to accelerate sales activity and encourage visitor involvement. Traditional sales promotions techniques are used, such as discounted prices, 'recommend a friend', 'buy one, get one free', limited availability, coupons and competitions. A website with a reputation for good sales promotions is likely to enjoy repeat visits. This is an important factor when convincing organisations to advertise on a website.

The Internet has the potential to revolutionise sales promotions for the following reasons:

- Offers can be tailored, depending on each individual's profile and sent to each person by e-mail.
- The website visitor or e-mail recipient incurs the cost of printing out coupons, thus eliminating production costs. This approach can reduce waste because an individual only prints out coupons that they are likely to use.
- Increasingly, coupons originating from the Internet can be redeemed in retail outlets (e.g. coupons from the website www.pigsback.com) and the originator can track the consumer. Usually, barcodes are included on coupons to facilitate tracking.

Direct marketing

If ever an element of the marketing communications mix was designed for the Internet, direct marketing was. At this point, it would be useful to revisit the characteristics of direct marketing, as described in Chapter 12:

- It is interactive.
- It allows measurable responses.
- It enables the target to engage at the location of their choice.
- It allows the organisation to test elements of a campaign in order to assess what does and does not work.

Using the Internet as a direct marketing medium is ideal because it displays these characteristics when used as a marketing tool. In practice, the Internet is being added to the direct marketing media mix. E-mail is considered the online equivalent of direct mail but, as we saw in Figure 14.2 on page 361, it is far more synchronous. It can be a vehicle for various methods of direct marketing on the Internet.

E-mail

Just as junk mail gives properly targeted, relevant direct mail a bad name, 'spam' gives e-mail an even worse name. Irish regulations and an EU directive define 'spam' mail as an 'unsolicited commercial communication' that is not identified 'clearly and unambiguously as such' (cited in *The Irish Times*, 7 March 2003). The article reports that the Internet service provider, AOL, 'uses filters to block some 780 million spams every day, an average of 22 per customer'.

Spam mail irritates and annoys Internet users and makes them less likely to even consider opening genuine e-mail communications. Kompass Ireland (2000) contend that spam mail has much greater consequences for the recipient than junk mail because there is always the possibility that it is carrying a computer virus. Their report goes on to outline best practice when using e-mail for direct marketing purposes:

- Always ensure that the person has given their permission to be sent e-mails. This permission can be sought when someone is filling out their details on an application form.
- Organisations can build their own opt-in mailing list. Kompass Ireland (2000) suggest that an electronic guest book be added to a website. Visitors can voluntarily add their contact details to the book – in effect they are giving permission for the organisation to contact them. Visitors can also be invited to subscribe to an online newsletter.
- Finally, when people give their details, they should be reassured that this information will not be given to any other organisations.

Recognising that many web users are highly suspicious about the content of their e-mails, some organisations have resorted to **viral marketing**. This is when an organisation sends an e-mail to existing contacts and encourages them to forward it to their friends, family and colleagues. This is based on the premise that people are more likely to open e-mails sent by someone they know, and plays on the power of word of mouth.

Viral marketing
When e-mail is sent to a contact and the contact is encouraged to forward it to their friends, family and colleagues.

Kompass Ireland (2000) go on to explain how e-mail can be used very effectively to:

- sell products and services
- up-sell and cross-sell to customers
- confirm orders
- welcome a new customer or say 'goodbye' to an ex-customer
- announce important information
- apologise
- encourage people to visit the website
- build a one-on-one customer relationship.

E-mail is a central tool for **webcasting**. When people subscribe to particular websites, they are usually invited to specify areas of particular interest. The website owner uses this information to send customised information to each subscriber, thus saving them time and money. This is known as webcasting. In some cases, a nominal fee might be charged for this service, for example, the *Financial Times* uses this method.

Webcasting
Sending customised information to online subscribers

The web is ideally suited to behaviour measurement. **'Cookies'** facilitate measurement on the web. Quite simply, cookies are text files that are saved onto web users' hard drives when they visit a site. This means that, every time these

Cookies
Text files saved onto web users' hard drives when they visit a site. Every time they return to that site, they are instantly recognised.

users return to that site, their computers send the files back to the website. This allows instant recognition and in certain cases, this means that the users do not have to enter personal information every time they visit the site. Browsing habits can be analysed and messages can then be personalised.

Testing, as discussed in Chapter 12, can demonstrate the difference between a low response rate and a high response rate. Testing on the Internet provides much faster feedback than testing a direct mail campaign. Testing in-use is a good way to think about testing on the Internet and some industry experts are saying that it can now be done in real time. 'During campaigns one can test and make instant changes. Ads can be run to appear immediately and you can switch target audiences mid-campaign. It is easy to see whether a campaign is bringing results and luring consumers' (Cody, 2000).

Selling

Chapter 13 examined the role of personal selling in the marketing communications mix. Figure 14.2 (page 361) shows that it is the most synchronous of all the elements of the mix and the highest ranking in terms of social contact. Selling on the Internet cannot directly compete with personal selling. However, it can be used to support the personal selling function and it can enhance the customer's buying experience. The following sales and sales support activities can be carried out on the Internet:

Price and product comparisons

Prospective buyers can compare products and prices by visiting various websites. This has been made much easier with the advent of intelligent agents software which searches for the best deals for the buyer.

Virtual showrooms and product demonstrations

Unlike printed communications, websites can provide a three-dimensional view of an organisation's products. This makes it easier for prospective buyers to assess them and may make a sales representative's job easier when it comes to closing a deal. While the term 'virtual showroom' applies to the concept of a virtual retailing unit, some estate agents are using websites to take house-hunters on virtual house tours. This is particularly useful when a housing development has not been built because many people find it difficult to visualise a house, apartment or office by looking at a two-dimensional architect's drawing or a computer-generated photograph.

Direct sales

Many websites enable customers to order their products or services during their visit. This offers some or all of the following benefits.

Convenience

A customer's lifestyle may mean that it is easier for them to purchase online as opposed to physically going to a retail outlet. Superquinn and Tesco both provide online shopping in recognition of this.

Access to products or services

When products and services are not readily available or cannot be purchased anywhere in the customer's country of residence, online shopping can be very beneficial.

Value

Some organisations provide financial incentives in order to encourage customers to purchase online. As we saw earlier, Ryanair and Aer Lingus deliberately encourage customers to book flights through their websites. They state that by doing so, cheaper flights will be the reward. Irish Ferries offer €6.50 discounts on all online car bookings.

Sales support

Customers can track their orders on the Internet as opposed to telephoning a sales representative. The organisation can also keep the customer informed regularly as to the status of their order.

Straightforward customer queries and user-support requirements can be addressed online. This means that sales representatives can concentrate on revenue-generating tasks as opposed to dealing with time-consuming queries.

When organisations sell their products and services on the Internet, they must address the following.

Security concerns

As stated earlier in this chapter, security concerns deter many people from purchasing products and services online. There are a few factors that help reduce these concerns:

- **reputation of the organisation**. If an organisation enjoys good offline and online reputations, people are more likely to divulge their credit card details.
- **constant reassurance throughout the purchase**. The organisation should inform the prospective customer of any steps they have taken to create a secure site. They must use software, which encodes credit card details, thus making them difficult to decipher.

Fulfilment

Fulfilment concerns delivering on any promises made to the customer at the time of purchase. If a commitment is made to deliver the product within a defined period of time, this must be adhered to. Also, it is essential to ensure that the following are done right first time:

- delivery address
- quantity
- specifications (e.g. colour, size).

The quality of the fulfilment process usually determines whether or not a customer purchases online again. A poorly executed fulfilment process damages online and offline reputations.

Summary

More than 1 million Irish people now use the Internet and, while the annual rate of growth in new users is slowing, it is still rising. The Internet displays pull and push characteristics. Its communication style is largely synchronous because of the small time lag that exists between the giving and receiving of information and the response to communication. Compared to direct mail, it is considered a relatively personal method of communication. With the Internet, consumers have control over contact. Their ability to control content makes it an interactive medium.

When designing websites, organisations should make them easy to use and should ensure that they provide interesting information. Sites should be updated regularly and should facilitate interactivity. The links they provide to other websites are important and, where possible, the sites should allow secure transactions to take place.

All elements of the marketing mix are being used on the Internet to varying degrees. Online advertising has enjoyed mixed success and a range of formats has emerged including banners, pop-ups and affiliate programmes.

The public relations function in an organisation can be enhanced with the Internet and it serves a range of publics very well. While sponsorship is relatively under-utilised, there is no reason to believe that content sponsorship will not become more common. Sales promotion techniques are widely used on many websites and can help bring visitors back to sites again and again. Direct marketing is the most obvious beneficiary of the Internet. Direct marketing's objectives appear to fit very well with the Internet and there appears to be huge scope for development in this area. The Internet can never replace the personal nature of personal selling. However, selling and associated activities on the Internet can enhance the work of sales representatives and make them more effective.

Useful websites

www.idma.ie	The Irish Direct Marketing Association
www.amárach.com	Market research company, specialising in the investigation of trends
www.kompass.ie	Provides tips on online marketing
www.enterprise-ireland.com	Contains case studies in e-marketing

Review questions

1. Distinguish clearly between the pull and push characteristics of marketing on the Internet. Go on to describe the other main characteristics of marketing on the Internet.
2. Using Figures 14.2 (page 361) and 14.3 (page 362), carry out an analysis of the following media – television, radio, newspapers, magazines, outdoor, telephone and ambient. You can also refer to Chapters 6 and 12 when answering this question.
3. Explain the main factors that should be taken into account when designing successful websites. Now select a website and, using your answer to the first part of this question, analyse whether or not you think it is a successful website.
4. Compare and contrast the merits or otherwise of using CPM impressions and clickthrough rates when charging for online advertising space.

Exercise

Select an organisation of your choice. Assume that it is preparing to launch a new product and that you have been invited to prepare an online, fully integrated marketing communications plan. Justify your recommendations. You should also consider how you intend 'pulling' potential customers into your website.

References

AC Nielsen, 'New websites 'Spring' forth in March', *Nielsen//NetRatings* (www.acnielsen.com, May 2001).

Armstrong, Gary and Kotler, Philip, *Marketing: An Introduction*, 6th edition (Pearson Education, 2003).

Ashcroft, Linda and Hoey, Clive, 'PR, marketing and the Internet: implications for information professionals' (*Library Management*, pp. 68–74 (Vol. 22, No. 1/2, 2001).

Cody, Pat, 'Hits and clicks' (*Marketing*, January 2000).

Elkin, Tobi, 'Kimberly-Clark, Colgate report online ad success' (*AdAge.com*, 21 October 2002).

Ellsworth, Jill H. and Ellsworth, Matthew V. *Marketing on the Internet*, 2nd edition (John Wiley & Sons Inc., 1997).

Hofacker, Charles F. and Murphy, Jamie, 'World Wide Web banner advertisement copy testing' (*European Journal of Marketing*, Vol. 32, No. 7/8, pp. 708–12, 1998).

Hoffman, Donna L. and Novak, Thomas P., 'How to acquire customers on the Web' (*Harvard Business Review*, May to June, pp. 179–87, 2000).

Kompass Ireland, *Direct Marketing on the Internet: Top 50 Tips for Your Net Success* (Kompass Ireland, 2000).

Maclaran, Pauline and Catterall, Miriam, 'Researching the social Web: marketing information from virtual communities (*Marketing Intelligence & Planning*, 20 June, pp. 319–26, 2002).

O'Malley, Lisa, Patterson, Maurice and Evans, Martin, *Exploring Direct Marketing* (International Thomson Business Press, 1999).

Peters, Linda, 'The new interactive media: one-to-one, but who to whom?' *Marketing Intelligence & Planning* (16 January, pp. 22–30, 1998).

Pickton, David and Broderick, Amanda, *Integrated Marketing Communications* (Pearson Education Limited, 2001).

Rowley, Jennifer, 'Remodelling marketing communications in an Internet environment' (*Internet Research: Electronic Networking Applications and Policy*, Vol. 11, No. 3, pp. 203–12, 2001).

Rowley, Jennifer, 'Information marketing in a digital world' (*Library Hi Tech*, Vol. 20, No. 3, pp. 352–8, 2002).

15

MARKETING COMMUNICATIONS IN CHARITY ORGANISATIONS

The aims and objectives of this chapter are to help you:

- to understand a charity's publics
- to identify the elements of the marketing communications mix most often used by charity organisations
- to appreciate the key success factors in the creation of charity campaigns
- to provide insights into the Multiple Sclerosis Society of Ireland.

Introduction

This book has primarily focused on the use of marketing communications in commercial organisations. However, as the number of non-commercial organisations grows, so too does their need for methods of reaching their target audiences more effectively. Like commercial organisations, they face more competition and many are turning to marketing communications in order to differentiate themselves.

This chapter focuses on the charity sector but it should be remembered that many other non-commercial organisations such as museums, third-level institutions, public transport organisations and hospitals have discovered the benefits of marketing communications.

The charity sector

Since the 1980s there has been a marked increase in the number of charity organisations, all competing for the hearts and purses of consumers and the private sector. Before exploring how this might be achieved, it is important to identify a typical charity's various publics. When dealing with the charity sector, publics are subdivided into donors, clients/customers, and the media.

Donors

The term **'donor'** refers to people or firms that give money or benefit-in-kind to a charity. There are different groups who donate to charities.

Donor
A person or firm that gives money or benefit-in-kind to charities.

The general public

The general public donates money to charities in a number of ways. They do it during street collections, or 'flag days', as they are known. Increasingly, people donate regularly by setting up direct debits with their chosen charity. A number of charities have retail outlets where the general public can donate items for sale and can purchase merchandise. Examples include St Vincent de Paul and UNICEF.

Time is another important resource and in an increasingly cash-rich, time-poor economy, it is in short supply. The services of the general public are used by charities across a range of circumstances:

- to collect on flag days
- to deliver a charity's core service. Many charities would not exist without the services of a committed team of volunteers, for example, the Samaritans, the Rape Crisis Centre (RCC), Childline, The Animal Foundation, and Aware. In circumstances where volunteers relocate and live in another country, they might be paid a nominal wage to cover basic day-to-day living expenses, for example, APSO and Concern
- to assist in the day-to-day running and the longer-term planning of the charity
- to work in retail outlets.

Corporate donors

A growing number of profit-oriented organisations align themselves with charities with very clear business objectives in mind. Gone are the days when a benevolent profit-making organisation might make a donation to a worthwhile cause without seeking anything in return. The more commercial orientation towards charity donations is known as **cause-related marketing**. This is done with a view to having a positive impact on an organisation's corporate or brand image. Therefore, it is intended that it will be beneficial to both parties.

Cause-related marketing
Marketing done with a view to having a positive impact on a firm's corporate or brand image.

The most significant example of cause-related marketing ever seen in Ireland was the Bank of Ireland's sponsorship of the 2003 Special Olympics World Summer Games, hosted by Ireland. Several other firms, including O'Brien's Irish Sandwich Bar, An Post and Eircom were involved in the sponsorship of the event, with a view to achieving corporate and brand objectives (see Chapter 10).

Corporate donations do not just take the form of financial support. Some firms provide services and expertise either free-of-charge or at a preferential rate. In return, their contribution is acknowledged by the charity and made known to the general public.

The Government

Charities often seek government funding. In times of economic prosperity this is easier to do. In the post-Celtic-Tiger phase of Ireland's economy, the charity sector is left with a large number of players, all competing for a smaller percentage of the Government's coffers. As illustrated below, the Government's involvement in the 2003 Special Olympics World Summer Games was based on well-researched criteria. While there was a very compelling social rationale, the commercial rationale was very important and the funding was given with a view to boosting the fortunes of Ireland's tourism industry.

The Government's role in the 2003 Special Olympics World Summer Games

In 1996, the Irish Government formed an interdepartmental group to examine the feasibility of Ireland making a bid to host the Special Olympics World Games in 2003. Eight Government Departments and two representatives from Special Olympics Ireland were involved. The group was chaired by the Office of the Tanaiste (Deputy Prime Minister). The report of the group cited several benefits for the country.

It was suggested that the Games would generate €14.35 million additional tourism revenues in 2003.

Including tourism-generated jobs, the total jobs impact of the Games was thought to be 1,600 jobs for one year.

The hosting of the World Games gelled with Bord Failte and the Department of Tourism and Sports policy called 'The International Sports Tourism Initiative' that aims to attract major sporting events to Ireland. The Games give Bord Failte an opportunity to show the world what Ireland is capable of.

The group acknowledged the social benefits, including the raising of awareness of the problems of people with learning disabilities and the promotion of inclusion and a positive profile. Since Ireland was awarded the 2003 Special Olympics World Summer Games, the Government has set up the Disability Authority and a Minister for Disability has been appointed.

In a sense, the governmental support of the Special Olympics was an element of a greater movement in policy and recognition of people with learning disabilities.

Inputs of the Governments

In financial terms the State provided between €9 million and €10.15 million to the 2003 Special Olympics World Summer Games. The money was drawn down through the Department of Tourism and Sport. According to Ciaran Sheedy, Assistant Principal with the Tourism Marketing and Promotion Policy Unit at the Department of Tourism and Sport 'the Irish Tourism Board acts as a conduit for the money.' If more finance was needed a memorandum to the Government came through this department. The finance was then issued to the 2003 Special Olympics World Summer Games through the Irish Tourism Board. The Government in Northern Ireland pledged €1.6 million.

The State also gave human resources to the project through its various departments and agencies, with the Department of Education giving four secondments. Also the Department of Health gave eight secondments from the health boards for 2003 Special Olympics World Summer Games while the Department of Agriculture was given one. In addition, much government time went into the World Games as An Taoiseach illustrated, 'a lot of my own key staff's time has gone into helping and assisting people. And we have hosted many functions to try and get people involved.'

Additionally, the European Union granted €6.35 million to the 2003 Special Olympics World Summer Games. The Games fell between the European Year of People with Disabilities and were marked as one of the designated events in the European Union to mark the occasion.

This excerpt is reproduced with kind permission from a case written by Peter McNamara, Garrett Murray and Carolin Grampp, UCD Business School, and with the help of Paul Brown, 2003 Special Olympics World Summer Games Limited, *2003 Special Olympics World Summer Games: managing a stakeholder network* (University College Dublin, 2003)

Clients/customers

Donors are a very important target audience for charities because they provide the funds and resources necessary for running charities. The people who benefit from charities are also very important and they must be made aware of relevant charity organisations and what they can do for them. The difficulty for charities is that they need to raise awareness of their existence but unlike commercial organisations, they have at their disposal only limited or, in some cases, no resources, to commit to awareness-building activity such as advertising and sponsorship. When charities engage in this type of activity, it tends to be for the purpose of attracting resources. Therefore, publicity is very important for charities in order to create awareness among potential clients and customers. While it requires hard work in order to make it happen, it incurs far less costs than advertising.

The media

As we have seen, media relations must be nurtured by charity organisations. For example, if a radio station is doing a feature on homelessness, a spokesperson from Focus Ireland might be invited to participate in the programme. Their presence highlights the issue, may serve to attract donations and may inform homeless people of their options. Another issue frequently covered by the media is depression. A highly qualified group of volunteers work with Aware, the charity that helps people with depression. They are often called upon to participate in radio discussions about the issue and at the end of the piece, they are usually invited to give a telephone number where people affected by depression can contact Aware.

As illustrated in the case study at the end of this chapter about the Multiple Sclerosis (MS) Society in Ireland, many charities organise high-profile fund-raising events. They often invite newspaper photographers or hire their own photographers to record the event. The photographs are then sent to newspapers with accompanying press releases, with a view to securing high-profile coverage of the event. Since there are so many charities running fund-raising events, celebrities are often invited to lend their support so as to improve the likelihood of the story being covered in the media.

Which elements of the marketing communications mix are most widely used by charities?

Advertising

Despite the costs associated with advertising, press and radio advertising is used by many charities, in particular, those helping people in the Third World, for example, Goal, UNICEF (Exhibit 15.1) and Concern.

Exhibit 15.1

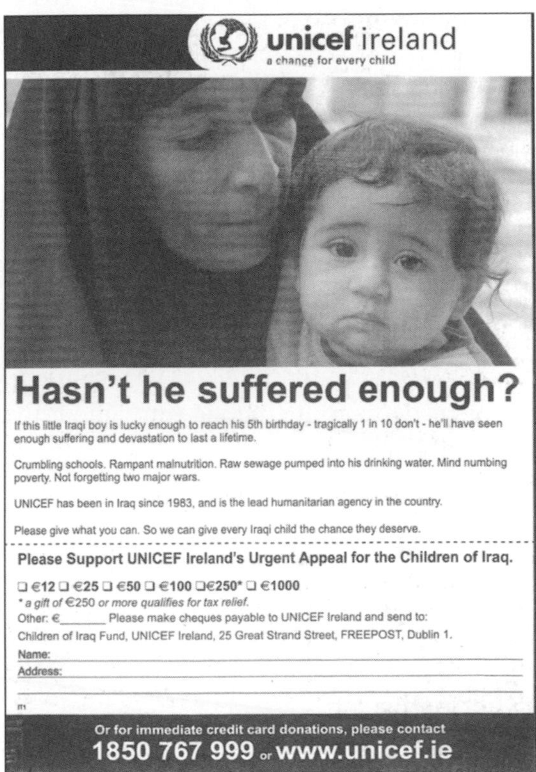

For greater impact, some charities use television advertising, for example, St Vincent de Paul in Ireland and both the RSPCA and the NSPCC in the United Kingdom. While television allows the advertiser to broadcast very compelling imagery, it is expensive and may give donors the impression that their donations are being diverted away from the deserving cause. This, in turn, may generate adverse publicity for the charity.

Direct marketing

Direct marketing is widely used by charities to target known donors. It is also used to attract new donors, as illustrated in the case study at the end of this chapter. Direct marketing is important because of the competitive nature of the charity sector. Like commercial organisations, charities are moving away from a transaction-based orientation towards a relationship marketing orientation. Techniques such as direct debit are encouraged to keep the donor for a long period of time. The Internet is important for some charities and informs potential customers or clients about a charity, and it is used to attract donations. However, as illustrated in the MS Ireland case study, the online donation methods remain crude in many situations.

E-mail is a cheaper alternative than direct mail and is used to communicate with present and potential donors and customers/clients.

Sponsorship

As illustrated in the Special Olympics case study in Chapter 10 and the MS Ireland case below, sponsorship is very widely used by charities. Profit-making organisations recognise that they can achieve particular objectives through the use of cause-related marketing techniques. Throughout the 1980s and 1990s, the Body Shop secured a high profile through extensive use of cause-related marketing and as a result, it did not have to spend money on advertising.

Many charities align themselves with a commercial organisation for a number of years. This allows them to plan and cover the costs of lucrative, fund-raising activity, for example, Vodafone's sponsorship of MS Ireland's Pen Day.

Public relations

A significant amount of a charity's marketing communications is devoted to public relations. Typical public relations activity includes the following:

- press releases
- publicity generation
- public talks
- open days to the public. For example, donkey sanctuaries around the country open their doors to the public throughout the year to highlight the good work being done by them.
- the provision of helplines, for example, the RCC and the Samaritans.

Sales promotion

As the number of flag days increased, some charities felt the need to offer donors something useful in return for their money. Traditionally, the feeling of having done something good for somebody or something else was considered sufficient. However, in an attempt to make their flag days more attractive and unusual, some charities employed sales promotion techniques. Many offer the donor a tangible object or the chance to win something in exchange for a specified sum of money. Examples of this approach are growing all the time and include real daffodils on the Cancer Society's Daffodil Day, a pen on MS Ireland's Pen Day and flower bulbs from Aware.

Personal selling

Charity organisations use personal selling to attract donations and support from the general public and the corporate sector. Sales representatives in commercial organisations are usually motivated by the lure of financial rewards. However, charities are usually dependent on a team of volunteer sales people who are not motivated by commercial gain. Instead, they are rewarded by feelings of personal satisfaction and fulfilment. It is difficult to find enough people like this because employment is more plentiful than it was in the 1980s. Therefore, most charities employ full-time staff who receive competitive salaries. Their personal selling activity is primarily aimed at the corporate sector and the retention of existing donors. Volunteer workers focus their sales activity on the general public on flag days and in charity shops. Some charity organisations use financial rewards to motivate volunteers. However, these schemes have been exposed by the media and have led to negative publicity for some charities.

Creating successful charity campaigns

One of the greatest challenges facing charities is reconciling the need to raise funds while having to spend money in order to do this. Donors want their money to go to those who need it and they want to see that it is not being spent on expensive marketing communications campaigns. Bird (1989) devised guidelines for charity advertising but they can also be followed when using other elements of the marketing communications mix (summarised in Table 15.1).

Table 15.1 Creating successful charity campaigns

- Ask for a specific amount of money
- Create headlines that contain three elements – the problem, the solution, and something that makes it sound easy
- Be direct
- Be personal and focus on the beneficiaries of the campaign
- Create a sense of urgency
- Capitalise on the Christmas spirit
- Suggest an amount
- Be very economical when creating and producing marketing communications material

Ask for a specific sum

It is better to ask donors for a specific sum and to illustrate how that sum could be used. In a 2003 direct mail campaign, Concern asked its target audience for €40 and explained that '€40 could feed 8 malnourished children for a month.' Later in the same leaflet, Concern stated that '€40 could help us feed 8 children who are weak and losing the battle against hunger for a month' and '€40 could provide 8 hungry children with specialised enriched lifesaving food for a month.'

Headlines with three elements

Bird contends that successful headlines usually contain three elements. Staying with the Concern mail shot, the front of the leaflet demonstrates this approach:

- a problem (emergency in Ethiopia)
- a solution the reader can supply (special appeal to the people of Co. Kildare – target €30,000)
- something that makes it sound easy (€40 could feed 8 malnourished children for a month).

Exhibit 15.2

This extract is reproduced with kind permission from The Irish Times

1984:

The generosity of the Irish people enabled Concern to save thousands of lives during the famine in which 1 million people died.

€40 could help us feed 8 children who are weak and losing the battle against hunger for a month.

Please help now.

Concern, 52-55 Lower Camden Street, Dublin 2. Tel: 1850 410 510
Fax: 01 475 7362, email: info@concern.net, www.concern.net
Concern – a non-denominational organisation working for a world where nobody lives in poverty, fear or oppression. Place of registration Dublin, Ireland.
Registered No. 39647. Registered Charity No CHY5745.

Exhibit 15.3

EMERGENCY IN ETHIOPIA

HORN OF AFRICA FOOD CRISIS

Special appeal to the people of Co Kildare. Target €30,000

€40 could feed 8 malnourished children for a month

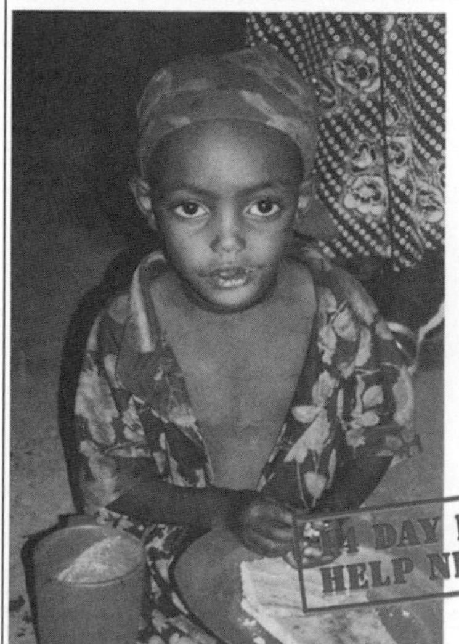

"If the 1984 famine was a nightmare then this will be too ghastly to contemplate."
Melas Zenawi,
Prime Minister, Ethiopia

The Spring rains have failed in 4 of the last 5 years. Please help Concern aid teams save lives.

Be direct

While subtlety may succeed in FMCG marketing communications, charities should not follow their example. Potential donors need to know the problem, the solution and what exactly is required of them.

Be personal

Charities need to stir emotions in order to motivate their target audiences to make donations. It is easier to do this by focusing on the individuals who will benefit from donations. Many charity advertisements and direct mail shots name individuals and tell their story. This technique is not limited to people but is also used by animal charities.

Create a sense of urgency

If the target audience is made to feel that their help is needed now, they will be more inclined to act on seeing, hearing or reading a charity's communication. Concern's 2003 leaflet starts with the words 'Emergency in Ethiopia' and goes on to state '14 day deadline – help needed now.'

Exhibit 15.4

Christmas spirit

According to Bird, Christmas is the time when people are likely to donate most money. He stresses the importance of using the word 'Christmas' in headlines if running a campaign at that time of year because it is more likely to focus the mind of the donor.

Suggest an amount

In cases where someone is responding to a press advertisement or a direct mail shot, always include a response coupon or form. One donation amount or a range of amounts should be pre-printed with tick boxes beside them. In cases where a range of amounts is suggested, the largest amount should appear first. This is because people do not like to appear mean and unless they really cannot afford the larger amount, they are more likely to opt for the first amount. However, a blank space should also be included so that people can donate a figure of their own choice.

Be very economical

Bird refers to this as being 'amateur'. It is important that charity marketing communications do not appear excessive or expensive to produce. When using press advertising, most charities use black-and-white print. If photography is used, it might be executed in such a way that it gives the impression that it has been taken by an amateur. Black-and-white photography appears less expensive. If direct mail is used, black and white is often used because it is cheaper to print. The paper stock chosen is almost always of an inferior quality. Since most charity marketing communications seeks a response, the reply device should not incur costs for the charity. Therefore, prepaid envelopes, free phone contact numbers and freepost addresses might not be used. They are essential catalysts for profit-making organisations but send out the wrong message if used by charities.

Summary

The Irish charity sector has grown considerably since the 1980s. This means that it is very competitive and utilises elements of the marketing communications mix in an effort to be heard. Charities usually subdivide their publics into three main groups, donors, clients or customers, and the media.

Donors are individuals or firms that give money or benefit-in-kind to charities. They can be broken down into the general public, the corporate sector, and the Government.

Charities might utilise all elements of the marketing communications mix to some extent. While advertising is expensive, some charities advertise on the radio or in newspapers. Direct marketing is widely used by most charities, and attention is now given to the database so as to build a bank of loyal donors. The corporate sector is demonstrating great interest in the concept of cause-related sponsorship. Greater use is being made of sales promotion techniques so as to differentiate the charity's proposition.

The creation and production of a direct marketing campaign requires a different approach to that used for commercial organisations.

Review questions

1. Identify and describe in detail the way in which most charities categorise donors.
2. Critically assess the role of marketing communications in the charity sector.
3. Prescribe a framework that would assist a marketing communications agency create and produce a campaign for a charity.

Exercise

Select a piece of charity direct mail and a newspaper charity advertisement of your choice. Use Table 15.1 (page 387) to critically assess whether or not they are effective pieces of communication. What, if anything, would you do differently?

References

Bird, Drayton, *Commonsense Direct Marketing*, 2nd edition (Kogan Page, 1989).

Polonsky, Michael Jay and Speed, Richard, 'Linking sponsorship and cause-related marketing: complementarities and conflicts' (*European Journal of Marketing*, Vol. 35, No. 11/12, pp. 1361–85, 2001).

Case study

MS Society of Ireland

Introduction

The MS Society of Ireland is over 40 years old and by 2002 it had over 5,000 members. Multiple sclerosis (MS) is the most common neurological condition affecting Irish adults and there are over 6,000 people living with MS in Ireland. The MS Society of Ireland exists to help people with MS control their lives and environment, to live with dignity and participate in the community. They provide support for the families and carers of people with MS and co-operate with the medical, scientific, social and caring professions to promote scientific research into the causes, cure and management of MS.

The Society exists to support people with MS, their families and carers. Services offered by MS Ireland are as follows:

- a support network of 40 branches nationwide, run entirely by volunteers
- community workers in all Health Board Areas
- counsellors
- respite care
- a news magazine
- a national 24-hour helpline
- information booklets
- emergency grants
- major funder of MS research in Ireland.

In addition to the above, MS Ireland offers individual donors the opportunity to feel better about themselves and offers corporate donors the opportunity to give something back to society while generating positive publicity.

Target audience

In order to attract donations, the MS Society divides donors into segments to allow for better targeting of appeals. Each group is not targeted for every fund-raising activity. The groups are:

- members of the MS Society (reached through MS branches)
- students and their families (reached through schools – primary schools distribute MS READaTHON sponsorship cards and secondary schools sell pens on MS Pen Day via transition-year students)
- corporations (reached directly)
- individual donors (reached directly)

- the general public (reached via retail networks – these have been responsible for distributing items such as Christmas decorations and pens for sale to the general public).

FUND-RAISING ACTIVITIES

Fund-raising is the main source of revenue for the society. However, fund-raising activities also create awareness of the Society's existence. For this reason types of activities affect how the organisation is perceived.

MS Pen Day

Pen Day takes place each May nationally, and gives people the chance to buy something of use, a unique selling point for the Society. Apart from the pens, a range of materials are produced to support the activity – posters, brochures, volunteer badges, collection boxes, 'thank you' certificates, balloons, T-shirts, press releases and advertising.

Vodafone (and previously when known as Eircell) have sponsored MS Ireland's Pen Day for a number of years. While on a personal level, the staff and managers at Vodafone might be interested in MS Ireland's cause, they must be able to justify their decision to sponsor the Pen Day. The presentation made to Vodafone in March 2002 articulated the objectives for the fund-raising event in a way that relates to both organisations. These objectives are detailed below in Table CS15.1. The presentation also emphasised the mutual benefits of the campaign (see Table CS15.2.)

Table CS15.1 Objectives of MS Ireland Pen Day 2002

- To generate donations in excess of €200,000.
- To identify additional, imaginative ways in which funds for the MS Society and sales for Vodafone can be generated.
- To provide the forty branches of the MS Society with a fundraising initiative that can help generate funds on a local level.
- To raise awareness of the MS Society on a national and local level.
- To alert newly diagnosed people with MS and their families as to the existence of the MS Society.
- To position Vodafone as an organisation that is an intrinsic part of Irish society, offering practical and compassionate support to Irish people.

Source: MS Ireland

The introduction of the Vodafone brand helped MS Ireland as both organisations have similar corporate colours (red). This has helped MS Ireland reduce printing costs as it can now successfully print a one-colour pen (white on a red-barrelled pen), where previously under the Eircell brand, they had to print a three-colour job to cater for Eircell's purple and blue. This makes the campaign more profitable.

Table CS15.2 The benefits of Pen Day to both MS Ireland and Vodafone

- Generate awareness for the MS Society
- Reinforce the Vodafone name
- Position Vodafone as a caring organisation involved with supporting people in a very practical way
- Encourage 'texting' amongst new target audiences
- Generate new sales for Vodafone

Source: MS Ireland

Christmas Star campaign

The idea behind the Christmas Star campaign is to invite companies to sponsor a star that would help light up the East Link Toll Bridge in Dublin with 1,000 stars at Christmas time, and to sell Christmas decorations to the general public. With two parts to this campaign, the Society uses direct mail to target sponsorship from the corporate sector and distribution through retail outlets to sell individual stars (Christmas decorations) to the general public.

Exhibit CS15.1

- **Individual segment**. This involves selling Christmas decorations to the general public, for example, a star for €2 through retail outlets. Customers were enticed to support the campaign through point-of-sale display boxes located near checkouts. The idea of locating the boxes near the checkouts was to capitalise on change given back after purchases. Direct mail is used to persuade retailers to take part in the fund-raising activity.
- **Corporate segment**. The corporate segment is contacted by direct mail. The East Link Toll Bridge in Dublin is decorated with 1,000 lights. Companies are sent

a letter asking them to sponsor a star (i.e. one light) for €300. The lights were grouped on four big stars (250 lights per star). The Society is looking into patenting this idea for a fund-raising activity with the hope that the campaign will grow and appear on more landmark buildings around the capital and nationwide.

Exhibit CS15.2

MS IRELAND

The Multiple Sclerosis Society of Ireland

The Royal Hospital Donnybrook
Bloomfield Avenue
Morehampton Road
Dublin 4 Ireland
Telephone (01) 269 4599
Fax (01) 269 3746
Helpline 1850 233 233

website: www.ms-society.ie
e-mail: mssociety@ms-society.ie

Mr AB Sample
Sample Position
Sample Company
Sample Street
Sample Town
Sample County

November 2002

Dear Mr Sample

With your help we would like to turn the East Link Bridge into a spectacular symbol of hope and generosity this Christmas. We want to light up the bridge with 1,000 stars. **Will your company become a star for us by sponsoring a star for €300.00?**

When you sponsor a star your company name will be added to the MS Society Roll of Honour. The Roll of Honour will be published in a national paper in early January – it will be posted immediately on the MS Society web site and will also be featured in a two page spread in MS News (mailed to 8,000 recipients). **Your company's donation will qualify for tax relief under Section 45 of the Finance Act 2002.** You can obtain more details on how to obtain tax relief at charities@revenue.ie .

Multiple Sclerosis is the most common neurological condition affecting young Irish adults. There are over 6,000 people living with MS in Ireland today. **In some parts of Ireland as many as 1 in 400 people are affected, one of the highest rates in the world.** Our funds are utilised to run regional offices around the country to provide people living with MS with support and advice on a local level. We also fund research to identify a cure for MS – a disease that is invariably diagnosed between the ages of 20 and 40 when people are the most challenging stage of their life in terms of career and family.

There are other ways in which your company can support our work. Instead of sending your clients, suppliers and colleagues corporate cards and gifts why not send them an MS Presentation Pack? The packs cost €100.00 and consist of 20 cards each of which contains a star – they are the perfect alternative to corporate gifts or cards. The MS Presentation Packs can be personalised with your company name and will advise your clients, suppliers and colleagues that you have made a donation to the MS Society of Ireland on their behalf. Or you may choose to simply make a donation to the MS Society of Ireland.

Be a Star! Complete the enclosed order form today so that we can be there for people with MS tomorrow.

Yours sincerely,

Maura McKeon
Head of Marketing

National Executive Committee: Allen O'Connor/Chairman, Louise Wardell/Deputy Chairman, M. Classon, O. Durkin, C. Fahy, E. Fenton, W. Lonergan, O. Hanlon, P. Hogan, B. Kenna, C. McDonagh, P. McCann, M. Crowley, P.J. O'Reilly, D. Power, A. Flynn.

Company Secretary Michele Kerrigan Charity Number 5365 Registered in Ireland No. 296573 Registered Office 29 Earlsfort Terrace, Dublin 2.

Member of the International Federation of Multiple Sclerosis Societies and European MS Platform

The amount of €300 was set so as not to exclude smaller companies. If a higher figure had been set, only the larger companies would have been able to donate. The letter was short and simple. According to Maura McKeon, Marketing Manager with MS Ireland, 'It had to be – you've only got a couple of seconds to grab the reader, after that you've lost them.' The opening paragraph explains the promotion and the following two paragraphs highlights the benefits for a company and the MS Society if they sponsored a star. Provision was made at the end of the letter for easy response either by faxing back a form or e-mailing a reply.

The campaign's success depended on the quality of the mailing lists. In 2001, MS Ireland used a list broker to compile contact names and addresses based on a list of criteria such as company size, location (near the East Link Bridge) and core activity. MS Ireland was faced with two alternatives when using the mailing lists. If they rented the lists they could use them only once. Alternatively, if they made adjustments (i.e. updated the information) the data was theirs to keep and use for ever. They opted for the latter option and undertook out-bound telemarketing to verify the data. This meant that the data became the property of MS Ireland and also ensured that the list was up to date and correct, thereby increasing the success of the campaign.

In its first year, MS Ireland achieved a 5 per cent response rate for the direct mail element of the campaign, which raised over €58,400. They also won the IDMA's Gold Award for fund-raising.

In 2002, they sent letters to more than 17,000 companies. These consisted of:

- 2001 Corporate Star sponsors
- IFSC companies
- Dublin 1 companies with less than five employees
- All Dublin companies employing more than five employees
- Companies outside Dublin with more than 20 employees
- Medical consultants/specialists
- Architects.

Swimathon

The Swimathon takes place in April every year and requires participants in the event to raise funds through sponsorship. It is not the Society's biggest revenue earner and largely relies on word of mouth for generating awareness. The Society tries to gain free publicity through local radio stations. For example, in 2002, FM104 promoted the event in its 'what's happening' event guide. Details given included location, time, and contact details for anybody interested in taking part.

Sponsored walks

The Society organises two sponsored walks each year, one in Europe and one further afield. In 2001, the Society headed for Northern Spain in May and Peru in South America in October. Participants are required to pay a deposit of €250 along with a completed application form. The sponsorship they raise covers the flights, accommodation, insurance and meals. There is a minimum sponsorship target to be raised that enables participants to go on the walk. This varies depending on the destination but it can be in the region of €1,500 for European walks and up to €4,000 for long-haul walks.

MS READaTHON

The Society's biggest annual earner is the MS READaTHON, which raised €825,000 in 2001. The campaign relies on primary schools for its success, so much so that it allows each school to keep 10 per cent of the money they raise. The MS READaTHON has been in existence since 1988 and has managed to raise over €5 million.

In 2001, over 28,000 children from all across Ireland read in excess of 500,000 books. With 726 schools involved, this appeal not only raises funds for the Society but also enables children to improve their reading skills while helping others.

The principle sponsors of the MS READaTHON are Coca-Cola, Bus Eireann and Penguin Books, with additional support also coming from Irish publishers and members of the book trade. DEN TV promotes the campaign during daytime children's programming on national television.

DIRECT MARKETING ACTIVITY

The majority, if not all, fund-raising activities carried out by MS Ireland contain some element of direct marketing. In particular, direct mail is used. Initial contact, especially with distribution channel members, is often by direct mail. For this reason, creative mailings are used to ignite initial interest among recipients. Care is always taken not to overwhelm readers with too many facts and figures. According to the marketing manager, easy response can greatly improve the success of the mailing and Society mail shots are designed with this in mind.

To facilitate relationship building, MS Ireland uses a database to hold donor information. In addition to databases bought from list brokers, MS Ireland has built up its own database of 22,000 names captured from unsolicited individual donations. The database holds information such as the donor's name, address and how much they donated. Top donors can be identified and are invited to view the projects run by MS Ireland, allowing the donor to see how their money is being spent. It is intended to develop this database into a complete contact history that will include further information such as when and how they made contact and their preferred method of communication, for example, by mail, telephone, fax or e-mail.

The database is also used to test various direct marketing approaches, such as the use of hand-written versus typed envelopes and the inclusion of a prepaid envelope versus the inclusion of a reply envelope requiring a stamp.

Exhibit CS15.3

Ongoing communications with existing donors

MS Ireland recognises that forming relationships with donors is crucial because the cost of recruiting new donors is increasing all the time and donor retention is much more profitable. Although the relationship held with individual donors addresses the benefits for them of donating, much more emphasis is put on the benefits of the donation for the MS Society. Every donation is always followed up with a personal 'thank you' letter. In the case of the Christmas Star campaign, the 'thank you' takes the form of a card with an individual Christmas decoration inside (a star), representing the star they sponsored on the East Link Bridge.

THE ROLE OF PUBLICITY AND PUBLIC RELATIONS

Publicity

Due to its low cost and high perceived value, the marketing manager never misses an opportunity to gain access to the national media. This involves keeping informed on current affairs and voicing an opinion on behalf of the Society where appropriate. She makes herself available to any newspaper, radio or television show that raises the topic of MS or the not-for-profit sector in general. She has forwarded her contact details to the relevant people in the media and tries to make sure that they will have no hesitation in contacting her. When the topic of MS arises, she ensures that the MS Helpline telephone number is also broadcast or published so that any listener, viewer or reader affected knows how to make contact with the Society.

Public relations

The Society's main concern is to make newly diagnosed sufferers aware of the disease and the Society as quickly as possible. This involves employing three full-time nurses to run the MS Helpline. Their role is to reassure callers, answer questions about the disease and inform them of the support that is available. It is also necessary to make general practitioners (GPs) aware of the Society so that they inform patients about it. All GPs are on the Society's mailing list for their quarterly publication *MS News*. One objective is to have the magazine in the waiting room of all doctors' surgeries.

The MS Society website

The Society's website (www.ms-society.ie) is an excellent tool for providing information to people with MS, their families, MS carers and medical personnel studying or working with the disease. Although this content is vital and should remain on the website, it offers fund-raising potential.

However, the donations page does not facilitate direct donations via the web. A form is made available and must be printed, completed and returned by post with an accompanying cheque or postal order.

Interest in the website is monitored by a third party and once a year they provide a report that contains information such as the number of hits, where they have come from and where they go after leaving the site.

This case study was written and prepared by Ian Lamon as part of his Degree at Institute of Technology Tallaght in 2002 and has been reproduced with his and Maura McKeown's kind permission.

INDEX